HUGH LYNN CAYCE:

ABOUT MY FATHER'S BUSINESS

HUGH LYNN CAYCE:
ABOUT MY FATHER'S BUSINESS

A. ROBERT SMITH

THE
DONNING COMPANY
PUBLISHERS
NORFOLK/VIRGINIA BEACH

For Libbie,

The spirit of grace and truth
Providence sent
To speak of signs and wonders
beyond my sight.
Light years ago,
Always.

The Donning Company/Publishers
Norfolk/Virginia Beach

The Donning Company/Publishers
5659 Virginia Beach Boulevard
Norfolk, Virginia 23502

Library of Congress Cataloging-in-Publication Data:

Smith, A. Robert, 1925-
  Hugh Lynn Cayce: about my father's business/
by A. Robert Smith, p.   cm.
ISBN 0-89865-723-7: $19.95
    1. Cayce, Edgar, 1877-1945. 2. Cayce, Hugh Lynn.
3. Psychics—United States—Biography.
I. Cayce, Hugh Lynn. II. Title.
BF1027.C3S58   1988
133.8'092'2—dc 19   88-29972
(B)   CIP

Printed in the United States of America

Table of Contents

Prologue 7

Part 1: About My Father 11

  Chapter 1   The Cayce Mystique 13

  Chapter 2   Loaves and Fishes 21

  Chapter 3   Model Boy: Selma 27

  Chapter 4   Country Boy: Hopkinsville 41

  Chapter 5   Preppie: Dayton 53

  Chapter 6   Young Skeptic: Virginia Beach 65

  Chapter 7   College Boy: Washington & Lee 71

Part 2: About My Father's Business 89

  Chapter 8   The Idealist 91

  Chapter 9   Cayce & Son: the A.R.E. 103

  Chapter 10 Mysteries of the Mind: New York 119

  Chapter 11 Eros and Philos: Sally and Tom 131

  Chapter 12 Off to War: Europe 145

Part 3: About My Father's Legacy 155

  Chapter 13 Plotting a Spiritual Renaissance 157

  Chapter 14 On the Road 167

  Chapter 15 Family Time 181

  Chapter 16 Public Awakening to the Sleeping Prophet 193

  Chapter 17 Hugh Lynn's Monuments:
               The Library & the A.R.E. Clinic 211

  Chapter 18 The Andrew Dilemma 227

  Chapter 19 Searching for Ra Ta 237

  Chapter 20 A New Edgar Cayce? 253

  Chapter 21 Passing the Torch 261

  Chapter 22 'It's Been a Good Life' 275

  Chapter 23 'I'll Be Back' 289

Appendix

  Life Readings: 'The Karma of Each Must be Met' 297

Books by A. Robert Smith

The Tiger in the Senate
  A biography of Senator Wayne Morse

Washington: Magnificent Capital
  with Eric Sevareid and Fred J. Maroon

An American Rape
  A True Account of the Giles-Johnson Case
  with James V. Giles

Hugh Lynn Cayce: About My Father's Business

Prologue

Edgar Cayce, America's premier seer, and his eldest son, Hugh Lynn, had a love-hate relationship which they believed had its roots in ancient Egypt. The elder Cayce never visited Egypt in this life, 1877-1945, but he seemed to return there countless times in an altered state of consciousness while giving the hypnotic-trance communiques for which he became world famous. His son visited Egypt frequently during the 1960s and 1970s in search of the evidence of their roots. The clues he discovered would not be admissible in court perhaps, but were profoundly moving to him nonetheless. They turned a skeptic into a firm believer in reincarnation—and in the idea that an intimate relationship is seldom limited to one lifetime.

While the story of their rivalry as high priest and ruler of an ancient kingdom on the Nile fascinates and entertains, it leaves one to ponder its credibility. Could the souls of these two Americans conceivably have started in this distant place and time and resurfaced as father and son in twentieth-century Kentucky? It is an intriguing question for the reader to consider while sorting out the implications of Hugh Lynn's life with his celebrated father.

Edgar Cayce's story has been told in greater biographical detail by others, but never in more intimate terms than by Hugh Lynn. No one was closer to Edgar other than his wife, Gertrude, who remained a silent partner.

This book, which Hugh Lynn asked me to write, is based largely on his recollections, and those of his family and associates, supplemented with new material from Cayce family letters and Edgar Cayce's own unpublished writings. Like his father, Hugh Lynn was essentially a storyteller, true to the oral tradition of his native South. In that sense this is a biographical memoir of Hugh Lynn's life which offers a fresh dimension to the character of his phenomenal father, while telling what it was like for Hugh Lynn, living with a man who could read his mind, forecast the future, and literally tap the wisdom of the cosmos. It is the remarkable story of an amazing family: America's most celebrated clairvoyant and his crusty, bungling father, Squire Cayce; his stoic, long-suffering wife, Gertrude; the family promoter, Hugh Lynn; Edgar's sweet, young live-in secretary, Gladys Davis; his lyrical biographer, Tom Sugrue; his stockbroker patron, Morton Blumenthal; and a DeMille-like cast of characters who were drawn to the Cayces from Wall Street to Main Street, from the worlds of business and the arts to the ashrams of mystics and academia, but mostly from ordinary households.

Hugh Lynn devoted his life to his father and to what they described as The Work. The Work became their mission, their life's purpose this time around, and it survives them in the enterprise that Cayce and Son built, the Association for Research and Enlightenment at Virginia Beach, Virginia, whose members now circle the globe.

Hugh Lynn's commentary revealed aspects of his father that may surprise those who think of Edgar Cayce as a saintly figure. Though no one was a bigger booster of Edgar Cayce, Hugh Lynn knew better than to worship him. Indeed, he astonished me by revealing the depths of his antagonism toward his father—and what Edgar Cayce had done to trigger such hostility—and the passion he felt for his mother. Earlier biographies, several of which Hugh Lynn had helped shape, had carefully sidestepped family conflicts. What one discovers in Hugh Lynn's experience is the touching humanity of these remarkable people. Despite their astounding abilities and spiritual idealism, they stumbled over personal frailties no less than we.

Hugh Lynn's reflections are both wise and witty, cheerful rather than maudlin, honest but never cruel, forgiving and informed by vast experience, both in and out of his body. They represent Hugh Lynn at his most candid, and at his best—a great teacher to the very end. By the time Hugh Lynn died at age seventy-five, on July 4, 1982, he had launched a renaissance of spiritual development that would overshadow his ambition to bring his father's work to public notice. He had fulfilled that purpose, and much more.

To have spent so much time with such an extraordinary human being as Hugh Lynn was my unmerited reward. He personified the higher self of the true spiritual seeker in much of what he did; but, like many of us, had to wrestle with his lower self no small part of the way.

In preparing this material for publication, I had the indispensable assistance of my wife Elizabeth McDowell, who was initially much more knowledgeable than I in the Cayce literature, and always a thoughtful analyst of the subject. It was she who first told me what an inspiring lecturer and fascinating person Hugh Lynn Cayce was. We began work together in 1980, little realizing that the clock was swiftly running down for this vigorous seventy-three-year-old. Before his death two years later, we conducted fourteen in-depth, tape-recorded interviews with him, most of them lasting several hours, usually on leisurely Sunday afternoons at our house, free of intrusion. Hugh Lynn reviewed his entire life, emphasizing what he thought significant, and responding to all our questions.

Like Hugh Lynn, we had much help from those who were close to him, especially his wife Sally and his sons, Charles Thomas and Gregory J. Cayce, as well as his brother, Edgar Evans Cayce, and his daughter-in-law, Leslie Goodman Cayce. The unofficial Cayce historian of Hopkinsville, Kentucky, D.D. Cayce, was also helpful. The generosity of the late Gladys Davis in sharing her memories and searching the archives of the Edgar Cayce Foundation was invaluable, for she said, "Hugh Lynn told me to give you everything." And she did. Gladys' successor archivist, Jeanette Thomas, faithful to this covenant, was enormously helpful.

Many others who worked with Hugh Lynn have shared the bounty of their memorable experiences. Among those who knew or worked with him for many years were Bob Adriance, Harmon and June Bro, Billie Babcoke, Marjorie Bonney, Joe Buchanan, Mary Ellen Carter, Nell Clairmonte, Helen Ellington, Joe Fiutko, Manley P. Hall, Anne Holbein, J. Everett Irion, Ursula Jahoda, William Lord, Gladys and William A. McGarey, Norrene and David Leary, Shane Miller, Arch and Ann Ogden, William Price, Meredith Puryear, Elsie Sechrist, Violet M. Shelley, Mae Gimbert St. Clair, Jess Stearn, and Mildred Davis Turner. Among the many others who were associated with him, I am indebted to Jim Embleton, Bob Jeffries, Jim Baraff, Verna Brainard, Lin and Tony Cochran, Tom Johnson, Sam Knoll, Tom Kay, Robert Krajenke, Avrum Levine, Mary LaCroix, Mark Lehner, John LaPrell, Bill and Lois Ann Newlin, Sue Newlin, Edward Morgan, Al Miner, Marilyn Peterson, Henry and Lyn Reed, Charlotte and Birley Schoen, Stephan Schwartz, Dee and Ed Sloan, Ken Skidmore, Gail Cayce Schwartzer, Claire Grant, Lindy Meunier, Diana and Barry Barrentine, Scott Sparrow, Mark Thurston, John Van Auken, Henry Vaughan, Adella Scott Wilson, and James C. Windsor. A number of other people contributed significantly, including Jim Bolen, Joe Dunn, Elaine Hruska, Ruth O'Lill, Dick Peterson, Francis Sporer,

Susan Lendvay, and my editor at Donning, Bob Friedman.

Having inspired this work, Hugh Lynn may also have had some part in its completion. After his death when the incomplete manuscript had gathered dust for too long, I began waking at 5:00 a.m., unable to think of anything but the desirability of finishing it. So each morning I resumed writing. A few days before Gladys Davis' death in 1986, I told her, "Something funny is going on, and I figured it was either you or Hugh Lynn doing it to me." Gladys laughed and said without a moment's hesitation, "Oh, it's him."

Thanks, Hugh Lynn, for that final kick in the pants—and so much more along the way.

A. Robert Smith
Virginia Beach, Virginia
July 1988

Part One

About My Father

Chapter 1

The Cayce Mystique

Five generations of Cayces are directly linked to the clairvoyant work of their celebrated kinsman, Edgar Cayce. The lives of these five Cayces span more than a century and a half, from before the Civil War to the close of the twentieth century. Their lives seem almost predestined, as though they were runners in a sacred relay, each preparing the way for the next, each passing a magical baton when his lap had been run.

This unmistakable Cayce mystique defies clear delineation or definition. It is more than tradition or close kinship, although there was and still is a strong sense of family among members of this clan whose roots go deep into the soil of Kentucky and Virginia. It was more than heredity, for genetics alone cannot explain the bond that formed among them. It was more than the occupational unity one finds, say, in a family of doctors or preachers. The Cayce mystique was not of this realm entirely, nor altogether removed from it either. Clearly, spirit was at work here and on the other side.

Earlier Cayces may have laid a spiritual foundation for this quintet, but limited knowledge of these ancestors cautions against pressing that claim. We do know that the Cayces came to colonial America, evidently from France, and settled in Virginia just west of Richmond. In those days they spelled their name "Caycey." Shadrach Caycey, the family genealogy has it, sired eleven children in eighteenth-century Virginia. His sons fought for independence, dropped the second "y" in the family name, and ventured west beyond the Appalachians into Tennessee and Kentucky after hostilities with the Cherokees subsided. The pioneer Cayce in Kentucky was Shadrach's tenth child, William, who in 1828 bought

29¼ acres for $145—the first of numerous Cayce homesteads in Christian County.

Like other Virginia farmers, they brought with them knowledge acquired from the Native Americans about growing two indigenous crops, tobacco and corn, and turned this mountain wilderness into a thriving agricultural region, noted ultimately for livestock and burley leaf, used for cigarettes, snuff, pipe smoking, and chewing. While other pioneers pushed farther west, the Cayces found Kentucky rich in the promise of the New World—cheap, fertile land, the opportunity to own it, to work it, to proliferate, to prosper, and to pass the promise down to their children.

Pioneer William Cayce and his wife Betsey gave eight of their ten children illustrious names. Their three daughters were Martha, Mary, and Elizabeth. Three sons were named for the chief Founding Fathers, all Virginians: George Washington Cayce, James Madison Cayce, Thomas Jefferson Cayce; one for the Yankee president of that period (1853-1857), Franklin Pierce Cayce; and one for an English scientist, Isaac Newton Cayce. The other two boys were Pleasant Cayce and just plain Will.

Thomas Jefferson Cayce, Edgar Cayce's grandfather, was the first member fo the Cayce clan who possessed clearly identifiable mystical attributes. He was surely the most important male figure in shaping the spiritual direction of young Edgar. By all accounts, the boy and the old gentleman were remarkably bonded, in spirit no less than blood. It was a bond for Edgar that survived his grandfather's accidental death, and carried their relationship into another dimension that surely shaped the impressionable boy and nourished his mystical inclinations.

A successful farmer and tobacco warehouseman, Tom Cayce was a tall, gentle, sensitive, bearded man who sired nine sons—too many for all of them to flourish by subdividing the family farm. He, incidentally, was more conventional in naming his progeny: six carried family or biblical names. But two of them, Robert E. Lee Cayce and John C. Breckinridge Cayce (named for Buchanan's vice president) continued the precedent of patriotism.

What set Tom Cayce apart were his mysterious powers. He is said to have been able to move objects at will without touching them—a rare feat, known today as psychokinesis. He also gained a local reputation as a dowser, using a forked tree branch to advise the neighbors on where to dig their wells.

His second son, Leslie Burr Cayce, grew up right after the Civil War, married an affluent farmer's daughter, fathered five children, disliked farming but liked the nickname Squire, worked as a country school teacher briefly, ran a country store, dabbled in local politics, served as a justice of the peace, and attempted several business ventures which failed.

Les himself showed none of his father's peculiar talents, nor did any of his four daughters, but his son, Edgar, was destined to gain world recognition for his clairvoyant gift. Edgar spent much of his youth on his grandfather's farm. "Among my earliest recollections," he later wrote, "are the conversations I had with my grandfather who, to me, was a most wonderful man." Their lives overlapped for less than five years—Edgar was born in March 1877, his grandfather died in 1881—but their spirits evidently communicated for much longer. "On a number of occasions I saw him do some very unusual things that I have since learned many people attribute to the working of disincarnate spirits," Edgar said of Tom Cayce. "I saw him move tables and other articles, apparently without any contact with the objects themselves. On such occasions he would say, 'I don't know what the power is, but don't fool with it.'"

Edgar became unusually close to both of his grandparents, especially after witnessing his grandfather's drowning: They had been riding Grandfather's horse, four-year-old Edgar sitting behind and holding onto the elder Cayce as he rode about inspecting his fields and crops. When they came to a pond, Edgar slid to the ground before his grandfather rode into the water to let the horse drink—and then watched in horror. "I saw the horse throw him, as the girth broke, and he disappeared" beneath the surface of the pond. Before Edgar could run and bring help, it was too late.

For some years after, the boy experienced periodic visits from his grandfather. He was not frightened but somehow reassured. Each time it happened he reported his conversations to his grandmother. She, too, was not surprised. Indeed, she encouraged her grandson by asking him what Grandpa had told him, thus inviting him to believe in spirit communication. "As a child I loved to be alone a great deal, and quite often had playmates that others coming upon the scene and hearing the conversation declared did not exist. Reprimands from different ones of the family as I grew up gradually made me ashamed of these experiences, but to me they were very real."

By his own account, Edgar was more serious than most children. His parents nicknamed him "Old Man." He wrote, "I did not know the pleasures of many games the others played at school—baseball, football, marbles, etc.—for I never could shoot a marble, spin a top, throw or bat a ball, as others. I preferred to sit and argue with the teachers, when they would listen, concerning the

15

mysteries of life. Often Professor Thoms and others insisted that I run out and play, but I could not keep up with the bigger boys and I was often in disgrace for wanting to play with the little boys and girls, if they would let me."

One day, however, while trying to keep up with the other boys in a ball game called "Old Sower," Edgar recalled, "I was the one who had to stand with my back to the others and have them throw the ball at me for having been unable to keep up with the others in the game. Someone must have struck me in the middle of my spine or the back of my head, for I remembered nothing that happened the rest of the day, though it was said that I rather mechanically went through all the activities throughout classes. It was nothing unusual for me to be peculiar to the rest of them, but in the evening my sister had to lead me home. I gradually seemed to grow worse, later throwing things at the table, and when I went in the kitchen, finding a pan of coffee that had recently been roasted, I told them it needed sowing and proceeded to scatter it over the yard. I was reprimanded and put to bed."

The boy apparently entered an altered state of consciousness—he had no memory of it upon awaking in the morning—during which he diagnosed his own difficulty as shock caused by the blow. Edgar prescribed that a poultice be applied to the back of his head. Puzzled and concerned, his mother complied, and Edgar slept on it. In the morning he was fine.

This experience may have triggered Edgar Cayce's extraordinary psychic talent, judging by the research findings of the Mind Science Foundation of San Antonio, Texas. C. V. Wood, Jr., co-founder of the foundation, says, "We have studied many persons who have had certain psychic abilities, and in almost all cases the ability developed after either experiencing a fall or being hit on the head, or after having an extremely high fever. This seems to imply that suddenly a person is able to use another part of the brain—more or less the same as suddenly fusing two wires—because of either the pressure from the blow on the head or the heat of the high temperature."

The famous Dutch psychic Peter Hurkos suffered a head injury in a fall from a ladder. Hurkos and Wood believe this was responsible for his talent. Whether Edgar Cayce was struck on the spinal column or the head, the shock may have impacted the brain, allowing him to tap another dimension of his mind to diagnose his own condition and prescribe a remedy—a remarkable feat he repeated for thousands of others as an adult.

He displayed another amazing talent as a child. A dull

schoolboy in the early grades, he stumbled in error repeatedly during spelling class. Then one night Edgar had what he later described as "my first vision." In saying his bedtime prayers, he had asked "that God would show me that He loved me, that He would give me the ability to do something for my fellow man which would show to them His love, even as the actions of His little creatures in the woods showed to me their trust in One who loved them.

"I was not asleep when the vision first began, but I felt as if I were being lifted up. A glorious light as of the rising morning sun seemed to fill the whole room, and a figure appeared at the foot of my bed. I was sure it was my mother, and called, but she didn't answer. For the moment I was frightened, climbed out of bed and went to my mother's room. No, she hadn't called. Almost immediately, after I returned to my couch, the figure came again. Then it seemed all gloriously bright—an angel, or what, I knew not, but gently, patiently, it said, 'Thy prayers are heard. You will have your wish. Remain faithful. Be true to yourself. Help the sick, the afflicted.'

"There was little sleep for me after the vision gradually faded away," continued Edgar in his memoir. "I could only rush out in the moonlight; and I will never forget that it seemed to me I had never seen it shine so gloriously as it did that May night. I went to my favorite retreat, or tree, and kneeling there I thanked God for letting me know He cared. I will never forget how, in the early morning after day began to dawn, two little squirrels came down that tree and hunted in my pockets for nuts I did not have. I couldn't even tell my mother what had happened, though she said, 'My boy, why are you so happy, yet look so very strange this morning?' I could only say, 'Mother, I will have to tell you later.'"

Still in a daze, he missed every word in spelling class that day and was kept after school to write "cabin" five hundred times on the blackboard. When he got home, his father was waiting, "and in no too good a humor for my being the dunce." Squire Cayce drilled him hard that evening, "but when I handed him the book my mind became a perfect blank—I had forgotten everything," said Edgar. Tired from so little sleep the previous night, "I began to fall asleep. Several times I picked myself up off the floor where I had been slapped for going to sleep."

An inner voice told the boy, "Rely on the promise," and he asked his father for time to take a five-minute nap. "My father told me to go to sleep. When the five minutes were up I handed him the book, for I knew that I knew the lesson. Not only was I able to spell all the words in the lesson, but any word in that particular book; not only spell them but tell on what page and what line each word could be found, and how it was marked." The slow student soon outpaced his classmates. "I only had to lose consciousness, even in school, to retain whatever I had read in the book." The following year, "no one was able to stay in my classes. I was accused of memorizing all my lessons; for I only read them, slept on them, and they appeared before my eyes as I recited."

He left school after the eighth or ninth grade—"All the schooling I obtained was in the little red schoolhouse in south Christian [County]."—and went to work farming for one of his uncles but soon quit to look for work in town. His family had moved from the farm to Hopkinsville, the county seat, so that his sisters could attend a better school. He was hired as a clerk in a book store. During his early twenties he learned commercial photography, the trade he was to pursue successfully for some twenty years. Thus Edgar was the first of the Cayce line to make a success of a white collar trade. His father had made the break from tilling the soil, but success eluded him and he ended up working for his son.

The Squire's marriage was also less than ideal. He lived apart from his wife for many years, assisting Edgar in his photo studio and later in his work as a psychic diagnostician. The Squire's chief contribution may have been in encouraging Edgar to use his psychic ability during his twenties when Edgar tried to escape it in order to lead a conventional life. In 1903 Edgar married Gertrude Evans of Hopkinsville, the daughter of a widow whose husband, a railroad man, had died in a train accident. The newlyweds began housekeeping in a rooming house in Bowling Green sixty miles from home.

The fourth link in the chain, Hugh Lynn Cayce, was born in Bowling Green four years after his parents' marriage. He spent much of his youth and all of his adult life outside his native state, but he was very much influenced by his father, with whom he lived until he married at age thirty-four, and for whom he worked, directly or indirectly, all his life. Hugh Lynn did not inherit his father's phenomenal gift—he showed a talent for telepathy, however, and used it effectively. What he inherited from his father was The Work, and through it he became a channel for healing as a teacher, counselor, organizer, lecturer, a friend to countless seekers, and the master builder of the Association for Research and Enlightenment.

Similarly, Hugh Lynn's eldest son, Charles Thomas Cayce, the fifth generation, perpetuated and built upon the foundation laid by his father and grandfather when he succeeded Hugh Lynn as president of the A.R.E. The physical overlap with grandfather Edgar was brief but significant for Charles Thomas. Only two years old when Edgar Cayce died in 1945, he has no conscious memory of his grandfather. But the connection was made nonetheless. Shortly after the birth of Charles Thomas, his first grandchild, Edgar gave a life reading for the baby. It said that Charles Thomas was the reincarnation of his great-grandfather, Thomas Jefferson Cayce.

Thus were their mystical links forged across the generations, bonding each Cayce to the other, uniting them in a common purpose that evolved and expanded through the endeavors of each of them. In the most sacred sense, these Cayces were *called*. The Work, the material manifestation of spirit, had called them all.

Chapter 2

Loaves and Fishes

It was hard to imagine Hugh Lynn Cayce, even at seventy-three, hospitalized, unless he had arrived all decked out in his favorite white suit to take command of the place. For his self-assured, regal bearing somehow conveyed that here was a man who was beyond such mortal annoyances as illness, if only because there was no time in his schedule for it. Manifesting more energy than most men half his years, he had transformed a well-filled-out frame of modest height and a restless nature into a towering figure of exuberance and ceaseless productivity. The years had touched him kindly, adding a flowing white mane, and a gentleness to his manner. His ruddy full-moon face, still capable of explosive dissent, more often bloomed into a cherubic smile of endearment. Age, too, had not slowed his pace. Until now.

Arriving at Bayside Hospital, tape recorder in hand to begin interviewing him about his life, Elizabeth and I wondered whether it would be best simply to pay a brief courtesy call and postpone our business until he had recuperated. We knew little about his condition except that he had been on a trip to Egypt when, suddenly taken ill, he had flown home from Cairo in great pain from a kidney stone. In surgery, the size of the stone had necessitated removal of his left kidney. Released after that episode, he had returned to the hospital in a few weeks for another surgical procedure. It sounded ominous.

We had come nonetheless at his invitation. "I'm flat on my back out here in the hospital with nothing to do," he had said on the telephone that day. "I thought maybe we could get started on the book." He sounded cheerful but impatient with confinement,

21

anxious to start the biography we had agreed months before to do.

When we found his room, Hugh Lynn was propped up in bed as though in anticipation. He hailed us with a jovial smile. His coloring was as ruddy as ever, made more so when framed by his white hair and white hospital gown. When we inquired hesitantly about his condition, he laughed it off. Since his first operation, he had been having these strange feelings, he explained, and the doctors had discovered they had left a plastic tube inside him. He was just in long enough for them to retrieve all their instruments, he joked.

We were vastly relieved and obviously led astray by the patient's lighthearted account of his condition. One family member later said that they felt that Hugh Lynn joked about it because he was "uncomfortable displaying [and thus admitting] his illness. It was sort of a skeleton in his closet, that he could suddenly be ill. He used all of his wiles to downplay it as much as possible. He kind of pulled the family into that because we sensed that he was embarrassed by it."

When he mentioned his kidney-removal operation, he focused on the metaphysical aspects, especially an accompanying out-of-body experience:

"I was knocked out. The drugs were heavy. It was a four-hour operation. I had bled rather heavily, and they had sedated me rather heavily. I had a lot of pain with that kidney incision. It was a big mass.

"I've had a lot of out-of-body experiences, or so I think, and so I know a lot about them, or at least I think I do. But this one was very interesting. They came and got me at the hospital, came to the window and yelled for me to come out. I was in the operating room. So I got up and went out.

"Some of them I knew and some of them I didn't. Then we joined a group of Japanese, somewhere, and we walked along and talked with them, and I understood them. They were talking in Japanese and I was speaking in English, but we all understood one another beautifully. It was very nice.

"Some of the people I knew were alive, and some were dead—or so-called dead. You know what Dad [Edgar Cayce] always said about that. Someone asked him, 'How do you know when you are dealing with a dead one or a live one?' And he replied, 'It's easy. The live ones are over here and the dead ones are over where you are.'"

Hugh Lynn roared in the telling of this anecdote, and we laughed with him. It was his way, one may conclude now, of whistling as he approached the grave. But he had a much more important objective in recalling his out-of-body experience. He had met the Christ and he was eager to tell us about it.

"I wanted to find Jesus. So this boy thought he could help me find Him, and he said to me, 'I think He is over there on the other side of the water. But I can't go over there with you right now.' So I told him, 'I'll go.'

"I went and He was there. I wanted Him to explain the loaves and fishes—how He did it. And He explained it. And when I came back to bed I was convinced that if anyone had given me a loaf and a fish, I could have multiplied the damned thing easily. I knew exactly what it was all about."

"How did He divide the loaves and fishes?" we asked.

"I can't tell you, but I knew then. What He did was explain that every grain and every piece of fish contained a replica of every other grain and every other fish in the universe. And all you had to do was divide them and they would keep multiplying.

"It has always fascinated me that He didn't make just enough for everybody but that he produced an *abundance*. It reminds me of something I did once. I had heard that morning-glory seeds, which are so tiny, produced prodigiously. So I planted one morning-glory seed in front of our porch trellis. After it came up and blossomed, I tied little bags on it and collected the seeds—*three quart jars* of morning-glory seeds from that one seed.

"There is an abundance of everything. It multiplies. There is a quality of creativity in it, and what He did was awaken that quality of creativity. And it just spread.

"Now He did the same thing with the fig tree, I think, only He reversed it. He told them that it was dangerous for man to work against the laws of supply. Remember the cursing of the fig tree when it didn't produce fruit? They pointed to it and asked him, 'Why is it?' And he spoke to it. Now I don't think they got all that He said there, but I think he was illustrating that if you put the same kind of energy in reverse that it destroys. Man is doing that right now with this world. We're destroying it."

We nodded in agreement, and he paused to take a drink of water. Surgery had not removed Hugh Lynn's pedantic bent. He quickly returned to his metaphysical theme:

"Things are not at all what we think they are. It's ridiculous what we consider the world to be. It brings home to me so vividly the little tiny statements scattered through the [Edgar Cayce] readings that I think are there just to pique your curiosity and to make you realize that maybe there is something else that you ought to take a look at.

"You've heard that statement, 'Man has chosen physical

consciousness as a diversion from the real life.' It's a by-path—not a punishment—but a by-path that God has provided. He has taken care of us by providing a way to lead us around to get back on the main path.

"We're not lost.

"We're not out here by ourselves.

"And we'll get back. But physical consciousness, what we call life, is just a diversion from the real life."

This Jesus experience was not Hugh Lynn's first. He had had three such encounters earlier in this lifetime, the first time as a teenager, the next time when he was about forty after the death of his father, and another time during a visit to the Holy Land. "I think I dreamed about Him several times, but these were conscious experiences—or at least I think I was conscious. You can call it an altered state if you want. But I was more conscious than I am now."

His first encounter with the Master as an adolescent was one of the most important experiences of his life because "it turned me around." Hugh Lynn declined to discuss it further. He talked freely about his second encounter as "a turning point in my life." He was in Texas not long after returning from World War II in the late 1940s. It was not long after his father's death in 1945, and Hugh Lynn was on a speaking tour to drum up interest in an organization based on Edgar Cayce's psychic readings. "I was in Rudolph Johnson's beautiful home in Dallas—he was our attorney. He had had readings from my father. He was an old friend, had been on the board, and had invited about forty people into their home. But I became ill before the meeting. I was burning up with fever."

Johnson considered calling off the meeting but Hugh Lynn wouldn't hear of it. A doctor was called. He gave Cayce a shot of penicillin. And after the people had gathered, Hugh Lynn got up to speak. "The penicillin was beginning to work as I was speaking to these folks. I don't know what I said, but in the midst of this talk suddenly on my left Jesus appeared. I thought at first it was my father. But Jesus was there. He grinned at me, laughed at me really, and said, 'It is I. You needn't be afraid.' He reached out and touched me on the shoulder, and the fever broke. I was drenched in perspiration. When I say He touched me, I felt it—I felt the energy from it. I was instantaneously drenched in sweat. I wasn't saying a thing, just standing there, and the people in the room didn't know what had happened to me. I think some of them thought I had seen my father because some of them said they had felt something there. I didn't tell anyone that night, or for years afterward, what I had experienced.

"Then He smiled at me and said, 'Get to work.' From that point on, I couldn't do anything that wouldn't work. I'd call people up and ask them to do something and they'd do it. Anything. I couldn't say anything, write anything that didn't work. Even my mistakes worked."

If Hugh Lynn had any doubt about what to do with his life, especially after the death of his father, it was resolved that night. He had thought as a youth that he might be a missionary. In college he majored in psychology. After college he worked as a librarian, real estate agent, master of ceremonies on a radio show, scoutmaster, director of lifeguards and director of recreation for the city of Virginia Beach, and general manager of the fledging A.R.E. Until he was called into the Army during the war, he helped his father—but when he returned his parents were gone, and there was no plan for what to do or how to carry on with an organization whose purpose had been to encourage folks to request psychic readings.

Hugh Lynn wanted to try to build an organization to research the thousands of readings that constituted Edgar Cayce's legacy, but he couldn't be sure that anyone would care, much less whether it would succeed. Now he had confidence that it would work. His life's purpose was clear at last: he would devote his life to building the A.R.E.

In his own mind, however, he had a different concept of it: "I never thought that I worked for the A.R.E. I worked for Jesus."

Such a conception did not turn Hugh Lynn Cayce into a pious young man—he was more on the earthy side, and seemed to enjoy this side of others—nor did he become a man of pretense. His father's psychic readings told him this was not the first life in which he had worked for Jesus. Nor the first time Edgar and Hugh Lynn had worked together. Early on in this life he had rebelled against all such ideas about past lives, but in due course he would come to accept this Eastern perspective—and accept his destiny. In setting out to spread the word, he would become an apostle for his father and The Work and, once more, for Jesus.

Those who have not walked in his shoes can never know what difficulties and hardships he encountered much of his life, even though "everything worked" for a time. Over the long years ahead many things would not work or come out the way he had hoped. But in some respects, he succeeded far beyond anything one might have imagined that night in Rudy Johnson's living room when the vision said, "Get to work."

He had much help—on this side and undoubtedly on the other. But without Hugh Lynn, it is quite likely that Edgar Cayce would have soon been forgotten and his legacy lost but to those who were helped by him personally. By getting to work, and sticking with it for a lifetime, Hugh Lynn was to do his father proud.

Chapter 3

A Model Boy

Hugh Lynn Cayce was born in Bowling Green, Kentucky at 3:15 p.m. on Saturday, March 16, 1907—a planetary junction, according to an astrologer, which stamped his nature as one "of very mixed influences, very dual." While late in life Hugh Lynn claimed to have little faith in astrology, he repeatedly referred to himself as a Piscean who exhibited a dual nature. He explained his duality in karmic terms, as opposing expressions of different incarnations. In one of them he had gained the royal power to command, in the other he had observed the spiritual power of love. He would spend much of his life trying to reconcile these rival instincts.

Astrologer Laurie Pratt's interpretation seemed on target in other respects: "Leo rising and the Moon in Aries make for leadership, pride, courage, initiative, self-confidence, mastery." She gave this reading in 1934 when Hugh Lynn was twenty-seven, long before he had begun to display these attributes as convincingly as he would in later years.

The astrologer went on to say of her young subject: "Sun and Mercury in Pisces are quite different in nature and indicate practically the opposite tendencies, so that there is often a struggle going on within the native to overcome timidity, fear, lack of confidence, worry, and indecision." Those who knew Hugh Lynn at the peak of his influence as an inspiring lecturer, author and head of the A.R.E., might regard this astrological reading as wide of the mark. Hugh Lynn's own account of his childhood indicates otherwise.

As he recalled his childhood, he began as a shy boy who was very attached to his mother, whom he called Muddie, an affectionate baby-talk nickname that stuck for the rest of her life. Hugh Lynn suffered teasing from bigger boys because of his father's strange behavior, but learned to be aggressive in fighting back. For most of his first eleven years, he was an only child who was forced to face death, family grief, serious family illness, and personal pain and fright, all before he was old enough to start school. Under the circumstances, it is astonishing that he wasn't permanently traumatized and that he remembered his childhood fondly. That he would survive without crippling emotional consequences is undoubtedly a tribute to the healing powers of his mother's affection and his father's attention. The intimacy of the Cayce family, their life together at work and at play, more than compensated.

A second son, Milton Porter, was born but died in infancy when Hugh Lynn was four. Caught up in the family's grief over this tragedy at such a tender age, introspective Hugh Lynn thought that he was to blame:

"I had the whooping cough. And I heard my Aunt Kate say to my grandmother, 'You know, I think the child caught it from Hugh Lynn.' Milton Porter had just died, and I felt so bad that I went outside and crawled under the porch steps."

When the family later missed Hugh Lynn, his father went out to look for him and found him under the porch.

"It was a tragic time for me because I thought I had been responsible for his death. He was just a baby. My father took me inside and comforted me and explained that my brother had to go to Heaven."

Edgar was terribly distressed, however, and blamed himself. "Dad felt guilty because he hadn't given the baby a reading in time. He was still scared of the readings even then."

Edgar Cayce, internationally recognized clairvoyant, *scared* to use his gift? Considering the wondrous cures he prescribed for thousands of people during his lifetime, it seems astonishing that at age thirty-four, the halfway point of his life, Edgar Cayce still was not sure that his strange talent could be trusted. It puzzled him no less than others. He had discovered the gift quite by chance, it seemed, when he had lost his voice in his late teens. With the assistance of a local amateur hypnotist, he discovered that he could cure his own ailing throat while in a hypnotic trance. Then others asked for his help, and reluctantly he gave trance readings for them, but not without anxiety that something might go wrong.

The loss of his voice caused not only his psychic gift to emerge but induced Edgar to change professions. He had clerked in several stores but switched to photography, a trade he could continue even while speechless. "He went to a school at McMinnville, Tennessee to learn how to be a photographer. He just took a short course. It began because there was an opening in a local studio. You see, photography was just beginning to come in. And after he went to school—it was job training, like training to work in a bank—he came back to Bowling Green to take over one of these studios." Photography, a trade he practiced for the next two decades, was to become his steadiest source of employment and family income.

The occasional readings he gave, on request, were for friends or relatives. Not all his relatives, however—especially in-laws—were receptive. Some of Gertrude's family looked askance at her new husband's strange powers. While his wife had no such misgivings and defended him as needed, Edgar aspired to be as conventional as the next small-town businessman. That quaint aspiration was not to be.

Hugh Lynn recalled stories his father told about these early years before his birth and during his baby years in Bowling Green. "Dad went to work for someone in a studio and the studio burned up. He went to work for someone else and another studio burned up, but this time he was running the studio and also had exhibited a lot of art work, paintings, which were for sale. They all burned up, and he had no insurance. He carried a debt of $5,000 to $7,000, which in those days was a huge amount of money for him. It had been lent to him by my grandmother's youngest sister. And he paid it back. All during those years, I never knew that."

The Cayces left Bowling Green when an unusual opportunity opened for Edgar in his home town. A new doctor in Hopkinsville, Wesley H. Ketchum, had heard about Edgar's success in diagnosing baffling ailments, so he sought his help with several problem cases. Impressed with the results, Dr. Ketchum made Edgar a business proposition: "He and Mr. Noe, a businessman from Hopkinsville who ran a hotel, would supply the money and buy Dad a photo studio in Hopkinsville. Dad would have his own business as a photographer; and in return he would give a couple of hours a day of his time at the end of the day to give readings for Ketchum's patients, maybe one late in the afternoon and one at night. And Dr. Ketchum would treat the people."

There was a fourth member of the new venture—Squire Cayce, Edgar's father, Hugh Lynn's grandfather. Squire Cayce, a tall, handsome man with an impressive handlebar mustache, had married Carrie Major, the daughter of a substantial farmer. Squire aspired to get into business on the strength of his wife's property holdings. "When she married my grandfather, she owned three of the biggest farms in Christian County. Her family was considered quite well-to-do. My grandfather ran through them rather rapidly—mismanaged them. He got into debt, started stores, borrowed money on them. He didn't want to farm because he wasn't a good farmer. My grandmother's family, the Majors, had been good farmers.

"I think she withdrew. She was dominated by the Squire. He wasn't doing anything to generate money." The Squire's brief tenure as a Justice of the Peace and as a country schoolteacher gave him status but scant compensation. "He tried selling insurance, and he organized an insurance company." He even suggested that Edgar sell insurance for him in outlying towns, before Edgar decided to give up sales and take pictures.

When Ketchum approached the Squire to join their partnership with Edgar, the Squire agreed and the three Hopkinsville entrepreneurs signed a contract with Edgar—the studio was his to operate and profit from, and his two daily readings were theirs.

"After they settled on this arrangement, we left Bowling Green and moved to Hopkinsville when I was just a baby. My mother's and father's families lived there, so Dad and my mother were glad to get back.

"Dr. Ketchum, as he later told me, built this studio for Dad on the strength of the Dietrich case." Dietrich, superintendent of the Hopkinsville schools, had a daughter whose growth had been stunted by a condition that had reduced her to a babbling, incoherent, apparently retarded child. The local physicians were stumped. Edgar, however, diagnosed the trouble as an injury to the spine caused by an accidental fall. The osteopathic treatment recommended in a reading brought complete recovery. Ketchum anticipated more remarkable cures with Cayce reading for his own patients.

He had more in mind than curing the sick, however. "They began to experiment with different kinds of readings. They wanted to see if he could trace missing people. Dad would experiment a little bit with it, and he helped find some people. They wanted to know if he could solve murders or not. He solved a murder in Canada—a woman had shot her sister, and he told them where the gun was.

"But they also began to get some other kinds of readings that Dad didn't know about. At the end of a reading, the secretary would type it up, and Dad could see those, but then they would ask Dad about the grain market, the commodities market, and then about horse races. Ketchum loved horses, and he apparently hit on more than one race because he bought Dad a house. They didn't tell him exactly where the money came from, just said they were doing very well and thought he ought to have a house because they wanted to share the proceeds with him.

"But Dad became suspicious. He was also beginning to get sick. He was suffering very painful headaches and nervousness and wasn't able to sleep. Mother got very upset. When he discovered that they were getting these readings he hadn't been told about, he got very angry. He sued them to break the contract. I didn't know this until years later, after Dad died and I met Ketchum."

Another factor that was to shape the destiny of the Cayce family was that the enterprising Dr. Ketchum turned Edgar into a major curiosity by writing a paper about Cayce's psychic cures. Ketchum intended delivering it to the prestigious Clinical Research Society in Boston. However, he was unable to attend because of marital trouble. Married and the father of a twelve-year-old son when he arrived in Hopkinsville from Ohio, Ketchum fell in love with a Kentucky schoolteacher. "His wife wouldn't give him a divorce. So he ran off with his sweetheart, taking her to Hawaii, which was just a territory then. He stopped on the West Coast long enough to write his speech, but couldn't get to Boston to deliver it, so he sent it to be read. He just reported his cases and Edgar Cayce's cures, and it made headlines all over the country.

"All this descended on Dad in Ketchum's absence. So Dad decided he would never give another psychic reading because he couldn't trust anybody. He left Hopkinsville and my mother and went to Anniston, Alabama, where he knew a Mr. Tresslar, who had a photo studio. Tresslar had a studio for sale in Selma. Dad had a good reputation, so at first he ran it for Tresslar and later bought it. We moved to Selma when I was three."

Hugh Lynn spent most of his boyhood in Alabama. "I think of my childhood as taking place in Selma. That's when I really began to remember.

"One of my earliest childhood memories is of what I thought was a ghost. Our family was living in an apartment combined with Dad's studio in Selma. The living quarters were on the third floor and my room was a little hall bedroom next to my mother and father's bedroom. One night I awakened to see a woman in white standing at the foot of my bed wringing her hands. She was obviously crying, yet I could not hear her. It took me about a minute to hop out of bed and leap into bed between my parents. They told me I was having a bad dream. A few nights later it happened again.

This time they listened to my story and again reassured me. The third time Dad asked me for details of how the woman looked and acted. He then told me I would never see her again.

"Years later, when I remembered this incident, my father explained that I had seen a ghost, and he had seen her also and had talked with her. She had died in that building before we lived there. Dad explained to her that she did not have to remain in the studio. And that was the last we ever saw of her.

"I could have been dreaming or just imagining in order to have a good reason for getting into bed with my parents. However, by the time I talked with Dad about this childhood experience, I had acquired a healthy respect for his psychic perception, and I accepted his explanation."

There was a shy, serious, introspective quality about Hugh Lynn as a boy, mixed with many high-spirited, rambunctious qualities. He matured earlier than many lads. One reason for it was his early encounters with grief and pain...and with fear. Beyond the stress caused by the death of his baby brother, Hugh Lynn feared for the life of his dear Muddie when she fell gravely ill following the baby's death. They thought initially that Gertrude had pleurisy, but she had one of the most dreaded killer diseases of the time, tuberculosis. There was then no known cure. Because Hugh Lynn, age four, was still so young, Gertrude, confined to her bed, spent much time comforting *him*—reading to him and talking with him during her lengthy confinement—while Edgar managed the studio downstairs.

Here again, Edgar was reluctant to give a reading for a loved one so dear to his heart—until her doctor said she was hopelessly ill and there was nothing to lose by risking a psychic prescription. Gertrude's reading suggested strange remedies, such as inhaling the fumes of apple brandy from a charred brandy barrel, but she was game—and after her recovery, she was sure they had saved her life. She was nonetheless months recovering. The effect of this frightening situation on her only child at the time was to draw him very close to her.

As she gradually regained her strength, Gertrude returned to helping Edgar in the studio. From a business standpoint, Edgar's move to Alabama turned out well. "Dad devoted a lot of time to extracurricular activities, but in the business I saw him make a tremendous success, with my mother's help. In Selma he probably became the outstanding photographer in the state of Alabama. People brought their children from all over the state. He became famous." When Hugh Lynn in later years visited Montgomery or other Alabama cities to speak, people frequently came up to him to say that they had had their pictures taken by his father. But The Cayce Art Co. was a family success, and their living "over the store" facilitated that success. "Mother was very much involved in the business, retouching photographs, which was necessary in those days with the cameras they had. You had a lot of lines in your face if you didn't retouch the negatives. Everyone came out prettier. Mother wiped out the lines. She also tinted pictures and helped with the books. And he was teaching me things. I began by learning to frame pictures—as a teenager, I did all the framing for him. Then I began to take on the development of Kodak prints. Kodak cameras were just beginning to get popular in those days. I made spending money that way—in the darkroom, developing pictures, mixing chemicals, processing them from the beginning right on through. I was paid for my work and didn't have to have an allowance."

Even before adolescence, Hugh Lynn was used by his father as a child model for commercial assignments. Pictures of the moon-faced boy featuring the advertised product had much charm. On one occasion, however, the boy's familiarity with photo equipment proved near tragic. "I was between six and seven years old when one day I decided to scare our black maid. She was cleaning the studio. I got some flash powder I had seen him use to take pictures. Dad would place a small amount of powder on a metal tray and hold it up above his head. By pulling a wire that hung down from the tray, he ignited a cap that flashed the powder. It was much more exciting than flashcubes.

"I found the powder in a wooden box and poured a bit of it on the floor and waited. The room was dark. When the maid opened the door, I struck a match. Evidently I hadn't put the top back on the box and a spark fell into the powder supply. It exploded in my face.

"Dad came running, picked me up and rushed down the street with me screaming in pain all the way to the doctor's office a few blocks away. My eyes were badly burned. The doctor covered them with bandages and sent for a specialist from Montgomery.

"The prognosis was poor, they told my parents. The worst of it for me was the itching—the pain was deadened with drugs. They tied my wrists to the iron bedposts to keep me from scratching my eyes. It was a nightmare.

"Days later our family physician, Dr. Gay, broke the terrible news to me. I could not see him but I remember he held my hands as he sat by my bed. Dr. Gay said to me, 'Hugh Lynn, you are a brave little boy (which couldn't have been further from the truth at that point). I'm going to tell you what we are going to have to do so that you can see again. We are going to have to take out one of your eyes in order to save the other one. I wanted to give you plenty of time to understand what we plan to do so that you'll be prepared for it.'

"I trusted Dr. Gay implicitly. He was 'family.' He had seen me through the measles and he had set my arm when I had broken it. But this time I dug in my toes. Even at that age, I knew about my father's gift for prescribing cures. Only two years before that my mother had been very ill and Dad had made her well by giving a reading. That much I was sure of. So I told the doctor that my father would know what to do for me because he was the best doctor in the world when he went to sleep.

"Perhaps to humor me, the doctor agreed, and Dad gave a reading immediately. It suggested that a different medicinal solution be used on the packs covering my eyes. It also recommended a different diet. I remember they gave me lots of grapes. The doctor feared that the new solution containing tannic acid could be too strong. But since they considered mine a hopeless case, they went along with Dad's reading and postponed the removal of my eye. The reading said to continue the treatment for fifteen days. At the end of that period when the bandages were removed I could see—with both eyes. I thought Dad was a miracle man, the most important person in the world. If you can imagine being blind for weeks, and having doctors tell you that you aren't going to see with but one eye and the other one must be removed, perhaps you can understand why I had no trouble believing in my father."

Hugh Lynn's confidence in the medical readings, like his vision, would never wane.

"When Dad went to Alabama he was going to give up readings entirely and stick to photography. But several things pushed him into giving readings again. My blindness was one. He saved my eyesight, no question about that. Then Dr. Gay introduced him to some of the people at the new little hospital that was opening in Selma. Because of Dad's ability as a photographer, they thought he would make an excellent x-ray man. They had installed one of the first x-ray machines. But when he tried to take x-rays, they were utterly amazed at the results. He would get two spines or two bodies on one plate. It never came out right, but the doctors were intrigued. He got the reputation of being a freak of some kind."

It was not the first time. In Bowling Green, Edgar had experienced a terribly painful experience when he appeared at a medical society meeting to give a reading, and one doctor jabbed him with a pin while he was in trance and then cut him. In Selma it was different. "The doctors were interested—of course, many of them scoffed and thought he was peculiar. But there was no attack. He was not doing many readings, he wasn't contending anything, he wasn't disturbing anybody, and everybody knew he was peculiar."

This time it was Hugh Lynn who came under assault. "Other boys heard about my father from their parents, and people argued over whether what he was doing was right or not. My peers translated their parents' stories into witches and devils. They began to call my father all kinds of names, to my face. They said he was a freak. They'd say, 'How's that freak father of yours getting along, Cayce?' I was a little fellow, and it was generally bigger boys who did this. The first time a classmate called him a witch, I hit him. He was bigger than I was and I ended up in a bruised condition. When Dad saw my left eye that night, he got the story out of me. I was scared. I didn't know what to do. My father said, 'Just don't pay any attention to them. Just laugh with them. That doesn't hurt me, and it doesn't hurt you.'

"But I couldn't do that. I'd fight every time. They'd do it again, and I'd fight them again. I was very shy, as I think of myself, very, very shy. I was very withdrawn, very introspective. I didn't really come out until I started fighting over Dad. The more I fought the better I got. I began to make an impression on even some of the big boys. They were the only ones who kept up the laughter and snide comments. I got a reputation for fighting. I got black eyes, and I got kept in the house for it. Dad and the family felt badly that I had got beaten up—I just got bruised, my feelings were more hurt than my body was. But I was so much happier after I got to fighting. Out of it came my interest in boxing—I boxed in high school and college. I've got a pair of adrenal glands that won't quit. So, I fought my way through a lot of that."

Boxing was the only sport in which Hugh Lynn felt competent. "I went out for football in my freshman year of high school but at the first scrimmage I broke my arm. So I never really got started. And I never could play baseball. I never was good at sports." He did play tennis in high school and college, and later he enjoyed golf but remained a duffer.

Despite the social and physical trauma that Hugh Lynn experienced in those preschool years, he thought of his childhood as "very happy—very, very happy. I remember then my whole family being involved in everything we were doing." Their life centered around the First Christian Church (Disciples of Christ) and the family business. "It was not my father doing one thing and my mother another and I doing something else. We did everything as a family. It was a lot of fun. Church, for example: We all went to church and Sunday school. My father was very busy with the Bible class he taught. He entertained them at home, which was part of the social life that we enjoyed. People that we knew were essentially related to the church in one way or another. They were our social friends, of all ages. There were only a few people who came in from outside the church."

Hugh Lynn recalled traveling to church meetings. "Christian Endeavor work was a great activity at the time with churches in the South. Dad was active in this and we would take trips to Christian Endeavor conventions and to evening meetings related to the church."

"We didn't have a car—never had a car until after 1925 when we got to Virginia Beach. We could walk to church easily, five blocks away." Church socials at the Cayces' home over the photo studio were frequent, usually for Edgar's class.

"Dad spent a lot of time with games of every conceivable kind. That's when he invented Pit, which is still on the market. He invented it for a Sunday school party, which is funny because it was a kind of gambling game, really, buying and selling commodities. He sold it to Parker Brothers [for $16]．

"Dad taught me to play checkers. He was very good at checkers. But we played every game that came along as a family, or with the people who were constantly stopping in at our house. The place was always full of people. Dad was very gregarious. We had a large downstairs entrance to the studio, and that's where they had a lot of activity."

Sometimes his father's peculiar talent led to some amazing stunts. One young fellow, Malcolm Williamson, a member of Edgar's young men's Bible class who worked for the railroad, was very curious about things psychic. "Williamson would come up to Dad and ask him all kinds of questions—could he do this or that? He was reading books and was curious what Dad could do. He deviled the life out of my father.

"One night he brought a Ouija board to a class social at our house and asked Dad whether he could work it. Dad said he could but he wasn't going to do it. Well, Williamson kept after him, arguing with him, and trying to make the board work. Finally Dad got tired of this and said to my mother, 'Come on, let's show them what this thing can do.' They sat down and put their hands on the board and I have never seen a piece of wood cavort like that thing did. It was as though there were a line of people, dead people, standing there in line waiting to be heard, and they would each have three minutes to give their speech, and then the next one would come in. The messages coming through that board were racing. Williamson could take shorthand, and he took all the stuff down.

"There was one message from a boy who had been in Dad's class but had gone into the army. He had given Dad a payment on some insurance. Dad had forgotten about it and had put it in an envelope in a desk drawer. Afterward, Dad looked and there it was.

"Since Dad had put the money there, you could say there wasn't anything very strange about this. You could say it was the subconscious.

"But there was one that came through from a teenage boy who had drowned in a pond on a farm in Ohio. His family didn't know what had happened and thought he had run away. But he had merely gone swimming, had hit his head on a stump and drowned, his body snagged on barbed wire beneath the surface. The message that came through from the boy was that he wanted them to get his body out so his family wouldn't think he had run away from home. So Williamson wrote to the family in Ohio, and they later wrote back and said they had found the boy's body in the pond.

"Well, this blew everybody's mind. But I never saw Dad put his hands on a Ouija board again, never touch one. It was an automatism [a suspension of the conscious mind to release subconscious images] that he said would short circuit. Like automatic writing, he thought it could hurt more people than it could possibly help. A lot of good stuff has come through Ouija board and automatic writing, but a lot of people have gotten disturbed through them too. The balance is on the negative side of it."

Determined as Edgar was to avoid giving readings, there were demands that he try to help in emergencies or seemingly hopeless cases. Besides those in his own family, there was one case that everyone at church knew about. It involved one of the Butler girls, a member of a large family. She was the sister of two friends of Edgar's, Alf and Roger Butler. "This sister was just out of college and teaching when she became ill. First she became neurotic and then psychotic and had to be put in an institution. Her brother sought my father's help." Edgar couldn't turn down a plea such as this, and the reading he gave diagnosed the trouble as stemming from a double impacted wisdom tooth that had in effect poisoned the girl's mind. "That was causing her strange psychotic behavior." Arrangements were made for dental surgery and the girl recovered. "This story got around and made quite an impression on the congregation."

"About that time Dad had a pain on his left side. Dr. Gay didn't think it was too bad, but Dad got a reading that said if they didn't operate right away he was going to die. When he operated, Dr. Gay found that Dad's appendix was wound around his intestines—one of the worst cases he had ever seen. And so Dad saved his own life, which kind of impressed him, I think.

"A few months after that my mother had appendicitis. Dr. Gay wanted to operate, but this time Dad wanted to give a reading for her first. It was appendicitis, but the reading recommended three specially-compounded capsules instead of surgery. She recovered and never had her appendix removed."

Hugh Lynn had no grave ailments as a child. His eyes recovered but he suffered from myopia and in due course was fitted for glasses. Except for his penchant for fisticuffs, Hugh Lynn, by all accounts, was a good boy, even a model son. "I went to Sunday school, I read the Bible, learned long passages that I recited, and I was very proud of how much I knew about it. I was active in church youth activities. And I was good. I didn't smoke or try to. Even in those days there were reefers [marijuana cigarettes], but I didn't know about marijuana or hashish."

It was a happy time for the Cayces as their various medical crises were overcome—and as they planned for a new baby. It was another boy. Edgar Evans arrived February 9, 1918 when Hugh Lynn was in the fourth grade. The baby soon acquired a nickname, Ecken.

As a schoolboy, Hugh Lynn brought home good report cards. Selma's schools used a numerical marking system. Students were given 1 for Superior through a 5 for Very Poor. The worst mark he ever got was Fair, in drawing in the sixth grade. His best was Superior in history in high school. He averaged between Excellent and Good in all subjects year after year. In deportment, his teachers rated him equally high. He seldom missed a day of school, and his reports show that he was never even late.

Entering adolescence, Hugh Lynn's natural shyness showed once more. "I discovered girls at the usual time, but having made the discovery was frightened out of my wits. I was slow with girls." And he was not a discipline problem for his parents: "Dad only spanked me twice." Hugh Lynn managed to avoid trouble. "I didn't lie. In fact, I couldn't lie, I discovered. I never got away with lying with my father—like the time we went swimming."

He and his buddies went skinny-dipping in the Alabama River one day, thus disobeying his father. When he returned home and tried fibbing it, Edgar shook his head and told him what he had been doing, what spot on the river—a new one—they had picked, and how one boy had cut his foot in the river and limped home bleeding. Astounded, Hugh Lynn knew there was no hiding the facts from or deceiving his clairvoyant father. "That scared the daylights out of me."

So the town boy was a model son. The country boy was someone else.

Chapter 4

Country Boy: Hopkinsville and Comyn

Gertrude's triumph over tuberculosis at the end of a long convalescence was sealed and celebrated when she became strong enough to take Hugh Lynn home on the train for a long family visit. It was to become one of his most cherished childhood rituals.

"I went back to Hopkinsville almost every summer from the time I was six or seven until I was about fifteen, into early adolescence. We did that as long as we lived in Selma. We kept going back when we lived in Dayton and even after moving to Virginia Beach, but only for short visits."

In his early teens, Hugh Lynn was allowed to make the trip without his mother when her brother Lynn, who had free passes as an employee of the Louisville & Nashville Railroad, stopped off in Selma to pick him up. Edgar made holiday visits too, but often as not Hugh Lynn enjoyed the domain of his wild country cousins without close male supervision. A sense of freedom he never knew in Selma awaited him there.

Hopkinsville, largest town in Christian County (population 9,419 in 1910), was the county seat, a trading center for the area's tobacco growers, the site of Western State Hospital, a mental asylum, and a railroad center. The town also supported a daily newspaper, the *Kentucky New Era*, a bookstore, and two motion-picture houses.

To Muddie and Hugh Lynn, their old Kentucky home was her family's place, which everyone called The Hill. "It was on a road out from town a little ways, about a mile and a half from the Western State Hospital. It was designed by the same architect who built the hospital. The house had beautiful columns and was set in a lovely

41

grove of trees. They used oil lamps—there was no electricity until I was in my upper teens. It had a well and we had to pull up the water. We put in electricity and running water. It was a nice place; it gradually ran down, but still it was a beautiful old place. It was home for Mother, and that's where she met Dad."

Its family occupants now were Muddie's mother, Elizabeth (Lizzie) Evans, and Aunt Kate Smith, both widows, and Kate's nephew, Gray Salter, whose mother had died. Kate's grown sons, Raymond and Porter, came by The Hill frequently—"they kept their hunting dogs there and hunted a lot." Hugh Lynn and Gray learned from them to hunt birds. Edgar also took him hunting occasionally. "He used to love to hunt—birds, rabbits, squirrels—in Hopkinsville. I used a shotgun and a rifle. And I was good. I liked guns. I learned to shoot a pistol, too. I became an expert marksman. When I went into the Army [during World War II], I qualified really fast at the top level with a carbine. I used to be able to drive nails with a .45—I'd practice all weekend as a teenager. I just loved to shoot. What stopped me was a reading I got while in college, my freshman year, that said the entity is too much engaged in the vibrations of violence as represented by guns, and if he doesn't curb this he will lose a part of his own body. So I got rid of every gun I had, and I never hunted again. Never shot one again until I had to in the Army."

The Hill was also where Hugh Lynn's parents held their wedding. Not everyone in Gertrude's family thought she should get mixed up with the strange Cayce boy who worked in the local bookstore. "My grandmother [Gertrude's mother] had two sisters, one favored Dad and the other one was antagonistic. My grandmother went along because Mother fell in love." And that settled it—their lengthy courtship concluded in marriage in Lizzie's living room one spring day in 1903.

Hugh Lynn's second companion in country hijinks was his cousin Tommy House, whose mother was Edgar's sister Carrie. Tommy's father, an osteopath, and Gray's father both worked at the hospital. When these three young musketeers got together, the model boy from Selma turned into "a juvenile delinquent," according to his own recollection. Mostly he and his cousins and cronies played pranks. They swiped melons and apples. "We'd steal dynamite, and we'd set off bombs to arouse people who got after us on the little farms around there—the ones who ran us out of their orchards and melon patches. We set off dynamite in a tree once, blew off half the leaves, and scared half the neighborhood—it was terrible. We could have killed ourselves very easily. It wasn't so much that I *did* this, but I *engineered* it. I did a lot of the planning

42

and thinking."

Hugh Lynn had one noticeable handicap as a gang leader. He hadn't learned how to cuss authoritatively. "I paid one of my cousins fifty cents to try to teach me how to swear. He was very good at it, but he got so disgusted at me—I'd given him the money, and he had worked hard with me, but he said, 'I don't think you're ever going to get the hang of it. You say the words but it doesn't come out right.'"

The town boy had also led a protected life as far as sex was concerned. "As we entered early teen age, I didn't get into a lot of sex in Selma, but on the farm and in that gang it was just rampant. The crazy things that gangs of boys will do are just out of this world. I think of it now as silly or ludicrous. No need to go into what was involved.

"We were organized like a militant gang, and we fought a group of black boys. This would happen near a spring where we would go to catch crayfish and they would go for drinking water. It was a fine spring and they hated it when we muddied it up. When we knew they were coming, we would mess it up. As soon as they got there, they knew that we were around. We would start throwing green walnuts and rocks at them. It was bad. We used barrel staves that had been soaked in water, and with them we could throw green walnuts like a bullet. It could knock anyone cold if it hit them in the head. The blacks would chase us, and when they caught us we fought. It became a neighborhood scandal, and someone would call the county constable."

Sneaking into the movies was a favorite challenge. "One of us would pay, and he would go to the back door and let the rest in. They'd catch us now and then, and for a while we'd have to go to the other picture show and do the same thing. We'd get money for the movie, but this way we'd have more spending money for candy and so forth. Some of the boys we ran with got into serious trouble, stealing, and one shot himself."

Did his parents know about his "delinquency"?

"Mother knew what was going on. People would call up and complain. They'd see us. The constable would come to the house. Then we'd be confined or thrashed or switched. They started with switching, and we got more than that."

Who did the switching?

"My grandmother. Or any of the sisters who could catch us."

The sister in residence, Aunt Kate, had lost her husband, like Gertrude's father, in a railroad accident. Discipline, left to two widows and Muddie, was evidently no match for two adolescent boys in residence at The Hill. Uncles Hugh and Lynn were also Hopkinsville boys, but Hugh died of TB—"it was that TB that I think my mother caught." Lynn, however, had become superintendant of the Hopkinsville branch office of the Louisville & Nashville Railroad. "He had pull and got jobs for people in our family, but they all died early."

Lizzie tried keeping the boys occupied with farm chores, but with scant success. "It was not a working farm. It had a big garden and a big orchard. Sometimes they would have somebody come in and put in a crop, and take part of it (sharecropping). They had lots of chickens. The chores included gathering eggs and feeding animals. I learned how to milk—they had two good milk cows—but I dreaded it. The cow didn't like me to milk her. I didn't blame her—I pinched her, and she kicked over a bucket of milk. We learned quickly how to get out of milking. You let a cow kick over a bucket of milk and they won't let you milk any more. They made butter with it. They were wonderful cooks.

"My grandmother would give me some money to ride into town on my bike to buy some steak, and she'd tell me to ask the butcher to give me any liver he had to feed to our dogs. I love liver, but in those days we'd feed it to the dogs."

Hugh Lynn often visited his paternal grandmother when he went into town. "We called her Grannie—a very gentle lady. She was wonderful to me, a typical grandmother."

But oddly he had no grandfather during those summers "back home." "My grandfather on my mother's side was dead then. He had died working on the railroad. The only grandfather I knew was the Squire, and he was never there. It was very strange. I never did experience him as a young person. He wasn't there in Hopkinsville very much, just off and on. I don't remember when he came to Selma, but Dad trained him to take pictures and put him in a studio in a little town called Marion, near Selma, where there was a big school. Dad got the contracts for the pictures for the school annuals. My grandfather was pretty good at it. But he wasn't in Selma very much, and I went to Hopkinsville in the summer. I didn't really get to know him until we lived in Virginia Beach and he came to live with us. He was a fine, wonderful old gentleman, very opinionated.

"The Squire had a life reading that showed one of the strongest drives from which emotional hatred comes that I've ever run into. In earlier years he tried selling insurance. He organized an insurance company that was based on the purity of the white race. He wouldn't sell insurance to anyone who had Negro blood. He and my father would have long involved arguments over the racial question.

Dad wasn't like that. I heard about that all my life. The Squire wrote long treatises on this, and he wrote the charter for this insurance company—a society for the preservation of people of the white race. He actually thought that blacks were animals and that they had no souls. They came up from Cain, and they were a branch off the tree that were just animal. He didn't mistreat them, but he had no feeling for them as human beings.

"What's interesting is that his life reading showed that he had been taken as a Roman youth of sixteen on a ship, captured by the Carthaginians, and spent the rest of his life until he was seventy-five, rowing a Carthaginian ship around the Mediterranean with a black man beating him when he was chained to the oars. So he decided they were beasts, and you just wouldn't believe his hatred." He was almost fanatical. Otherwise, he was a very capable person."

Hugh Lynn's aunts Annie and Sarah, Edgar's sisters, also lived in town, operating a millinery business. "I would go by to see them, and could always count on getting some money for a picture show or an ice cream cone. These were real good people, nice and wholesome. I thought many times that I was the only unwholesome one in the family because I fought a lot, and I worried a lot. I guess I had a conscience, and there were conflicts within me. But it didn't stop me from getting involved in all those things. Sometimes they'd hear about it but not too often. We didn't get into the papers or anything like that, although we sometimes almost got shot."

Of his three living grandparents, he enjoyed the closest relationship with Lizzie. "She was a beautiful woman with a fine mind. Later I used to write her long complicated letters. She had opinions on everything. She was very proud of me when I was going to college, and came to my graduation at Washington & Lee. She hadn't been to college—my mother had—but my grandmother had a sharp mind and I was very close to her."

Over this bucolic scene of carefree adolescence a dark, threatening cloud formed, turning their Hopkinsville holiday into a family crisis during Hugh Lynn's sophomore year in high school.

It all started when a Texas newspaper editor wrote Edgar in December 1918, wanting to know if a psychic reading could be obtained for a floundering oil venture in which he and a few friends had invested.

"It was while I was a high school freshman that the telegrams came from Texas for Dad to give the readings on the oil wells. And he hit the first oil well right on the nose. They had a dry hole and told him where it was, sent him a map of it, and he said go back so many hundreds of feet and shoot it with so many quarts of nitroglycerine and you'll get so many barrels of oil. And they did it, and they got it. They sent him the money to come to Texas, and he got all excited over that.

"He didn't have anyone to go with him. Mr. Williamson had been moved by the railroad or I think he would have gone. Dave Kahn had come home from the war—he was on leave, all dressed up in his captain's uniform.

Kahn was the eldest son of a family from Lexington, Kentucky that had requested a reading for a younger son, Leon, who had been badly injured in a fall from a moving wagon. Dave had arrived home from Army service only to discover that the death of his father had left his mother $65,000 in debt. He consulted Edgar on how he might raise the money. Why not try oil, suggested Edgar. Oil fever was high in Texas, the automobile was catching on, and fortunes would be made for those that had the foresight and enterprise. If they made enough money, he'd operate the hospital free of charge, Edgar told Dave. But they needed some investment capital to start it.

"I've got friends all over the East, North, South," boasted Kahn. "I can get backers for us." Kahn was thrilled. "For Cayce and me, the gushing promise of the Texas oil appeared to hold the answers to all needs," he wrote in *My Life With Edgar Cayce*.

Leaving his photo studio temporarily under the management of his father, Edgar began what promised to be a shortcut to wealth—and ended as a long detour to near disaster.

In Johnson County, Texas, in 1920 the Cayce Petroleum Co. of Texas was formed by three trustees: Cayce, Kahn, and Texas driller-investor M. C. Sanders, who put $5,000 into the venture. Several other Texans, on the strength of Edgar's psychic soundings for hidden oil deposits, joined a coterie of investors who put up some $50,000. Among them was Edgar's uncle, Clint Cayce, who ran a thriving mill supply house in Hopkinsville. He put $5,000 cash into Cayce Petroleum.

A New York securities dealer, W. H. Martin, was engaged to sell stock but had little success because of lack of proof of oil where the company was drilling. Martin said that, "outside of Cayce's personality, we had nothing else to sell."

In September 1920, they made an agreement with Live Oak Oil Association of San Saba, Texas, to drill a 4,000-acre tract that Live Oak had leased. The agreement specified that if oil were discovered, the Cayce Company would get the 640-acre tract on which the well was located. The remainder of the property would be divided into 160-acre checkerboard squares, with each company getting alternate tracts—and whatever oil was found on them. The agreement

46

was extended several times and modified during 1921—giving the drilling company one-fourth of any oil discovered—but it never brought in the gusher of their dreams. This was not their only property—they obtained leases elsewhere in Texas, Arkansas, and Oklahoma during this time.

Drilling first one site and then another, by 1922 Cayce Petroleum's bank account was as dry as its wells. Various reports suggest that technical problems, personal conflicts, even suspected sabotage frustrated the venture, despite readings that identified the location of great reserves of oil. Like so many hopeful ventures, it was undercapitalized from the start. So were Gertrude and her sons.

Initially, the company, with Edgar as president, had authorized $100 a month for the Cayce family's "home expenses" while he was gone. Actually, much less was sent to Gertrude from this account—$360 all told during one year—in sporadic payments of $30 to $75. Squire Cayce's management of the studio apparently was also less profitable than expected. Consequently, Gertrude had passed a difficult winter in Selma, Edgar being absent much of the time, and was obliged to take her boys to Hopkinsville and live with her mother. She was aided by occasional cash donations from her brother Lynn, who worked steadily for the railroad. What began as an adventurous attempt to acquire a small fortune for a good cause turned out to be an impossible dream for Edgar and Dave, and one long nightmare for Muddie and Hugh Lynn. "That experience went on and on, and it was horrible. It was a fiasco."

After the first year or so, his family began to suffer financially and emotionally, wondering what the future held for them. Hugh Lynn bravely confronted his father. "I wrote to Dad finally, and of course Mother wrote to him often, but he didn't come by Hopkinsville very often. He came once that first year, and he promised that the following summer he would take me out there."

What did Hugh Lynn say to his father in that letter?

"What was he going to do with his life? Where was he heading? Was he giving up the family? I was very direct."

The result was that Hugh Lynn got to spend a summer in Texas the year he was fourteen. "I went out there on the train to be with him. I was thrilled to death. I'll never forget arriving in Comyn. It had rained the night before and the mud was a foot thick. I stepped off the train and sank into this black mush that covered my new white sneakers. I never got them really clean again.

"The Sam Davis well at Comyn was a mile or so from the town near a Humble Oil tank farm. Shacks surrounded the well. This is where we lived, with the drillers and men who worked on the well.

They were about the biggest, toughest, roughest men I'd ever seen. One of the driller's wives, Lenora Ringle, made the best fried chicken I'd ever eaten and wonderful potato pie, almost as good as my grandmother's.

"I was thrilled to be in Zane Grey's Purple Sage country, riding horses. I grew up quickly out there. They were a rough gang of young men working on the wells, hauling pipe and handling all the rough work, but they took a liking to me, and they'd slip by at night and knock on my window and I'd slip out and go skinny-dipping with them in the reservoir. I thought I'd been well educated by the gang back in Hopkinsville, but I had never heard such language or such stories. I never heard better curse words than the oil gang used until I heard General George Patton when I was in the Army. He had a few that nobody had ever manufactured before.

"Dave Kahn wasn't married then, and he was a good-looking man. He kept that captain's uniform on longer than he should have, because it got him into places and around. He was a promoter of the first water. He'd get on a crowded elevator in a hotel with Dad. As it started rising he'd say, 'You know Mrs. Jones told me today of the wonderful reading you gave for her catarrh.' Things like that. By the time they got to their floor and got off, everybody in the elevator would follow them off into the room to make appointments for readings.

"Dad used to fuss with Dave about it and say, 'Dave, you know that isn't true. You made that up.' Dave would reply, 'Well, there are true cases just as good as that one. I just changed their names a little bit.'"

The young bachelor knew nothing about the oil business but persuaded friends in Atlanta to invest in the venture and convinced his elders to name him executive vice president. But Kahn couldn't keep his mind on business, and had a run-in with the chief oil driller, Cecil Ringle. "He had a very good-looking wife," Hugh Lynn said of Lenora Ringle. "Dave looked at her a few times too often one night, and her husband almost shot him. Dad got between the two of them and calmed him down. I watched that awful mess. So when I say I grew up out in Texas, it was in several directions."

Hugh Lynn also got acquainted with a different side of his father. "Somehow Dad was different from the father and Sunday school teacher I knew in Selma. He was easy and quiet with the men. They respected him and yet seemed to accept him as one of them. It was as if he had forgotten Selma, yet he didn't raise his voice even when the others argued violently."

If Gertrude hoped that Hugh Lynn would bring his daddy

home, she was only momentarily satisfied. They returned in time for school, but Edgar stayed only a few days and then went on to New York to meet with a stockbroker. He needed more capital to continue. By September he was back in Texas for a third year of wildcatting.

In later years Hugh Lynn said repeatedly that his father had been a poor manager and was unrealistic with money. Not only was his wildcatting for oil a failure, but the Cayce Art Co. no longer supported the family. Edgar had asked the Squire to look after it while he was gone and told Gertrude, who kept the books, to collect the due bills. "He had just walked off and left a business," recalled Hugh Lynn, shaking his head. "My brother, Edgar Evans, had been born and there just wasn't any money. Dad wasn't sending any money back. So Mother took us, as she usually did during the summer, to my grandmother's in Hopkinsville. But there was no money to come back to Selma in the fall, and Dad wasn't back in Selma. So we stayed on in Hopkinsville that winter [1922-23], and I went to high school there, my sophomore year. Uncle Lynn had to support us. We didn't have any clothes. We had food only because we were out on a farm. It strained everybody.

"And I think it hurt my father a great deal because he got mixed up with a very difficult group of people. There were a lot of shenanigans. And that's why they didn't get any oil, I'm sure, because there was oil out there."

Material hardship was the least of it. After all, with a garden and chickens and milk cows, no one would go hungry. The emotional strain was something else. Only yesterday, it seemed, their life had been so happy in Selma, with church socials in their home, his father telling stories, his mother baking for the crowd, all of them working and playing together. Now it was all so different, so empty in a way without his father—emptier beyond his imagining for his mother.

"This was a tragic period because my parents were separated." Gertrude suffered her pain stoically but could not hide her loneliness and heartache. What had begun as a venture that would take only a few weeks, or months perhaps, kept Edgar away from home for four years.

When Cayce Petroleum's capital ran out in 1922, Edgar traveled north, east, south and west in quest of money, giving readings. "Mother couldn't understand Dad's running around the country like that. He kept grasping at a will-o-the-wisp that looked like it was going to materialize any day, and didn't."

For all practical purposes, he missed out on Hugh Lynn's early adolescence. The boy, discovering the evidence of his manhood, matured quickly, his passions becoming noticeably intense. Whenever he noticed that Muddie was depressed, he felt a rush of anger toward his father. "Whenever he hurt her, I hated him. Whatever he did, if he hurt her it hurt me. I got angry."

But the boy's feelings were complicated further by his growing physical attraction for Muddie and jealous antagonism toward his father. "The very fact that he had hurt her, I didn't think he should have her. I was jealous of him, horribly jealous as a teenager, and fascinated at the same time, and very much in love with her. I felt ashamed because it was a physical attraction—I wanted her as a woman, not as a mother. It was horrible. I thought I was absolutely the only person who had to suffer like that. It started in early puberty. I always loved her and was always fascinated by how much they loved each other. I couldn't understand it—it was painful, and it grew more painful through the years. I was going to run away from home—I was about fourteen or fifteen—because I had reached the point where I didn't think I could stand it. But I had to stand it—and he [Edgar] ran before I did."

In reflecting on his life, Hugh Lynn mentioned repeatedly his adolescent desire for his mother. She had been the first great passion of his life. And it did not end soon. During college he still preferred his mother in some ways. Once he said he invited her to campus for a weekend prom, then paid a classmate to dance with his date so he could dance with Muddie. His love for his mother did not, he made clear, interfere in later years with his romantic attraction for young women, including the woman he married. He eventually concluded that his desire for his mother had not been abnormal after all. "It was years before I took enough psychology to discover that half the world was in the same position."

Did his father's long absence become a family catastrophe?

"For my mother. She was the one hurt by it. I could figure out lots of things to do without my father. That wasn't my problem. I never felt very young, or suppressed, or incompetent. I'm not like that."

Lizzie took advantage of the extra teenager in residence that year and put Hugh Lynn and Gray to work with pick and shovel digging a trench for a water line to the house. When the job was done, rendering the outhouse obsolete, the three musketeers decided to celebrate by torching the privy—an occasion recalled by the family less for the advent of indoor plumbing than the stench of that dramatic bonfire.

Edgar returned home to Selma finally in August 1923. Gertrude came back from Hopkinsville with Ecken and Hugh Lynn, who was now sixteen, and they reopened the studio and set about reviving the family business. Edgar had not given up his hope of underwriting a hospital with oil profits, but for now at least he was back home. Gertrude accepted him, welcomed him. In a few weeks she even agreed to pull up stakes in Selma and move to Ohio with him, leaving behind friends and what material security they had once derived from the Cayce Art Co. No one would have blamed Gertrude if she had told her husband that it was time he settled down again in Selma and revived the family business and paid some attention to his family's personal needs. But she must have known that if she and Hugh Lynn and Ecken were to have Edgar at all, it would have to be on his terms, uncertain and unconventional as they were.

As for Hugh Lynn's feelings, the good times he had had in Texas did not really offset the anger he had developed toward his father. "Oh, there were times when I could have killed my father without batting an eye because of the way he treated her [Muddie] at different times. That may sound like a drastic statement, but it isn't at all."

Under ordinary circumstances his parents had an "absolutely beautiful" relationship, Hugh Lynn thought. "In fact, it was too beautiful. That bugged me worse than his hurting her. It drove me wild, upset me terribly. When they were getting along, and when he was there, they loved each other very, very much. She absolutely worshiped him. And without her, he would never have got through the front door. She was the strength, the willpower behind him. He would go off on tangents. She always stayed still, whatever he wanted to do.

"When he left Kentucky and went off to Selma and said he was giving up the psychic business, she supported him. She didn't object to the psychic business at first because he was helping so many people. She supported it and faced her family down—her mother, aunts, everybody in Hopkinsville—faced them down, with the result that he saved her life, and their life together in the process.

"There was just a rapport there. She just worshiped him. And it was Mother who told Dad there was something wrong with Ketchum. She didn't know what it was, but she knew intuitively that Ketchum and Noe were mistreating him. She was scared of Ketchum and Noe and kept telling him they were going to destroy him. She was warning him.

"She was practical. She kept track of money. He couldn't. He spent money just like Jesus gave out the fish, like there was plenty of it, when in fact there never was. He would spend money on things

51

that shouldn't have been bought at all. She supported that, but she kept after him about it. And she kept him from being overly verbose and exaggerating and would call him on it, not in front of other people but by himself. She praised him when he was good at something, and he looked to her to know whether or not he was good when he gave a talk.

"She had a life reading which was fascinating because it said that when her soul entered the body it was twenty-four hours after she was born. I used to kid her that she took one look at Dad and the future with Dad and me and my brother and she couldn't decide whether she wanted to try it this time or not. She didn't have an easy life. But she did love that man, and without her, anybody would tell you, Dad would have gone off into left field. She just loved him into focus, keeping ideals and principles in focus. It was beautiful.

"I realized that as I grew up, but it didn't keep me from being upset. It was my jealousy of my father that bothered me, not my doubting his integrity.

"She was just a wonderful mother, a wonderful person. We were very, very close. She would help with lessons—she had been to college. She was very supportive. She loved me very much. They both loved me. I had more love in my life than the average person by far. I had no complaints in that direction. I was the one who had trouble in that direction."

Chapter 5

Preppie: Dayton

Hugh Lynn's father returned home penniless but possessed by a new sense of purpose. Overshadowing his failure in oil was his success as an itinerant lecturer and psychic. Wherever he went, people flocked around to request readings or listen to his talks and wild stories. He had spent one winter in the big city of Birmingham, living in a hotel, where he gave readings and held court for admirers and the curious. He had been written up in the Birmingham newspapers, which treated him like a visiting dignitary. To return to the confining routine of a small town photographer was no longer enough.

Although he reopened the Cayce Art Co., he had no intention of devoting full time to it. He no longer doubted the importance of the readings, and he seemed just as determined to raise the money for a hospital. He decided to give readings at his studio on a regular basis, and thus hired a Selma girl, Gladys Davis, as a salaried stenographer. She was a tall, pretty blonde, and at eighteen only two years older than Hugh Lynn, who knew her only slightly because Gladys, a Methodist, attended a different church. The daughter of a poor farmer and a direct descendent of Jefferson Davis, she had dropped out of high school to work and help support her family.

In some respects, Edgar's decision to hire a secretary was another example of poor financial judgment when he had no idea whether the business would support her. He might have managed with part-time help or volunteers. During earlier years his father or Dr. Ketchum or Al Layne usually scribbled notes during his sporadic readings. At best he might engage a local court reporter to take down a reading or two. Consequently, few of his early readings were preserved.

Now, however, it would be much more businesslike: Miss Davis would take it all down in shorthand and systematically type up her notes, making two copies—one for the client, one for the files. It was her penchant for saving "one for the files" that made the hiring of Gladys one of the more beneficial decisions of his life. From that point on, during the most productive clairvoyant years of his life, virtually every reading—some 14,000 of them in all—was preserved, indexed, and eventually computerized and carefully analyzed for hidden truths. If Edgar had found oil, it might never have happened that way.

Hugh Lynn was glad to be back home, starting his junior year at Selma High. He had missed his best friend, David Pierson. "We were inseparable. We discovered girls together. We were both in love with the same girl, and both knew it and talked about it, and she knew it and everybody else talked about it—a fun kind of thing. David's father was a dentist. They were in the church, and rather affluent—they had one of the first Model A Fords in Selma, and got into the auto business. When David grew up he had the Ford agency in Selma."

Hugh Lynn would inherit his father's business too, but it would not be the photo studio, which Edgar abruptly closed once again that fall, never to reopen. During his wildcatting in Texas, Edgar had met an Ohio businessman, Arthur Lammers. Clinging to the hope that he could find investors for Cayce Petroleum, and thus realize his dream hospital, Edgar went to Dayton to visit Lammers, who owned a printing business and seemed well-to-do. Lammers was also fascinated with astrology and other esoteric studies, and he had an imaginative idea for founding a research institute and using Cayce's gift to gather information on philosophical and metaphysical subjects. During their visit Lammers made a startling proposal:

"Lammers offered to set him up in a Dayton hotel—he wanted what he called "horoscope readings"—and he wanted Dad to just devote time to the readings and give up photography, and Dad did it—just walked out of the studio he owned. He left my grandfather in it for a little while, but he just got nothing out of it at all. He had all this equipment, and his negatives. A man came along and offered to run it for him because my grandfather wasn't really a good photographer—he could take pictures but he wasn't good at running the business. So Dad said to this man, 'Fine, do that,' but he never made a contract and never got paid. He just ran away. He could turn loose of physical things as well as anyone I know. And yet he loved money, too. He wanted it for the hospital. It was almost as though he knew instinctively that he had to move on."

While Edgar's decision was sudden, it was consistent with his itch to do something bigger than become Selma's best picture man. Lammers' institute to investigate psychic phenomena might answer his questions about the readings.

This time, however, Edgar took the family with him, including his new steno. But rather than disrupt Hugh Lynn's school term, he suggested that Gertrude arrange with friends for Hugh Lynn to remain in Selma and join the family in Dayton at Christmas. The Piersons were glad to have him. "When I left Selma a few months later that friendship stopped, but it was very intense and we had a great rapport. Friendship, beginning with David and moving on to others, became a very important part of my life—a commitment to a friend, a trust in a friendship. I've done this all my life—had a few intimate, very close friends, in Selma and everywhere I've gone."

Edgar's work in Dayton had no sooner been started, however, when Lammers suffered a crippling financial setback. Embroiled in a lawsuit, he was unable to meet his financial commitments and went bankrupt. Their only source of income suddenly stopped. The Cayces were stranded, barely making ends meet with contributions from a few people who obtained readings. They tried to shield Hugh Lynn from worrying about this setback but he was not fooled. "I knew from their letters that things were not going well. I was supposed to be paying the Piersons for my board but I hadn't paid them for a month or two. They were very pleasant about it. I don't know whether we ever did pay them. There wasn't even any money to bring me to Dayton, so my mother used a couple of gold coins she had to pay for my ticket."

When school let out and the Piersons put him on the train, Hugh Lynn left Alabama and his childhood behind for a whole new life up North. Young manhood lay ahead now, beginning, of all places, in a Yankee prep school.

"When I got off the train in Dayton, I don't know when I've been more depressed. My father was distraught and looked gaunt and tired. It was snowing but he wasn't wearing an overcoat. When I hugged him as I got off the train I heard crackling sounds. It came from newspapers he had stuffed under his clothes for warmth. I was dumbfounded."

It was the Cayces' first encounter with the cold of a Midwestern winter. In their financial straits, they lacked even the price of warm winter clothing.

"We took the trolley to their apartment on the second floor of a small private home. It was not in a good section of town—it was the cheapest one they could find, Gladys later told me—but it was on the streetcar line. Dad had an office in the old Phillips Hotel where he gave readings. He hadn't given up the office because he couldn't settle up on the back rent he owed, and he was afraid if he moved out he'd be arrested for non-payment of rent. He stayed on and promised the manager it was coming."

Despite their difficulties, the family celebrated Hugh Lynn's return. Muddie fixed a nice dinner.

"The dinner was sparse. There just wasn't a great deal of food. There was a chicken—such a little chicken that you could put your hands around it—and it was for all of us, my brother, Gladys, my mother and father and me. It was good because Mother was a good cook. I felt the tension at dinner, but they didn't talk about it. Dad avoided any questions by saying they were getting along all right, people were getting readings, and things were going to work out. And then he'd ask me 'How is everything in Selma?' to keep me away from what was going on.

"Finally, I asked them what went wrong, why were we so poor? Dad said Lammers had gone bankrupt and they hadn't seen him for a month or more. He did all the printing for the National Cash Register Co., which had been closed by a strike. So suddenly there was no money.

"But along with this bad news I sensed that they were excited—I didn't know what it was. We had hardly finished eating when they began talking about life readings. I had never heard of a life reading. They presented me with this document and told me it was my life reading. I read it while they sat around the table waiting for my reaction—and I went into shock.

"They were so excited about it—Mother was excited, and Gladys was excited. Dad was weighing it, but excited about it. This was a new thing that had happened for his readings, and indeed a new thing that happened to the United States."

These new readings had been inspired by Lammers' request for a "horoscope reading." A student of mystical philosophy, Lammers had been delighted when his first reading hinted at a previous incarnation. The Cayces were astonished but intrigued, for Lammers' reading suggested that he and Edgar had been associated in a previous life. As more such information came through Cayce, they began calling them life readings, because they focused on people's lives, past and present, rather than just the physical ailments of this life.

Hugh Lynn's first life reading identified several earlier lives he had lived in other countries in centuries past, most recently as a monk in medieval England. The reading said he had also fought in the Crusades. He read part of it, then paused.

"I asked my father, 'Do you believe this?'

"He said, 'Well, I don't know. I'm having to think about it. What do you think of it?'

"I said, 'I can't believe it. This is ridiculous.'

"I had never heard the word reincarnation before that I could recall. I certainly had never heard my father mention the word. I knew there were such beliefs as past lives, but I thought it was only by ignorant Hindus who were in so much trouble all the time. I had no true concept of it at all.

"But one of the things about my life reading that shocked me—and I didn't say anything to anyone about it—was that it explained my attraction for my mother."

Among the boy's previous incarnations, said his reading, was one in ancient Egypt—indeed, it claimed that he and both his parents had lived in that time. Hugh Lynn had been a monarch named Araaraart. Edgar had been the high priest, Ra Ta. And Muddie had been a beautiful young dancing girl named Isis, who was Araaraart's favorite. A great rift developed between the king and the priest over the girl. The priest, although married, had a child by the dancer—and the king, infuriated, had exiled the priest and the girl. Furthermore, a life reading for Gladys said that she had been that baby, which might explain why Gertrude and Gladys in this life had so easily assumed a mother-daughter relationship.

It sounded like a fairy story, entertaining but unbelievable, and yet Hugh Lynn wondered—could this be the reason that he was so tormented by passion for Muddie and jealousy toward the man she loved? After 12,000 years, the "priest" still had the "dancing girl"—and there was not a thing the "king" could do about it.

Hugh Lynn tried hard to hide these strong feelings from his family. He didn't think he had ever given himself away, but now he worried about being exposed. "I thought these readings were an invasion of privacy. I didn't think they knew about it, but I thought maybe he was using this reading as a way of getting at me without saying anything himself. This idea hit me and grew on me, that it was a way of warning me, because we were all involved, everyone in the room.

"I began to question everything about these new readings: How did they start doing them? How many had they had? Who had had them? They had started because Lammers was curious about astrology, and the reading Lammers received said that his impulses were not nearly as great as they had been in a past life when he was a monk. That opened the whole can of peas.

"Of course, they all got readings after that, and they fit together like a tight puzzle. The more I read them, the more disturbed I became. But they romanced it, made it into a romantic tale, saying wasn't it interesting that this and that and so forth. They were very free with what you would think of as difficult."

There was one more astounding element in the scenario of past lives laid on young Hugh Lynn. His reading said he had lived "in the days when the Prince of Peace walked by the seashore. This entity answered the call, and was one of those followers." His name: Andrew. The only other detail given was that he had "brought his brother to the Master."

Hugh Lynn rejected it completely, suspecting his father of trying to control his behavior by suggesting that he should be as pious as he felt sure Jesus' followers had been. How could he live up to their standards?

He also rejected the reincarnation concept. At the customary age for challenging the conventional wisdom, the boy ironically protested the unconventional wisdom of the readings. The reincarnation idea troubled him because the life readings suggested that everyone was responsible for his own life situation, based on what had occurred in prior lives. Anyone who had wronged another person and failed to correct it, the readings indicated, was destined to have an opportunity in a subsequent incarnation to make amends. The purpose was for each soul to gain greater awareness and a higher consciousness.

If Hugh Lynn and his parents had known one another in ancient Egypt, the reverberations were still being felt.

"The reading explained very clearly that what I felt for my father and for my mother was memory. And I was responsible for what kind of memory I had. I was imposing on my father a whole set of ideas that didn't exist. I was jealous of him, but I had no right to be jealous in the present-day situation. I distrusted him in relationship to my mother, but I didn't have a right to do that. You see, I was putting on him my own weaknesses, my own problems—and we all do it. I would get angry with him, easily, over her—but rarely got angry with him over other things. I would delight in making him angry over little things just because it was a way of hurting him. It hurt me and I knew it hurt him. I took advantage of him, imposed this on him, and I didn't want to accept reponsibility for that, or for what I had done in the past as the root cause of my present attitude. I didn't want to accept the idea that she preferred him to me."

Gladys was just the opposite of Hugh Lynn—most eager to

know about her earlier incarnations. So was Gertrude. During that impoverished winter in Dayton, with few outside requests for readings, Edgar had ample time to give life readings for everyone in the family. One reading filled in the poignant details of the tragic outcome of the ancient Egyptian love triangle: When the king [Hugh Lynn] exiled the priest [Edgar] and the dancing girl [Gertrude], he took their baby [Gladys] away from them—and the child had died without her mother. Hugh Lynn found this scenario further reason to scoff at the whole business.

"I didn't want to accept the idea that I kept a child that they had, and that the child died after I separated it from them out of anger toward them, and that this child had come back and was sitting there in the room.

"I wanted the readings to be a nice practical thing, like diagnosing illness, and I thought my father was wrong to start these life readings. I thought he'd gone around the bend. I became more and more confused. I was pretty young. I didn't know what to make of my feelings, but I just wanted to cover them up—or run away. But my reading focused it in just a few pages. It showed me where my anger and hate came from. I wasn't supposed to be a person who got angry or hated people to the point where I could kill them—I didn't want that at all. I didn't want to see myself like that, but that's what the readings said I was like, very clearly.

"In the long run my life reading helped me. But it overwhelmed me in the beginning because it simply said, 'Hugh Lynn, you are responsible for the way you feel.' That didn't sit well with me. And I don't think it really does with most people. They don't want to take responsibility for that condition that is bothering them, whether it is physical or emotional or mental or whatever. People are loath to accept that responsibility."

Edgar Cayce had opened an entire system of philosophical thought for western minds to one day contemplate. But it was over the objections of his eldest son.

Hugh Lynn escaped by throwing himself into school activities, which were very challenging because his new school was so different from the rural school in Kentucky and even Selma High. Through the intercession of an inventor who had been helped by a reading, he was admitted to an innovative Dayton academy, Moraine Park School. "It was an advanced, experimental school set up by wealthy industrialists in Dayton for their children. They let a few others in so they could associate with the hoi polloi. It had a limited enrollment of about 120 students in the upper school. I don't know how in the world I got in. The headmaster interviewed me and I got a full scholarship—it was very expensive. I went there for a year and a half until I finished high school."

Was the poor boy from Alabama admitted to this Yankee prep school because he was so different perhaps? "Yes, I was sort of a token Southerner. I was a novelty—they loved to hear me talk—but I was sharp, and I beat the daylights out of them in debating.

"They took me in. They were not snobbish, those that I knew, even though they were all much better off than my parents. We were almost starving. I had only one good pair of pants and I took them off when I came home from school. It was rough, but the other boys were good about it and I soon became very close with several of them. We had clubs—I was in the Grandfell Club—and everybody in the club was very close. I was also in the Shawnees. Each student had to perform a job or run a business. You had to learn how to do something. The two Patterson boys—their father owned National Cash Register—ran a taxi service for other students. They had a car and every morning they came by and picked me up and took me to school, which was held in a greenhouse given by the Pattersons and converted to classrooms. Dick Funkhouser, whose father was president of Delco, ran the school bank. Everybody had an account in the bank, and we had checkbooks and were supposed to learn how to use them. My job was to be a secretary to one of the professors.

"I also went out for debate and was on the Shawnees' debate team. We debated all over town. My key man—there were four of us on the team—was Gene Kettering, whose father invented the self-starter. Gene was sharp. I played tennis with Gene and we became good friends. One of the most fascinating conversations I ever had when we lived in Dayton was with Gene's father."

Charles F. Kettering, an engineer, was an inventive genius. In addition to the auto self-starter, he developed a high-compression engine for autos, a diesel engine for trains, ethyl gasoline, and accounting machines for National Cash Register, a major Dayton industry. When Hugh Lynn met him, Kettering was vice president for research at General Motors, which had bought the Charles K. Kettering Laboratories in Dayton.

"When we got to Gene's house his father was sitting on the living room floor and—I'll never forget that—he had taken their organ completely apart and had every piece of it out on the floor. I couldn't imagine that he was ever going to get that back together. When we came in, he stopped to talk to us. He seemed delighted to just sit there and talk, nobody was going to bother the organ—it could sit there for months if necessary. We had a fascinating conversation.

60

"Everybody in the Ohio industrial world was in that school—the Sieberlings of the rubber company, and lots of people like that that I never thought I'd get mixed up with. I went back to Dayton years later and had lunch with a batch of them—all very affluent. Gene was a multi-millionaire, had guards for his children. When I make friends, I make friends intensely. I became close to the headmaster's son, Leland Slutz, the Patterson boys, Funkhouser, and Gene. We drifted apart later, but we were very close then.

"My friendships in Dayton were not as deep as my earlier friendships. I never shared the same kinds of things, but I shared a lot of intellectual curiosity with them. I delighted in taking opposite sides in debate on such issues as the fight that was going on between capital and labor. I was for labor, and the big unions were just beginning. National Cash Register was closed by a strike, and there was a furor over that. Our team debated labor questions, aided and abetted by the headmaster.

"We had topflight judges for our debates. One of the Wright brothers was a judge and wrote a critique of me that I never forgot. We were debating a girls' team—there were two girls' clubs in the school—and were in the final debate on this labor issue. I had memorized my speech, and the debating coach was very proud of it. He said I had written a good speech and delivered it with great style. I got up to talk without a copy of my speech. We had a prompter behind us who had a copy if we needed help. I started by saying, 'The . . .' and my mind went blank. The speech had vanished from my mind. I walked over to the edge of the platform, so nervous I didn't know what to do, while the prompter ruffled through the papers looking for my speech—he couldn't believe I'd stalled after the first word. At the other side of the stage I began again, 'The . . .' but drew a blank. So I returned to the other side of the stage and this time gestured with both hands and tried again, and it came rolling out just as I'd memorized it. When the judges' reports came in, Mr. Wright—I don't remember whether it was Wilbur or Orville—said about me: 'The third speaker for the negative had one of the most pregnant pauses I've ever heard in a debate.' "

What did his classmates think of his father's business—or did he not speak of it?

"They were very much aware of it. I talked about it in class and was asked questions about it. But I wasn't making much noise about it—I was overwhelmed with those life readings. They had hit me full blow and I didn't want to talk about that. It was on my mind constantly as I stewed and worried about it, but I wasn't talking about that."

Hugh Lynn's report card that year was as imaginative as his school. Instead of merely identifying the courses each student took, Moraine Park School rated each student in fifty-six categories clustered under ten objectives: Body Building, Spirit Building, Society Serving, Man Conserving, Opinion Forming, Truth Discovering, Thought Expressing, Wealth Producing, Comrade or Mate Seeking, and Life Refreshing. The only marks were for work of exceptional merit or unsatisfactory work. Hugh Lynn received E for exceptional merit in Body Building (he had gone out for boxing), in Mathematics, and in Project work, a category under Wealth Producing. He was rated highly satisfactory in English, and satisfactory in all other categories.

At the bottom of his report card, headmaster Fred Slutz added his own evaluation of Hugh Lynn: "He is a real treasure! We cannot afford to lose him." Slutz added a reference to the student's scholarship status: "We shall do everything in our power to make it possible for Hugh to graduate at Moraine."

The larger question was whether the Cayce family could survive without Edgar going back to photography. They had made it through a tough winter on the strength of Edgar's few acquaintances who got readings and recommended him to others. Edgar had no fixed fee for a reading, giving some for nothing, but occasionally received a generous contribution from an affluent client. By the end of their first year in Dayton business had picked up considerably—enough for the Cayces to move from their apartment to a duplex on Grafton Avenue in a pleasant residential neighborhood closer to the school and near a lovely city park.

"We could walk to the park. The whole family would go on Sunday afternoon and play croquet and bowl on the green. Dad was good at any kind of game, especially bowling—bowling on the green, ten pins, duck pins. I never saw him lose at ten pins."

They also found a Church of Christ and attended regularly but didn't become heavily involved as they had in Selma.

"We always went to church, wherever we lived."

After moving into the house, Edgar closed his office in the hotel, set up shop in the dining room at home, and periodically visited other cities for a week or two—Columbus and Chicago particularly—to give prearranged readings.

During one visit to Columbus, he received a telephone call from a New York stockbroker, Morton Blumenthal, who had an earache. Dave Kahn, who had gone into the furniture business in New York, told Blumenthal about Cayce. The stockbroker was helped by a reading and became so intrigued that he went to

Dayton to meet the psychic. Like Lammers, he had a strong philosophical bent and was captivated by the potential he saw in Edgar's trance readings. After returning to New York, he began requesting readings regularly for medical, philosophical, and financial reasons. Blumenthal was in business with his brother Edwin. Pleased with the results in all three categories, Morton invited the whole Cayce family to New York at his expense. It was Hugh Lynn's first visit to the big city and his first experience with anyone quite so worldly.

Blumenthal, a handsome, dark-haired man in his late twenties, lived in a hotel apartment with his mother. Hugh Lynn stayed in his apartment while the others were lodged in rooms in the hotel. For all the wealthy boys he had encountered in Dayton, Hugh Lynn had never met anyone like Morton. Despite his youth, Morton was a big spender from Wall Street, a man about town with a show girl for a sweetheart, a seat on the Stock Exchange, and a burning desire to understand everything in this realm and beyond. He took the Cayces and Gladys to visit the places where he worked and played, the Stock Exchange and the Silver Slipper, a Manhattan night club, and to a shocking Broadway show.

"Morton had sent for tickets from his ticket broker to whatever show they had seats for, and so we saw, "Ladies of the Evening." It was quite exciting for a teenage boy—all about prostitution."

Although a New York sophisticate, Blumenthal had not come to wealth easily. Born in Altoona, Pennsylvania, he had worked his way through college, and urged Hugh Lynn to continue his education. Hugh Lynn felt confident of getting into a good college on the record he was making at Moraine Park, but he wondered where the money would come from. Much taken with the bright Cayce boy, Morton promised financial aid.

Blumenthal's ideas for Edgar were even more magnanimous. He proposed creating an organization to sponsor Edgar's work, pay him a salary, and move him to the East Coast. Morton thought he could raise the money to start it, and people who requested readings would pay the organization to keep it going. The family would be moved to Virginia, where the readings said they would build a hospital. It sounded wonderful to his visitors, who returned to Dayton with a new optimism about their future. Was poverty behind them at last?

Blumenthal organized the National Association of Investigators, which put Edgar and Gladys on salary early in 1925 and offered to pay the family's expenses for their move to the East coast. Since the readings had recommended a small summer resort town,

Virginia Beach, Virginia, as the best location for the hospital, Morton laid plans to make Edgar's dream come true. Edgar said they would wait until Hugh Lynn finished his senior year in the spring of 1925.

Graduation exercises at Moraine Park were so formal—no routine cap and gown would do—that his mother had to rent a tuxedo for him. Hugh Lynn, now eighteen, suddenly looked very grown up, but then his adolescence had been an uncommonly maturing experience.

Late that summer after Blumenthal's check ($540) for moving expenses arrived, the Cayces packed their meager personal effects, climbed aboard the train, and left Ohio with few regrets. They were headed for Virginia where Edgar—and Hugh Lynn—were destined to do their most important work.

Chapter 6

Young Skeptic

When the Cayces' train reached Norfolk, Virginia via Hopkins-ville soon after Labor Day 1925, they spent the night in the Southland Hotel on Granby Street waiting for Gladys, who had gone to Alabama. Rejoined, they boarded a trolley for the last lap to Virginia Beach. The summer-resort village they found at the end of the streetcar line was virtually deserted, an autumn ghost town. Vacation cottages stood empty, many of them boarded up. The house that Blumenthal had rented for them, a two-story dwelling facing a line of sand dunes near the sea, was larger than many and commodious enough for its five new occupants. But typical of beach houses, it had no central heating system, only a fireplace in the living room. The autumn nights were so warm, however, that it was not until late fall that they realized their plight.

Their first night in town, with no food in the house, they set out on foot to find a restaurant. The Casino, four blocks away, was the only one open. Spot, a small local saltwater fish, was in season but the Casino had only a few left, enough to serve the newcomers one fish each. Next morning, looking for a grocery, they found one open at 17th Street, several miles from their house. They could walk or take the trolley, which ran every two hours. The town's tiny post office was there, too, so Gladys began walking "into town" for the morning mail. The business section included a drug and hardware store run by the mayor; an active Coast Guard station manned by a year-round crew; and a choice among three churches: Baptist, Methodist, or Presbyterian.

On the first Sunday they tried the Baptist Church. They enjoyed the service and afterward Edgar approached the minister about their joining the congregation.

"The preacher said he'd discuss it with the congregation, and asked us to step out into the vestibule. Well, Dad stepped out into the vestibule and kept right on going out to the sidewalk, and we never went back."

Edgar felt offended that his family had not been welcomed with open arms without further adieu.

"Next Sunday we went to the Presbyterian Church, just a little mission church. But the minister, Dr. Scattergood, welcomed us, and he became interested in the work—later served on the [A.R.E.] board of trustees."

From that day until the last year of Edgar's life, the Cayces stuck with the Presbyterian Church. Eventually it would become an important element of their social and community life, for Gladys joined the choir, Edgar taught a Bible class, Ecken joined the church's scout troop, and Hugh Lynn taught Sunday School and became the scoutmaster. But for the first few months in this resort town, Hugh Lynn felt uncertain about his future.

"I really wasn't prepared to go to college right then—the money wasn't available."

Pondering his father's advice that he learn something practical, Hugh Lynn signed up for a one-year general course at Norfolk Business College. As an example of practicality, Edgar took his sons to the beach below the dunes in front of their house to scavenge for driftwood and poles that floated ashore. They dragged them home and chopped them up for firewood. Evenings were spent huddled around the fireplace until bedtime. "Sure does make us wonder about the heat in this house, and about our being able to get some electric heaters or oil heaters or both," Edgar wrote his patron, Blumenthal. "$200 this month is not going to carry me over...I wish you would send me $50 or $75."

Blumenthal had paid the first month's rent of $50. The stock market was doing well by him and he sent Edgar an extra $100. By late October the Cayces bought several small kerosene heaters that they carried from room to room, even to the bathroom, as the nights grew cold.

Ecken, just seven, was enrolled in the local school and Hugh Lynn commuted by trolley to business school.

"I knew that I was going to have to work while going to college and I needed some skills, particularly typing, so I took shorthand, typing, business, and spelling—I needed the spelling badly.

"I learned to type, and that helped put me through Washington & Lee, where I got a job in the library my freshman year and worked

66

there four hours a day for four years, typing index cards for the card catalogue, as well as moving books in the basement, dressed in dust clothes."

Business school also brought the boy his first serious romance—"a girl who was playing in the Norfolk Symphony. I fell in love with her. We both went to Norfolk Business School. She was smart as she could be, had light brown hair and ivory skin. We became engaged and were quite serious. She was one of the most talented women I've ever known—but cold as a marble statue. I thought she was a goddess on a pedestal."

Hugh Lynn brought the young lady home to meet his parents. When he had told her about his father's strange occupation, she was intrigued. Hugh Lynn described his father's life seal—an oasis scene including a well and three palm trees—and the girl sketched it for his father. Edgar was so touched that he gave her a life reading in return. It was now two years since Edgar had given Hugh Lynn his first life reading, and the boy was still not reconciled to the concept of past lives—particularly one life: the disciple Andrew. He mentioned it to no one and refused to believe it.

His fiancee's reading said she and Hugh Lynn and Edgar had all known one another in ancient Egypt—and she had chosen to go with the high priest when he had been banished by the king. She later returned and married the king and gave him a son.

Hugh Lynn's girlfriend responded quite positively to her life reading. As she put it: "I saw it taken down in shorthand, as he gave it, and heard it. As I read same, I recognized it as just the words I heard. Now, have I fooled myself, or is it not true that truth is stranger than fiction? For I feel within that everything I have been told is true, and I thank my friend [Hugh Lynn] for having brought me in touch with what appears to me to be such a wonderful phenomenon, and a source of help to many seeking to know themselves; for this is an actual experience, and not fiction."

Her enthusiastic acceptance of his father's clairvoyance, even though Hugh Lynn remained skeptical about life readings, seemed to augur well for their romance. He was nonetheless most intrigued by the idea that she also had been a member of that ancient Egyptian circle when Hugh Lynn was supposed to have been king. Hugh Lynn said her reading indicated that she had been one of the king's lovers, but had been stolen by the king's brother. The story lacked nothing in melodramatic romance and adventure. This appealed immensely to Gladys, who read romantic dime novels, but not Hugh Lynn. It gave him an idea, however.

"It occurred to me that this was a marvelous opportunity to

test the life readings."

Fred, a high school friend from Selma, had written, requesting a reading. To Hugh Lynn's astonishment, Fred's reading said they had been brothers in ancient Egypt when Hugh Lynn had been the king, and they had got into a big quarrel that had split the kingdom. In Selma they had been close buddies, often double-dating, Hugh Lynn with Fred's sister. Here again, this reading sounded like a fairy story to him.

"Neither Fred nor my girlfriend had ever met in this life, and they knew nothing about the other's life reading. So I decided to bring them together. She was at the Beach, with her mother who had come from Long Island to meet my family, and I invited Fred to come for a visit at the same time. Mother and Dad liked her and her mother. She was also wealthy.

"After the first night that we were all together I asked Fred, 'What do you think?'

"'She's the worst you've ever picked,' he replied. 'You can't marry this girl. It's absurd. She's cold as ice.'

"'But she dances beautifully and plays the violin,' I said.

"'She's terrible for you,' Fred insisted.

"Fred was there a week before she and her mother returned to their home in New York. Fred stayed another week before returning to Selma—by way of New York. He went there to see my girl.

"Within a few days I got my pin back from her and an apology from them both."

Had the king's brother and the king's lover repeated a pattern?

"She called their relationship an affair, and he told me exactly what was going on. Every night that he was there in Virginia Beach he had borrowed our car for a late date—his date was my girl whom I had taken out earlier. They were having intercourse from the first night on, and he admitted it.

"I had loved him like a brother. He was a wonderful friend. But I hated what he had done. I experienced love and hate. He was a wonderful guy, but after that I wouldn't trust him as far as I could throw him by his hind leg. And I concluded, 'By golly, these life readings are right.'"

Nearly twenty years later Hugh Lynn had a series of experiences which seemed to him to validate his reading. "I began to choke regularly"—and on three occasions had to be taken to the hospital emergency room to prevent strangulation. Afterward, he dreamed of seeing his former fiancee's face. "This was in another life, in England, and I was choking her. She was having someone else's child."

In other words, he and his pretty violinist had evidently made music together in several lives, never harmoniously. In this karmic reenactment of his life as a Norwegian invader of England, it became apparent to Hugh Lynn that he had strangled her for her unfaithfulness. It seemed to be the key to his own near-strangulation in this life. He prayed for the strength to forgive her and for forgiveness for himself. When he awoke next morning, it was as though a great weight had been lifted from his soul.

A few days later Hugh Lynn received a telephone call from the woman, his first contact with her in all those years. She had married and divorced twice and was calling from New York on a whim to say, "I do hope you've forgiven me by now. I did treat you so disgracefully." Hugh Lynn assured her that he had. He never heard from her again, nor choked on any more stew bones.

Chapter 7

College Boy: Washington & Lee

What prompted Hugh Lynn's choice of Washington & Lee, a very proper, quite old, and exceptionally good school in Lexington, Virginia?

"I didn't choose it. The readings selected it. I had planned to go to Columbia University. Dave Kahn had said he could get me a job somewhere in the furniture business in New York while I went to Columbia. When I got a reading on what I ought to be studying, it said if I really wanted to prove reincarnation to myself I should go to Washington & Lee. I had never heard of it. I had come recently from Ohio, and my focus was on something commercial and practical. I was trying to get work—things were very tight for us financially. So when it said go to Washington & Lee, I went. And I got in."

His choice of a college was certainly significant in one sense.

"Tom Sugrue was one of the first people I met there. He, too, was a freshman; and he, too, had changed schools at the last minute."

Did Hugh Lynn consider their meeting providential?

"It was certainly providential in the sense of looking into the future. It meant a great deal to both of us because my father saved Tom's life, I'm certain, and he and I worked through one of the most difficult pieces of karma that I have ever seen. And we became friends at a level well beyond the average friendship. It was beautiful."

Their relationship was pretty rocky to begin with, however.

"Tom was shorter than I and redheaded. He talked through his nose—a damned Yankee, I thought. The first time I saw him on campus he was wearing a beanie, strumming a ukulele, and singing an Irish ditty. He asked me where I was from and I told him Virginia Beach. 'Where in the world is that?' he remarked. When he told me he was from Naugatuck, Connecticut, I said, 'Where in the world is that?' So we started off very ungracefully. He was rooming next door to me in the oldest and most ramshackle dormitory at Washington & Lee. His roommate, Leon, was an ardent Baptist. Tom was an ardent Catholic, and had considered studying for the priesthood. But he was kind of a rebel, very much in line with modern Catholic activities [challenging the Vatican]. He later wrote a book, A *Catholic Speaks His Mind*, that he thought he would be excommunicated for.

"My roommate was Bill Meredith. Bill was big and tall and slow. Tom was short and fast and thought like lightning—without question, one of the finest minds I've ever known. In his four years at Washington & Lee he held every major position on campus—we elected those—he was a politician. He wrote school plays, musicals, both the book and the music. He resurrected the literary magazine that had been dead for years. I wrote for it and Tom edited it. He was admitted to a fraternity his freshman year, Phi Kappa Psi, and later wanted me to join too. The management of that frat was wild. We had some politicians and athletes and some brilliant guys. Politics was a terrible thing on campus in those days, and we were right in the middle of it.

"While this was going on, Tom and I tried to join forces and put our beds in a side room. With that we began a continuous argument that never stopped. The other boys used to get after us about it because whenever there was nothing else to do we argued, mainly about two subjects: He was running down Edgar Cayce and psychical research, and I took the Catholic Church apart piece by piece.

"I found a picture of a magnificent altar, covered in gold and jewels, in a Catholic cathedral in some South American city. Millions of dollars had been spent in ornamentation. So I looked up in the World Almanac the poverty and illiteracy figures for the same city, and I mutilated the World Almanac by tearing out these items and then pasted them on the wall over Tom's desk and shellacked them so he couldn't get them off. He came in, sat down and read them, and didn't come back for a week.

"But we didn't just argue. We fought, and some of the things we fought over were childish. I had put up a Virginia Beach pennant in our study room. He came in and said, 'Take that thing down. I'm not going to have a Virginia Beach pennant in here.' And I said, 'There are four walls here, you can put up whatever you want, put up one of Naugatuck so people here will know how to spell it.' But he said, 'I'm going to make you take it down,' and I told him what would happen before that went on.

"Next morning when I got up I didn't have any pants. During

the night he had stolen every pair, even my tennis shorts, everything. And remember, in those days you appeared in class in coat and tie. You couldn't even wear a sweater. I had a nice coat and tie, but no pants. So I went down the hall looking—I had to get to class—and found a pair of duck pants, too long, but I rolled them up and put on my coat and tie and went to class. That afternoon I tracked down my pants in somebody's room across campus. When I got back to my room there was the most horrible smell, and everybody in the dorm was looking at my Virginia Beach pennant. It was saturated with this stuff that Tom had got—horrible smelling stuff. You could not stay in the same room with it even with the windows open. There was an upperclassman there who was supposed to manage the floor. He was yelling, trying to get someone to take down my pennant—it was saturated, and the stuff was all over the wall. He told me to take it out but I refused. Tom came in and was ordered to do it, but he wouldn't touch it. He said, 'It's Cayce's—let him do it.'

"We were sent to the V.C. (Vigilance Committee), which was made up of football players. Any upperclassman could turn in a freshman's name to the V.C. Rushing was just plain brutal—you had to have a tie on, you couldn't walk on the grass, you could hardly breathe except so many times. Well, we had defied the upper-classman's orders by refusing to take down my pennant, so Tom and I appeared together before the V.C. and were punished for disobedience. We were stretched over chairs and the football boys got paddles as thick as your finger and broke them over our rear ends. They did that three times—it was terrible. And they bet among themselves over whether they could break the paddles—it was inhumane. But that's the way it was done in those days.

"We still wouldn't touch the pennant. So the sophomore in charge of our floor got a pole and hooked it on the pennant and threw it out the window. Neither Tom nor I had given in. Neither had won either, and we went on fighting.

"A few nights later we had one of our most violent battles while playing cards. I was wearing a ring that my grandmother had given me—a beautiful white sapphire. Tom said, 'Let me see it.' I held up my hand for him to look at it. He said, 'Take it off and let me see it.' And I replied, 'You can see it without my taking it off.' He said, 'Take it off,' and started pulling the ring—and the skin down to the bone of my finger. I hauled off and hit him in the face, three times, as hard as I could hit him, bruising his eye and the side of his face. I never had so much fun in all my life. I went to the hospital and my ring finger was bandaged up, and he got some ice for his eye and face.

"It was ridiculous the way we got into arguments in the middle of the night. Tom would get so mad that he wouldn't sleep in the same room with me. He'd throw his mattress out in the hall and sleep out there. Before our freshman year was over we broke up and he moved to the fraternity house.

"We also did crazy things like bet $100 on our grades—neither of us had any money, the bet had been made in a moment of anger. Realizing that he was a brilliant guy, I worked myself into a froth. When the reports came out we had identical marks—all A's in our four subjects and a B in conduct. So it was a stalemate. But that got me on the dean's list, which I liked."

Although only a college freshman, Hugh Lynn was treated as an adult by his parents. Edgar constantly wrote to keep him informed of developments, often asking his advice. Edgar sent him a copy of the application for a state charter for the National Association of Investigators, saying "It's the first application of the kind that has ever been filed in any state in the union, so we're making history if we don't do anything else—and possibly will set a precedent. Our charter, if granted, allows us to do most anything except build railroads, and operate steamship lines—though it mentions the readings specifically—but merely calls them readings—doesn't say kind, character, nor qualify them in any way—but sets forth, of course, that it is a psychic research association—and while there have been and are psychic associations, there have none as yet been organized that have asked to be allowed to do the things that are allowed in this charter."

There was also some bad news from home during Hugh Lynn's first semester at college: Ecken was seriously burned when he got too close to the fireplace. "His pajamas caught afire," wrote Edgar, "and no one being in the room he was pretty badly burned before his mother or I could get to him. He is burned, however, on the back side of his leg, from the ankle to the hip, the worst part being, of course, under the knee. . . It's been pretty trying on the little fellow. He's such a nervous child anyway. It seems that both of our boys have been tried so as by fire, anyhow."

Adult memories of this childhood episode differ a bit, but they agree on one key element: on this occasion, Edgar had no hesitancy about following the advice of a reading. Edgar Evans has no recollection of a doctor attending him, but of his parents applying various oils as suggested in his reading. Hugh Lynn recalls talk of surgery:

"His leg was doubled up and the doctors wanted to cut the tendon. They said he would limp for the rest of his life, but he would

74

be able to walk. Dad gave a reading that said the operation wasn't necessary. It said he would be all right."

A month after the accident, Ecken was still unable to walk. "It's right pitiful to see him sliding around on the floor, trying to do some of the things that he normally does a lot of," Edgar wrote a friend.

Although he was scarred for life the length of his leg, Ecken healed and grew to become the most athletic member of the family, a football player at school and an avid golfer in later years. The use of his leg was not impaired.

On his father's birthday that year, Hugh Lynn wrote him a touching, admiring letter wishing him a happy celebration, then added: "Perhaps, Dad, you remember when I was a little fellow how I used to say that I wanted to be like Dad—except I wanted a little more money. Well I have changed a bit. I prize one thought, one idea above most of the rest I have gained by your teaching. There is something other than money to look out for in the world. Time and time again have I seen all go wrong—the world almost come to pieces—and you fell back upon that inner sense of the realization of aid, that fountain of strength which flows only from within and through Him. Try and try and try, oh, if I can get this idea into my being to the fullest extent of its meaning. This is but a poor expression of only a very little of the strength that comes to me from the person who comes to my mind when the 18th of March is mentioned. May God grant me the privilege of knowing better the man who is 'my Dad.' Greetings, Dad, on this another birthday [Edgar's fiftieth]."

Later that spring, as his freshman year drew to a close, Hugh Lynn wrote his folks a reflective letter in which he said in some ways he was pleased and in others disappointed in himself. He had met some "fine fellows and some perplexing ones. In all, the reading [294-81] was about right—some of the fellows here have had a hard time getting along with me and I with them. There have been times when I can almost feel the old tendency to withdraw from it all, shut myself away and just think—the monastery idea again."

In a word, Hugh Lynn had begun to see parallels between his own traits and what he perceived he had been like as a monk in medieval England. The life readings didn't seem so far out after all.

"The fellows haven't been able to understand that attitude and it has been a rather hard one to apply with so many around so much. I haven't made many real friends, therefore, no enemies but just acquaintances. I'll see some of them again, will remember them but never very close. They will all forget me but never some of the ideas I have brought out. I rather count time lost if I haven't made friends—that is one failure.

"I have, though, met one fellow at least who will someday be well known as a writer and I am bringing him home for a day or so, I expect. You won't like him but he will be interesting, perhaps."

Edgar replied: "I reckon your mother wrote you about bringing the boy home with you. I, personally, think it would be very nice—be very glad for you to do so—be glad to have him."

"Tom," replied Hugh Lynn, "wants to get a life reading while there if possible. He is very interested and I am anxious to get him placed. We get along miserable together, both too sarcastic and disagree on many big ideas yet must have had some attraction somewhere else. I too want a reading while he is there to help check up on my self."

During his first year away at school Hugh Lynn tried to think how he could test the life readings for accuracy.

"I began to figure out all the things I must check on. This led me to get life readings for boys at college—boys whom Dad did not know—and try to follow through on them to see how accurate he was about their personalities, habit patterns, and weaknesses—all the things I could examine. I'd ask if they wanted a reading. They'd do it out of curiosity. They had to write a letter asking for one. Two of these boys turned out to be quite astonishing.

"Leon was right out of the First Baptist Church of an Alabama town. He was studying for the ministry. He was the most aggressive Baptist I've ever known and the most Baptist Baptist. He thought I was absolutely nuts, and I thought he was narrow-minded. We enjoyed each other but we argued at the top of our voices over psychic stuff and religion. I didn't interpret the Bible like he did—he was much too literal. It seemed to me that he was so closed, and yet his life reading said he was very broad-minded, a universal kind of figure. I thought it was the damnedest reading I'd ever seen. I marked it up against Dad, a big, black mark. I thought the reading was wrong.

"Many years later his reading proved to be the reality. Leon became an outstanding social-service worker in New York. Then be became the minister of the second largest Baptist Church in St. Louis—I spoke in his church several times. He took that church out of the Southern Baptist Convention, he had blacks in his church, he marched at the head of the peace movement in St. Louis, he put together a program in that city for bringing ministers and psychiatrists together to discuss case histories. He turned out to be the most broad-minded person, and his reading was right on the nose. But you would never have known it when we were in school. Dad's reading for him saw all these things. This later impressed me.

"There was another boy whom Dad had never met. He was a brilliant student, but his reading said he faced real problems with karma. He was later thrown out of Washington & Lee and got into every conceivable kind of trouble. He had four marriages and divorces."

While most of the information in the life readings about past lives was beyond checking for accuracy, Hugh Lynn, the skeptical sleuth, found nothing glaringly incorrect with which to fault them. He believed in his father. He believed in his father's work. Even the wild stories of past lives in faraway places seemed increasingly authentic.

Hugh Lynn's growth at Washington & Lee was not limited to the curriculum.

"I began to drink by the end of my freshman year. Everyone at Washington & Lee was drinking. It was during Prohibition, and we drank this horrible stuff that came out of the mountains—you couldn't stand it except on weekends." It was the resumption of Hugh Lynn's youthful sowing of wild oats, which continued into the summer when he returned to the Beach.

"Growing up in Virginia Beach in the summertime was quite something—it was wild in the summer, with lots of college students and college parties. Tom and I were very much involved with girls and the whole Beach crowd."

"Tom also fell in love with my father. He told Dad he had the most cantankerous son he'd ever met, but he was charmed by Dad. And Mother and Dad both liked him. He even asked for a reading."

And so the classmate who had scoffed loudest at Edgar's work was turned in another direction, destined to become an eloquent interpreter of Cayce's work with *There Is a River*, published nearly two decades later. Always welcomed by the Cayces, "he'd come and stay weeks or a month. We played at Virginia Beach for all it was worth."

Making the dean's list his freshman year entitled Hugh Lynn to academic privileges: "If you were on the dean's list you could take any number of courses as long as you passed them all, and you didn't have to attend classes when you didn't want to. So in my sophomore year I took seven courses—courses I liked, from professors I liked, as well as the courses I had to take."

Hugh Lynn may have bitten off too much, for his report card that sophomore year was more spotty. He got an A in English and in Comic Spirit in Literature; a B in Principles of Psychology and in Hygiene; a C in Abnormal Psychology and in Roman Life and Thought; an E—a conditional failure with a chance to draw the mark up before the end of the year—in both Physics and Spanish. "There are no excuses," he wrote his folks. "I simply quit when I got tired and I found that I just couldn't do that—successfully." Hugh Lynn recovered academically, but never matched Tom. "I learned how to study, how to work. Tom made Phi Beta Kappa—he just got A in everything. I got excellent grades but they were not quite that good. Tom also did all this extracurricular stuff, too—and drank heavily."

During his sophomore year, Hugh Lynn wrote a reflective letter home that was remarkable for its candor about his behavior:

"For two years now I find that I have made mistakes and I certainly hope that the coming two years will see an improvement. These mistakes which I refer to are those I have made with regard to getting the most out of college. The first year I took a few easy subjects and failed to touch the material for which I was looking, something new and different. The year passed and I found myself dissatisfied with what I had failed to find, so I started in to see if I could find any interest in the social side of life that I had failed to contact during the school year. Well, you both know the result of last summer in regard to my finding true or lasting satisfaction in the pace which I ran. At the end of the summer I realized that I had wasted my time and energy and that the rush and tear of things did not hold an interest for me which answered that craving which had possessed me. You both commented on the change in me, seeming for the worst. Well I came back to school this year with the idea of working and playing at the same time but with the idea of really getting some work done."

Hugh Lynn had not given up having a good time, however. He thought having a car would help. When the Cayces bought a new Ford with a rumble seat, they gave Hugh Lynn their old car. In his senior year, Hugh Lynn had a wreck one Saturday night while on a triple date. It was scary and expensive, but caused no serious injuries. He, cousin Gray and another boy had taken their dates to a football game and dance in Roanoke. After the accident, he wrote his parents:

"You probably have about four or five stories of the accident by now and probably are not any surer than am I as to just what happened. Anyway this is *my* story and I'll stick to it.

"We had a lovely time up until Sat. morning about 1 o'clock or between 1 and 1:30. The girls enjoyed it very much I think as did Gray. Everyone was very nice to them and the dance went off smoothly.

"After the dance we went down to have a bite to eat, then out for a ride before taking the girls in. We drove out the road toward Clifton Forge. The road for some distance out is very straight over low hills, rolling. As we turned around it began to rain just a little. We were driving between twenty-five and thirty [MPH]. Around just a slight bend and down a little hill, very *little* hill, I met another car coming pretty fast. I turned out and the car began to skid, I foolishly put on the brake and the car began to skid and the car came completely around. In turning, or after it had completely turned, the back wheel struck a low rock on the side of the road. The weight of the car and the speed of turning carried it over. It turned over once and half over again with the wheels against the wire fence. The bank fortunately was not steep, just a gentle slope to the fence. As you know no one was seriously hurt but all were scared badly. Several cars stopped and rushed us all to the hospital as Vivian had fainted and Gray was cut, Hazel hysterical. Lois was worrying about Gray, Roby about Vivian and I about the car. It looked terrible there in the dark and I was about ready to dispose of it for 50 cents if I could have gotten that much. I got a very small scratch on the hand getting Hazel out. I came right back with a wrecker and they got the car out inside a couple of hours. As the next day was Sunday they didn't work on it. In the meantime I had to pay the fare for Lois and Hazel as they didn't have enough. But I'll itemize the bills and let you see them later.

"The car was bent up pretty badly, 3 fenders, the top torn and one corner smashed in. It didn't show on the inside however and believe me I am glad that it was a strong top. The mechanic here checked over the car carefully and found that nothing about the motor, chassis or other parts (mechanical) were hurt. On Tuesday morning the car ran perfectly, not a rattle, knock or anything. Two glass [windows] were broken, how the others failed to be I can't tell."

The letter itemized the following "expenses to date of one H.L. Cayce (un inc.)":

Hospital bill	9.00
Lois ticket	10.00
Hazel ticket	10.00
Gray ticket	10.00
Wrecking bill	24.50
Cash	5.00
Laundry	3.00
Repair bill	106.00 (estimate)
Grand total	$180.50

(for today's dollars multiply by about 10)

His father took the news with amazing grace. "When you get ready for the machine, or go over for it, why you can give a check for it and I'll try to arrange to take care of it here at the bank. You notify me of any overdraft. They notified me of one today—haven't been up yet, but I'll attend to it tomorrow and see if I can get enough to take care of it."

Undoubtedly his parents agreed with Hugh Lynn when he wrote, "It was a miracle that some of us were not hurt badly. It makes one wonder." As for who was to blame, he added: "You can't imagine how sorry I was that all this had to happen. I do not feel that it was entirely my fault—nor anyone's, that's the trouble. It seems almost one of those necessary things that some good God kept from being too serious."

As much as Hugh Lynn liked a good time, he responded as well to classical music and to great literature and to the silence of contemplation. "For the last three Saturday nights now I have been going over to the Y to listen to those records of Dr. Stevens. He certainly has a wonderful collection and for the first time I am beginning to be able to appreciate real music. Ever so little but I find that I love it more than I ever realized. It is beautifully quiet and restful over there with everything quiet and only the strains of a symphony or the clear notes of some great singer's voice to break the stillness. It is there that I have found rest and peace and quiet of late and I find that I cannot live without those periods of loss of contact with the rush of the world. Truly it is the quiet that one can find only in prayer and, when I lose myself in the heights of emotional feeling over some beautiful piece, God is much nearer, it seems, and I am ashamed when I realize that I had to come away to find the beauty in the really good records that we have."

He discovered great literature with Professor Fitzgerald Flournoy, a Rhodes scholar who convened the Hibiscus Club evenings at his home. Hugh Lynn and Tom attended. "We not only took every course Fitz gave but we got him to make up new courses. He made up one on humor. It was a reading class, and we'd meet at his home. He enjoyed it so. We drank tea and read, going back to Rabelais, coming right on through the literature."

"We are reading poetry and short stories now after having just finished 'Faust,' he wrote home. "It is at these meetings that I see Tom on the plane that we can come together and enjoy the same things. For that reason alone the meetings are worth a great deal to me."

The Cayces both wrote letters to their son, Gertrude in hand, Edgar dictating to Gladys, who typed them up and filed a copy.

Hence only his father's have been preserved. Typically, they were chatty: "Well, I got my rose garden all prepared. . . .Tunney still holds the bag. Jack [Dempsey] put up a good scrap but wasn't equal to the battery from the marine. . . .Mr. Ramsey, of the Presbyterian Church, you know, has asked me several times to take a class up there. It seems that they have no teachers. So he gave me what is supposed to be the adult Bible Class. He has a very small congregation—I've never seen more than fifteen or twenty there at any one service. Yesterday we had four in the class—your mother, Eckin, and a man and his wife, but I think I'll like it. . . .Well, most of our flowers we planted have come up, but the UP was principally done by the chickens I think. . . .I have a lot more little chickens but we had our old rooster for dinner yesterday—put him up and fattened him and he sure was good!. . . .I guess your mother told you about Edgar Evans winning his testament. He still sticks to the class, and we go over the Sunday School lesson together nearly every Sunday morning. . . .Our strawberries are getting ripe. I've had enough to have on my cereal a time or two. . .we have been a heap busier this week than usual, and the better part of the appointments were for new people—some in New York, some in Birmingham, some in Chicago. . . .I sent you the reading for [roommate] Robison yesterday, and I guess you all have had time to cuss it and discuss it considerable."

On his twenty-first birthday, however, Hugh Lynn received a philosophical letter from his father:

"Now your life is just before you, as man has been taught to consider same. You are in the midst of your own development, for you are in the midst of life. Civilly you are your own man, with the right to think, act, and express yourself in your own right without fear or favor from any man. In our study of the phenomena of life we know life is a growth. As we apply that we know, day by day, we grow to be that we build with our mental being. As to how much in accord we build with all the laws pertaining to man's life, whether spiritual, mental, or physical, just that much do we really grow. We become lopsided by trying to develop some one phase of that life, disregarding as a "WHOLE." We may separate it, we may dissect it to understand it the better, but in the application of any law pertaining to life, we must consider it as a whole.

"Sugar, I know you won't think I'm preaching, for you know I love you too good to even ever want to say a cross word—I am in hopes that my life has been such that you will not censure or blame me for anything that I should have done that I haven't, or for doing anything that I should not have done—but I know from experience that after we pass our twenty-first birthday we begin to more and more live a portion of our life in retrospection. This part of our general make-up I am sure is correct, and I am hoping that as you build on and on, you will always keep in mind that your mother and your father, in this experience at least, have tried to the best of their abilities to keep you and your future ever in mind and we are hoping and praying that from time to time you will bear with us and will keep us in mind at times also. Set your hope in Him, who *is* the way and the light. Let your foundations be laid in Christ—for there is no other that is safe, and keep your heart singing, and smiling, all the way through."

Perhaps the most remarkable aspect of his relationship with his father and mother while he was away at school is that they treated him as an adult. They asked his opinion, they sought his advice, they took seriously his suggestions concerning the work of the Association of National Investigators and the launching and running of the Cayce Hospital. And Hugh Lynn responded maturely, even when his father needed a pep talk, for there were times when Edgar's self-doubt crept into his letters. Once Hugh Lynn noted "a lag in events, a period of seeming gloom, inactivity, and general hesitation" on Edgar's part. He wrote to his father:

"Think back for just a moment and everything becomes understandable. All the people were quiet. The revolt and the personal affairs of the king had been put into order again. Messengers were going back and forth between the king and the exiled priest. The greatest statesmen of the country had been bending every effort to find some point of reconciliation and had found it in a joining in of both the king and the priest in one of the greatest institutions ever known to man. The king was in favor of the enterprise, and had settled himself to the straightening of the disordered details about him. Still the high councilor had not given any words of favor. To him the people turned to see his reaction to this new enterprise which had grown under the hand of the statesmen without his aid. It seemed that he still fought to uphold against the priest whom he had fought so long and so hard. Another outbreak of the old disturbance seemed certain. So far he had been left out; considered yet in a distant manner. Now he was needed for the work to go forward. Stillness settled over the land like a giant cloud, darkness, doubt, then light. The high councilor threw himself into the work and progress began again."

While Hugh Lynn mentioned no names, he was referring to the ancient Egyptian Ra Ta story found in the family life readings, which said Edgar had been the priest and Hugh Lynn had been the king.

Young Cayce added in his letter:

"Fanciful, doubtless wrong, yet this, I think, is a background for the reasons of the present conditions. Dad, this thing is too big to expect it to run off in marked time; it is too mixed and tied up with men's lives and souls not |to| meet here and there a contest of mind, spirit and matter; it is too deep for those who do not understand to grasp it and carry on; it means too much for those who have not had a direct part in the establishment not to say proudly, you started without us—continue. Yet once the spirit, the urge, the understanding, the light comes to those who are needed, there will, there must come a response. The purpose is His purpose, and He stands behind His purposes and drives as well as calls, for He used the whip as well as the calm word. Against such, physical sins have no power—jealousy will fall with the rest. Upon yourself you have taken the task of bringing together all that you tore asunder. It is not easy. There is a lot to fight but O what a lot you have to fight it with...this is but a pause, a bit of dark cloud and there is lots of bright sky back of it all."

The young skeptic of yesterday had become an ardent believer. Edgar responded immediately: "You drew a picture that seems to fit the conditions exactly...you have worded it wonderfully well."

Hugh Lynn also took the readings seriously as a source of advice. He urged his parents to buy a lot on which to build a home "as early as possible for things there are bound to go up in the location we want it." But, he cautioned, "Don't jump before you check on *anything* with a reading...I think it will be a good thing nevertheless for us to begin to think and plan and things will turn up—we should realize by now that we have got to think and hope and wish first—for anything the sooner the better—but be sure to get reading first before decision."

In his junior year, Hugh Lynn's letters took an introspective turn.

"It is hard to come to the time and place where one begins to realize that he must give up and sacrifice on an altar of opinion, great parts of his individuality—to become a social creature; a benefit to society as well as just to a few and himself. One like myself who has always placed so much importance on individuality, on being different, who has always abhorred becoming just a middle to nothing person, like the general rabble—finds it hard to laugh at myself when the world—society—reaches into me and takes what it calls its due in respect and fear of its established conventions. Two outstanding examples in my recent life near past, present and near future come to me.

"First there has come my tearing up and patching up of my

conception of friendship. That thing called friendship, a kind of love, meant more to me than most anything else. I prided myself on its importance in my life, on the beauty of my conception of it, sacred and very great to me. With George Rutledge, whom I cared and still care as much for as any boy I know—I have ruined its very essence. I have sacrificed and stand ready and determined to sacrifice him for an ideal—it was hard to decide which was greater, the individual or the ideal—society said the ideal. If he will not play as the ideal directs then—it will all break up between us; even now he doubts me—and I can do little but try and explain that I think it is best when deep down in me I know that for him the way I have chosen is not best.

"Then there is, has been another little matter that reminds me of society's power over even the part in me which I considered above it. You remember the Morris girl, the younger one who was unfortunate. You possibly remember too that for a time I went with her. She always seemed more like a pal than anything else, I knew her so long. Then later of course she grew attractive and I was interested in her. (It happens like that in books, long overlooking, then seeing for the first time someone who has been close to you all along.) She was pretty, uneducated, lacked background, and all that, but I liked her. I was attracted of course by her body, which was indeed very beautiful—too beautiful as it has proved. I came I guess to love her in a way, loving just her body. It was a healthy, clean, straight love—sex—yes, but I understood it and myself. We were very happy for a short time, and for one who was supposedly so ignorant she understood very well and responded beautifully to a person who acted quite differently from the average person she went with. My desire to remain master of myself and her understanding of me kept things between us on what the world calls a fair, clean basis. I knew that she had and would go much further with others than she did with me, and she knew that I knew. We remained interested in each other enjoying a very peculiar yet very perfect companionship—for a short time. (Incidentally this young lady danced in a temple once in Egypt.)

"But all this is just background and explanation. She suffered and I forgot to think of her—society demanded it. Deep down in me I know that I do not think she did terribly wrong—I cannot hate her—in fact I still love her body—beautifully—I guess. In the future society says forget, regardless of what you really think and feel— and I know that in the end, I shall—though at odd moments I curse myself for it.

"Odd isn't it. I hope that on paper this isn't too crude and has not bored you. It is truly real feeling and real thoughts. I think you will understand—and I think I understand. Don't try to answer it unless you realize that you do understand how I feel. If you do please answer it for I believe that I am not alone in feeling this necessity of conformity with the rules of society and that each thinking individual must find such a time in their life when they feel much in the same way as I have expressed, so brokenly above. I know that I feel better for having written this. It always helps to express in some way what I feel and think. I am sorry that I could not say this in person and hope that the writing does not spoil it. In any case it is good to know that I can express myself and receive from you, Muddie and Dad, a reasonable and sympathetic understanding. All are not so fortunate, especially at my age |twenty-two|."

Edgar replied quickly:

"I think I fully appreciate and understand much of what you are talking about as respecting yourself, your relations with others; ideals and ideas. Of course, in the last few years I haven't had the opportunity—or possibly you haven't felt inclined to talk with me as much concerning your own personal affairs of every nature as you once did, yet I have always felt, and I think I have tried to conduct my life in such a way and manner that you would always feel at liberty and privileged to talk with me about anything that was on your mind.

"Of course, we all realize that the thing that is paramount in an individual's mind, and ideas and ideals, is the thing that interests them the most, and unless the other person—who may be a friend, a pal, or associate—can in some form at least become interested in that which is uppermost in the individual's mind, then he can never be just as close as he should be. That is the vast difference in people being interested in things and individuals, also in people being pals, friends, or just associates and acquaintances. When one tampers with another's ideas, one may be excused. Only when one reasons and discusses conditions regarding another's ideals may one be considered attempting to be of service. To find fault with such a discussion, in a quiet way and manner, is to create a gap and dissension that also breeds and grows into divisions. So, I think, from my little experience—though sometimes I think it has covered and does cover as broad a field as most people, and I'm wondering often how I have any mind at all, or if I really have one—but I think I understand what you mean. I think I would love for you to talk with me personally concerning these things. I would like to discuss them with you. We are always hesitant in approaching such things unless we are very sure the individual desires that they be discussed."

Hugh Lynn had a love-hate relationship with the campus

fraternities.

"I spent a lot of time at Tom's fraternity house—I wasn't a member at first but he took me there—and finally they said, 'If you are going to eat here all the time, why don't you join?' So in my sophomore year I joined. Tom and I roomed together, deliberately. We both chose it. We fascinated each other. We were intrigued by how much we disliked one another, but we enjoyed each other too. But when we drank, either in the dorm or at the frat house, we'd involve everybody in the building in our arguments. They would all take sides, the wildest thing you've ever seen.

"The third year, Tom wanted to live off campus in an apartment, so we tried it together. It didn't work. This time I moved out. I couldn't stand it."

Hugh Lynn's ambivalence about trying to become a big man on campus like Tom was reflected in his attitude about campus politics. During elections, he wrote, "Everyone is terribly friendly, passing out cigars, etc. It is impossible to study for people dropping in to politic at all times. Even here in this 'gentlemen's' school there is the usual dirt which seems to enter most political campaigns. Block voting, giving away everything from show tickets to dance places in next year's Fancy Dress [an annual ball] are in order with numerous side favors like the 10 gallons of liquor that were distributed in the two dorms last nite. They don't buy the votes outright—not quite."

He flirted with the idea of running for secretary-treasurer of the student body his junior year. He said "people have asked me why I didn't and since the political week has rolled around I see that I might have had a fair chance, as the strongest candidate is in bad with several frats—anyway I didn't and have few regrets as I see all the cutting and slashing that is going on."

Hugh Lynn became an extroverted leader later in life, but in college he still had a tendency to hang back socially. Near the end of his junior year he wrote that "only now and then" did he "succeed in getting a sense of being a part of the college life" such as at a football game or in a Saturday night bull session. "It is nice when you do though. You can just relax and feel all collegiate." College "hasn't been exactly like I thought it would be but it has been wonderful in many respects."

He also had dark days, such as one period at the start of his senior year, which he described to his parents:

"For the past few days I have been in a fog. I have been lonesome, more so than ever before, I have been miserable. I have been through conditions which I would have refused to believe I would pass through, I have met circumstances which I could not control for the first time—that hurt. Let me tell you about it.

"I have spent three years building up a kind of wall of reserve in my relations with other than a comparatively few fellows on the campus. I have a few real friends—a slightly larger number of acquaintances—the rest I do not know. I have never tried to make myself liked—I did not care. Through the influence of others (the friends) and my own work (books) I gained many of the little honors which the average frat man doesn't have. I found many on the campus who naturally I didn't like and they in turn didn't like me—I ignored them."

Tom had an easy time socially and was admitted to what Hugh Lynn considered "the most sophisticated club on the campus." Although the members were "high hats," Hugh Lynn wanted in too. One night he tried to crash one of their parties and was humiliated because he got bawled out. He wrote to his folks about it, admonishing them to tell no one. He realized it would be expensive if he were admitted but he "wanted it, yes—for reasons—hated it for other reasons but that is a long sad story—one of those regular college sob tales. It is now time to become college hero, etc., and win the fair daughter of the president—she happens to be ugly— and I am going to fool them and continue to hide."

Through Tom's influence, Tommy House got in also and they tried to grease the way for Hugh Lynn. "Three or four times they have tried to get me in. Each time they failed" because he had been blackballed by one member. Separated from his closest friends, he felt "cut off from the world" and "somehow it got to me. I had found something I wanted and couldn't get except by allowing others to help me. They did."

One last push got Hugh Lynn in.

"They tell me that few have received such praise and curses all in one breath as I in a meeting this afternoon. After a rather stormy session they passed me, thanks to Tommy, Tom and a few more. I accepted. Thus I am pledged to the oldest, high hat-edest, possibly the richest club on the campus. It will mean I'll spend more money than usual, perhaps. Socially and politically it means everything. I wanted it worse than anything I have ever wanted before. All that I could do in acting 'nice' for the past few days was useless and badly done—I could not erase in a week three years' habits. Others had to do it all for me. They did.

"Maybe I was wrong but you don't know how much it means in 'just the feeling.'"

Hugh Lynn had gained an objective, not without cost. "I have lost a bit of individuality or independence," he acknowledged, but "I have gained a feeling which is peculiar, there is a change in the way others look at me, even today. It seems worth it—just to be near Tommy and Tom. I never needed people before."

To fulfill his destiny, he would need people far more than he ever dreamed on that triumphant day—for he was going to learn more from difficult relationships than was offered in his splendid college curriculum. What he found was that he was connecting with people such as Tom that he had associated with in earlier lives, not always in love. As he put it near the end of his span, "Quite frankly, a lot of my life has been ironing out, one after another, these difficulties, these karmic patterns. I've dealt with them, I've faced them, I've cleared them up, I've learned how to love the people that I hated and fought with, and I've deliberately gone about doing exactly what Jesus said to try to do, and it's been plain hell at times."

Part Two

About My Father's Business

Chapter 8
The Idealist

Edgar's dream of building a hospital finally materialized while Hugh Lynn was away at college. Construction began during his sophomore year, concluding near the end of his junior year, and the summer in between he worked construction on the project. Facing the sea from the top of a knoll north of the business section of the town, the handsome four-story facility resembled an antebellum Southern mansion with its wide porch across the front and sides. Dedicated on Armistice Day in 1928, the thirty-bed facility opened for patients in February 1929. The chief of staff was Hugh Lynn's great-uncle, Dr. Thomas B. House, who left his position as medical head of Western State Hospital in Hopkinsville to come to Virginia Beach. Dr. House had gained great respect for Edgar's diagnostic gift because his own wife, Carrie, many years before had insisted on obtaining a reading from Edgar before agreeing to surgery for a painful abdominal condition. The reading, which revealed that she was pregnant, turned out to be right.

During the Cayce Hospital's first year of operation, 3,000 visitors came to see it and to inquire about its unconventional treatments, which included hydrotherapy, electrotherapy, colonic irrigation, and even recreation—the hospital had tennis courts, a croquet ground, shuffle board, a club room for cardplayers, and bath houses for those able to enjoy the therapeutic benefits of the seashore. The hospital also offered more conventional procedures such as osteopathy. While each patient had diagnostic readings from Edgar, the hospital was equipped for such standard diagnostic procedures as x-ray, blood tests, spinal smears, urinalysis, and others used to "confirm the diagnoses and prove the efficacy of the treatment as outlined by

Mr. Cayce's readings," the chief of staff reported. The hospital was equipped to handle patients suffering from anything but contagious or mental diseases. Sixty patients were treated the first year, with an average of ten patients signed in at any one time.

Part of the holistic therapy for body, mind, and soul was a lecture given each Sunday afternoon in the hospital lecture room by Edgar or Morton Blumenthal, Edgar one week on his experiences and interpretations of the Bible, and Morton the next on such topics as "Creative Evolution" and the "Fourth Dimensional Viewpoint." The lectures proved so popular that Morton began teaching a philosophy class on Saturday afternoons and the hospital added a library. Thus marked the beginning of the educational thrust of the Cayce work, which was to expand considerably in years hence under Hugh Lynn's direction.

Even while still in college, Hugh Lynn moved the organization a big step in the direction of publishing educational materials. He teamed up with Tom Sugrue to publish a quarterly for the Association of National Investigators called *The New Tomorrow.* Tom was editor, Hugh Lynn managing editor. The inaugural issue, in December 1929, had a strong philosophical flavor, including texts of lectures given at the hospital by Edgar ("What Is Truth?") and Morton ("My Concept of God"). Hugh Lynn contributed an article entitled "Life Readings—What They Are and How to Use Them." It reveals a good deal about the transformation of Hugh Lynn's thinking concerning reincarnation since his initial shock five years before. The family skeptic had been converted into an ardent believer, judging by what he wrote to explain the nature of a life reading:

"It is a discussion of you, of your abilities and faults, of your likes and dislikes, of your peculiar characteristics that make you an individual. It is a picture of you from an angle that an Olympian God might use, should he have reason to summarize the progress of your development and the point to which you had attained. It is a history of your existence, an explanation of why you are playing the part you now portray in this great little comedy we call 'Modern Civilization.'"

He illustrated his comments by interpreting one woman's reading. The reading gave her previous incarnations in "the Ukranian country," the Holy Land, and ancient Egypt. Hugh Lynn explained: "These appearances are taken up in backward order as one would back down a ladder. This appearance (in Russia) was just previous to the present." The reading said the woman had been a peasant leader who gave much to the people through music, to which Hugh Lynn commented: "Musical ability was here developed. It is an outstanding accomplishment in the present."

In Egypt, said the reading, she had been a "brilliant musician to the king" and had "the ability to act and sing and the ability to wind an individual about her finger." Hugh Lynn's comment was terse: "Another talent shown in the present and hard to explain in any other manner." The reading said the entity had "gained through service in the first of these [abilities] but lost through misuse of the latter ability." And it added that "the entity will find that the principles apply in life as in death." Hugh Lynn's comment was: "Consider this well for herein lies a universal truth."

His commentary, in short, was that of someone who had overcome his initial doubts by comparing various life readings against the character and personality of people he knew well enough to draw conclusions.

By this time, also, Hugh Lynn had seemingly accepted the prior identities given him in his own life readings. A note from him to Gladys Davis was kiddingly signed, "Well thanks again from all of us—Hugh Lynn, Ericson Olif, Arat, Edgar, Andrew—puff, puff."

Moreover, he, Tom, and Gladys formed a Historical Committee to study the life readings of other members, including the officers and members of the board of trustees, and to understand the relationships of various members to one another. Hugh Lynn and Tom concluded that they had been fellow monks in an English monastery around the time of King Alfred and that some of their antagonism and new-found friendship could be traced to that earlier relationship. From this new perspective, Hugh Lynn found that he had more incentive to work things out with Tom. Indeed, instead of collegiate horseplay, they found themselves preoccupied with serious questions of common interest.

"Things we had once argued about now drew us together. Tom wanted to know more about my father and I wanted to know more about the Catholic Church. I had softened up on the Catholic Church, too, and Tom took me to visit a priest there in Lexington, but he was a young football boy who didn't know beans. So we went to Washington, D.C., and saw some Jesuits. I had questions about Catholicism and we really got into it. Tom also had questions, which led to his book, A Catholic Speaks His Mind, years later."

While finding a reincarnation link seemed to strengthen his relationship with Tom, Hugh Lynn feared that the Historical Committee's analysis of past-life ties among board members spelled trouble. The board consisted of Blumenthal and his wife Adeline and brother Edwin Blumenthal, who had joined in helping to underwrite the hospital; Lucille and David Kahn, who had contributed the hospital's furniture; Tim Brown, a Dayton inventor;

Franklin F. Bradley, whose Chicago paint company had contributed the paint for the hospital; and Edgar, Gertrude, and Hugh Lynn. At the next meeting, held at the new Cavalier Hotel just down the beach, his fears were realized.

"They were going to have a beautiful meeting. All the wives were there, and we were going to have a dinner dance. They had all had readings but had never met one another. According to their readings, they had had great conflict with each other in previous lives. But here they were, greeting each other and hugging.

"Within thirty minutes after they sat down and started talking, you could hear them all over most of the Cavalier Hotel, Morton and Bradley screaming at one another. The argument was about the garage roof. One of them favored a tin roof and the other wanted a shingle roof. They expounded the advantages of each at the top of their voices. They got mad.

"I had warned them in a letter before they came to the meeting. I said, 'Now be real nice. You fought one another in another life.' But, 'bang,' it went off like a firecracker. It just exploded, and Morton and Bradley were never on the same side of a vote from that time on."

Less than a year after the hospital opened, its superintendent, Dr. House, died. He was succeeded by a Dayton, Ohio, physician, Lyman A. Lydic, leaving the Cayces to ponder whether to make a place within the hospital staff for Dr. House's widow, Carrie, who had been so helpful to Edgar in his youth. Carrie and Edgar's sister Annie, who was already on the staff, were antagonistic to one another. Hugh Lynn, devoting an entire ten-page letter to this family problem, concluded: "It is a situation worthy of a great diplomat, worthy of a great mind, a broad mind and a noble and honest heart. It is not mere flattery to say that only you would be capable of handling it." Edgar found places for both women.

Four months after assuming his post, Dr. Lydic was able to report that the hospital was treating patients with congenital incoordination of mental and psychical faculties, stomach ulcers, acute gastritis, general pruritis, mucous colitis, spastic paraplegia, tabes dorsalis [syphilis of the spinal cord], optic neuritis with partial blindness, shell shock with its typical manifestations, hysteria, acute osteomyelitis, and all types of gynecological cases. Dr. Lydic added that "some of these cases are considered beyond help by the medical profession, and I must say that we haven't a case which is not responding in a very encouraging manner."

Whatever the practical problems of running such an institution, the realization of Edgar's dream after so many years of frustrating setbacks and family sacrifice evidently had a powerfully inspiring impact on Hugh Lynn. For when his parents asked him what he wanted to do after he finished college, he said: "I am going to begin work or fit myself to work in some department of the Association of National Investigators, Inc." When speaking of a career he repeatedly referred to "The Work." And his description of what he visualized doing coincided remarkably with the life he eventually led. He told his parents:

"I am going to maintain active work and connection with every department, making myself useful to everyone as much as possible. Particular interest is going to be paid to the library, museum, archaeology, historical, lecturing and teaching...fields I feel I am most capable in. I am going to try and make myself indispensable to each individual in the Association, those now interested and those later to enter. Plus this: I am going to use all my influence to bring men who I feel will carry on the principles on which this whole work is laid. Ultimately I will study, travel, organize and assist in an expedition to Egypt and other places to prove our historical conclusions. On this I will write and lecture and teach. I believe that the work of the association can be brought to a point where it will change the thought of the world and bring to civilization a solution to the critical period which is going to arrive in a comparatively short time in the history of the world. We can, I believe, bring on the millennium—just as any age might—those are gathering who can bring this to pass—I believe we will. In every field we will be in a position to push forward the principles of the Master and bring to the world an understanding that will draw Him to recognize His work. I intend to prepare myself to aid in every way to bring this about, to help every man to maintain his balance and thereby maintain my own. Thus my story and I'll stick to it."

Thus was Hugh Lynn's vision at age twenty-three. He did, indeed, stick to it.

His immediate options, he thought, included: working under his father at the Beach in some capacity; going on to graduate school; or seeking employment elsewhere to gain business experience that might later assist his father's work. He decided that his career must meet four conditions:

- Help the world as a whole.
- Be of some help to Muddie and Edgar.
- Help others who meant a great deal to him.
- Offer him an opportunity to "rise to the highest point"—not, he explained, "power or fame but a bigness within, the highest point of my present development."

"Work in the Association fits all of these very well," he decided.

"It offers possibilities that nothing else does." As Edgar Cayce's son, he enjoyed "certain advantages," but they could "become hindrances very easily, and how well I know it," he told his father. "It is a work that is dear to me for many reasons. First, it is His. Second, it is yours. To become one with Him, that is the goal, you, we are to reach, are reaching.

"This may sound like a bunch of conceits. It isn't conceit but shall we say ambition. I believe rather strongly in my own ability, yes, but also very strongly in the Forces that are back of 'the work.'"

His father was very receptive. Indeed, his reply suggested that he saw Hugh Lynn as destiny's child: "I have the faith and the confidence in your ability to carry on that which is for a better understanding of man's responsibility to his Maker. Even as your close relationship with the Master [an apparent reference to the Andrew incarnation] brought you in contact with all sides of human nature, yet your knowledge you first applied in bringing your brother [Peter]. Then, you did not falter in the service you gave throughout that period. Again you will keep many together. You will mentally prepare yourself for the place you should occupy, if your abilities are guided in the right direction. We must be circumspect in our walks before men, but being ever ready to give an answer for the faith that lies within, knowing He is able to keep that which we commit unto Him against that day when it will be *necessary* for His aid to keep the ties that bind."

Hugh Lynn's adolescent anger toward his father had been dissipated, perhaps by the enormous respect he had for him and for The Work. As he wrote:

"One of man's greatest mistakes is to underestimate other individuals, particularly if you are matching wits with them. I learned a bit of this in Egypt and I shall not forget. At another time I learned humbleness to offset the self-praise, that too I shall remember. Please don't think that I shall ever overlook and forget the hand that has engineered this from a beginning that pre-dates any of the rest's [others'] thoughts on the subject. I refer of course, Dad, to yourself."

Edgar Cayce, the psychic diagnostician, was coming into his own during this period. The visible monument to his work, the hospital, brought not only personal satisfaction. It brought a deluge of clients. During the first three months of 1930 he gave 210 readings—more than his usual two-a-day quota. Moreover, he had a two-months' waiting list. Those difficult days in Dayton when clients were few and money was tight seemed gone forever. There was every reason to believe that the institutionalization of Edgar Cayce's psychic gift was at hand.

By the time Hugh Lynn approached graduation day at Washington & Lee, he had become eloquently philosophical for such a young man. In a paper entitled, "A Champion of Imagination Against a World of Reality," he wrote:

"It is peculiar that the civilization of a race or nation is made of the understanding and appreciation of the people of two conflicting attitudes toward life. Either one looks at life through the glasses of reality or through the glasses of imagination, if he is not fortunate enough to have that understanding blend of the two which is a priceless treasure and a requisite for contentment. For, if one looks too much to the material hardness of the world about him or loses himself in the realm of imagination too often there comes in either case a failure to achieve the most out of this little understood state which we call life. Imagination is the word which spells progress but the vanguard of progress is the reality of achievement which stabilizes advancement. The dreamers, it is true, are the saviors of the world yet it is also true that the man who understands the realness of things and applies them to practical use is the man who makes possible the enjoyment of the ideas of which the dreamer has only dreamed. Thus hand in hand these two views of life come down together to make life worth living, and it is ironical to see that throughout the ages the supporters of each of these views have ever fought the other, condemning it as the cause of human suffering and discontent."

He also became reflective. "It is quite funny to look back and try and see the boy who came here four years ago," he wrote his parents. "In some respects he was a finer boy than the one who is leaving. There has been an outer layer placed over him, he seems changed a bit but I believe at heart he is the same. He has learned—well, I wonder just what he has learned. Of one thing I am sure—he is not afraid, after this long period of hiding, of trotting out into the world and seeing what it is all about. Something tells him that it won't be much different from the life he knows already from a few angles. Human nature is human nature whether it be in the schoolroom or the office, on the dance floor or at the bridge table. And after all, he has tried to study people—just a little. That study has made him love them more, love them all in spite of what we call sin and faults. College has not taught him to be a snob, it has made him a bit radical in some ways. It has cost him a part of his individuality, it has destroyed a great part of his natural openness, it has left a few memories that scar. In all it has been worthwhile. With the pain of parting there will be a mingling of eagerness, of looking into the future."

Hugh Lynn, evidently the first of the Cayce clan to finish college, was delighted to hear that his grandmother was coming all the way from Kentucky to join his parents in Lexington for the great occasion. In a letter home, however, his mind was very much on the practical side: "Please be careful driving up. I had a terrible dream last nite about your being killed. I woke up crying. Please be careful. Please bring Hazel. Expect a rush, crowd etc. Don't forget the tux."

Upon graduation, returning to Virginia Beach, Hugh Lynn got a job that expressed both the dreamer and the practical side of him. He went to work in yet another idealistic venture Blumenthal had underwritten, a fledgling college, Atlantic University, which opened in an ocean-front hotel in September 1930, a few months after Hugh Lynn's graduation. He was hired as school librarian at a salary of $150 a month. Having worked in the college library at Washington & Lee, he had obvious qualifications. But why would he want to work as a librarian? In a letter to his father he explained his idealistic motive:

"It is time for us to approach the real reason that I am to become the librarian at the Atlantic University. You have possibly read the article of Bradley's in *The New Tomorrow* on just how a young man should obtain a real education. He suggested that one pick out a man who they felt could lead them into the right channels and under whom they could rise to the highest point in the profession of their choice. I thought his idea was a pretty good one so I picked me out just such a man whose profession was the profession I wanted to enter and who I felt was the best in his line that I knew. The profession I wanted to enter was that old but much misused profession of 'helping the other fellow.'

"I found that this man had a pretty large business and that his peculiar situation was going to make it very hard for me to get in direct contact with him but on looking about I found that I had certain natural advantages. I contrived therefore to get into this man's business. Seemingly it was in a place a long way from the man himself but in other respects would be closer than appeared. I intend to stay very close to that man, to study him, to work with him, to become a part of him so far as it is possible. I know that through his development, through his intent and purpose this man has become the channel for a force that can do more good for humanity than anything I have ever contacted. I would learn of that spirit, that purpose, that will that has made this man such a channel for good works to his fellow man. I shall come thoughtfully, prayerfully, humbly, considerately to this man asking that he only allow me the privilege of becoming a student at his feet. I got a long

98

jump ahead when I picked that man as a Dad. I'll be there."

The president of Atlantic University, William Mosely Brown, was a favorite of Hugh Lynn's. He was a popular speaker and known as a scholar with unfulfilled political ambitions. He had been on the faculty at Washington & Lee. "Dr. Brown had been our psychology professor. Tom and I took every course he gave. We liked him. He was very good. We didn't care what the course was, we took all the courses he gave."

Dr. Brown left Washington & Lee and became a high-level lecturer and then ran for governor of Virginia. He was soundly defeated by Harry Byrd. After his defeat he became president of Atlantic University.

A.U. was underwritten by essentially the same financial sources that backed the Cayce Hospital—the Blumenthal brothers. While Edgar was elected to its board of trustees and credited by Blumenthal with inspiring the idea of establishing the college, the board opted for a conventional liberal arts curriculum. "We have no idea of having any course or department on mediumism, spiritualism or anything of the sort," said Dr. Brown. A.U. ambitiously established departments in English, history, languages, mathematics, political science, science, philosophy, psychology, art, drama, public speaking, plus pre-law, pre-medicine, and pre-engineering programs. Only one department might have raised an eyebrow: A.U. taught astrology.

The school also boasted a football team, women's soccer, a dance orchestra, a student newspaper, fraternities, and even a school mascot, a three-legged dog named Tripod.

Dr. Brown nonetheless "got interested in the readings. Every head of a department he hired had to have a [psychic] reading. It was the most amazing selection of a university staff you ever saw. They were topnotch people, paid fabulous salaries for those times."

What A.U. lacked most conspicuously was an endowment to assure its survival. Having opened in the wake of the stock market crash, it was in financial trouble from the start and foundered fifteen months after it opened. Although funds were diverted to it from the hospital, A.U. declared bankruptcy in December 1931.

Worse still for the Cayces, the hospital closed soon afterward. Hard times—and bitter feelings—led to its collapse. "My father was on the board of the university, and of course he was on the board of the Association for National Investigators that was running the hospital. A lot of patients were paying but the hospital was just getting started and needed money. So the conflict came to a break between my father and Blumenthal, who had put up a lot of

99

the money."

What caused the break?

"It wasn't just that the collapse came with the stock market crash. Morton's interest began to be pulled aside by another psychic. There was a little Irish girl named Patricia Devlin who worked in Morton's office on the switchboard, and she began to manifest considerable psychic ability. She began to give readings and Morton began to get information from her when he couldn't get it from Dad because of the number of patients at the hospital who needed physical readings. Morton used to get a reading every day from Dad but this had to be tapered off because of readings for the patients. Morton agreed to this but he still wanted psychic information."

Morton's turning to another psychic evidently did not in itself create a rift with Edgar, for Hugh Lynn recalled that Patricia came to the Beach with Morton on a number of occasions and participated in the Sunday lecture program with Morton, giving psychic demonstrations. She also received a reading from Edgar.

"She was a very good psychic," conceded Hugh Lynn. "But she differed with Dad on a lot of the basic stuff that was cause to worry."

Morton's relationship with her led to several traumatic conflicts.

"Morton became very involved with this woman, whether romantically I don't know, but she was the basis of Morton's wife's divorce suit—but also his brother's wife's divorce suit. And they all, both the Irish girl and her husband and Morton and Edwin, moved to Virginia Beach and all lived together in the same house. It was a strange pattern.

"Morton converted from the Jewish to the Catholic religion. His brother also joined the Catholic church at the Irish lady's instigation."

Hugh Lynn said he didn't know the whole story, but he surmised that Morton got conflicting financial advice from Patricia and his father.

"My father didn't discuss this with me. Morton told me that she was giving readings. I only surmised that they disagreed [with Edgar's]. I think they disagreed over the break in the market and lost a lot of the money."

In any event, Dave Kahn sued Blumenthal over the stock broker's handling of Kahn's investments.

"Dave had put money with Morton in the market and they were accusing each other of everything under the sun. The story is that they both showed up in court and were confined in jail overnight.

100

"The entire board of trustees was investing with Morton in the market, and when he got caught and the market went down they all lost large amounts of money. This created a real furor but also cut off the flow of money to the hospital, not only from Morton but from everybody else on the board."

Hugh Lynn estimates that Morton invested close to $1 million in the hospital and Atlantic University, counting construction costs and salaries.

It was the lawsuit between Kahn and Blumenthal that led to the break between Morton and Edgar, for it forced Edgar to choose sides.

"Dad received a telegram from Morton saying, 'In the name of Jesus Christ, you are to desist from giving any more readings for David E. Kahn.' Dad refused. That was the break. No one could tell him who to give readings for. No one. Not even Jesus Christ and Pat Devlin."

In the personal chaos that ensued, the organization and its hopeful enterprises were abandoned.

"Dad and Morton broke, they split, they wanted to close it out. They split over many things but that telegram was the final straw.

"They closed the hospital—it was turned back to Morton. The Association of National Investigators owned all that property, three blocks of it, but a lot of it was mortgaged. Morton wiped that out. And he stopped paying on the house we were living in, so they asked us to move out.

"We had a faculty that was still here at Virginia Beach. They were suing Morton, and they were starving. Some of them couldn't get jobs and were destroyed. Dad felt responsible for it. So we dissolved the National Association of Investigators in the quickest trial you ever saw. We had a big battle with lawyers. We put Dad on the witness stand and the judge asked, "Mr. Cayce, what is all this about?" Dad said, "Judge, we would like to dissolve the ANI. It's come to an end." The judge said, "It is dissolved," and that was the end of it." Then Morton sued Dad for taking a stove |from the house| and the storm windows off the porch. Morton just had to have a suit.

"Suddenly everything was gone. The hospital was closed, I didn't have a job, the university was closed, and Dad wanted to die. His dreams had been shot, and he just wanted to die. Literally. He was finished, depressed. He just didn't want to go on."

It seemed a bleak prospect for the idealistic college grad who had been so eager to devote his life to his father's work.

Chapter 9

Cayce & Son

The collapse of the Cayce Hospital had a profound influence on the direction of Hugh Lynn's adult life. Had the hospital succeeded, his father, then fifty-four, might have happily devoted his remaining years to giving readings for patients, to lecturing, teaching his Bible class, and fishing. Had Hugh Lynn felt free to chart his own course, he might well have pursued an independent career in psychology or archaeology. It was one thing to express idealistic goals as a college student, another to subordinate himself to his father. But he couldn't disentangle himself.

"I would have left after college, I think, if things hadn't collapsed. When they collapsed I felt that I wanted to help Dad. Mother was just so committed to him. He was so proud of my willingness to try to help him. It wasn't just my support as a son—he called it that—but my support of his work, consolidating it, stabilizing it, so that we could do the job."

Disbanding the original Cayce organization, the National Association of Investigators, did not mean that the concept was flawed. After the hospital closed, Edgar invited about seventy-five friends from all over the country to meet at his house to discuss how to carry on The Work. Many responded by letter with encouragement. Those who crowded into the Cayce cottage on 35th Street shared their feelings, each with a unique slant.

Edgar's sister, Sarah, urged that some means be sought to continue operating a hospital because, "the physical work is the most important." Francis H. Greene, a professor, agreed, saying, "We owe Mr. Cayce and the hospital for saving the life of our boy whom we brought to him in a very critical condition." But Wallace H.

McChesney, a chiropractor, said, "There is a greater work here than the physical side of life. That is only the shadow of the greater thing." His life reading had made him aware of it: "Simply the realization that you are part of the eternal scheme of life, that you are everlasting and perpetual and will never die is tremendous." H.H. Jones agreed that, "the spiritual is very much greater than the physical, but in the physical you have something you can show in a tangible form. And I heartily agree that the hospital work should go on." Esther Wynne told how the hospital had drawn her to The Work, and she thought, "the hospital is a means whereby a great mass of people may be reached. The mental and spiritual growth will come also in its own good time."

Mina Kerr favored an emphasis on research to discover "new truths." An admirer of the Quakers, she said, "So many times we quote, 'Where there is no vision, the people perish.' I like to turn it to, 'Where there is vision, the people live.'" Edgar's minister at the Presbyterian church, the Rev. Frank H. Scattergood, said, "Any other movement with which we may associate ourselves will also be benefited by this work of Edgar Cayce." Helen Ellington also took the broad view: "The one thing that I remember from The Work is that God is only where His instrument manifests Him. Well, this work, it seems to me, has made some wonderful improvements in my soul."

Edgar's sister, Annie, who had worked at the hospital, stood up and told how she had taken action on her own after she had asked in a reading, "if I should take a house and take care of the ones that have been begging to come." The reading approved her nursing-home idea. "The house is small, but the best I could obtain at this time. I have two patients who were anxious and waiting to come, and I am taking care of them as well as I can."

After most folks had spoken, Dave Kahn gallantly mentioned Gertrude's self-sacrifice: "There is always someone who has to stand the brunt of everything. In the business world, it must be the credit man. I know what it is to back up this kind of work—days of trial and criticism and worries—and one person here has been connected with The Work through it all. She will tell us how she would like to see it carried on." Dave beckoned to her in the next room, but Gertrude shyly said, "Dave, we had agreed that Hugh Lynn would talk." Kahn insisted that she tell the crowd, "how many fields should we touch?"

"All of them," replied Mrs. Cayce. "I think we have to reach as many people as we can."

Kahn asked Gladys what her ideals were for The Work, and she said that after seven years of taking the readings in shorthand, "It seems that all of my life up until that time I was waiting for just such an opportunity. I hope to give the rest of my life in the same manner."

Waiting until last, Hugh Lynn asked the crowd to forget whose son he was. "I am just a soul hunting for something, going somewhere, most of us don't know where—looking, searching for something. By the very presence of each of you here, by the words that you have spoken, you have manifested an interest in something that will make others' lives more worthwhile. Each of us, as we have contacted this man, just a man—a highly-developed man, it is true, but just a man—are here, each and every one of us, to promote and carry out the information, to give to the world the information that comes through this man. If to me, to you, it is worthwhile, as each of us gets a glimpse of the life, of the understanding we are to carry on to the others, then each of us is going to get what we are looking for. Our lives are going to represent the purposes and ideals that we believe in. We are the representation to the world of this work.

"Now, let us all get together. Let us think together. Let us be of one mind. Let us try to give to the world a little of life, of understanding, of truth. Let us try to help each individual that we contact to realize the spirit of the Creator that is within each and every one of us."

What began as a discussion group turned into a spiritual pep rally for The Work, and for organizing anew.

"You can't possibly know what this meeting has meant to me," said Edgar before they adjourned. "To hear so many people express themselves about The Work being something glorious." Then turning to Hugh Lynn, he said, "And there is one more thing: there are few men who live to be a hero to their children. To see the love that has been expressed by that boy this evening, to know what The Work has meant in his life, has made my life more worthwhile."

Three months later, after several readings seeking guidance, the new organization was born. Esther Wynne suggested that it be called Seekers of Divine Truth. Other ideas included Universal Brotherhood, Life Society, Inc., Cayce Research Society, and Cayce Sanitarium for Psychic Research. Hugh Lynn's cousin, Gray Salter, came closest with National Association of Research and Enlightenment.

Chartered by the Commonwealth of Virginia, the Association for Research and Enlightenment comprised about three hundred members who had received readings. Without an endowment or wealthy backers, however, it remained largely dependent on volunteers. It had no funds to pay office rent or staff salaries. As a practical matter, its headquarters would continue to be the Cayce house, and the Cayces would go on as before, living on contributions. The question was, what should Hugh Lynn, the college grad, do?

"I was caught. How could I leave them at that time? I thought I'd stay on and help them get started again and then I'd go on about my business. I wanted to be an archaeologist—it was in the back of my mind—because history and archaeology always appealed to me, even though I had majored in psychology. So I got caught in the transition. And Dad loved me so much that he wanted me to have a part in it, and he was very proud that I devoted time to it. He used to say, 'This thing can't be all wrong if my son is interested in it.'"

Hugh Lynn, in a word, feared the A.R.E. might founder if he didn't pitch in. He looked back on that decision philosophically later:

"Dad depended on me to help make decisions and to move along. You see, that's what happened to me in Egypt, according to the readings. There was an old king, and I was his son. He turned over the throne to me and backed off, put Egyptian counselors around me to give me support. I was very young, only sixteen years old. So I took on a lot of responsibility and must not have done very well with it in the beginning. Most of the time was spent fighting, getting people in trouble, getting myself in trouble."

Edgar's dependence was never more obvious.

"We were renting the big, old house facing the ocean on 67th Street, and freezing in it during the winter. It was a struggle for Dad to look at the hospital building he had lost and to see the remains of the Atlantic University foundation that had been started in the block directly across the street from us."

Edgar had a dream that alarmed the family terribly. It was interpreted by a reading to mean that he was so despondent that he might "enter the spirit world" if he no longer felt needed in this realm. "The reading scared us to death because we thought he was going to die," recalled Gladys. "Everyone started working to stimulate his interest in staying here and carrying on his work. If any one of us heard of someone who was ill, or needed help mentally or spiritually, we would dash to them and tell them about Mr. Cayce. Gradually, he began to feel needed, as he was helping people and getting results."

He had a very loyal local core group, perhaps a dozen, who had begun to meet regularly, initially to study ESP. Hugh Lynn and Gladys were members of this group. Edgar frequently gave readings to guide their study of metaphysical concepts. Thus the first Study Group was conceived and formalized in 1931. It had an immediate effect on Edgar's spirits. "The Study Group rallied around him and group work became very important to him," recalled Gladys. "He could see and feel that he was being a channel." Hugh Lynn said flatly: "That first Study Group saved his life."

The group's impact went far beyond Edgar personally. It helped galvanize Cayce and Son to undertake together a new mission through the A.R.E. Hugh Lynn was twenty-four and Edgar fifty-four when they teamed up to breathe life into the A.R.E. Originally appointed to the board of trustees, Hugh Lynn was now named business manager. Edgar would be, in effect, the high priest, giving readings on the direction of the work, while Hugh Lynn tried to implement them in a practical way.

As librarian for Atlantic University, he had been paid a weekly salary. As business manager for the A.R.E., his compensation was chancy.

"I got a little spending money when there was any. And that was all. Gladys didn't get any salary. I didn't get any salary. It was years before that developed. There wasn't any money. The family had a little income from readings. People gave a little money, but nobody had much money in those years."

Along with the collapse of the hospital and the university, and the feud with the Blumenthals, the Cayces suffered a feeling of being dispossessed. First, Blumenthal had them evicted from 35th Street in July 1931, then he sued Edgar for removing the stove; they moved to the beach house on 67th Street, but it overlooked the hospital, which had been turned into the Cape Henry Hotel for tourists. As cold weather set in, they found the drafty unheated beach house impossible. Finding affordable quarters suitable for both household and offices challenged them repeatedly. Hugh Lynn could find nothing better than two small houses next to one another at the opposite end of the beach on Lake Drive; a few weeks after they moved in, the property was sold out from under them, forcing them to move once again that spring. They moved three times, chickens and all, within one 11-month period. Between the 4th of July 1931 and Memorial Day 1932 they occupied five different houses, none of them as comfortable as what they had once known.

Lacking funds to buy a house—Gladys had promoted the idea among the Cayces' friends that they put up enough money to purchase property, to no avail—Hugh Lynn found another house for rent that was spacious enough for their enlarged family and business needs. It was the house on Arctic Crescent which the elder Cayces purchased four years later and lived in for the remainder of their lives. Although functional, it afforded little personal privacy. Hugh Lynn shared a bedroom with his teenage brother, and Gladys shared her room with her cousin Mildred, who performed secretarial duties. Only Squire Cayce, now a crotchety widower, had his own room.

The main office of the A.R.E. at the head of the stairs was

jammed with small desks for Hugh Lynn and the two young women. Edgar put his couch in a tiny room on the first floor where he gave readings and answered his mail. Years later a wing was added, providing much more spacious accommodations, but initially it was a lot to expect all of these people to cohabit harmoniously, especially since none of them left the premises to go off to work. Only Ecken was gone during the day at school. Edgar escaped to his garden or to the edge of Lake Holly behind the house for a little fishing, but all of the family's work and play, and A.R.E. business, visitors included, were centered under one roof.

Hugh Lynn enjoyed the most imaginative escape of all by dreaming up a transcontinental motor trip for his Boy Scout troop to Yellowstone National Park in the summer of 1933. It turned out so well that he proposed to expand on it the following summer. According to his application to the Boy Scouts of America to "conduct a moving camp," it was a fifty-day 12,000-mile journey costing $110 per boy, which he told the boys' parents was "less than one cent per mile." It would probably be, he confidently assured them, "the finest educational investment for your boy that you will ever have the opportunity of making."

Setting out in the Cayce family Buick, with packs strapped to the running boards and a "Pike's Peak or Bust" sign on the side, they had an adventure the scouts, Ecken included, never forgot. Not least of all was the Chicago World's Fair which they visited on the way. As Hugh Lynn later told the story, he let the boys wander on their own for awhile so he could take in the show of Sally Rand, the famous fan dancer. When he looked around the audience, the scoutmaster was astonished to see a row of familiar young faces, more attentive than usual for this rare educational opportunity.

Most of the tour, however, was spent in the great American outdoors, from the Petrified Forest to the Great Salt Lake, from the Badlands to the redwoods—"the greatest travel adventure of my life," said Norfolk attorney Berry D. Willis, Jr. "Every young man who had any association with Hugh Lynn came away from the experience richer in character and imbued with a desire to help mankind." The sturdy Buick and their leader brought them safely home in time for another school year and the rituals of family life.

The Cayce household rituals usually included all of the adults. Twice daily, once before lunch and again in midafternoon, they gathered for a reading, Edgar stretching out on his little green couch, the others clustered close beside him. They convened three times for meals and to speak with visitors, who dropped in frequently. Gertrude cooked and the young women helped with housekeeping

108

chores. When Edgar gave readings, Gertrude served as conductor and Gladys as the stenographer. Hugh Lynn, the Squire, and Mildred observed. When Mildred returned to her home in Oklahoma in 1935, Gladys resumed carrying the full secretarial load.

Despite the personal turmoil of the Cayces' lives during the early thirties, Hugh Lynn made remarkable organizational progress. The first Study Group also experienced internal personality clashes. But, united in prayer, it did more than survive; it spawned other groups that in time would become a worldwide movement. The first of these spin-off groups was foreseen in a reading which advised starting a healing prayer group. Hugh Lynn was one of its founding members, too. So were Gladys and Mildred. Thus was born the Glad Helpers, a group that still holds a weekly healing prayer meeting in Virginia Beach. Through the work of these initial groups, the pain and sense of loss suffered by Edgar over the failure of the hospital slowly healed.

"In the years to come," said Gladys, "he realized that it was a good thing that the hospital failed because as long as it was in existence he wasn't doing this sort of work. He was always intent on helping the people who were ill. He gave the physical readings preference over the life readings. When we began to study together and receive group readings, it was as if his family had been enlarged."

Hugh Lynn was intent on enlarging the A.R.E. community beyond the few hundred people who had readings. So in 1932 he launched a monthly publication, *The Bulletin*, which contained extracts and health hints from readings, philosophical articles, and book reviews. He also organized the first annual meeting of A.R.E. Congress, open to all members. His challenge was to generate enough enthusiastic interest in the A.R.E. as an educational vehicle for it to survive without a major financial angel.

Although small, the organization was not destitute, for it had several generous patrons such as the Kahns. David's furniture business in New York had done very well despite the Depression, and he never ceased attributing its success to Judge, as Dave called Edgar. He shipped the Cayces a dining room suite for their new home on Arctic Crescent. Lucille Kahn devoted much energy to organizing metaphysical lectures in New York, raising interest in psychic phenomena and in Cayce's work, and raising money for the A.R.E. The Cayce family periodically took the train up to New York, often staying at the Kahns' house in Scarsdale while Edgar gave readings. Edgar visited other eastern cities to give readings, but seemed to do best at gaining new clients in New York. Some of them learned firsthand what an extraordinary mortal Edgar was.

109

"We were in New York once, staying with the Zentgrafs at their mansion on Staten Island. Mrs. Zentgraf and Dad both liked to bowl. But on this occasion Dad had taken a cold. It was a very cold night and he choked up and became very hot. The Zentgrafs called a doctor who came and examined Dad—I was in the room with him. The doctor left the room and went downstairs and told the Zentgrafs, 'We've got to get him to a hospital immediately. He needs oxygen. I think he's going into pneumonia.'

"They called an ambulance and I went upstairs to tell Dad what the doctor had said. He told me to lock the door and not let anyone in until he waked up.

"As I locked the bedroom door, he went into an altered state. It was just like he was giving a reading, except that he did it himself. Almost immediately he began to perspire. It saturated the sheets and ran off the bed onto the floor in puddles. The ambulance arrived and the doctor came and knocked on the door. I told him through the door that my father was asleep. The doctor pounded on the door. The Zentgrafs came upstairs. There was a great furor—it was crazy—and I was just sitting there not knowing what to do.

"In about twenty minutes Dad came out of it, and his voice was just as clear as mine. His fever was gone. He was saturated, but he had no more congestion in his head or lungs. He got up and took a warm shower. Mrs. Zentgraf changed the bed while Mr. Zentgraf tried to explain to the doctor that my father can do this sort of thing. The doctor finally sent the ambulance away because there was nothing for it to do.

"Watching Dad do that made me realize what control is possible over the human body."

The New York police, however, suspected that Edgar was up to no good. While he was giving readings in a Manhattan hotel room in November 1931, a woman detective made an appointment that set the stage for the arrest of Edgar and his "pretty blonde secretary," as the New York tabloids described Gladys. Gertrude, who was also arrested, was cropped out of the newspaper photos. They were all three charged with fortune-telling.

At least one reporter who covered the story was sympathetic. Tom Sugrue, not long before this embarrassing incident, had moved to New York, at Edgar's suggestion. "Dad said, 'Tom, you should go to New York and get a job on a newspaper, and if I had your skills I'd go to the Herald-Tribune.' Tom did get a job as a reporter on the Herald-Tribune. And he wrote a real story [about Edgar's arrest]."

Hugh Lynn and Mildred, not knowing of the arrest, had gone to the train station to pick up the returning travelers but waited three hours in vain. Next morning when they read the papers, they knew why. Instead of being angered or alarmed, Hugh Lynn treated it as a joke. "I do hope they gave you a nice cell with plenty of light, running water and whatnot," he wrote. "Be sure and save us all the printed details in the papers there. It is quite thrilling to have parents in the papers, especially in jail." Turning serious, he said the Study Group would pray for them. "There have been many people treated this way, you know, from 10,500 B.C. to now anyway....The world is not kind to people who are different. Keep smiling and remember, 'Father, forgive them for they know not what they do.'" When the accused came to trial, the magistrate listened to the evidence and dismissed the case.

The incident left Edgar puzzled. "Just how or why information concerning us should be so worthwhile to newspapers is a thing I haven't been able to quite figure out," he wrote to Dave Kahn's mother. "We are actually hearing that little newspapers over the country are still carrying articles that we are in jail—when for weeks we have been home and trying to go on with our work."

The Cayces visited New York frequently, drawn there by friendship as well as business. It was still touch and go for Edgar to make a living just by giving readings for clients at random. Until his split with Blumenthal, he had done well for seven years simply because Blumenthal had paid generously for a steady stream of readings. All told, Blumenthal received 468 readings—more by far than Edgar gave for any other single individual.

Although others were equally enthusiastic, his gift was known to a relatively small circle. And the bad press had not helped. Edgar said "one could not blame people for not believing them or for feeling that the whole thing was a lot of 'bunk.'"

A growing number of New Yorkers, however, had benefited by following the suggestion that they consult Dr. Harold J. Reilly, who ran a gym in Rockefeller Center. Reilly, a tall husky man in his mid-thirties, was a physiotherapist who had also been trained in chiropractic. His clientele, primarily the business and professional crowd, included the rich and famous as well. Reilly had never heard of Cayce until people came to him with typed copies of their readings. He tried Cayce's suggestions and used them effectively. After they met, Cayce and Reilly became close friends.

Occasionally, a lecture program was arranged in New York for Cayce and Reilly to talk about some of their favorite success stories and to get the word out. Edgar liked to lecture.

"One rainy night Dr. Reilly and Dr. Dobbins, an osteopath, and Dr. Henry Hardwicke were speaking about their experiences with Dad.

The title of the program was "Three Physicians and a Psychic." They had a hall full of people. Dr. Dobbins told a story of a man who had been in a mental institution. His cousin had gone to Dad to get a reading for the man, who was so violent—he had beat up his wife and almost killed his child—that he was in a straitjacket. Dr. Dobbins, the osteopath, went to see the man and to give him an adjustment recommended in the reading. The reading said he had slipped on the ice in front of the post office and injured his spine, knocked it out of alignment, which had caused pressure that resulted in his mad behavior. The man let Dr. Dobbins work on him and quieted down, and the doctor made some more adjustments—and he recovered and was as sane as anyone.

"When Dr. Dobbins told this story that night he had no idea the man was in the audience. But when he finished, a man stood up in the back of the hall and came walking down the aisle. He was a great big fellow. He walked on the stage, turned to the audience and said, 'I just want you to know that I'm the man the doctor told about, and every word of it is true. I'd be in that mental institution yet if it weren't for this man.' And he turned around and shook hands with my father, and tears came to Dad's eyes.

"Well, you can't have much more than that in one night, but while the program was going on a little lady came into the hall to get out of the rain. She was all wet and came in just to get dry. Knowing nothing about the meeting, she took a seat in the front row. When the meeting was over, she was the first one to get to my father. Within moments after she grabbed hold of him, I had a note from Dad which said, 'Make this woman an appointment for tomorrow morning. Cancel whatever you have to.'

"She had just come from visiting her daughter who was also in a straitjacket in a mental hospital. Next day Dad gave a reading for the girl, who was an artist. The reading said that the girl had sold a painting to a man, and when she delivered it he had raped her. During the assault, she had been injured in the spine, resulting in her seemingly insane behavior. Two days later we had Dr. Dobbins in that hospital to see her. He gave her a spinal adjustment, and she recovered—and got out of the hospital—and painted a portrait of my father."

Such remarkable happenstance as the woman coming in out of the rain only to stumble upon Edgar Cayce as an answer to prayer apparently fulfilled Edgar's soul purpose.

"I think the readings suggest that the people who got to him for readings were the people he had met before or had hurt before with his psychic ability when he was misusing it. He had misused it as a gambler in early America. That's why he never played cards for money, never gambled. It wasn't because he *couldn't* do it, but because he *could.*"

Hugh Lynn, no less than his parents, derived a sense of divine purpose in The Work as one experience after another of this sort unfolded. Indeed, even harassment by the police for a second time, on this occasion in Detroit, didn't diminish their dedication. But it did sidetrack them and alarm their friends.

They had gone to Detroit to give readings in a private home. A man who got a reading for his daughter Betty, who had asthma, filed the complaint. The reading suggested using the wet-cell appliance and spinal manipulations to relieve her respiratory trouble.

"The man did not understand the reading. He was stubborn and insisted that the treatments suggested were in no way connected with his girl's trouble. Dad was completely tired out after this reading, indicating a difficult mental attitude."

Two days later, on a Saturday morning, "four officers came in and arrested the four of us on a charge of practicing medicine without a license. They questioned Dad for half an hour trying to get him to admit the work was a fake. It seems that Betty's father had taken the reading to her doctors and they told him it was worthless."

Edgar, Hugh Lynn, Gertrude and Gladys were booked in a Detroit police station, the men in one section of the jail, the women in another.

"My father and I were fingerprinted and we turned over our wallets, keys, and everything in our pockets with the exception of three dollars, which we were told we could use for candy and cigarettes. He was bewildered by the indignity rather than angered by it; and I think what grieved him most was the shock to my mother and Gladys."

Because it was a weekend, their friends had difficulty arranging for their release immediately.

"We were taken into a large confined jail space in which there were a number of small cubicles with double bunks. As soon as we got into this large enclosure, some twenty or twenty-five inmates gathered around us. Apparently one man had been elected as the head or captain of the group. He was the person to whom we gave the three dollars. He asked my father, 'What are you in for?' He answered quietly but was very straightforward. He said we were charged with practicing medicine without a license. The other prisoners wanted to know if it was true, and Dad said it was quite true—but that was not the real reason we were there. He said, 'Like all of you, there is back of what you are accused of the *real* cause, the

113

real reason for your confinement.'

"He turned then to one of the men and began to talk to him personally. Everybody sat down in a circle on the floor, including me, but Dad remained standing in the middle. He looked at this man and said, 'You are accused of hitting a child with an automobile. That's why you are here. But the real reason for your confinement is a conflict with your wife that's been going on for a long time. You were very, very angry after an argument with her. Because of this anger, you got into your car and pulled out quickly without being very observant and struck a child.'

"The man turned white. Several men who knew him gasped. The captain said, 'My God, do they put people like you in jail?'

"He then ordered the men to get us the two best mattresses and put them in the cell Dad and I were supposed to occupy. But we never used them because we were bailed out later that evening by the general manager of the Buick plant, who had received very wonderful relief from an attack of kidney stones the week before, and a furniture dealer from Flint whose son had received a reading. They each put up $400 to post bail of $200 each for the four of us, thus saving us a night in a very modern but rather filthy jail."

A pretrial hearing was set for the following Thursday. The Cayces and their friends discussed the effect that publicity might have on Edgar's work. The arrest and the questioning by the police had so upset him that he could give no more readings while awaiting the hearing. A friend in New York prepared some press releases providing background material which played up the Cayces' connection with psychical research, as well as a copy of the A.R.E charter issued by the Commonwealth of Virginia. Hugh Lynn favored calling the newspapers and giving his side of it, but "the people in New York and the lawyers in Detroit felt that such publicity would do us more harm than good.

"The charges against everyone but Dad were dropped. The judge called in my father and explained to him that the whole situation was most unfortunate and he was very sorry that it had happened. He suggested, since it was necessary to impose some sentence, either a fine of a few dollars or a return of the original membership fee of the complaining witness and a short period of probation. We accepted the latter. Dad was put on probation and released to the custody of a Norfolk parole officer.

"Not one reporter showed up during the whole proceedings. So far as we know nothing appeared in the papers regarding the trial.

"On the way home from Detroit on the train, Dad had an offbeat dream, a sort of compensation for the degrading humiliation he had
114

undergone. He dreamed that he had been born again, around the year 2100, in Nebraska, which was now a seacoast state. Unfortunately, no one asked him whether the sea was west or east of the state. While a boy in that life he insisted he was Edgar Cayce, he had lived before and been arrested in Detroit. He said if someone would take him to Detroit he could lead them to the police records.

"So these scientists—tall, bald-headed fellows with thick eyeglasses—put him into a cigar-shaped flying car and set out for Detroit. This machine had no conventional means of propulsion, it just flew very swiftly and silently. They arrived in Detroit and found the records. They proceeded to New York, where he remembered some records of another arrest; but New York had been razed to the ground and was in the process of being rebuilt. I don't know the cause; nobody asked him that either. So they continued on to Virginia Beach, where everything seemed to be in fine shape, business booming. No disaster area here. This work of ours was still in progress. The A.R.E. was going great guns. His scientist friends took copies of the readings back to Nebraska via the flying cigar, and the dream ended.

"In his interpretation, Edgar Cayce said these things could come to pass. It should be very stimulating."

When Edgar reported to his probation officer in Norfolk, "he just happened to be an A.R.E. member. Instead of Dad's having to report to him once a month, the man came out to the beach to take his statement—and get a reading at the same time."

The worst result of the Detroit incident was that it laid Edgar low physically. As he later told a friend in a letter, "I proceeded to have, well, one pain after another and really was quite ill." A reading diagnosed it as gallbladder trouble, but he recovered without the necessity of surgery and reported that "now we can laugh at it all."

Despite the humiliation and pain of his arrests, the Cayces were encouraged by the growing interest in The Work, notably the formation of additional Study Groups in other areas. By 1934 Study Group No. 5 had been started on Long Island. Hugh Lynn knew from his experience in the first group that strong wills among its members often clashed and disrupted group harmony, but that it could contribute to real personal growth. Aware that groups may disband over disagreements before realizing such rewards, he sent a letter of guidance to all Study Groups: "You are a group of strong wills. You have many points of view. That is good. Each one of you, almost without exception, thinks under the surface that everybody else in the group is just a little off the track. I expect God considers each of your souls just as important in the scheme of things as the individual sitting next to you. Do you not have time to help one another?"

Personal growth, Hugh Lynn continued, was to be found in group relationships. It was not surprising that when the group developed study materials, the first lesson was titled "Cooperation." Hugh Lynn added:

"Spiritual growth can never result from our attending a thousand lectures, studying with a multitude of teachers, or listening to an infinite number of readings. It comes only from our own thought and action expressing what we know of universal laws. What you discover will be important, but in the beginning not nearly so important as your attitude toward the group and the individuals who compose it."

The Study Group movement was spurred greatly by the lessons compiled from Edgar's readings for Study Group No. 1, ultimately published as a lesson book. Hugh Lynn directed the project, encouraging Esther Wynne, a Norfolk schoolteacher, to compile the material and draft the manuscript with input from Study Group No. 1. It was entitled, A *Search for God*. Hugh Lynn defended this curious title by characterizing the Study Group effort as personal research. Although his father had actually given psychic trance readings at a number of the initial Study Group meetings, Hugh Lynn wanted to avoid any suggestion of the occult—a word he "hated with a passion," said one associate. The preface of the book defined its purpose in the familiar terminology of Bible school literature: "Try living the precepts of this book. Here is a unique compilation of information dealing with spiritual laws of daily living." The information in the book, it added, came from "general 'readings' given by Edgar Cayce" as well as experiences of the Study Group members during meditation. "To these individuals it brought hope, peace, a better understanding of their fellowmen, and an inner joy in a greater awareness of attunement with the Creator."

The revolutionary aspect of the book perhaps was its focus on meditation as well as prayer. Meditation, a familiar practice in Eastern non-Christian cultures, had attracted little interest in the United States then. The book therefore broke ground by explaining the purpose of meditation—"the emptying of ourselves of all that hinders the Creative Force from rising along the natural channels of our physical bodies to be disseminated through the sensitive spiritual centers in our physical bodies"—and describing how to meditate: "Meditation is not musing or daydreaming, but attuning our mental and physical bodies to their spiritual source," it said. "It is arousing the mental and spiritual attributes to an expression of their relationship with their Maker."

Hugh Lynn didn't want to scare off anyone who might consider this an alien practice. The book's preface added: "There is nothing new here. The search for God is as old as man. This book is passed on in hope that through it, during the trying times ahead, many may glimpse a ray of light; that in other hearts it may awaken a new hope and vision of a better world through application of His laws in daily life."

While the topics addressed were as familiar as the teachings of Jesus and the epistles of Paul—faith, virtue, fellowship, patience, love—the book was a primer for personal change. "The first and last obstacle to overcome is understanding ourselves," it declared.

A *Search for God*, Volumes I and II, was destined to become the most widely used educational material ever issued by the A.R.E. Those two little books have gone through many printings and today are used throughout the world by groups from Ireland to Japan, from Brazil to Germany. While the Study Group movement was thus to become an international phenomenon, and the heart of the A.R.E. in many respects, it remained primarily a vehicle for individual spiritual growth.

If Hugh Lynn had done nothing else to preserve his father's legacy, this in itself would have been a notable achievement. The Study Group movement gave The Work a focus and its members a framework for personal spiritual growth. That, as much as anything, gave the A.R.E.—and Hugh Lynn for the rest of his life—a high sense of purpose.

Chapter 10

'Mysteries of the Mind': New York

The growth of the A.R.E. in the 1930s stemmed largely from two major efforts: the personal readings Edgar gave in Virginia Beach; and the public activities—lectures, articles, testimonials—centered in New York City. To manage both ends of the axis Hugh Lynn shuttled back and forth constantly. His own growth, professionally and socially, can be traced to this experience. In 1938, while spending weeks in New York trying to promote a publishing project, a wonderful opportunity opened for him. Radio station WOR, the flagship station of the Mutual Network and one of the most prominent broadcasting outlets in America, offered him a weekly Sunday afternoon program about psychic phenomena. Part drama, part talk show, it was called, "Mysteries of the Mind." Hugh Lynn, then thirty-one, was master of ceremonies. This splendid opportunity fell his way seemingly by chance.

"The son of a woman who had been greatly helped by a reading became the manager of WOR, and he gave me a chance to develop the program. They put it on the Mutual Network as a sustaining program and were looking for a sponsor."

The show was designed to be both entertaining and educational. It began with a dramatization of actual psychic episodes such as dream premonitions, mental telepathy, and clairvoyance that people had told Hugh Lynn about. After the actors finished each skit, Hugh Lynn led a discussion of the incident by two professors.

"Lucien Warner, a Ph.D., was one, and Henry Hardwicke, an M.D., was the other one. Warner would attack the story and explain how it couldn't have been—though he frequently believed that it could—and Dr. Hardwicke would support it and explain how it could have happened, in accord with the laws of psychical research. I got to know them well, working with them every week. I was paying them good money. They were very knowledgeable.

"There's an interesting story about Warner. He got a reading from Dad that gave him an incarnation in France, one in ancient Persia, and one in the American Revolutionary War during which he had trained Tories on Long Island, which was controlled by the British.

"Years later, after Warner's death, his wife came to Virginia Beach and told us that during World War II he had trained American spies to be dropped behind the German lines after the Normandy invasion—and he did it from a house on Long Island. He spoke fluent French, and he went right back and did the same thing all over again—some coincidence, and all documented."

The radio program gave Hugh Lynn his first important job outside of his father's work. Although his qualifications for conducting such a program stemmed from experience he had gained in association with his father, the program's content was entirely his responsibility.

From his own personal experience as a Scout leader, Hugh Lynn knew that the mind was capable of fascinating feats. When he took over the troop a few years before, he was confronted with the task of teaching many skills no one had taught him.

"When I did so, I began having a series of dreams that were like a television series about an Indian friend. In these dreams, he and I were growing up in one of the early frontier settlements in Kentucky in the time of Daniel Boone. I heard about Boone but never saw him. I was just a kid, nine or ten years old, in these dreams, playing with an Indian boy in the woods. And he taught me all kinds of things—how to build a fire to cook on, paddling canoes, the use of the bow and arrow, identification of trees, tracking animals, all kinds of wood lore—and I loved it. After I would dream these things, I'd use them to teach the Scouts. This was true of archery, true of canoeing. I don't do canoeing like the average paddler, I do an Indian canoe; and all the Scouts in Troop 60 did it that way because I taught them.

"The cooking was a lifesaver. I was probably the only scoutmaster in Virginia Beach who didn't have to eat raw meat. My scouts could cook. They knew how to build a fire. We never lost a firebuilding contest in the history of the troop. No flint and steel, we used the bow and rotation method. We could do that faster than anybody. My Indian friend had taught me, and I transferred it right over to Troop 60."

Having benefited from these psychic phenomena, he was strongly motivated to pursue the experiences of others, too:

"I was running all over New York digging up stories for my show, tracking them down, putting them together and writing them up. I had a writer who did the dramatization, but I had to provide all the details. The writer was Harold Sherman, who has written all kinds of books on the psychic. He didn't believe in reincarnation but I liked him. He had a physical reading but the doctors didn't follow the directions very well, and he blamed the reading for failing to help him, and we argued about it."

Each half-hour program covered several incidents, such as a woman's story of the ghost who always appeared at lunchtime after the gentleman who previously owned the house, Frank Barton, had been killed in an explosion. The apparition, seen by guests as well as his widow, always wore a straw hat like Barton had. In his commentary, Dr. Hardwicke said the evidence suggested that "this man's mind continued to function, after death, as it functioned when he was alive." He noted that "in almost all reported cases of so-called haunted houses, violent deaths have occurred."

Dr. Warner, however, saw it as a case of "the power of suggestion. People of hysterical nature quite often imagine they are hearing or seeing things." He noted that Barton's widow and daughter were the first to "see" him, but they could have been suffering from the shock of his sudden violent death and imagined that he had returned for lunch, as had been his custom.

Another case involved a woman who lived in Brooklyn and had a son, Abbott, in the Army at Fort Monroe, Virginia. Unknown to her, he had become critically ill with flu but requested that his mother not be notified lest she worry. After taking a turn for the better, Abbott told his doctor that he would notify his mother. That night she was awakened in her bedroom at home by a "visit" from Abbott, who told her he had been ill and had recovered. Then her visitor vanished.

Hugh Lynn asked the woman, "Are you sure this was not just a vivid dream?"

"I am positive, Mr. Cayce. I waked up suddenly. The room was in darkness but I seemed to see my boy walk right through the door into my room."

"How did he look to you?" asked Cayce. "Was he in uniform?"

"No, that's one of the strange things about it. No, he appeared to be wearing the blue serge suit that he'd left at home, hanging in the closet, when he went in the service."

Hugh Lynn asked, "What makes you think you actually saw him in your room that night?"

"Because, Mr. Cayce, he came over and sat on the side of the bed. I didn't feel him sit down but I did feel his kiss on my lips."

"When your son left, did he again seem to go through the door?"

"No, he just seemed to fade from sight."

The woman later told her two sisters about this incident, and they told her that they knew Abbott had been ill because he had written one of them but asked that his mother not be told. She had no idea that he had flu.

Did Abbott know about his "visit"? No. He said he had gone to sleep thinking that he would get word to his mother, but he was surprised to hear what she had experienced. Hugh Lynn told the experts that he had affidavits from the boy's doctor and the hospital concerning his illness.

Dr. Hardwicke said: "Abbott was undoubtedly worried about his mother and desired to communicate with her...this emotional desire furnished the force for impelling or sending his soul or mental body to the room where his mother lay sleeping. She actually saw this mental image of her son."

Hugh Lynn asked, "Then you believe that humans under certain highly emotional conditions can really project their souls or the image of their bodies so that they can be seen by another at a distance—and even talk with them?"

Dr. Hardwicke said, "There have been many such cases of record."

Another possible explanation, he added, is telepathy: "Abbott's mother may have received his thought impressions while asleep. Awakening suddenly, thinking of him, she may have seen the memory pattern of her son, dressed as he had been before he left for the service."

Dr. Warner remained dubious. He noted that "her sisters knew of her son's illness. It is quite possible that they might have let some word of it drop to her or have shown by their actions that they were worried about him. She could have sensed their thoughts or attitude unconsciously. She must have known of the general sickness at soldiers' camps. And she must have been anxious about her son, hopeful he would not get sick, or if he did get sick he would get well. Such feelings when they become strong enough are sufficient to bring on a hallucination or desire experience. Our unconscious mind plays strange tricks on us sometimes, and in my opinion, this case is evidence of it."

122

On one program Hugh Lynn told of a dream of his that had baffled him for years.

"I dreamed I was going into an old house which had been turned into a nightclub. I was escorting a young woman whose facial features were unfamiliar to me. The place was almost completely dark, with candles burning throughout the room, and there was music. We sat down at a small table. A white waiter who wore glasses and had on a short white coat with brass buttons came over to take our order. I gave him our order and then turned and looked over my shoulder and was startled to see a former friend with whom I had had a falling out. I awakened and was so impressed by the nature of this dream that I wrote it down. The following year an old house in my home town was turned into a nightclub. I did not go that entire season, but I heard later they used colored waiters that season. At the beginning of the second season—two years after my dream—I was given tickets to the opening of the nightclub. I went to the club with a girl I had not known when I had the dream. As we entered the club . . ."

Hugh Lynn's narration ended at this point and the dramatization took over with actors portraying him and his lady friend. "Hugh Lynn" tells the girl that the nightclub is just like a scene from a dream he had, even the same music. "In my dream I was taking a girl I had never seen before to this night club. That girl is you!"

When the girl mentioned that the waiter was coming, "Hugh Lynn" closed his eyes and said, "Tell me, Ellen, I want you to witness this for me—is this waiter a white man wearing a short white coat with brass buttons, and is he wearing glasses?"

"Why, yes."

"Then my dream's come true."

The script failed to include the experts' analysis.

Hugh Lynn narrated many amazing cases and concluded each broadcast with an appeal:

"We are interested in determining the true explanation behind the mysterious happenings of the mind. When you consider that man's mind has given the world all its great inventions and all that goes to make up our modern civilization, is it unreasonable to suspect the existence of even greater hidden powers which are operating under certain mental laws, still not understood by us, which powers are often referred to as psychic phenomena?

"Science is pointing the way now to great discoveries in the realms of mind, and you can aid science by sending in reports of any psychic experiences you may have had. You must have had one or more such experiences. Would you like to have it investigated and explained? A dream that came true; an apparent message from a friend or relative who has passed on; a telepathic communication? Please write up your experience and mail it to the 'Mysteries of the Mind' Hour, station WOR, New York City. I'll read the account of what happened to you and, if it is one we can present on the air, for our board of distinguished scientists to pass judgment upon, I'll get in touch with you. Wherever possible or practicable, we want to bring the men and women who have had unusual psychic experiences before the microphone so they can tell their own stories. Help science solve the 'Mysteries of the Mind' by cooperating with us. This is Hugh Lynn Cayce bidding you 'Good evening.'"

As a result of this appeal he compiled a list of names and many stories to try to verify. One common experience had to do with dream guidance. For example, a thirteen-year-old boy who had received a ring for his birthday lost it while playing in the yard with his older brother. A family search failed to find it by nightfall. That night the boy dreamed that it was behind a rock in the driveway. Next morning he went to the spot and found it. Hugh Lynn noted that this dream had "a simple psychological explanation in subconscious memory."

Many other dreams foretold tragedies, often death. They included the mothers of infants who perished accidentally after an earlier dream warning. Or children who had visions of parents at the time the parent was taken, unknown to the child, by death.

Hugh Lynn was quite proud of his show and considered it a turning point in his career. As he wrote to the headmaster at Moraine Park School in Dayton, "Considerable interest has been manifested already, and I believe we are going to be able to build up some real public interest." But he also still maintained the ideal of service upheld by his father. As he told headmaster Slutz, "The Association work is progressing very nicely, also. My father was here with me, in New York, for several days, and lectured to a very enthusiastic audience. We are continuing the work of assembling our confidential records and case reports, and I am confident will some day be able to make a real contribution to the whole field of psychic research. As I have told you, it has been for me a real opportunity and privilege to see almost daily miracles."

Working directly with people who had psychic experiences was really just another dimension of working with his father. The whole field of psychic phenomena fascinated him so much that earlier that year he had applied and been accepted at Duke University for a graduate program in psychology under J.B. Rhine, the noted parapsychologist. But after launching the radio show, he withdrew and invited Dr. Rhine to appear on the program. "I had looked forward to your joining us for some work at the Parapsychology Laboratory," Rhine responded. "I appreciate your invitation to appear on the program, but I shall probably not get around to that, since I am rarely in the city."

Fascinating as the show may have been, WOR couldn't find a sponsor to keep it on the air beyond the initial thirteen weeks.

"There was a very charming lady in New York whose husband was an executive with a New York advertising agency that had the Texaco account. They lived in a big, beautiful apartment where she would entertain and invite me when I wanted to meet people. I met the Chryslers and other people, and they were getting readings. Her husband tried to help us but it didn't work out."

Although he was a product of the Bible Belt and a straitlaced church-oriented family, Hugh Lynn enjoyed the cosmopolitan life of Manhattan. It introduced him to such new customs as social drinking, which became popular with the end of Prohibition. More refined than the collegiate guzzling of illegal moonshine a decade earlier, social drinking had snob appeal, which was no less intoxicating than the alcoholic content. The charming lady whose husband was in advertising made it easy for him.

"I knew them quite well, and I used to drop in for a drink. They served excellent sherry. I enjoyed cream sherry."

Relations with unattached women also were freer in New York. While he began his stay in New York by bunking with family friends, he soon made other arrangements.

"I lived with the Kahns in Scarsdale for a while. David Kahn took me on because of my father, but I would have to say that we didn't particularly like one another in the beginning. We got acquainted in Texas [during the search for oil] and I didn't like what he was doing and the influence that he had over my father. But we came to like each other. My family stayed in their home repeatedly and became close to their sons, knew them when they were growing up. Dad gave readings in their home. Lucille Kahn became a very good friend and still is today. They helped me many, many times, giving me a place to stay, and even giving me spending money in New York in the beginning. When I began to make my own money I moved into town.

"I was getting $350 to $400 a week. That was a lot of money, but it didn't last too long."

His short career as a national broadcaster had a dramatic impact on Hugh Lynn. Although his tenure was brief, it was more than a challenging, well-paying job. It was a maturing experience in every respect. By not working for his father, he was proving to himself that he could find his way in the world professionally and socially, make valuable contacts, and enjoy the sophisticated life.

New York nonetheless left him confused. "Life here is one long follow-up," he wrote Tommy House. "People, people, people, people. Rich, sick, crazy, charming, worried, poor, tormented, smart people...sometimes I move blindly through a haze, a turmoil of thoughts."

But Hugh Lynn didn't lose his hopeful idealism. "Always ahead there is a ray of hope, though, a seeming brightness in helping those about, day after day. God grant me the vision that it may always be help and not harm."

After seeing a Broadway play, "Our Town," he told Tommy that it was "a picture of life, love and death in a small New Hampshire town, a typical country town." It brought back many memories of growing up in Hopkinsville and Selma. "My emotions are running rampant, tumbling back over the years, all mixed up with my thoughts of life."

For one so young, Hugh Lynn was remarkably philosophical about his New York adventures. "There isn't much we can do but hold on to our faith and hope; faith in a Divine plan, hope that we may reach out to a clearer and clearer perception of that plan. There are periods of doubt, trial and testing that are hard, but we know the way if we can just hold to it."

Had his radio show been a commercial success, one can only speculate how his later life might have been changed.

"I made a lot of friends in New York because of the readings"— including Charles Schwab, one of America's biggest industrialists of that time.

"I met him through his mistress. She had had a life reading. I think he had a physical reading. She came to lectures. She was interested in the psychic. She was a very beautiful woman, a lovely lady, and didn't look at all like a mistress, or how I thought a mistress ought to look. She had a gorgeous apartment on Park Avenue. She played bridge with Schwab, and it was known that she was his mistress. His wife had been ill for years.

"She had me over for breakfast one morning with him. He ate four hard-fried eggs, burned toast, and drank a glass of Scotch whiskey straight—I've never seen such a breakfast in my life. We couldn't say anything—he wouldn't give it up. The steel magnate had an iron stomach. His reading told him to quit. He refused. He later had a heart attack or something, I think, and died.

126

"Another friend of mine in New York was Judy Chandler, an amazing, highly talented lady syndicated columnist. She was in radio, too, doing a fifteen-minute daily program from the Empire State Building tower. She interviewed every celebrity who came to New York. She was also a playwright, and at one time had a couple of plays running on Broadway.

"Judy had life readings that took her back to Palestine—it is her story that is told in the novel by Mary LaCroix, *The Remnant*. She was an Essene. Her readings also said she had been in Egypt and in Persia.

"I used to go with her to the New York art balls and to the theater if she didn't have a date. She had a beautiful apartment and would entertain Dad and Mother when they came to New York. Later on I helped her obtain good real estate buys in Virginia Beach, using my psychic ability. It was weird.

"Judy had $25,000 to invest and asked me to find a place with two or three apartment units so she could live in one—she wanted to move to the Beach for a while—and rent the others. So one morning I turned into a street and saw a lady out sweeping the sidewalk. I asked if she knew of anything with several rental units for sale on this street. She practically dropped her broom, then asked me in for coffee. She told me that her daughter, who had two children, had just learned that she was going blind. 'I'm going to have to sell my place here and go live with her and take care of the children,' she said. 'I have three units here.' I asked how much she wanted and she said $25,000. I bought it."

Hugh Lynn had tried selling real estate while attending Norfolk Business College. As an agent for a developer, he sold several lots—one to an old family friend, Mamie Gray of Selma for $1350. But while fortunes were to be made in buying and selling beach property, Hugh Lynn's less remunerative interests were stronger. It was not his destiny to acquire wealth in this incarnation.

Was he thinking of making a career in radio?

"At first I was thinking of the money"—his first experience at earning a big paycheck. "I was being pulled away from The Work and from helping Dad. I'd started out with the idea of introducing his work on the radio eventually. I probably could have, but I realized that I was coming apart. I was being pulled away from The Work rather than being able to help The Work. I was living it up in New York, living with a woman—it was bad."

Hugh Lynn was not without a sense of purpose, however, even in carnal pursuits: He explained that he had been attempting to exorcise his secret passion.

"So many of my affairs, the women I had before I married, were all attempts to free myself of this passion for my mother."

During our interviews with Hugh Lynn, once he had opened the door to this secret passion, he kept returning to it, sometimes expressing doubt that we appreciated how much emotional anxiety and turmoil his feelings for his mother had caused him. "I knew when I went to Dayton [in 1923 at age sixteen] how much I was involved with my mother, at a physical, at a thought level. I was in turmoil, and so I hung this on it in that connection. But that is the most dramatic thing in my life. And one of the most difficult things because I felt so guilty about it for so long. Adolescence is turmoil anyway, but for me it was a violent kind of turmoil. It involved things that I could never talk to anybody about. I could never discuss, for example, that I was fascinated when my parents had sex. I couldn't leave the next room—I couldn't drag myself away—even though I knew I ought to go. It was absolute torment, but also absolute fascination.

"I tried all kinds of ways to push it down away from me except the right way. When I began to reach out at the sexual level, I did so in order to get rid of those feelings for my mother. I tried to give them some other outlet. I was violent about it, promiscuous, not in number but in depth of relationships. That was what I got into in New York."

Hugh Lynn said he never completely rid himself of such feelings for his mother during her lifetime but, "I gradually got them under control, because they [his parents] kept them under such control and their love was so different for me. My father was never jealous—and he had no reason to be. He was never antagonistic with me on that level—never touched me. Neither did my mother."

Hugh Lynn, nonetheless, had no doubt that his mother realized something of what he was going through. "I know she was aware of it," he said, recalling the occasion when he invited her to a college ball.

"She was a magnificent dancer. I have danced with her when it was absolutely terrific. I had a girl but I invited Muddie to a Fancy Dress ball at Washington & Lee, and I paid boys to dance with the girl I had lined up so I could dance with my mother. I wanted my girl to have a good time and I needed a cover, so to speak. Mother would ask, 'Where's Hazel?' But she was delighted."

During his attempt at sexual exorcism, Hugh Lynn invited one of his New York girlfriends to the Beach to meet his folks. "She was a very capable gal, head of a department of a magazine, making good money, had a nice apartment. I had moved out of the Kahns' house

128

and moved in with her. I didn't intend to marry this woman, I was just living with her. When I brought her down to Virginia Beach for a week, she really dressed up to meet them, and they were very gracious, absolutely beautiful. But when I left I knew that they knew the whole story."

Hugh Lynn made no effort to hide the intimate nature of his relationship with the woman. But he was the one apparently most troubled by the affair.

"I felt so guilty for having imposed on them this character whom I didn't intend to marry."

Returning to New York with his girlfriend, he carried his remorse like burdensome excess luggage. The libertine life had not freed him after all.

"I got drunk one night and had an experience that turned me around. I was in a bar and I dropped something and leaned over to pick it up. My head hit the floor—not hard, for I was already leaning over—and I stood on my head. The whole thing spun like a top, and that whirling began.

"When I stood up again, I was sober. I knew that my life in New York was all washed up. I knew I had to get out before I got in further, because I was well in then. I knew that I had to stop it or I was going down the drink, disappearing. I got on the train and came home."

Returning to Virginia Beach, to his parents' home, to his job as manager of the A.R.E., Hugh Lynn never again would be diverted from his father' work.

"Years later, after Mother and Dad were dead and I was married, I walked into their living room and sat down in the chair that I had sat in, and that scene with the girl from New York came back to me—and she sat there, and Mother there, and Dad over there. How guilty I felt for dragging them through that when they knew that this was just an affair.

"Then suddenly they were there in the room—I saw them like I would see another person who was alive. My father grinned at me but didn't say anything. Mother smiled at me, and in my head I heard them say, 'We forgave you a long time ago. Let it go.'

"And finally I let it go."

Chapter 11

Eros and Philos: Sally and Tom

Hugh Lynn was drawn back to Virginia by another, more persistent force, the tug of his heart. Four years before going to New York he had been smitten by an engaging young Southern woman named Sally Taylor. They had met on a blind date. Tommy House had asked him to go along and meet this friend of his girl, Doris. As Sally recalls it: "I had come to Virginia Beach from North Carolina to help my brother, Waller, who was a doctor and wasn't married. I answered his telephone and kept house for him. One day I was walking on the beach and I met a young woman who told me about the art class she was in, and she thought I might enjoy that—they were painting seashells. I was new and didn't know anyone, so she asked if I'd like to come along dancing, that her friend could get me a date. So that's how I met Hugh Lynn."

The two couples went to the Pinetree Inn, a popular, inexpensive establishment that had a jukebox.

Hugh Lynn asked her for another date. While she had enjoyed herself and liked his looks, Miss Taylor refused. She was, alas, engaged. Hugh Lynn wouldn't take "no" for an answer. Sally, a slim, dark-haired, soft-spoken beauty with smoldering eyes, took on an aura of forbidden fruit. She was twenty-nine that summer, two years older than Hugh Lynn.

"She was engaged to a man from Oxford, North Carolina. She wouldn't give me a date because the man she was engaged to was here [in Virginia Beach]. She told me to call her later."

Her fiance was a teacher: "We had something in common, and I didn't know anything about this psychic stuff," she recalls. But obviously Hugh Lynn had something special if a proper young schoolmarm entertained thoughts of dating him later on. His strong suit was not subtlety, however.

"I didn't wait until later, for I knew that this was the girl I was going to marry. I was so happy I went out and got drunk. And I called her at the Cavalier Beach Club, paged her, got her off the dance floor and told her I loved her and was going to marry her. She said, 'You're drunk and you're crazy.' She wouldn't speak to me for a week or ten days. I chased her for the next seven years."

Sally was one of eight children, seven girls and a boy, of an affluent North Carolina tobacco grower. They lived about forty miles north of Raleigh in a historic plantation house, "Longwood," until it burned to the ground when a maid carelessly allowed sparks from the kitchen stove to set fire to the place. Her father built a modern house in nearby Stovall, but continued to supervise his 2,000 acres and twenty tenant farmers.

A graduate of Duke University, Sally taught school for several years before her brother asked her to go to Virginia Beach with him. By the time she met Hugh Lynn, both her parents had died. Within two years, Dr. Taylor married and Sally returned to teaching high school English and history, in New Bern, North Carolina. To pursue her, Hugh Lynn had to drive nearly 300 miles round trip for a weekend date. It was no small test of his desire.

Sally's delight in her ardent suitor was not without its problems within her family. Before meeting him she had never heard of reincarnation. She didn't want to hear about it, either—and Hugh Lynn soon realized that The Work was not a winning topic. Sally thought her new beau was great fun, though, and she liked him for that. They danced a lot—"Did you know that Hugh Lynn was voted the best dancer in his class at Washington & Lee?" she recalled—and played a lot of bridge and had such a good time together that she could overlook his peculiar vocation, at least when he didn't get serious.

Hugh Lynn wanted more than fun—he wanted to get married. He even got a reading in 1937—the year he turned thirty—to find out whether Sally would make a good wife for him. The reading said "yes" but the girl kept saying "no." Sally liked him, indeed, found him almost irresistible. He certainly was sure of himself for a man with no money. One story Hugh Lynn had told her about his collegiate adventures captured his self-assurance.

He had run out of gas while driving home from Washington & Lee, and was parked by the side of the road. A policeman came along and threatened to arrest him for negligence. Hugh Lynn said that would be fine with him because he could catch up on his sleep in jail.

132

Instead, the cop filled his tank and sent him on his way. "He had that kind of effect on people," said Sally.

But Sally was no pushover. She just wasn't sure about a man whose work was so unconventional. Her old boyfriend might not have been as much fun, but at least his life as a teacher required no adjustment on her part. Bright, educated, and engaging as Hugh Lynn was, what kind of a future did he have to offer? Even his getting into radio in New York didn't convince her, for he was still involved with all this strange psychic business. And that job didn't last as long as one school term—none too impressive to a teacher.

While in New York, Hugh Lynn said in disappointment, letters from Sally were "infrequent" and he felt pretty disheartened about his prospects with her. "There is so much between us preventing a complete cooperation; yet so much that is attraction," he said in a letter to Tommy. "It will end as all have ended, a cruel futile gesture on my part, unless I can pull out of the temporary emotional slump and see something besides a world going mad." While he enjoyed the bachelor life in Manhattan, he met no one he liked quite so well. He knew also that his father felt bad about his working and living in New York, all of which contributed to his decision to return to the Beach.

Doing the radio show had stimulated his interest in investigating psychic phenomena. It was a subject that could be pursued almost anywhere. After returning to Virginia, quite apart from his father's psychic work, he began looking into the mysterious Crump case, which had intrigued and puzzled local residents for years.

"I heard about the Crump phenomenon when we first came to Virginia Beach. There were two boys who had grown up together in town, one named Henry Stone and the other Woodland Burroughs. When they were teenagers this phenomenon began—it was something like a big cat which in the beginning walked over top of them in bed. Then it pulled all the covers off. Then it began to move things.

"One time they took a hotel room and charged admission for people to come in. Everyone was seated in a circle in the room and they were all dumped from their chairs—chairs were pulled out from under them [by some unseen force]. Now that's a lot of energy.

"Stone was blind, blind since a childhood accident, but he overcame the handicap and made his living as a fisherman. And Burroughs became an electrician working for the Norfolk Navy Yard. Burroughs drank, and the more he had to drink, the better all this stuff worked. I talked to about twelve people who were with them during different seances. They have moved stoves full of fire on hunting trips when everyone was drinking. I think the drinking released their inhibitions.

"I had sixteen sittings with them. I never got that phenomenon but twice, once in our house and Dad was present. Stone and Burroughs were men then, but they started as boys. I used to have to take beer to Burroughs, and after three or four bottles of beer he'd talk. He told me that this thing started with sex play between him and Stone when they were children.

"The same thing was true of Arthur Ford and his control, Fletcher, I learned later. Fletcher was a boyhood friend of Ford's, and when they were teenagers they had a lot of sex play. And it set up the connection for Arthur and Fletcher to be tied together [psychically]. So here are two cases that I know of where this is true. You see, everything that happens in the psychic operates through the glandular system, as Dad's readings made so clear. We don't have any psychic phenomena without the (endocrine) glands being involved.

"Stone was one of a group of adolescents—twelve, thirteen, fourteen years old, it was a gang kind of thing. All of them were involved in adolescent sex play. One of the boys died. I talked to people who swear that this incident really happened:

"Stone and Burroughs went to the Pungo store. Stone had been drinking and he got boisterous and threw somebody around, even though he couldn't see him. The storekeeper asked them to leave and got them out of the store. Stone and Burroughs were standing outside when Stone said, 'Crump, let's fix these people.' And within five minutes every piece of canned goods in the Pungo store was out in the street.

"Now that is phenomenal if that really happened. There were witnesses. I interviewed them. I wrote a lot of this stuff down. Nobody ever knew whether Crump was the boy who had died. They never identified Crump."

Years later, writing about it in a magazine article, Hugh Lynn concluded that, "as an unexplainable poltergeist, he serves by reminding us that only a fraction of the infinite universe is explainable."

Hugh Lynn and his whole family witnessed another phenomenal incident in their own home. It involved his grandfather, the Squire, who had lived with them for years.

"My grandfather died during a visit to Hopkinsville. He was buried there, and Dad went to the funeral. A week later my grandfather showed up in Virginia Beach. He had had a room in our house. We began to hear things in his room. We heard him breathing—he breathed heavily. We heard things moving, although

134

nothing ever moved in the room. We heard him walking. Dad said, 'He's back. He'll be here a few days. In his mind he is trying to straighten out his papers before he dies. He'll not be here long. Don't bother him because it will upset him that he can't communicate, can't make himself heard.'

"Mother heard him. Gladys heard him. The mailman heard him. We all knew the mailman, and he knew my grandfather because he used to meet him at the door to get the mail. On this day I opened the door and as he was handing me the mail I said, 'Come in a minute, there is something I want you to hear.' I told him to walk halfway up the stairs. When he reached that point on the stairs he heard my grandfather breathing. He looked at me very strangely and said, 'Isn't that where your grandfather stayed?' I said, 'Yes.' He said, 'What is that sound?' I replied, 'It's my grandfather. He's back.'

"The mailman turned white and ran out of the house. And from that day on he wouldn't come to the house with our mail—he left it in the hedge.

"A few days later my grandfather was making a lot of noise up in his room and I ran upstairs. Dad said, 'Hugh Lynn, don't do that.' But I was running up the stairs and before I could stop I ran into Grandfather on the landing. I could feel him, and every hair on my head went straight up in the air. I don't know how I knew it but I just knew it was my grandfather—it was cold, but quite a different chill, and it was like running into cobwebs in the dark woods, very fine when they touch you, but when you wipe them away there is nothing there."

His interest in such phenomena didn't make things smoother with Sally, who remained an inscrutable challenge. For all Hugh Lynn's self-assurance and newly-gained worldliness, Sally refused to get serious with him. Here he was back home without "a real job." Besides, the subject of the paranormal remained an awkward obstacle. When she introduced him to her brother, Sally mentioned nothing about Edgar Cayce's trance readings, much less the idea of past lives. Her family liked Hugh Lynn as a man—he was intelligent, amusing, rather sophisticated now, a good dancer and bridge player. Not a bad catch. So when they did learn about his work they thought it strange but raised no objection to Sally's dating him. Dr. Taylor's attitude was simply that he didn't have time to look into it, and the less said about it the better.

Sally liked Hugh Lynn's parents, however. She admired Gertrude's sincerity, determination, confidence, loyalty, and her energy and ability. Without her, Sally thought Edgar would have been helpless. "She cooked and never knew whether she was cooking for

135

three people or ten," observed Sally, "and she cleaned house, and twice a day she had to get herself together to conduct a reading. Often the people requesting the reading were there and she had to deal with them. Her manner while conducting the readings gave people confidence in what Edgar was doing."

Whether Sally recognized it or not, others saw a strong resemblance between her and Gertrude. "If you want to know what Gertrude was like," Gladys Davis told me, "she was very much like Sally." Hugh Lynn, in a word, wanted to marry a woman older than himself who was a younger version of the mother he so adored.

Perhaps Sally's admiration for Mrs. Cayce helped wear down her resistance. But there was a principal snag. Sally was unsure she wanted to marry a man who, in his thirties, seemed so dependent on his parents. "I told Hugh Lynn before I'd marry him he had to get a regular job, a permanent job with a permanent salary coming in—he was just working for his father, and he was paid very little, and living at home. So he took that to heart."

Not long after Hugh Lynn returned from New York, Tom Sugrue became desperately ill and needed help.

"Tom was working for *American Magazine*. They sent him around the world as their roving reporter. When he came back they offered him an editorship, and he took it. He got married—he married a beautiful woman, Mary, who was a very strict Catholic. They bought a house on Long Island and he would commute into New York to work. His illness began in his knee—it would get stiff and painful. Mary by then was pregnant and she suggested that when she went to the hospital to deliver the child that Tom enter the hospital too and find out what the problem was.

"He walked into the hospital—it was painful but he was walking. They gave him sixteen fever-machine treatments. They put him in a cabinet and raised the temperature to a very high degree to kill the germs. They burned him, according to Dad. They burned the lining of his intestinal tract, which absorbs food for the body. And he withered away.

"Mary came out of the hospital with a baby girl, but she was frantic because Tom came out of the hospital looking like a skeleton. His arms and legs had no flesh on them—he was a horrible looking sight—and he had no control over his arms and legs.

"Tom wanted to ask Dad for a reading but Mary refused. The readings were not scientific and she thought they might be the work of the Devil. It wasn't until she feared that he might be dying that she agreed.

"Tom got a reading and it said that he was dying but that it could be prevented. It recommended Epsom salt baths, very light massage, Atomidine, and the use of the wet-cell appliance. It was a very complicated reading. I took the appliance, the reading, and everything and went to New York and stayed in Tom's house for a week or ten days and started him on these treatments."

Mary thought their moving to Florida might help, but she chose Washington, D.C., where her parents lived, instead. She thought she could get someone to help with Tom. Hugh Lynn would train him.

"Then her father had a brain tumor, and she had Tom and her father—an impossible situation. I asked whether I could bring Tom to our house to continue the treatments. Mother said, 'Oh, by all means.' So he came to our home in June 1939—and lived there for two years."

That month marked another important event in the family life with the graduation from high school of Ecken, or Edgar Evans. Tall like his father, he went off to Duke University in the fall to become an electrical engineer. In Ecken's absence, Tom Sugrue became the second son of the household. But unlike the strong, athletic Ecken, Tom was frail and physically dependent.

"He was so thin and his arms and legs were stiff. Dad continued to give readings to prescribe treatments. At one point a reading recommended snake venom so that he could break loose the joints. I went to a local doctor who said, 'Hugh Lynn, I never heard of it but I'll look it up and if I can get it I'll let you know.' About three or four days later he called and said, 'Hugh Lynn, your father has been reading the medical journals. I just got my A.M.A. *Journal* and it's got an article on snake venom.'

"So I rolled Tom up to the doctor's office in a wheelchair and he gave him an injection. He and Tom hit it off beautifully, and then he began to come by the house to see Tom. They both liked baseball, and Tom knew the batting averages of every ballplayer in America, and he and the doctor would discuss baseball endlessly."

In New York, Hugh Lynn had got acquainted with Harold Reilly, who operated a health clinic in Rockefeller Center and had been recommended in readings for many people. Reilly taught Hugh Lynn massage, which now proved most helpful.

"I did everything for Tom in those years, and I learned to love him and really, really care for him as a soul. I massaged him every day. I'd take him out and get him into the ocean. I was running the scout troop [at the Presbyterian Church] in those days and the Boy Scouts would come by and carry him anywhere I wanted to go. He and I prayed and meditated together. We played chess—and I got good at chess because I had to beat Tom.

"We were living across the street from Star of the Sea Catholic Church, and Tom developed a wonderful friendship with Father Brennan, who was a beautiful man, one of the best educated men I've ever met, a scholar. He got along wonderfully with Dad, too.

"Father Brennan would come over to the house to give Tom mass. He would always bring Mother pies, bread, cakes, groceries he received from his parishioners—too much for him, so he'd bring it over to us. When he did so he always went around the house and sprinkled holy water—everywhere except where the readings were. He wouldn't bless the readings. Dad wanted a picture of him for his study—he had pictures of lots of friends on the wall of his study. Father Brennan gave him one but he chuckled and said, 'Now you must be sure, Edgar, that you don't stick any pins in it.'"

Tom continued to write, but this time he went inside for inspiration and wrote fiction. As the months passed, he worked at his first novel, which he finished within a year. *Such Is the Kingdom* was an autobiographical story of a boy growing up in Tom's home town in Connecticut.

After completing his novel, it occurred to Tom to write a book about Edgar Cayce. The Cayces agreed to help. So Tom stayed on in Virginia Beach. Apparently he never visited Hopkinsville or Selma to gather material. He had the benefit of living in the house of the subject, who was a very good storyteller. And Hugh Lynn offered to help pull together and check the facts.

"He interviewed my father, he interviewed my mother, he interviewed my grandfather who was living there at the time—they'd go up to his room and talk with him, answer his questions. So during the next year he wrote *There Is a River*."

More than an authorized biography, the book was an adoring portrait. The author was hardly in a position to write anything less flattering, for the Cayces were giving him the sort of tender loving care—plus psychic guidance—that was unavailable elsewhere and apparently was essential to his survival.

"By the time he finished the book Tom was much better. Mary's father had died, meanwhile, so after sending the manuscript to his publisher in New York in 1941, he went to Florida with Mary."

Hugh Lynn continued his long-distance dates with Sally during the two years that he played nursemaid to his best friend, but the hardship was intensified. Tom didn't like it when Hugh Lynn left town to court Sally. "Tom was jealous of Sally," he explained. Hugh Lynn's devotion to Tom and his idealistic impulse to help people through his father's work finally spoke to Sally, however. She had never met a man with such a strong and sincere desire to be of

138

service. "His dedication really knocked her over," said one family member.

Tom's departure gave Hugh Lynn more time to devote to romance—and to satisfying Sally's insistence on his obtaining a "regular" job. As she recalled the sequence of events: "One night they were having a meeting down at City Hall where Hugh Lynn had left his umbrella. When he went back for it and learned that the city council was going to hire someone to be in charge of the lifeguards, he told them, 'Give me that job. I know every lifeguard out there because they've all been my Boy Scouts'—so he was hired."

Although it was only a seasonal job, Hugh Lynn was given an impressive title, recreation director for Virginia Beach, in May 1941. That was enough for Sally. She finally said "yes." They set a wedding date for that fall after the tourist season when Hugh Lynn could get away. Sally Taylor married Hugh Lynn at her family home in Stovall on October 10, 1941. The nuptials were performed by a Presbyterian clergyman, Joseph Clower, a Washington & Lee classmate of Hugh Lynn's who now was his minister at Virginia Beach. The wedding was followed by a honeymoon trip to New Orleans.

Two and a half weeks after the wedding, back in Virginia Beach, Hugh Lynn and Sally asked Edgar for a reading. Gertrude, conducting the reading, said: "These entities seek at this time mental and spiritual guidance which will aid them in living and working successfully together. If there are urges from past incarnations which have not been given please explain them now, indicating how such urges may be directed for the best interests of all concerned."

A reading before their marriage had indicated they had known one another in China. Hugh Lynn found confirmation in the wedding gifts they later received—seven were Chinese in design. The reading now said China had had a major influence over them materially, but that "the mental status of each comes through other periods" which had brought "the awareness of each."

"It has been indicated that each, from material associations in the past, from abilities of each in this present, may be a complement to the other," the reading went on. "Let the ideals and the principles of each be one. Their manner of approach, their manner of thought need not necessarily be the same, but the purpose, the desire, the hopes, the welfare of each should be as is indicated in such a union—one for the other. Each should be ever mindful as to the welfare of that as may be for the glorifying of the truth, beauty, love, hope, self-sacrifice in their relationships not only to one another but to their problems, their joys, their sorrows, their blessings, their downsittings. All of these, let them be with that attitude as of a helpmeet one to the other.

"This then will bring—as we have indicated oft—the closer walk with Him, who is the truth, the light, the hope of the world. In this manner may there come to thee that blessing, that hope, that assurance of a life, of an experience that may bring a constant well of joy, of happiness. Not that there will not be periods of disturbance, but let it always be from the other—not from self. Do not both get angry at the same time. This ye can control, if ye walk with Him.

"Let thy ideal, then, be as it was in the days of old; that ye bring one another closer, closer to that spirit of truth, of love, of life, that is the hope, that is the way that each may contribute to the other that which is pleasing in His sight."

The first question they asked was: "Does our marriage and desire for children provide a possible outlet for expression of any particular entity or type of entity?"

The response was:

"This is most desirable. As has been indicated, the purpose, the desire, the hope of each in the preparations of the body and the mind for such an advent as the entrance of a soul, a spirit into the earth, must be from mutual desire of each. This should be that purpose—to each fulfill that purpose the divine influence, God, has for thee. Then let it come as the fulfilling of that hope, that desire, that purpose. Thus the type soul will be given thee that is in keeping with thy abilities to contribute to mankind, to the world, the channel for a soul needed in the present."

Next they asked: "Explain in detail what mental, physical and spiritual preparations we may make in order that our first child may have advantage of the best influences from all sources which our individual development and union of purposes may provide." The reply was:

"Let thy mind, thy body, then be kept as a continuous source of influence for the purpose that God through the Christ may have with thee. For He knoweth thee by name. He *will* give that work, that purpose thou must do now. The understanding comes in prayer, in meditation, in purpose, in hope, in *living*. Be not merely an outward but an inward expression of that thou would have the spirit of truth be with thee. For, as ye treat thy fellow man day by day, so ye do unto thy Lord, thy God, thy Christ."

"Can and should we pray, desire and in any way try to make it possible for the first child to be a boy?"

"Let that be in His keeping. Choose, rather, to be the channel; and let thy prayer be: Lord, have thy way with us.

"This will bring the purposes, the activities, the *best* in each to

140

that desire that He may walk, He may talk, He may have His way with thee. Let that mind ever be in thee as was in Him, the Christ: 'Lord, use Thou me—my body, my mind, my purpose—as a channel of blessings to others.'

"Materially, make preparations, provisions, now, for the future by the daily care for providing for body, mind, soul. Live as ye would have thy son, thy daughter live. This will bring the consciousness the more oft of His purpose with thee."

Before that winter was over, Edgar and Gertrude learned the good news that they were to become grandparents—Sally was expecting—and that Edgar Evans also was planning to marry. Ecken had finished college at Duke University, graduating in engineering, and taken a job in Virginia Beach with the local electric utility. When the war broke out, however, he joined the Army. He was twenty-three.

In Florida, Sugrue was in despair. *There Is a River* had received a cool reception by his publisher. Struggling against his infirmity, Tom felt ill-equipped to cope with a skeptical publisher. Again, he turned to his best friend. Again, Hugh Lynn dropped everything to help him.

There was much more at stake than Tom's success as a writer, and Hugh Lynn knew it. If the book were published, his father's work might become widely recognized—and the A.R.E. might turn into something more than a handful of faithful admirers. Barely home from his honeymoon, he hopped a train to New York to see Tom's publisher.

"The editor at Henry Holt Publishing Co. was William Sloane, who later was to become very influential in the field of para-psychology—he published J.B. Rhine's books and Gina Cerminara's *Many Mansions*, and he was responsible for publishing *Bridey Murphy*. He got a reading from Dad which gave him information about a trip he was about to take to China.

"Sloane said, 'Hugh Lynn, Tom's book shouldn't be done this way. This could be a very popular book, it has a lot of excellent material, but you've got to get Tom to rework it. Can he do it?'

"I said, 'I don't know. He's flat on his back but he can write. What would you do with the book?'

"Sloane told me and I took notes. I returned to Virginia Beach where Sally and I got in the car and drove to Florida. We got there at 2:00 a.m. Mary Sugrue was crying—her sister had just developed a brain tumor similar to the one her father had. Their little girl, Patsy, was then about five or six. Tom was in a wheelchair. With effort, he could get up on crutches but it was much easier for him to use a wheelchair.

"So Sally agreed to take over the running of the house and Mary left that day. And Tom and I went to work rewriting *There Is a River*. I told him from my notes what Sloane wanted—detailed descriptions, a new opening, a flashback. It had been a straight chronological biography starting with Dad's birth. We talked and talked, and I gave him the details he wanted, about the man who used to drive the horse and buggy who took Munsterberg [a skeptical professor from Harvard] out to see Dad, and about the studio in Selma. Tom wrote it, but I worked with him for about two weeks. It became more readable, the philosophy section was taken out and put in the back, the physical readings were taken out."

In the preface, Sugrue acknowledged his debt to Hugh Lynn "who not only led the horse to water, but made him drink"—an oblique reference to their freshman quarrels about his father's clairvoyance.

Within weeks of their return to Virginia Beach, the nation was plunged into war with Japan. At thirty-four, Hugh Lynn was not eager for the adventure of war. Surrounded by the evidence of mobilization in the shipyards of Norfolk and the new military bases being constructed around Hampton Roads, the newlyweds hoped that their new life together would not be drastically disturbed. The war affected Hugh Lynn's job with the city, as Virginia Beach expanded its recreational program to include the servicemen pouring into the area. His job, the Cayces hoped, would be considered essential to the war effort and spare him from the draft.

Sugrue's crippling affliction did not impair his faculties. Completing the task of rewriting, he added an acknowlegment of thanks to Hugh Lynn and "my wife who acted as typist, proofreader, editor, and nurse to my crotchets and doldrums. To them I am deeply grateful. If I have done a good job it is because of them and despite myself."

In fact, however, the content of *There Is a River* had kicked up a family storm. It had to do with articles of faith. The Cayce philosophy, which Sugrue had eloquently sketched in the book, upset his wife while she was typing the final manuscript. She considered karma un-Christian, at odds with the beliefs she had acquired during her strict Roman Catholic upbringing. If her husband had sought family harmony by accepting his publisher's rejection and filing his manuscript away in the bottom drawer of lost causes, Edgar Cayce might have remained virtually anonymous. But the philosophy of life that had come from Cayce's lips had found an eloquent and courageous messenger in Thomas Sugrue. In a poignant letter from Clearwater Beach, he wrote Hugh Lynn: "You and your father will understand that 'they' have fought me tooth and nail, all the way. I come at last to the work I want to do with my bridges burned behind me. The book is my Declaration of Independence to family, friends, and church. This is what I am. This is what I believe. You may follow me; you may ignore me; you may fight me, as you have in the past; you cannot dissuade me.

"You have no idea what a great relief it is to me to have it over—the period of trial and test. Looking back over the period of preparation, I am convinced that it was all wise, necessary, and adequate.

"I believe I am well prepared. I have, I hope, a little patience and a little understanding now. I am shriven physically. I will not smoke or drink again, and by an odd twist of circumstance, the monk's cloth has again fallen over me. I accept it now as part of the plan. But I cannot help laughing at myself for thinking that this time I would escape it. . .I have no one but you to turn to now for understanding and friendship. . .Wish you were here for some chess. . .I haven't even an enemy in Clearwater.

Love, Tom."

When *There Is a River* was published a year later, a crate of books arrived at the Cayce home. Hugh Lynn was ecstatic. After all the freak stories in the tabloids, a very respectable New York publisher had finally given Edgar Cayce his due. Respectability at last! The hardback edition carried a simple dedication: *For Hugh Lynn*. After all that he and Tom had been through together, he said, "I appreciated that deeply."

Hungry for recognition for his father and for their work, Hugh Lynn emptied the crate and proudly set out in the family auto passing out copies all over Virginia Beach. This prophet would be not without honor in his own town.

The prophet picked up the wooden crate, went out back to fetch his ax and chopped it up for kindling.

Chapter 12

Off to War: Europe

From the outset of their marriage, Sally and Hugh Lynn consciously prepared themselves for parenthood by praying and meditating that they might attract a soul who would be compatible with their souls' purposes. "Sally prays a lot," said Hugh Lynn, and meditation had become a way of life with him. He took seriously the business of attracting the right soul for them.

"I think there is a great deal that we can do in the kind of souls that we attract into the earth. I'm absolutely convinced that there are thousands and thousands of souls that die in all kinds of wars and pestilence, just casualties, who have no desire except to live in the earth. They want to experience the earth again. They want to eat, be able to have sex, be able to have power, to have money, they want to live in the flesh, and they want to get into the earth again. So anybody who happens to be having sex |without love and commitment| is a vehicle they can use because there are no ideals other than for physical gratification. So they attract each other. That's why we have such a hodge-podge.

"When you prepare, and there are ideals and principles and planning, I don't think they are attracted by that pattern unless they have a strong karmic pattern with the parents and are drawn by such ties. Sometimes they come for need because of the balance the parents can provide. I think my brother |Edgar Evans| was such an entity. He needed my parents desperately to balance the kind of patterns that were in his life. And they did it. My mother particularly was just beautiful in balancing the materialism that was just wrapped up in him."

When Sally delivered a son almost a year later on October 7,

1942, they felt that their prayers had been answered. At Hugh Lynn's suggestion, they delayed naming the boy until his father could give the child a reading. Most of his clients went to the foot of the line to wait their turn for one of his twice-a-day communiques. But not Edgar's first grandchild. Four hours after the birth, Edgar gave the baby a reading. At its suggestion, they named him Charles Thomas Taylor Cayce. "You've given him so many names you won't have any left for the next one," Sally's family teased. On one occasion Sally told me the "Charles" was also for a close family friend and benefactor, Charles Dillman, a local builder who later remodeled the old Cayce Hospital building when the A.R.E. bought it for its headquarters; and the "Thomas" was for Thomas Sugrue. Her maiden name, Taylor, accounted for the third surname. In any event, he would grow up being called Tommy, and later insist on the more formal Charles Thomas.

The reading said that in his previous incarnation he had been Thomas Jefferson Cayce, Edgar's grandfather, his own great-great grandfather. Edgar told Hugh Lynn that he knew he would be close to this baby, as he had been to his grandfather.

The birth of a son not only turned Hugh Lynn into a family man but also, he hoped, would improve his prospects of avoiding the draft. "I did everything under the sun to stay out of the Army. I got out of it the first time my number was called, and I put it off until I don't know how long." In the spring of 1943, at age thirty-six, the draft board ordered him to report to Fort Meade near Baltimore for basic training. The Cayces thought it unfair, for they had already given one son to the military. Moreover, they felt need of Hugh Lynn's help more than ever, for *There Is a River* had turned Edgar into a symbol of hope. While the book did not become a best-seller, publicity and book reviews triggered an enormous increase in letters and visitors requesting readings, many of them on behalf of boys overseas.

The war thus impacted all of the Cayces heavily. While both soldier-sons survived it, their parents did not.

Shortly before Hugh Lynn left for the Army, he was sitting in their living room talking with his father.

"He said to me, 'Hugh Lynn, we won't be here when you get back.' I said, 'Of course you will.' But he said something about knowing things I didn't know. Lots of things he wouldn't explain. It was very hard for me to leave under those circumstances. They took me [away] screaming."

Hugh Lynn came home on leave from Fort Meade, but after basic training his unit was ordered to England for the war in Europe. He didn't want to believe that his father would not live to greet him when he came home, but when he looked at him he suddenly noticed how old his father, now sixty-six, looked.

"He was tiring. He was pushing much too hard. It wasn't the readings he was giving, although he was giving too many—sometimes six and eight at a time, talking very fast—but he was wearing down from the pressure of people who wanted to see him."

He saw his father for the last time "at the bus station in Norfolk, just across from the post office. Dad and Mother had driven me in. Sally was with us, and Charles Thomas [who was about nine months old] was in her arms. We got out of the car and were standing on the sidewalk and Dad took Charles Thomas while I was saying goodby to Mother, and then he handed Charles Thomas to me and I told him good-bye and handed him back to Sally, hugged her and got on the bus. And that was it."

The public recognition he had sought for his father took a heavy toll.

"Marguerite Bro—Harmon Bro's mother—wrote a review for *Christian Century* that blew the top right off the church-minded people, for Mrs. Bro was the author of a number of religious books. She then did an article for *Coronet*, then a very popular magazine. It was called 'Miracle Man of Virginia Beach.' It came out after I had reached England. The article brought thousands of letters, and the membership of the A.R.E. skyrocketed out of all proportion. People came and camped in the front yard—sick people waiting for a miracle. That pressure was just horrendous.

"The mail was delivered in sacks, telegrams in packages, the phone had to be disconnected—it rang all the time—and Dad had to hire lots of girls because people were sending money for readings. He would deposit their money but when he reached a certain number he'd send their money back because he couldn't take any more—he didn't want to make any appointments more than two years ahead, and he was giving ten or twelve readings a day."

The Cayce home was never quiet. In addition to greeting visitors seeking readings, they had rented their empty rooms to military wives whose husbands had gone overseas. Sally moved back to Stovall to live with her sister in her family home. She and Tommy occasionally returned to Virginia Beach for a visit with her in-laws, but the Cayce house was always so crowded with people that Sally, a very private person, never stayed longer than a week.

Hugh Lynn adjusted to the wartime Army—civilians in uniform—quite well after receiving his assignment. As recreation director for a city, and a former radio commentator, he was assigned to a company that provided entertainment for troops.

147

"We were a special services unit to provide recreation—movies, books, live entertainment—for front-line troops. We had all the latest films and field generators to provide electricity so we could show them in the field. We had a library of about a hundred movies. They would drop the latest films to us by parachute. We had music, books, complete shows—singers, magicians, all kinds of entertainers. We did this in England for a year for troops stationed there before the invasion of Normandy. Then we were attached to General George Patton's tank corps."

Bypassed by the war, Sugrue went to work on another book, *Starling of the White House*, the memoir of the head of the Secret Service who had just retired. William Starling was from Hopkinsville, Kentucky, a friend of Cayce's, and through Dave Kahn he got Sugrue to write the book—as recommended in a reading Edgar gave for Starling. The book was published a year after *There Is a River* and hit the best-seller list. While the royalties and success were gratifying to its crippled author, his loneliness in Florida concerned his friends. The Kahns persuaded an editor friend at the *Saturday Review of Literature* to hire Sugrue, despite his physical handicap. They found lodgings for him in a little hotel in Manhattan across the street from the *Saturday Review* office so that Tom could get back and forth to work in his wheelchair.

Separated from his wife, Tom depended on the Kahns, particularly Lucille, who "gave him at least fifteen years of added joy in New York," her husband reported in his own memoir. As Lucille put it, she and Tom "clicked" from the moment they met fifteen years earlier—and a Cayce reading explained that they had been together in a prior life in India during which they had had their "greatest spiritual unfoldment," said Lucille. "This we accepted as our bond." In New York the former actress and the author went to the theater together, gave metaphysical lectures, and even did a radio program for a time called "Conversations at Eight." It was a fulfilling relationship for both of them.

Hugh Lynn's non-combat assignment to "Special Services" did not guarantee his safety, for the job of his unit was to follow close behind the combat troops once the long-awaited invasion of Europe began.

"On June 22, 1944, sixteen days after D-day, we landed on the beaches of France with a complete band, including four pianos, and all our equipment. We raced across France to catch up with Patton's tank corps and then settled down and began to service them. We had USO people attached to us—Bing Crosby, Mickey Rooney, and other movie stars.

148

"Mickey was attached to the company for a while and when he left he took with him every shred of money in sight. He was the best crap shooter I've ever seen—he really took us, just cleaned us. I shot with him. Everybody in the company did. He would get hot, and when he got hot he would just clean up. And he'd give it back, but keep gambling, never stop. It went on all the time he was with us. He was a real energetic guy, a lot of fun, and he did a lot of good work entertaining troops. He was really good."

"When we reached Germany and the bombs started falling on us, we got caught there and had some frightening experiences."

Hugh Lynn's introduction to death under wartime conditions came before the invasion. It was while en route to Europe.

"I was on the Queen Mary crossing the Atlantic, it was night and in the darkness we sliced through another ship—and we didn't even stop to pick up survivors. We were in the middle of the Atlantic, we had 15,000 troops on board, and German U-boats were waiting and watching for us. We knew they were out there but the Queen Mary could outrun them. But we couldn't stop. We just radioed for other ships to come."

Hugh Lynn's acceptance of reincarnation insulated him somewhat from the shock of encountering death, for his military experiences sometimes took him beyond this life into other incarnations. It began during basic training.

"I was sitting in the barracks at Fort Meade. Since I am a Pisces [a water sign], I always ended up in a bunk next to the shower room, not by any choice of mine. One day I heard this clunk, clunk, clunk of a fellow coming down to take a shower but I didn't pay any attention until the boy got opposite me. I'd seen him before—he was in my company—but I hadn't paid any attention to him. He had a towel over his shoulder, a bar of soap in his hand, and was wearing clogs and that's all. I looked at him and it came out of me just like an explosion—I blurted out, 'I haven't seen you since we were caught stealing camels together in the Gobi desert.'

"He looked at me as though I was crazy. With that statement I visualized a scene—there were three of us, all teenagers, and we had stolen someone's family car, so to speak. That is, we had taken camels without permission. They were racing camels. We were sitting around a little fire, and we could see the families—brothers, fathers—coming after us. They caught us and I had this memory of being whipped.

"It was something that had happened thousands of years ago. It was crazy. I had no control over it. It just swept over me, kind of a flash."

The other "camel thief" was an eighteen-year-old recruit named Sam Benesch. Although twice the boy's age, Hugh Lynn felt a kinship with Sam and they became close friends after they got to England.

"Sam was a brilliant boy, but the Army feared he might be too nervous for combat duty. But he wanted to go."

During the long months of waiting in England for the invasion of Europe, Hugh Lynn got better acquainted with Sam. They were in different platoons in the same company, and remained so even after the invasion. One night when a group of soldiers began fooling around with hypnosis, Sam volunteered to be hypnotized.

"He was a very good subject. He was one of three boys whom we hypnotized who went back in time and talked in foreign languages. Sam met his grandfather while he was under hypnosis. His grandfather had died before Sam was born. While he was under, he began talking to his grandfather and he wanted to go with his grandfather, and we had an awful time getting him out of it. His grandfather had taken him on all these trips, to initiation ceremonies in India and Egypt. This went on in front of fifty GIs in a crowded room. And we couldn't wake him up. He had been talking with his grandfather, whom nobody else in the room could see, of course. I had to slap him and do all kinds of things to get him out. He left the room immediately, and he was upset for days.

"I was walking guard that night between 2:00 and 4:00 a.m. and Sam came out and walked guard with me and we talked. He had remembered, as a result of the hypnosis, all these trips to Egypt and India with his grandfather. He had the wildest knowledge. I wrote to his mother about this right after this incident. She remembered that, as a little boy, he had told her about his grandfather coming and taking him on these trips. They had taken him to a psychiatrist, who had hypnotized him and wiped it all out. And we had opened the door again on this whole thing. He never knew his grandfather except in these dreams. Sam and I hardly left one another after that."

It was the beginning of a lifelong friendship—or the continuation of one that had spanned several lives. This time it was between a middle-aged sergeant and an adolescent private. In the style of comrades in arms, Hugh Lynn and Sam took care of one another.

"We talked philosophy and the whole thing. He had never read a book, and yet he had the most unusual knowledge of the mystery religions. I knew something about them, but he had never read anything about them, and I was amazed."

Hugh Lynn's second closest Army buddy was more his age, Bill Epstein, a weekly newspaper editor from Maryland's Eastern Shore.

"He was a drinking friend, a warm, gregarious, delightful character. We drank together a lot. We ate together a lot, too. Sam's parents had a grocery business, and Sam had two duffle bags, one of which was constantly filled with food—his mother sent him food packages every day. So we always had sardines and crackers and cheese. Sam was a very popular man in the company.

"So it was Bill and Sam and I. Sam didn't drink very much, but I drank and Bill drank."

One fringe benefit of their work supplying films was that they were in a position to exact tribute from company commanders who wanted the latest movies.

"We had access to all the motion pictures you could conceive of. To get the best pictures from us—they would come in and sign up for them—they would just happen to bring along a bottle of good cognac. It was bribery of the first water, but these captains had a lot of money, and we stayed very well furnished with everything that was drinkable all the way across France. We liberated a champagne factory on the way, and every man in the division was issued three bottles of champagne. You should have seen that column of troops winding its way around. It was wild."

The company, still trailing General Patton, had survived the Battle of the Bulge of December 1944. As winter wore on, they waited in eastern France for the push on into Germany. That's where Hugh Lynn was when the news he had dreaded caught up with him. As his father had predicted, his time had come.

Writing about Edgar's last days, Tom Sugrue said: "He had been ill since August 1944, when the strain of overwork pressed him down to a sickbed. For more than a year he had worked under unbelievable handicaps.... Often there were more than 500 letters in the daily mail. The library [an addition to the house] which had seemed so large when first built, was jammed with stenographers working at correspondence. Mr. Cayce himself examined every letter, and worked late into the night dictating answers.

"During the morning and afternoon periods he gave not two but from eight to twelve readings. Still he could fulfill but a small portion of the applications. The others, with their tales of misfortune and suffering, weighed heavily on him. For the first time in his long life of service he could not help every one of his fellows who asked for aid. He worked harder and harder, but the appointments ran on and on, until they were more than a year ahead of him.

"His own diagnosis, given in a reading last September, was that he had reached a point of complete nervous exhaustion. From this he did not recover."

That fall he had gone to Florida, where Sugrue was still living, in an effort to regain his strength. In addition to physical exhaustion, he was depressed by an unexpected development at the First Presbyterian Church the Cayces had been attending for nearly twenty years. The publicity Edgar received as a consequence of Sugrue's book caused some of the influential Presbyterians to complain that this man with his "un-Christian" beliefs was teaching in their church. For nine years the Cayces had been close to their minister, Joseph B. Clower, and had enjoyed many church activities with other members who had no objections to Edgar's work, perhaps because they knew little or nothing about it or his philosophy; they knew him simply as a good Christian gentleman and churchman. But soon after the biography came out, Reverend Clower moved on and was replaced by a new minister. The result was very painful for Edgar: He was relieved of his Bible class. After all his years of personal study of the scriptures and teaching Bible classes, he was uncere-moniously defrocked.

He retreated from the hectic, painful scene in Virginia Beach, spending some time in Roanoke, but returned to the Beach in time for the holidays. He died at home on January 3, 1945.

Joe Clower came back to conduct the funeral service. It was held at the Cayce home, not the church. Edgar was buried five days later in Hopkinsville, after a second service there conducted by the minister of the local First Christian Church.

"The roll of those he served is long," Sugrue wrote. "How many he reached through his readings is incalculable. His only ambition was that after his death even more people be reached and given whatever in the readings was good and helpful . . . .

"Truly he fulfilled the Christian ideal; he laid down his life for his friends. He was a great man. We shall not see his like again."

Muddie, herself gravely ill, had written to both her sons, knowing that neither of them could get home for the services. When Edgar Evans, stationed in the Caribbean, got his letter, he wrote to Hugh Lynn, who got the word weeks later. Muddie's letter had not arrived.

"A V-mail letter from my brother, the first word of my father's death, mentioned that Dad had been buried in Hopkinsville. And our mother was dying. I got up and went out into the hall of the old bomb-damaged French chateau where our company was quartered. I pushed aside the heavy canvas hanging across the hall and went outside to be alone. It was cold and drizzling, getting dark. Feeling depressed, I tried to pray. How could a loving Father let this happen to His children?"

Death had stared Hugh Lynn in the face for months, from the bloated bodies lying by the roadside as his unit pushed across Europe. But the dead were strangers. Now death was ever so personal. Worse still, Hugh Lynn received a message through the Red Cross that Sally had been hospitalized. Her brother, Dr. Taylor, warned that her condition was very serious. She had a tumor that required surgery. Hugh Lynn's personal island of security back home suddenly seemed as threatened as the American troops in the Battle of the Bulge.

"Thousands were dying there in France, I realized. But I thought maybe God had gone away to another part of the universe. Maybe there wasn't anything out there to pray to. This madness in which we were involved made no sense. Suddenly all that I had believed in—God, love, Jesus, service—were washed out of me. Empty, alone, cut off, I felt desolate. Afraid. Life had no meaning."

Hugh Lynn, yearning for someone who was close, turned to young Sam Benesh.

"I was drinking heavily, and he took care of me. He kept me out of trouble, got me into bed when I'd had too much to drink."

Hugh Lynn forced himself to pray for Sally, for his baby son, for himself. It was two weeks before the news caught up with his unit—Sally's operation had been successful, the tumor had been benign.

After recovering his equilibrium, Hugh Lynn faced the prospect of losing his mother, too. On Good Friday he wrote her a beautiful letter:

Dear Muddie,

It is important for you to realize how much fun it has been being your son. So many times I have seen you faced with problems, conditions that I have known to crumple up so many people, and you have risen above them—and (the important thing) carried others with you. These things Ecken and I will not forget. To few people has been entrusted the guidance of so many lives—not in the outward way to be seen by men, but in the background where the going was tough. These things I know, and will not forget. Never have I known of such unselfish love for two human beings as you have always shown toward Ecken and me. This, too, I will never forget. It would be easy to go on and on.

It makes me proud to think of you. It makes me deeply happy to know how ready you are to pass through that other door. There is so much beauty in your living, my dear, that I cannot be sad at the possibility of you joining Dad. You held up his right hand—sometimes both hands here, so it does not surprise me that he may

153

need you now.

We have come, Muddie, to an understanding of karma in a way that we have for a long time been explaining to others, and I find that your life represents so much that is fine and beautiful that I cannot allow my selfish desires to mar this period of waiting and wondering.

My prayers are that you will not suffer, my dear. I know that you must realize how much love has been, is, and always will be, yours.

Hugh Lynn

Muddie may have received her son's loving message subconsciously, but she never received his letter. Two days later, at sunrise on Easter Sunday, Gertrude Evans Cayce, sixty-five, slipped through "that other door."

By the time Hugh Lynn received notice of her death, the Germans were in flight and the war in Europe was nearly over. Soon he would be going home. Going home to Sally and Tommy. And to a house brimming with poignant memories of the two great spirits whose work he was destined to carry on.

Part Three

About My Father's Legacy

Chapter 13

Plotting a Spiritual Renaissance

Home from the war in the fall of 1945, Hugh Lynn received a hero's welcome. Sally and three-year-old Tommy, and Gladys and a homecoming gathering of A.R.E. members put on the celebration at the Cayce house. While his joy was complete on one level, there was an underlying sadness to his triumphant return. The emotional impact of his parents' recent passing was inescapable once again as he walked through the house and saw his father's couch, his mother's china. And Gladys, too, sweet, devoted Gladys, still answering the mail, renting out rooms to service wives to keep herself and the A.R.E. afloat, holding things together until he got back. There was also the larger question of the future, if any, of the A.R.E. "You know, in two years overseas there was nothing I could do about the Association but think," he told the gathering. "So you needn't be surprised that I have a few ideas about the work to be done." In fact, he was unsure what he should do.

Business had not been put on hold until his return, however. The board of trustees had authorized the purchase of the Cayce home and its furnishings. They wanted it turned into the Cayce Historical Memorial, provided $11,000 could be raised to purchase it. As Gladys reported in the *Bulletin*, "Thus there will be presented for the study and use of members the exact setting in which Edgar Cayce carried on his work. The home and offices will continue to remain open to visitors who come daily asking to see where readings were given, what books the Cayces read, and other items of personal interest."

Several thousand dollars had been contributed by the time Hugh Lynn got home. When he climbed the stairs to his old office, he found his desk still there but his files gone. They had been hauled out to the garage by a well-meaning volunteer who had cleared his desk for a lanky, gregarious graduate student from Chicago, Harmon H. Bro, who came six months after Hugh Lynn joined the Army. Hugh Lynn found his files gathering mold in the damp garage. It was an inauspicious beginning for what was to become a challenging relationship with Harmon.

Bro and his pretty bride, June, had assisted immeasurably during Hugh Lynn's absence. For one thing they helped cope with all the visitors inspired by the magazine article, "Miracle Man of Virginia Beach," Harmon's mother had written. They also helped Gladys stage the first and only A.R.E. Congress without a Cayce in attendance, in June 1945, barely six months after Edgar's death. Determined to carry on, Gladys had invited a group of speakers. It was to be business as usual. Several dozen members attended. Afterward Harmon wrote a brave, upbeat report to all the members—there were 525 names on the rolls, but only 185 were still active—appealing for funds. He also reported the creation of the Edgar Cayce Publishing Co. It consisted of one hand-cranked mimeograph machine.

The board of trustees had voted a whopping budget of $62,000, half of it to endow an Edgar Cayce Foundation that was supposed to launch a research program. Most of the other half was to go into publishing booklets based on the readings, to buy the Cayce home, and to hire a librarian who might start indexing the thousands of topics found in the nearly 15,000 readings. Until they were indexed, only Gladys knew where to find anything—and that from memory.

The big issue that had faced the board—Is there a future for an organization based on the work of a dead psychic?—now faced Hugh Lynn, too. Members were asking him: What services can you offer us now that we can't get a reading from your father? It was not easy to answer with any assurance.

Bro's report assured the members that an active search had begun for psychics who would carry on in the Cayce tradition, for the readings had promised that "new channels, new individuals will be provided." But where would another Edgar Cayce be found?

"We were whistling in the dark," Bro conceded years later. "The little A.R.E. had no money. After Cayce's death, the funds paid by individuals for over 1,000 readings scheduled two years ahead had to be returned. Those using treatments prescribed in Cayce's last years had required letters and calls to help them continue, and the cost had drained the organization's resources. Six months after Cayce's death the A.R.E. was sinking."

What could Hugh Lynn do to save it?

"I didn't know what I was going to do."

Harmon, a thoughtful young man, eagerly laid out the issues as he saw them for Hugh Lynn. "Though a dozen years his junior, I had sought as a young college instructor and minister to stand in for him where I could, and had been forced to face all the questions of the meaning of his father's gift and life which I knew Hugh Lynn faced."

Bro's questions were: Should the little A.R.E. be disbanded? Should its files of readings be given to a college or medical school for possible research? Should the A.R.E. try to become a research foundation, an adult education fellowship, a quasi-religious lay order, a healing center, a publishing firm?

"Hugh Lynn had to search his soul for answers," said Bro. "Finally, he made his choice. He would, he told me with some passion, 'make the name of Cayce known everywhere.' It was a bold choice. He meant his father's name, as the bearer of a record of unusual service to the ill, but also as the source of a body of coherent, little-studied concepts on the human condition. Yet 'Cayce' was also Hugh Lynn's name, and the effort to establish his father's rightful stature might mask from him his own ambition as a bright, energetic, competitive, and sometimes impatient young man."

Hugh Lynn had no doubt about perpetuating his father's name and legacy and promoting the reputation that Sugrue's book afforded. But by the time he got home, another point of view had surfaced within the board of trustees.

"The board of trustees favored giving the readings to Harvard University for their library, and I got very upset over this—the thought that they were going to give them away." Rudolph Johnson, an attorney from Dallas, Texas, recalls "one of Edgar's oldest friends" advocating giving the readings to Duke University, where J.B. Rhine had made a reputation for parapsychological research.

Hugh Lynn was still overseas when the board first discussed this idea, and Gladys got so upset that she locked up all the readings in the vault and put the key in her bosom. Nobody would have access to Edgar Cayce's legacy until Hugh Lynn got home to take command.

"But the board members said, 'Well, what are you going to do with them?' I said, 'I don't know, but we'll have to find out. We'll have to do something to preserve them. They'll have to be used."

The readings, 14,265 of them, consisted of Gladys's carbon copies, filed under each person's name. Later they would be given code numbers to protect the identity and privacy of those who got the originals. With the readings were letters between Cayce and the recipient. Edgar's correspondence, 145,000 pages of it, overflowed file cabinets and storage boxes crammed into the tiny headquarters. Hugh Lynn recalled an earlier crisis over protecting the readings:

"I went upstairs one day and pulled open the cardboard cases where we were storing the readings, and in the back of one of them was a nest of mice. They had eaten away the corner of about twenty-five or thirty readings, and it scared the daylights out of me, the thought that we were going to lose them all."

As a consequence they raised enough money in 1940 to build an addition to the house which included a library and the vault in which Gladys had locked them. But the postwar crisis was much more difficult.

"The only thing I knew to do was to dash out and talk about it to anyone who would listen to me. I'd ask people to invite friends to their homes so we could talk about these readings and what we should do with them."

It was harder than anything he had ever attempted. Without his father, alive and giving readings, providing direct answers to individuals in need, it was difficult to arouse much interest beyond the loyal remnant. His most valued ally, lending moral support and brain power, was his best friend, Tom Sugrue. Although confined to a wheelchair, and living in Florida and later New York, he served as editor of A.R.E. publications. Sugrue suggested that the post-Edgar role the A.R.E must play was to search the readings for nuggets of value to the public: "It will take many years to do this, for as information is extracted and studied it will suggest theories and truths which will set up new problems of research. There is no doubt that these readings comprise one of the richest legacies ever left by a human being. In them there is a potential of wealth for everyone."

Hugh Lynn had no doubt of this either, hence his immediate opposition to surrendering this great treasure to others who would value it less, if at all. But the means of realizing the ideal voiced by Tom was not simple, even the approach to take. As Sugrue said, "The question for the Association to decide is whether it wishes to prepare itself for that larger task, or whether it wants to be satisfied with the smaller service of extracting the information without attempting to integrate, correlate, and synthesize it."

Hugh Lynn chose the "larger task," which for him was a personal, lifetime commitment.

As for preserving the readings, some of the New York businessmen proposed creating the Edgar Cayce Foundation to take custody of them and prepare them for public research. The idea created a furor of violent opposition from some of the Virginia Beach

160

Edgar's eldest son, Hugh Lynn Cayce

Hugh Lynn and his mother

Thomas Jefferson Cayce, the first seer of the Cayce clan

Edgar Cayce and his father Leslie B. Cayce

Hugh Lynn (second from left) got into
Christian Endeavor activities with his father
in Selma, Alabama, where they lived over the
Cayce Art Co. studio; but he got into mischief
with his buddies in Hopkinsville, Kentucky,
where he spent many summers.

The death of their second son
made Hugh Lynn an only child
until Edgar Evans (right)
completed the family in 1918
when Hugh Lynn turned eleven.

Hugh Lynn's favorite photo, age sixteen, just before the family moved to Dayton, Ohio, where they lived in a second-floor apartment of a private home. Edgar's new secretary, Gladys Davis, eighteen, who lived with the Cayces, and Hugh Lynn enjoyed teen talk in a nearby park. Hugh Lynn (second row, third from left) was graduated from a fancy prep school in Dayton in 1925.

Two New York stockbrokers, Morton and David Blumenthal, invested $1 million in building a hospital and starting a university at Virginia Beach, where the Cayces moved in 1925 and lived close enough to walk into the surf.

Hugh Lynn went off to Washington & Lee University in 1926.

*The Cayce Hospital, built while Hugh Lynn
was away at college, closed shortly after his
graduation—but twenty-five years later
became A.R.E. headquarters.*

The Search for God Study Group was invented in 1931 by this group of people: Standing, left to right, Esther Wynne, who later compiled the Search for God books; Gladys Davis, Fannie Freeman, Helen Storey, Florence Edmonds, Helen Ellington, L. B. Cayce, Mildred Davis, Mary Louise Black, Hugh Lynn, Edith Edmonds, Hannah Miller, Frances Morrow. Sitting, left to right: C. A. Barrett, C. W. Rosborough, Jeanne LeNoir, Ruth LeNoir, Eloise Potter, Minnie Barrett, Gertrude Cayce, Leona Rosborough.

The Cayce home on Arctic Crescent was A.R.E. headquarters for over twenty years until the hospital bulding was regained in 1956.

Hugh Lynn, as a scoutmaster in 1934, led his troop on a memorable camping trip to Mount Rushmore and other national parks.

Around her dinner table in New York, Lucille Kahn (left) gathered the A.R.E. brain-trust at Thanksgiving, 1937. To her left, Gertrude and Edgar Cayce, and Mary Sugrue. To her right, Tom Sugrue, Gladys Davis, and Hugh Lynn Cayce.

Hugh Lynn lived with the Kahns in 1938 while working in radio in New York, and enjoyed the social life with a New York columnist, Julia Chandler, whose reading said she had been a woman in Biblical times named Judy, a story depicted in the novel The Remnant by Mary LaCroix.

Tom later became ill and moved to Virginia Beach (here with Edgar Evans Cayce on boardwalk) but remained in good spirits.

Hugh Lynn lived at home until he was thirty-four and married a Southern belle, Sally Taylor from North Carolina, after a seven-year courtship.

Drafted into the Army in 1943, Hugh Lynn said farewell to his bride and year-old son, Tommy, and his parents, who died before he returned from the war.

Sgt. Cayce's unit provided entertainment for General George Patton's troops from the Normandy invasion to the German surrender.

Vaughan Shelton (right) was one Army buddy whom Hugh Lynn hired at the A.R.E. after the war.

When Hugh Lynn and brother Edgar Evans returned from the war their sons were no longer babies.

While Hugh Lynn was gone, the A.R.E. managed with Gladys Davis (far left), Mae Gimbert St. Clair (far right) and June and Harmon Bro (rear), all of whom would remain dedicated to The Work for decades, and many volunteers.

Hugh Lynn and Tom planned a spiritual renaissance after Edgar Cayce's death.

With a smile and a shoeshine, the A.R.E. salesman hit the road, lecturing, selling books, and spreading the Cayce message. He was often accompanied by Mrs. Elsie Sechrist, whose life was saved by Edgar Cayce.

Publication of his book, Venture Inward, *in 1964 attracted attention from the media.*

In 1963 he went to Egypt and returned many times in quest of the evidence for *Ra Ta.* Other journeys took him to China, India (where he met the prime minister), to Tibet for an audience with the Dalai Lama, and to Israel where he meditated by the Sea of Galilee and required medical aid by a fellow traveler, Dr. William A. McGarey, founder of the A.R.E. Clinic.

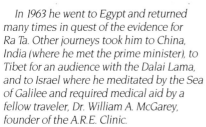

In 1974 Hugh Lynn bulldozed neighborhood opponents to build a modern library-conference center, then mounted the 'dozer in hardhat to break ground.

He also worked with youth and started a summer camp in western Virginia next to a national forest (top left).

Hugh Lynn and Sally had two sons, Charles Thomas and Gregory. Charles Thomas (left), a psychologist, made his father a happy man by agreeing in 1970 to join the A.R.E. staff as director of youth activities.

In 1977 Charles Thomas took a bride, Leslie Goodman, and became president of the A.R.E. following Hugh Lynn's heart attack, giving his father more time for gardening.

Another psychology professor recruited by Hugh Lynn for his staff was Herbert Puryear.

The lad who started out posing for his father ended up an inspiring teacher of his father's spiritual concepts and a visionary pioneer of the New Age.

members who didn't want the A.R.E. to lose control of them. A split in the board of trustees ensued until 1947, when a majority approved the plan. The Foundation, chartered in Virginia in 1948, had its own board of trustees, whose selection was carefully orchestrated by Hugh Lynn. In later years, at least, he apparently controlled the A.R.E. by influencing the election of new board members. As one board member put it, Hugh Lynn appointed the committee that picked the board members and they never picked someone he didn't approve. If Hugh Lynn was going to devote his life to this organization, he was going to run it his own way.

Another dimension of his commitment was his trying to comprehend the nature of his father's gift.

"I went to all kinds of psychics to try to understand Dad, sometimes to ask about him, but just to understand psychic ability. I wanted to be sure he wasn't really a freak, that it was a universal quality with many facets to it. I began by reading the literature. I went back to the early British Society for Psychical Research and read everything that had been published, and then came on into the American Society and read all that. Then I began to read the people mentioned in the readings. D.B. Holmes was a famous one, an American who went to England and spent a lot of time there studying William James's work. I spent a great deal of time checking out his psychical work with Mrs. Piper. I didn't go to England or meet anyone until much later. But I talked to people who had investigated the Marjory case in Boston, a famous mediumist case. I also got involved in the Andrew Jackson Davis material, and the man who had influenced Mary Baker Eddy, the founder of Christian Science."

Hugh Lynn's review of the field gave him a fresh perspective on his father's work, and certainly fortified his respect for Edgar Cayce's extraordinary gift.

"The thing that is unique about Dad that you won't find in others were his medical diagnoses, his consistent medical treatments. There are few medical clairvoyants that are any good.

"There are some healers that pray for people or put their hands on people. And there are people like Dora Kunz of the Theosophical Society who diagnose by looking at auras."

Hugh Lynn recalled the occasion when he and his father met the famous Irish medium, Eileen Garrett, in New York. They agreed to each give a reading for the other.

"In the morning Dad gave a reading on her. We asked where her ability came from."

The reading said: "A portion is from the soul development of the entity. . . . Also from those influences from without that are either in those attitudes of being teachers, instructors, directors, or those that would give to those in the material plane the better comprehension of the continuance of a mental and soul activity."

Hugh Lynn asked Edgar about Mrs. Garrett's control, Uvani, who identified himself as an Arab.

"Dad said he'd look him up. And we sat there for about ten minutes waiting for him to look up Uvani. He finally said, 'Yes, I've found him. He's on the fifth level.' He found Uvani was an all-right guy, a dead one but all right.

"After lunch she gave a reading for Dad, and I asked the questions. Uvani said he found Dad 'peculiarly intuitive, supersensitive, and yet not using all the power that is within him.'"

Uvani also thought the most influential incarnation for Edgar had been in India. "But I am very certain that he must have suffered great torture and great sacrifice during this understanding, with the result that a contact with him is almost, as it were, blocked out—and that is a pity, because I think they came back to make something very right for him that has been a wrong, and I believe he can use this greater power.

"If that can be lifted, behold a new channel, a new understanding in work can be accomplished," added Uvani.

"I told Dad that if he would let him, Uvani could clarify the language of his readings. And Dad said, 'That's true. He would be able to smooth out the sentence structure. But Uvani wouldn't be able to go nearly as high or as far.' He meant that Uvani didn't have the reach that he had."

Most of Hugh Lynn's energy was devoted to pumping life into the A.R.E. Tom Sugrue began a weekly lecture program in New York's Willkie hall to generate interest. Sitting in his wheelchair in the front of the hall, Tom developed into an accomplished speaker himself, and he brought in other speakers to discuss parapsychological issues. When they got Eileen Garrett as the speaker in 1948, he introduced her. "Like many mediums, in fact like all sincere psychics, she tried many times to run away from the power she had, to deny it and to refuse to use it," Tom began. "In the end, however, she determined to study it and use it for the advance of scientific investigation of extra-sensory perception."

It was this educational approach that Hugh Lynn and Tom thought best for building a community of interest in the A.R.E. They would turn to scientific inquiry, to research, to testing the readings to see how generally applicable they were. If an unconventional remedy proved successful for one person's ailment, would it prove helpful to others? There was still so much that medical science did not know about the cause of diseases, if any of the answers were found in the Cayce readings their value would soon be recognized.

The dual objectives of this strategy were apparent. One objective was to demonstrate to the world that Edgar Cayce had not been a freak, but a man of profound psychic powers and spiritual perception.

"I had told Dad that I considered him the greatest sensitive the world had seen since Jesus, and that before we were through with this he would be known as that."

The second objective was to "prepare the ground for a spiritual renaissance among people of intelligence and perception," as Tom put it. This had been their goal when they launched the magazine *The New Tomorrow* twenty years earlier. They had hoped Atlantic University would become the seed ground for this renaissance. "We wanted a small school for the study of psychic phenomena and the examination of the esoteric tradition in religion from an objective point of view." They were keenly disappointed when its financial investors chose an orthodox liberal arts curriculum instead. In a letter to Mrs. Garrett in 1949, Tom reviewed their strategy:

"Atlantic University had a short life, as did the Cayce Hospital, and we were back where we started—with a dream. We then divided the job. I went out on the rim, in the world, and Hugh Lynn remained at the axis, in Virginia Beach. During the long years of the Depression and World War II we did what we could. The intellectuals with whom I worked were for the most part too clouded by ego to perceive the spiritual wave which is forming from the pressure of world events, and the simple, good people with whom Hugh Lynn worked lacked still the intellectual development which, added to their unspoiled nature, would give them a wide and inclusive viewpoint. Things are a little better with both types of people now, and we feel, with his father gone, that the time has come to begin. There is not, in fact, too much time left. Something must be done."

As between the intellectuals and "simple, good people," there seems little doubt who played the dominant role. "The people who kept the A.R.E. alive were the ordinary folks, the not-very-educated true believers, some of them tithers, who felt that it was the work of the Lord," says author and lecturer Violet M. Shelley. "Mostly, they were strong women." They responded not only to his father's legacy but to Hugh Lynn. They were his constituency.

The A.R.E., however, had to find a hook, a new reason for people to join. Hugh Lynn favored education, self-improvement, as the magnetic power. The readings were loaded with wisdom which anyone might benefit from studying. If he could get that message across, it just might work. The primary approach to rallying interest was through publications. The A.R.E. had issued Hugh Lynn's newsy, mimeographed *Bulletin*, monthly since 1932, even during the war when volunteers such as the Bros helped get it out. When he returned from the Army, Hugh Lynn received considerable help writing *Bulletin* articles from a student volunteer from the University of Wisconsin, Gina Cerminara of Milwaukee, who was living in the Cayce house. During 1946 and 1947 she and Hugh Lynn wrote many *Bulletin* articles, while laying plans for a more impressive publication. In the tradition of the magazine, *The New Tomorrow*, that Hugh Lynn and Tom had launched in 1929, they started a new little magazine in 1949 called *The Searchlight*, with Tom as editor. By focusing each bi-monthly issue on a main topic—reincarnation, dream interpretation, psychic research, an essay on the Kabbalah—they introduced the members to the idea that great wisdom was to be found in that vast storehouse of knowledge that was the legacy of Edgar Cayce.

The same objective was served by changing the format of the annual A.R.E. Congress meeting in 1948. Until his death, Edgar himself had been the chief attraction at these gatherings, usually giving a reading that everyone in attendance could watch. Now Hugh Lynn substituted a week of lectures and studies of the sort they had hoped Atlantic University would offer. As Sugrue explained it later to Mrs. Garrett:

"Congress has been run as a school, with regular classes each day for the week of its duration. The classes have been conducted on the plan we originally devised, examining facets and aspects of the spiritual and psychic life with information drawn from the general literature and tradition, and with the Cayce readings on these facets and aspects as commentary."

By stimulating wider interest in the Cayce literature through topical booklets based on the readings, and reaching the members through the *Bulletin*, Hugh Lynn hoped that the flock would multiply.

"The next step," Sugrue went on, "is to extend the school through the whole summer, with courses arranged to suit the normal vacation period of individuals. The Beach provides an ideal campus for this plan—people like to go there for a few weeks or a month during the hot season; cottages and hotels provide ideal dormitories and dining halls. The Association has merely to set up a curriculum and provide the classrooms and the teachers."

These were visionary young men. While not immediately realized, their dream would be fulfilled in the form of summer conferences, which have become a principal outreach of the organization.

164

The success of the educational approach, however, depended on researching the readings to discover what they had to teach. They obviously would have to be read, their topics identified, and everything indexed. It would be a mammoth undertaking.

Gladys clearly was the key person Hugh Lynn relied upon in fostering this renaissance. Having typed most of the readings from her shorthand notes, she had developed a proprietary attitude toward them. The readings had become her personal mission. If she had left to find a well-paying secretarial job, as surely she might have during the war after her boss died, instead of devoting her life to this cause, it is quite likely that the framework Hugh Lynn found upon his return would have been too fragmented to rebuild. But Gladys, as Bro put it, "held her ground" and held things together. Harmon added: "She had never been married nor borne a child in this lifetime, and Cayce had clearly been the overshadowing male figure in her journey into her late thirties [she was thirty-nine when Cayce died]. But she knew how to love. She could relate to people, and draw out the best in them. She kept the board members, the staff, and potential helpers and donors talking, by listening to them, asking serious questions, and constantly making notes. She humored some, challenged others, hugged many, and teased and laughed often. . . . Gladys reached us all."

When Edgar had been inundated with requests for readings, paid secretarial help was added. But now, with no salary funds left, Gladys had to rely on volunteer help. The project was formidable. It meant typing up a separate cover sheet or two listing the topics alphabetically. A typical reading might begin with: Akashic Records, Angels and Archangels, Bible, books of: Galatians 6:7, etc. It continued through Religion: Zoroastrianism, Spirit Communication; and Work: E.C., Readings et al. It would be twenty years and more before Gladys and her volunteers had listed all the significant topics mentioned in each reading.

Once the contents of each reading had been identified, it would take another decade to index the entire collection. Then all of it would be microfilmed, so that copies could readily be produced and distributed.

"Then it will be available for study, not only at the Beach, but everywhere else it is desired, and photostats of any or all the sheets can be made quickly by anyone wishing to study a particular subject—arthritis, immortality, marriage, leukemia, the Gospel of St. John, etc. The medical information will be assembled and studied by doctors, and we hope eventually that it will be used by men in research medicine; there is a great deal of information, for instance, on the relation of the endocrine glands to disease. The readings on telepathy, clairvoyance, and man's psychic powers in general will be gathered and studied along with everything printed and known on these subjects. The religious and mystical information will be paralleled with all the known systems, both Oriental and Occidental, and students will be exposed to all of it."

Hugh Lynn and Tom, in a word, had developed a blueprint for the future so that the A.R.E. could survive his father's death and become beneficial to millions.

It was not risk-free, of course. Harmon Bro sized it up this way: "Cayce had opened up directions of thought and practice relatively new in the West, such as reincarnation, or meditation, or ESP for everyone. But the obvious danger of an association to promote his concepts, as some pointed out, was 'crystallization' of ideas into a cult—seemingly a mocking outcome for his lifework. Better to let the enterprise die peacefully."

Hugh Lynn would have done most anything, and made any personal sacrifice, to prevent its dying. His ultimate goal was to transform people's lives no less than their philosophy. As Sugrue put it:

"What we want to do is to give people guidance in the spiritual field, information and interpretation in the parapsychological field, and help in the physical body. The three together will stimulate them to seek along the proper lines for inner peace, mental stimulation, and unfoldment of the soul faculties."

Edgar Cayce's legacy would take on greater stature than ever simply because of the readings' uplifting effect on people's lives. If life begins at forty, as they used to say, certainly it was a new life that beckoned to Hugh Lynn Cayce when he crossed that temporal threshold shortly after coming home from the war. He was about to foment a spiritual renaissance, nothing less, and the sooner he got going, the better.

Chapter 14

On the Road

Launching a spiritual renaissance, a heady enterprise for two middle-aged fraternity brothers turned metaphysical intellectuals, demanded originality, initiative, and a willingness to fail no less than an impulse to succeed. Although he credited Sugrue with being more brilliant academically, Hugh Lynn was also an idea man, a visionary who succeeded in the end because he beieved in his cause more than his personal comfort. In achieving his objectives, he willingly sacrificed himself—and others—and therein lay a problem he would struggle with for most of his life.

Recognizing that he could not carry out this plan single-handedly, Hugh Lynn recruited several former Army buddies. Publisher of a Maryland weekly newspaper, Bill Epstein seemed ideally qualified to help upgrade the A.R.E.'s attempts to publish. How could they move up from the mimeograph machine to the printing press without any money? That's where Bill's expertise, and generosity, came into play.

"He was a wonderful guy, wrote a history of Kent County, Maryland. I didn't have a publisher, so I got Bill to publish the *Searchlight* and our other publications, booklets, for a while. But it became impossible to keep going after he sold the paper and turned it over to somebody else—so we had to stop that."

Sam Benesch came to the Beach after the war, too, before heading for college. He stayed long enough, however, to marry Edna, a volunteer in Hugh Lynn's office. They had two sons but later divorced. Sam ended up earning a Ph.D. and working for a major defense contractor in California, where he was active in study group work in later years, helping financially when Hugh Lynn asked for contributions—"a close, close friend."

A third Army buddy, Vaughan Shelton from Pittsburgh, agreed to work with Hugh Lynn as a writer and editor.

"I met him at Fort Meade. We became drinking buddies when we couldn't get out of camp. He was interested in the psychic and was a writer on a little magazine in Pittsburgh and married to a wealthy, beautiful woman. After the war they moved to Virginia Beach and he became editor of our press. He put together the Black Book that later brought us so many members after Jess Stearn mentioned it in his book, *The Sleeping Prophet*.

"He was a brilliant writer and a good editor. But he couldn't handle the finances. [Vaughan evidently paid writers advances; Hugh Lynn didn't know where the A.R.E. could raise the money to meet these literary obligations.] I had to fire him. It was one of the most painful things I've ever been through, because he was a warm personal friend. We used to play poker together, in the Army and here at the Beach. Bob Adriance used to play poker with us."

Bob Adriance was an insurance company executive from a wealthy family who had walked in and volunteered his services when Hugh Lynn most needed someone with business acumen. Adriance, too, was an Army veteran, about ten years younger than Hugh Lynn. He was a godsend for the A.R.E. because he had a keen understanding of the financial world and considerable business experience, which Hugh Lynn lacked. He also had sufficient private means to work without a salary. Hugh Lynn made Adriance business manager and treasurer. "Hugh Lynn and I took a piece of yellow legal paper, drew a line down it, put his name at the top of one column and mine at the top of the other and listed who would be responsible for what," explained Adriance. "The finances were pretty simple, too. We had a pile of bills on one side and the contributions stacked on the other. And when the money came in, we'd pay what bills we could."

As Hugh Lynn mustered help where he could find it, Sugrue finished another book, *Stranger in the Earth*, a very personal testament to his own unconventional faith, his personal involvement with Edgar Cayce, and his difficulties with the institutionalized church. He later expanded on his disenchantment with the church in A *Catholic Speaks His Mind*, for which he was criticized by Cardinal Spellman of New York.

When Tom contracted to write a book on the birth of the new nation, Israel, he asked Hugh Lynn to go with him to gather material. His publisher agreed to pay the expenses of a traveling companion for the crippled author.

"I couldn't go, I was busy with the A.R.E. So he got an editor from *Harper's* to go with him, and this man had a stroke on the ship going over. Tom went on nonetheless, with Israelis taking care of him in a wheelchair. It was one of the most courageous acts. He traveled all over Israel for six months and came back and wrote *Watch for the Morning*, a beautiful book that became a best-seller.

"Tom returned from that trip determined to walk but he began to have sciatica. He started taking cortisone. His publisher wanted him to make a publicity tour when the book came out, so this time I went with him, and I set up A.R.E. conferences all along the way. We went all over the United States, just hitting big cities where there were large Jewish organizations. I'd carry him on and off the plane. He'd speak at the Jewish organizations that paid his expenses, and then he'd speak for the A.R.E. He sold books like hot cakes, and I got to go along free. It went very well."

Most of Hugh Lynn's travels were done the hard way, however, by car or train over long weeks away from home. "Each winter after Christmas he began an extended lecture tour which would keep him away until as late as May—not easy for a family man," recalls Harmon Bro. "He went up and down the East Coast, through the Midwest and South, on to the West Coast, stopping in cities large and small to lecture to anyone who asked him—and incidentally to sell the A.R.E. publications. He spoke on campuses, in churches, in Theosophical lodges, in hospitals, community forums, at retreat centers, at A.R.E. gatherings, in meetings of Spiritual Frontiers Fellowship, in research centers, and in many homes. It was a principle with him to honor every request for a lecture if he could, whatever the fee, and often there was none."

Hugh Lynn initially traveled by auto, his trunk loaded with booklets and copies of *There Is a River* to be displayed and sold at the meetings. It was essential to sell enough publications to pay for his transportation to the next stop on the tour.

"He told me they would scrape together enough money in Virginia Beach to get him to the first place, and they would hope to raise enough money there to get him to the second place," recalls Violet Shelley.

Hugh Lynn was so poor himself that he didn't have to take a valise, because he didn't have anything to carry but a few notes, recalls one friend. His suits were shiny and his shirt collars frayed, so that one admirer gave him an anonymous gift certificate for $100 at a men's clothing shop. His appearance seemed to improve after that, the donor observed. Elsie Sechrist, who had received a reading from Edgar, often accompanied Hugh Lynn but could afford to pay her own expenses. "We would charge 25 cents for a lecture," said Elsie. "I remember once Hugh Lynn went up to the desk to pay his hotel bill with a fistful of quarters and spread them on the desk. The girl said, 'I can't take those,' but Hugh Lynn said, 'It's either the quarters or nothing, that's all I have.' So she counted out enough of them to cover his bill."

Some people who first encountered Hugh Lynn in those days remember him less as an able salesman for the A.R.E. than as a charismatic missionary for living a new kind of life. He was not a polished speaker; he stammered through his text, but he imparted sincerity and attracted people who were seeking something. Early on he had strange encounters with people who claimed to have been in communication with his father.

"In 1947, in Chicago at one of my very first lectures, I was confronted with the dilemma of how to react to people claiming to have communication with Edgar Cayce. After the lecture several people came up to speak to me, one of them the minister of a local spiritualist church. He said he was sorry to have to give me the message but that Edgar Cayce had been at my lecture, standing at my right, and he had communicated that he was sorry he had ever given many of his psychic readings. He wanted me to burn all of them and stop the work which had been launched to study his records. I thanked the man, and moments later was confronted by a woman bearing another message. She also was a minister of a spiritualist church. She, too, said Edgar Cayce had attended my lecture, standing to my left, and he wanted me to know that he wanted me to go forward with the work of the A.R.E. You pay your money and you take your choice."

Hearing many such "messages" over the years, Hugh Lynn developed a test for those who came bearing them: "Ask Dad what were the occasions on which he whipped me," he would tell them. There had been two such occasions. No one ever answered the question correctly.

On one occasion, though, he believed that Edgar Cayce had come through an English medium, Mrs. Ena Twigg. He had a dream in which Tom Sugrue advised him that there was going to be an event of psychic importance that would startle a lot of church people. "I said, 'Well, Tom, what is it going to be?' He just laughed and held up a fish. I recognized the fish as a pike, a species that had been in our little lake and had jumped into my brother's canoe one time. Shortly after that dream, Bishop James Pike announced that he had communicated with his son, who had committed suicide [in 1966] in an LSD experiment, through Ena Twigg. [An Episcopalian, whose church was in San Francisco, Pike recounted the experience in his book, *The Other Side*.] When Bishop Pike got his son, he also got Edgar Cayce. He didn't write about or talk about that part except to me later."

Hugh Lynn had a different test for alleged communications from his mother. A member of the first Study Group, Florence Edmonds, told Hugh Lynn that shortly after his mother died she dreamed about Gertrude, who told her, "When I communicate with Hugh Lynn, tell him that I will give him two red roses." Hugh Lynn asked her to say nothing about her dream to anyone else, and he kept a watchful lookout for the red roses. About twenty-five years later he received a call from a man whose wife had begun to hear strange voices after playing a Ouija board and doing automatic writing. For a time she had been in a mental hospital, and after she was released, still hearing voices, she called Hugh Lynn and repeated the strange, confusing pattern of words she was hearing— dirty stories, dire forecasts, gossip, and teasing comments about the woman herself. Suddenly she stopped the gibberish and said, "Mr. Cayce, your mother says to give you two red roses." With that the strange voices fell silent.

Not all of his experiences while speaking made sense to him. One time while talking to a group outdoors beneath an enormous spreading tree, "I said, 'I've had a thing with trees,' and I pointed at the tree—and I moved from my body into the tree. I'd never had such an experience. Ruth Lenoir, who was there, said I just stood there with my hand out like I was paralyzed for several minutes, and then I shook myself and went on."

Did he talk to the tree?

"I didn't say anything to it at all. I was just a part of it and caught up and just dispersed in its energy pattern. It's a very disturbing kind of feeling because you are scattered, blended, like you are getting beat up in a milkshake."

How could this happen?

"There is an energy pattern there and when you tune yourself to that energy, you get involved in it, you know it is alive, you feel it, you hear it, you are a part of it, you are in it, so to speak, you move with the sap and you feel what is going on with the roots and the leaves. The tree is a living entity, it has life and it is going places, and it perpetuates itself through its seeds and all its connections with its brothers of the same kind in the forest, but it is also part of a bigger pattern of all trees, part of an energy network."

Was that an out-of-body experience?

"I don't know what you'd classify that as. I never had anything like it."

A more understandable experience while lecturing was occasionally recognizing a person in the audience from a past incarnation and suddenly reliving a vivid experience with that person. Once at Virginia Beach a young man in the audience loomed up in his mind's eye as another of the boys he had known in the Gobi Desert—that same camel-theft experience he had recognized when he met Sam Benesch years before in the Army. More often, his lecture tours brought him in contact with people who were in need and sensed that he and his message offered something beneficial. Some people who worked with him believed Hugh Lynn was quite psychic in identifying people in need. Hugh Lynn believed that he was partially gifted in telepathy. "I never talk about it," he said, but his readings suggested that he had telepathic powers. He thought it was something most people could develop. "I tried to refocus the telepathic ability so that I would use it in connection with prayer for healing. I try to know when to pray for people. I've found that when I use it in that direction, it will come and frequently be very, very timely and very helpful. If difficulties arise and I know that prayer will help soften or go through something, I try to use it in that direction. And that works.

"I also use it every day if I'm talking with someone. You know people never ask you the question that is troubling them. They'll ask you something else, trying to get themselves up to the point of asking what's really on their mind. People would come to me because they were actually in trouble, when I was on the road or at the Beach, particularly young people. To be able to know when you answer their first question what they really want to know, you can do it without startling or disturbing them or waiting for them to ask the paramount question. It takes time for people to talk about what is hurting them. So I try to answer some of that right off and get into it, and I pray while I'm talking or while they are talking. Light is the key to quickening the Divine within the person. So if you use light and surround the person with light instead of using the kind of prayer that says, 'God, heal this man's legs so he can walk again,' for he may not need to walk at all. He may need a rest and you may be upsetting his pattern considerably. He may need something else. Using the light, that's the way I pray for others, for myself. It's not new, it's ancient. I connect it with the illumination."

Author Lin Cochran recalls one time while chauffeuring Hugh Lynn during a visit to Florida that he asked about her family, and she expressed concern about her son, Tony, who had been released from the army for disobedience and sent home from Germany. "Bring him to the meeting tonight," Hugh Lynn insisted. Much to her amazement, Tony felt compelled to accompany her even though "the A.R.E. just wasn't my thing." He said "it was as though I knew there was a purpose for going—something said to do it. I don't remember anything else about that conference except the few minutes I spent with Hugh Lynn. That few minutes changed my life."

They had simply taken a stroll together, Tony talking about his strange experiences in a haunted house in a German town, where he had had a strong sense of deja vu. His landlord's account of wartime bombing of the area matched a dream Tony had experienced repeatedly. His mother had also dreamed of a connection between the boy and Nazi Germany. "Hugh Lynn said I could have been a young soldier in the Nazi army, killed in that air raid."

But Hugh Lynn reassured him "that there had been a purpose for everything I had done" and he shared some of his own youthful rebellious experiences. "He made me feel there was a bond between us, a brotherhood of rebellion. He talked about man's idea of success and moral fiber. I felt acceptance from Hugh Lynn. He said, 'Stick to your guns. Follow the light wherever it leads.' I've never felt that connected to another person—not the personality, but the spirit. He gave me the courage to follow the light."

Jim Baraff, another young man who felt an immediate connection with Hugh Lynn upon meeting him in 1968 when Jim was twenty-three, said he was treated "like a son" and given a job in the press. He soon had no doubt of Hugh Lynn's telepathic powers. "I was working on the folding machine one day and thinking, 'I've got to talk to Hugh Lynn.' A few minutes later he walked in and said to me, 'Jim, you've got to stop doing that. Make an appointment when you want to talk to me.'"

Another young man who heard Hugh Lynn, in Detroit one night in 1950, asked for a private appointment.

"Hugh Lynn said, 'Certainly,' and then I thought he added, 'Come to my room at one o'clock.' I figured he must have a lot of others to see and how nice of him to volunteer to see me so late," recalls Wym Price.

"So at 1:00 a.m. I went to his hotel room. I couldn't see any light under the door but I knocked anyway. There was a pause and the dear man opened it, tying on his bathrobe and rubbing the sleep from his eyes. He looked at me and said, 'I said ten o'clock, not one o'clock.'

"I was so embarrassed that I tried to leave but he insisted that I come in. So we sat there on the edge of his bed in the middle of the night for an hour while he answered my questions. Is it any wonder I have always loved him?"

The experience was so moving to Wym that he moved to

Virginia Beach and, with Hugh Lynn's continued counseling, organized his life. "He was my father from when I moved from Michigan, best man at my wedding, godfather to my two boys, counselor, and one of the sweetest, kindest, most caring humans I have known."

Occasionally these virtues complicated Hugh Lynn's life, as in the case of a woman from California who became openly, boldly infatuated with him after attending a lecture in Los Angeles in which Hugh Lynn appeared with Manly P. Hall, president of the Philosophical Research Society in Los Angeles and author of *The Secret Teachings of All Ages*. The scholarly Hall held Edgar Cayce in high regard and respected Hugh Lynn. "We had many talks on serious problems," he said. "Hugh Lynn was a wonderful, cultured, charming gentleman, very sincere and very dedicated and deeply involved in the problems of spreading the message."

Jessica Madigan, a thirty-nine-year-old widow, had never heard of Cayce until that night. She was so impressed that she went to Virginia Beach in 1950 and spent considerable time at the old Cayce home studying the readings and talking to Hugh Lynn and Gladys. She thought it highly significant that she and Edgar Cayce shared the same birthday, March 18, especially after she found a reading predicting that someone would be born on his birthday thirty-three years after him, as Jessica had been, who would come into The Work. When she excitedly told Hugh Lynn, he is said to have dismissed it by saying that thousands of people had been born on that date who might become interested in The Work. "I know that, but did you ever meet one?" she insisted. Hugh Lynn just shrugged.

Convinced that she was born to fulfill a prophecy, Jessica became a serious student of metaphysics and developed into a lecturer and teacher for the A.R.E. Dr. William McGarey recalls learning about numerology from her at Virginia Beach in the 1950s. She spoke at the A.R.E.'s Asilomar conferences in California for some years. Hugh Lynn thought well enough of her to write a glowing recommendation when she applied for admission to the University of Hawaii: ". . . a person of integrity and one possessing many fine qualities. . . a fine, creative mind. . . a good writer and an excellent lecturer. . . has devoted much of her time to talking with and lecturing to groups in penal institutions in California."

Jessica also developed her psychic sensitivity, and eventually wrote and self-published fifteen books based on her experiences and insights. A colleague of Jessica's, Jery V. Stier, says she wrote her books as though in an altered state: "As Jessica would type utterly absorbed, with great emotion and feeling and interest in ferreting out the story, she would see unreeling before her inner eye, just like a movie with color and sound, exactly what she was writing." She became convinced that she and Hugh Lynn not only had been together in prior lives but were twin souls, as Edgar Cayce and his secretary, Gladys, were said to have been. She was convinced that she and Hugh Lynn had been Adam and Eve. Actually, Jessica said there had been five Adams, which corresponds to the Cayce readings' account of the origin of the five races. Hugh Lynn and she had been "the yellow Adam and Eve," Jessica claimed, and Edgar and Gladys had been the Caucasian Adam and Eve. Jessica also thought that she had been the beautiful Egyptian queen Nefertiti and that Hugh Lynn had been Amenhotep III, a strong ruler of ancient Egypt.

In this life, however, she bore no resemblance to the exotic Nefertiti. Four years younger than Hugh Lynn, Jessica was "a dumpy brunette, and not especially attractive," recalls Hugh Lynn's secretary of that period, Marjorie J. Bonney. Jessica thought that she understood Hugh Lynn better than anyone, including Sally, possibly because he confided some dreams to her. While his side of their relationship was Platonic, it became a problem when she returned home to California and began writing him love letters.

Hugh Lynn had never been taught, as ministerial students usually are during their seminary training, to cope with infatuated parishioners. During his lecture tours, however, he was usually accompanied by a woman chaperone, either a retired schoolteacher, Esther Wynne—"Miss Wynne," Hugh Lynn always called her—a spinster who had been in the first Search for God Study Group for many years; or Elsie Sechrist, a tall, no-nonsense, Germanic woman of strict Lutheran upbringing who had converted to Catholicism. A registered nurse, Elsie was devoted to the A.R.E. because she believed Edgar Cayce had saved her life when she had been given only six months to live due to a heart condition. These two women served not only The Work but helped Hugh Lynn deal with his mostly female constituency.

Elsie said that his relations with female admirers were a concern, but not for the reason one might expect: "Hugh Lynn had quite a problem at first with women because he was so stiff and formal. I don't know what it was with him, but he acted as though he was afraid they were all going to jump on him or something. People always said, 'He still thinks he's king.' So one day I said to him, 'Why don't you just relax, you're so formal, you act as if you are king.' He said, 'Oh, Elsie, stop it.' I said, 'I'm just telling you what's wrong with you.' Nobody dared talk to him like that, but he had to put up with me because he didn't have anybody else who could afford to pay her own travel expenses."

He resisted the advice initially but gradually became more relaxed, she said, "and he got to the point where he could shake hands with the girls and even hug some of them." Marj Bonney said she never saw Hugh Lynn touch a woman during the years she worked for him, and was quite surprised years later when he greeted her and another woman with a hug and a kiss.

Perhaps his experience with Jessica had made him guarded. Elsie said, "I know she made life miserable for him. She sent him these long, voluminous letters, and he finally got to the point where he said to me, 'I just tear them up, I don't even open them.'"

Elsie thought Jessica, who claimed to have had visits from Edgar Cayce, had some psychic ability, but that she "just went overboard." Elsie was confident the relationship had been "all one-sided."

"She was in love with Hugh Lynn and was sure he loved her but didn't want to show it. I had a vision about her about the time she was trying to get involved with Hugh Lynn. She was standing in the middle of a hall with urine running down her leg as though she had no control. And that said to me that she was losing control of herself. From then on her letters became such that he just tore them up. And she became angry with me and started writing letters about me as well."

Hugh Lynn tried to redirect her energies. In a remarkably compassionate letter in the spring of 1960, he wrote:

"Dear Jessica:

"Through a number of years I have come to know you as a fine person, talented and capable in many ways. This year it seemed to me that you had grown in balance and have begun to find a place, through your college work, enabling you to extend your capacity to help others. Hold to this and do a good job.

"The flow of thought and imagery from your subconscious is a remarkable operation to observe, and so long as it relates only to your inner life it can be directed and controlled if you are able to discipline yourself enough. When it begins to create and build false patterns as to the way I feel, act or believe, it becomes dangerous to you, to me and the Association.

"All that Angie wrote you and a great deal more is true and has been true for a long time. You should not give others confused and inaccurate impressions which have no basis for truth except in your mind.

"I have tried in many ways to help you to help others, which is

176

the good that both you and I should strive for. I will continue to try.

"Stop the letters, Jessica. I am not reading them. Close the door of your unconscious, love Jesus and work for Him.
Hugh Lynn."

Stier speculated about Hugh Lynn's motivation: "As an upright, very married man, he had been fascinated (if more than a bit dubious) about maintaining such secret communications with a woman who seemed to know him so well—much too well. I suspect Hugh Lynn may eventually have felt rather emotionally threatened psychically and psychologically by her insights—and her enthusiasm. And thus he may have sought consciously and unconsciously to sever this unorthodox, if Platonic relationship." Jessica experienced some bitterness and resentment—"she had a strong temper and could become very, very impatient and sharp-tongued"—but Stier said she eventually worked through it. Cut off from official A.R.E. sponsorship, Jessica held her own conferences at Asilomar and conducted a weekly discussion group in a Los Angeles restaurant which Stier reports was "dedicated to the work of Cayce following her ouster from the A.R.E." Hugh Lynn, however, kept his distance, refusing in later years to take phone calls from her. Their estrangement apparently was never resolved. She died in 1986.

If such an experience made Hugh Lynn tense, he learned one technique in order to relax while on the road. That was self-hypnosis.

"I think hypnosis is a tremendous therapy tool. If I was in a situation where I thought it would help, I would go to a good hypnotist. But I just wouldn't play with it. Unless it was someone I had known and worked with, I wouldn't want them hypnotizing me."

Hugh Lynn said he had never let anyone hypnotize him, but he had learned self-hypnosis in order to relax.

"It takes two or three months to learn this, but every day taking a couple of times out it just takes a few minutes to go over the body, relaxing it. I even went to the trouble of learning the names of some of the muscles and nerves so that I could talk to them. I speak to them and tell them to relax. I go over each toe and up the leg and body to the head and then get up. It's a very relaxing exercise. After you've done this for quite a while, you can go to sleep anywhere in about two minutes. It's amazing, the body does exactly what it is told to do. It's just plain suggestion.

"The technique for dealing with tension is to go over your body and see where you are tense, where your muscles are tight. Just speak to it, relax it. You can become a much more relaxed kind of person as a result of that. You can go to sleep quicker, sleep for twenty minutes, and wake up on a dot. I visualize a clock when I want to wake up. I never use an alarm clock. I set the clock in my mind. It works beautifully. I do it while riding in a car. People pick me up at the airport and we have a long drive into town, I'll talk with them for a few minutes and then ask them to excuse me while I sleep for a few minutes as they are driving me. It has saved my life. I've done it for years. The only time when it won't work for me is when I get to stewing about something, or writing something, or I'm worrying."

During his long road trips, Gladys managed the office with the help of several volunteers, notably Gina Cerminara and Mae Gimbert St. Clair. Miss Cerminara, a graduate student who lived at A.R.E headquarters and helped Hugh Lynn write the *Bulletin*, started writing a book about the fascinating reincarnational theme of past lives found in the readings. Sugrue had deliberately omitted this information from his Cayce biography because he and Hugh Lynn believed that it would be poor strategy to hit the public with too much in *There Is a River*. So Tom had left out the dramatic scenario about the Cayces in ancient Egypt. But now that the public had been given the highlights of the "Miracle Man's" life, Hugh Lynn thought it was time to develop further details of the extraordinary story for mass consumption. He encouraged Gina and helped her piece the story together, while Tom gave lectures in New York to raise funds to help pay her living expenses while she wrote.

"That was one of the main sources of Gina's income."

Sugrue's own literary success was won despite his increasingly painful handicap. Never able to conquer his physical ailment, he fought a losing battle, retreating slowly, bravely. Limited to writing five hundred words a day to preserve his strength, "he mentally composed, rewrote, then memorized those five hundred words, so that not a moment or an ounce of precious physical energy would be wasted," said his daughter, Patricia Channon.

Swimming in the Gulf off Florida seemed to help, but when he returned to New York he never regained the use of his legs.

"I traveled back and forth to New York quite a bit in those days and I'd stay in a little hotel downtown around 45th Street off Park Avenue. Tom was writing for Eddie Condon, the jazz guitarist. When I was there we were out every night at all-night clubs, and I listened to more good jazz by Condon and his friends. After hours they would sit and play and improvise. It was fun."

Patricia would later say that her father was "constantly in pain" and took aspirin three times daily and an injection of cobra venom, recommended in a reading, to deaden the pain. But "he could hardly begin to be angry or depressed before his unshakable optimism would bring off-setting good points to mind. Oddly, the only parts of his body not affected by illness were his arms. They could still be used for writing, although crooked at the elbow."

But optimism was not enough to save him. After the holidays in 1952 he became critically ill. As Hugh Lynn described it:

"He was in a New York hospital, and I had arranged to go see him. But I went in a dream first, the night before I was scheduled to go to New York. I got to the hospital in my dream, went into his room and no one was with him. He greeted me and said, 'I'll be with you in a minute. Tom got up from the bed, left his body, and we walked down to a room where we sat down by ourselves and talked. He said, 'I'm going and I'm very happy to be going. I can't deal with this pain any longer. There is no use your coming up here, spending the money. I won't know you. I will hear you but I won't consciously recognize you. I know you would come, and now you have come.'

"Then we talked of other things, and he said, 'I'll try to continue to help if I can.'"

Tom Sugrue died in January 1953. He was forty-five.

"I never loved another man like I loved Tom. I never hated anyone more thoroughly either, nor enjoyed hating anyone as much as I enjoyed hating Tom. That's different from just enjoying or liking or caring for someone as a friend.

"I've had some very deep friendships but I've never known one with all the kinds of ambivalence and of change that this one had. I certainly never worked harder at a relationship, and neither did he. He trusted me and I trusted him and we were absolutely frank with each other."

Hugh Lynn said this experience, against the background of their life readings, was the most convincing case for reincarnation he ever encountered. He was convinced they had fought one another more than once before.

"In Egypt, where we fought, he was a native and started a rebellion [when Hugh Lynn had been the king] and there was a great deal of persecution. Again, in the Crusades, when I was a crusader and he was a Moslem. I ended up attacking his village. Apparently I was trying to climb over a wall and he took one of those swords and whopped me across the hand between the thumb and the index finger. When we argued, the scar would reappear there. It was weird—just a reminder. Then after attacking me, he took care of me—it says I was taken in captivity and that he became curious from our conversations about the purpose of the Crusades, and who was this man Jesus? So next time around he ended up in a monastery in England—the same one I was in—we were both monks, and we

179

spent a lot of time philosophizing and discussing.

"That's four incarnations together. We had a joint reading about this, one of the most satisfying readings of my life. It was toward the end of our two years together at Virginia Beach, when Tom lived with us. It indicated that together we could do a great deal, but that if we constantly argued—we enjoyed that, too—we wouldn't get anywhere. It said we had wiped out the memories of our karma with each other, and we were free."

Chapter 15

Family Time

For a time during the winter of 1948, Hugh Lynn was less anxious about the A.R.E.'s future than he was over family matters, Sally's condition in particular, as they awaited the arrival of their second child. It was not an easy pregnancy for either of them, for Sally was then nearly forty-three and her doctor, brother Waller, had prepared Hugh Lynn for the possibility that she might lose the baby. It was a time for daily prayer and meditation in the cause of preserving human life. As she neared her time, Hugh Lynn dreamed that his father came to him with a reassuring message that Sally and the baby, a boy, would come through just fine. And in May, she delivered their second son, Gregory Jackson Cayce. Like Tommy, who was five, the baby favored his mother.

After recovering her strength, Sally went to North Carolina with Tommy and the baby to stay with her older, unmarried sister, Mary, in the family home. Mary had just adopted a baby girl, who was the same age as Tommy. Sally said she found this more agreeable than the crowded rental conditions that prevailed in Virginia Beach during and immediately after the war.

Hugh Lynn's solution was for them to build a home. What made it financially possible for them to build was the A.R.E.'s purchase of the old Cayce home on Arctic Crescent, which the organization had been using as a headquarters for fifteen years. The elder Cayces had bought the Arctic Crescent property in 1936 with a mortgage loan for $4600. In 1940 the A.R.E. constructed an addition for a library and fireproof vault, over which a private apartment had later been added. In 1945, after Edgar and Gertrude Cayce died, an $11,000 A.R.E. fund-raising effort was launched to purchase the property from the estate.

Under the Cayces' will, Hugh Lynn and Ecken shared equally. Other than the home, the Cayces had acquired little. While their boys were away at war, Edgar gave each son a building lot, which then cost about $800, recalls Edgar Evans, so that they might build their own homes when they returned from the service.

Other than real property, the modest Cayce estate consisted of $1794.51 in a joint savings account; a five-year-old Pontiac, which sold for $800; a diamond ring and a pin valued at $50; Series E Victory bonds redeemable for $838; and household furniture appraised at $1500. By the time the executors, who were Gladys Davis and a Norfolk accountant, Theron A. Helms, had paid funeral expenses of $606 and other miscellaneous bills and minor debts, sold the car, redeemed the government bonds, and the sons had divided the jewelry and furniture they wanted, Hugh Lynn's inheritance, including the value of the building lot and his share of the Arctic Crescent place, came to a grand total of about $8,000.

With this working capital, he hired an architect and a contractor, who bid $15,530 to build a contemporary three-bedroom brick rambler shaped to fit the corner lot that Edgar had given him. It was well situated near a lake on 53rd Street two blocks from the ocean, one of the city's most desirable neighborhoods. It would be the first and only home he ever owned. Sally left Hugh Lynn to supervise construction while she was living with her sister. "I came back when the house was livable," she recalls.

Gladys Davis had left the Arctic Crescent place, too. After living in the Cayce household for twenty years, she had moved out during the war to share a house with her brother, Burt, and sister, Lucile. In 1949, she built her own cottage next to the office on Arctic Crescent. She had the help of contributions from A.R.E. members, to whom Hugh Lynn appealed, to reward her more than twenty-five years of faithful service to The Work. Three years later, she married Albert E. Turner, a retired Pennsylvania stockbroker. Turner had come to Virginia Beach to learn about Cayce and been smitten with Gladys, who at forty-seven was still a lovely woman. Gladys, however, had no intention of giving up The Work for Al—indeed, she was married not in church but at A.R.E. headquarters, in Lydia J. Schrader Gray's apartment over the vault containing the readings. Fortunately, her husband became enthusiastically involved in A.R.E. activities. She had a happy marriage by all accounts until Turner's death sixteen years later.

Gladys subsequently married a retired Virginia farmer, Les Wilmore, much to the surprise of colleagues at the A.R.E. "He makes me laugh," she explained. She was widowed once again upon Wilmore's death five years later when she was seventy-five, but her marriage to The Work continued uninterrupted.

During those years as Hugh Lynn's boys grew up, he routinely took time off from office duties to be with them, perhaps to compensate for his absences. And he joined in activities where he thought it would count. Charles Thomas recalls: "He taught Sunday school, he was president of the PTA when I was in elementary school, he was a scout leader when I was in the Boy Scouts. I don't know any Dads [who did more] and I'm sure part of it was showing us that he was normal and not stuck up here on the hill doing strange things. He was getting right into it with us with both feet. He did everything he could without overly protecting us, like putting us in private schools or not letting us ride the school bus—there was none of that.

"He would notice when I was playing football or wrestling— sports things like that—and he would take off in the afternoon and come watch that, talk with the other boys and parents, extending himself to make sure there wasn't added uneasiness on our part because of the strangeness of his work. He wasn't strange as a parent. He was the best parent I can imagine. He went out of his way to be normal."

Charles Thomas thought of their scouting adventures as the highlight. Young Greg followed the tradition by joining the Cub Scouts, and Sally became a den mother.

"Dad loved to hike, so his major focus while I was in it was taking overnight hikes," said Charles Thomas. "Boys loved that. We would hike out to areas of undeveloped land, points on Lynnhaven Bay or somewhere, and spend the weekend, take tents and food, and hike for several hours and he would be right with us. We'd play, 'Capture the Flag.' I never saw him take a book or anything to read, and he would be right with us 100 percent, maybe twenty-five or thirty boys.

"He was terrific at telling ghost stories. The high point of those hikes was sitting around the campfire listening to his ghost stories, and he would scare the pants off us. We loved it. I think there was a grain of truth in them that made them so scary.

"He told stories about the old Wilder house [a stately mansion] about a block from where we lived. It used to have a moat around it, and there was a drawbridge over to the island where the house was. It used to be a club—Hugh Lynn used to take Sally dancing there. Before that it was owned by a man named Majory, who had a black servant who was a deaf mute—his tongue had been cut out. And Majory had all these animals—an anteater and some monkeys—on the island. After he died, bootleggers would come up there and use the deserted house, making whiskey and taking it out by boat. And there were people shot in there—revenue agents would come. There were no other houses at all around there, and Hugh Lynn would take us boys camping around there—we wouldn't go on the island but we'd camp where we could see it—and he would talk about ghosts in the house or blue light floating through the house, and he'd grab somebody and it would scare the daylights out of us."

Greg recalled his father's enthusiasm for games of all kinds. "He would come home from work and want to relax. He would always change into what we called his play clothes. He would always want to do a game or a sport—ping pong, tennis, badminton, horseshoes, swimming, or a board game. He loved all kinds of board games—Monopoly, Parcheesi, checkers, chess—anything where you had to have a little strategy to beat the other person and figure out how to win. He was good at almost all of them."

Hugh Lynn had said the same thing of his father. "Dad was good at any kind of games, especially bowling. I never saw him lose at ten pins. In Dayton we used to walk to the park and bowl on the green and play croquet."

Greg marveled at how deeply involved Hugh Lynn became when they played together. "He would get into it and really be a child with us, not a parent pretending, but really child-like with us."

A generation later his first grandchild, Charles Thomas's daughter, brought out the same quality in him. Leslie Cayce, his daughter-in-law, recalls his playing with two-year-old Corinne: "He would just sit right down on the floor and he loved to do these building blocks with Corinne. I was struck by that because by the time you are a grandparent you usually forget sitting on the floor, but he was right down there."

Greg said his dad's playfulness was one of the traits he most treasured. "He would laugh and joke and really be a companion. I think we had every game in the world. He would just wait for new games to come out to try. He watched us grow up and realized that he could teach us new games. Eventually we graduated to bridge. He taught us to play bridge when we were eleven or twelve years old, because they wanted bridge partners. It was fun for us. We played bridge more as children than we did as adults. Nobody else we knew could play bridge."

Bridge was Hugh Lynn and Sally's favorite social activity, with neighbors, close friends, and once a week with Edgar Evans and his wife, Kat. "Sally had a rule. She wouldn't talk about A.R.E. matters in her home, so that Hugh Lynn could relax," said one friend. But he used those occasions to keep his brother abreast of new developments at A.R.E.

Both Greg and Charles Thomas recall lots of talk with their dad on the subject. They both grew up feeling some discomfort about the A.R.E. because of playful taunts or questions from schoolmates. "They would ask, 'Do people really reincarnate up there?' Greg recalls. "I would go to my parents and ask, 'What do you say to people when they ask what Edgar Cayce did?' They would tell me what they would say, or suggest things I might read. They used it as a way to introduce me to the material. That wasn't always comfortable. I wanted answers and they gave me books." Another factor was that Hugh Lynn was tired of explaining the A.R.E. Greg surmised, "He gave it to others but he didn't give it to me. That's not a big gripe for someone who was giving as much as he gave. He just got tired."

Charles Thomas and Greg, five years apart, seldom talked about their father's unconventional occupation between themselves, but they experienced the A.R.E. in similar ways as boys helping their dad when he took them to his office, emptying his wastebasket and doing other odd jobs. During the summers while he was in high school and college, Greg often worked in the A.R.E.'s little library or the bookstore or in the maintenance department. "I sensed early on that he was looking for ways to make me feel comfortable being around the organization, around the people, around the philosophy, to help me step into it," says Greg. "He did that very quietly, almost ingeniously." Charles Thomas worked elsewhere, as a lifeguard at the private Cape Colony Club his last two summers in high school, saving his earnings for college.

Although Hugh Lynn was very active in the Presbyterian Church, as Sunday school teacher, elder, and deacon, and he was running an organization which emphasized personal spiritual growth, he and Sally did not inflict the "preacher's kid" syndrome on their boys. "I found it very hard to embarrass my parents, and I gave up very early," says Greg. "They didn't provide a front against which I could rebel, which confounded me. They were so kind and gentle and understanding that it was kind of like trying to rebel against Jello. There was no 'You must do this' or 'You must do that,' or 'This is the rule.' It was more a bending, sort of like they were saying, 'We know you are going to try some things, and some of them are going to be fun. But some of them you are going to pay a price for. But we aren't going to preach to you about it.'"

Writing in his diary when Greg was sixteen, Hugh Lynn expressed regret that he and Sally sometimes both "confront Greg about his activities with his friends waiting for him. Reason, quiet discussion, and agreement are far better than breaking off communication through forcing an impossible decision. It takes a great deal of wisdom to know when to insist."

Greg recalled how his parents enlisted his older brother: "They used Charles Thomas as an advocate, particularly when drugs came along. They had no idea what to do when it came to drugs. They didn't want to forbid them and they certainly didn't want to advocate using them, so they told Charles Thomas, 'Talk to your brother and explain to him what can happen when you use drugs. Tell him that it may seem exciting or fun, but that you can become schizophrenic and be checked into a mental hospital.'

"That was really helpful. He [Charles Thomas] did that. He sat me down and said there are certain experiences that a large number of people have that can be kind of interesting and frivolous, similar to alcohol, somewhat more intense sometimes, but he warned me to be very careful, especially about driving with anyone who used drugs or getting into a situation which endangered anyone's life. He told me, 'Beware, there are some people who use drugs and don't come back to a normal state, even after just smoking marijuana. The percentage is higher for people who use LSD.' That sort of set some fences for me. I felt that I had a little room to experiment, and so I never felt the need to seriously rebel. I felt sort of understood. Charles Thomas's willingness to talk about it satisfied most of my curiosity. So I didn't need to declare or fight for my identity. I'm really happy about that."

While Hugh Lynn was an adoring father, Greg grew up feeling closer to his mother. Sally was *always* there for him, and Hugh Lynn at times was not, especially when he went out on the road. "I remember vividly his tours. It was an annual event in late winter or early spring. He would just disappear. There was this huge vacancy because there were no more games," recalls Greg. "There was a real sense of loss. It was talked about and explained and rationalized, so I felt like it was his duty, helping other people. But looking back on it as an adult, I sort of regret and am jealous of the amount of time he gave to A.R.E., because so much of his passion went into the organization and the people in the organization. He gave [us] a lot, but his tank was half empty when he got home."

To help compensate, Hugh Lynn usually returned from his tours bearing presents. And when he forgot, Sally was prepared to slip gifts into his suitcase before his sons caught him empty-handed.

186

His greatest gift to his sons was his example. Both boys marveled at his way with people. "His greatest strength that I saw was his unconditional positive regard for people," said Greg. "When I was a child he would teach me that everyone was a person of great worth and that I should smile at the person before they did anything for me at all, even before they said 'Hello.' And if I was going to do something with someone, I should always look for the good that person had to offer. People just drink that up, they love it. And of course a lot of people who came to the A.R.E. didn't have a very high opinion of themselves and had some kind of need. That's been a help to me, the belief in the goodness of people."

Charles Thomas admired his father's ingenuity in working with people to help them and to achieve his own goals for the A.R.E. "He had a love of life, a sparkle that made him attractive to people. He used that to get people involved. His genius was in working with people, not in the classic psychotherapeutic sense, but in touching them right at their core, often over an extended period of time, working with them on projects they would get excited about and that helped him do what he needed to get done. He would involve them—he would use that phrase—involving people was his genius, getting them involved to use their own talents in ways that were helpful to other people. I saw him do that, not just with A.R.E., but with all kinds of people, in the Boy Scouts, in Sunday school."

Greg was also impressed by his father's "loyalty to people. If he tried to help someone, he would help that person as much as he could. And people would wear him out. We'd say, 'Why do you keep putting up with this mess? Hasn't this person made you angry, don't you just want to get rid of them?' And he'd say, 'No, let's try something else.' It was amazing."

Hugh Lynn was also notorious for his outbursts of anger, but he evidently restrained his temper at home. The reading he and Sally received shortly after their wedding had advised: "Not that there will not be periods of disturbance, but let it always be from the other—not from self. Do not both get angry at the same time. This ye can control, if ye walk with Him. Let thy ideal, then, be as it was in the days of old; that ye bring one another closer, closer to that spirit of truth, of love, of life, that is the hope, that is the way that each may contribute to the other that which is pleasing in His sight." Neither son can recall their parents quarrelling in their presence. When Sally was angry she showed it in less volatile ways. "I loved and respected Hugh Lynn a whole lot and I didn't want to bother him. He was working with people and problems all the time, and I didn't think I wanted to be a problem," Sally explained. But she didn't always let Hugh Lynn off without an instructive word or two. Confiding in his diary not long before their twenty-fifth anniversary, Hugh Lynn wrote: "Sally certainly helps me see faults, recently it has been easy—perhaps I am getting worse or careless." On one occasion Sally became so put out with her husband that she didn't speak to him for three days. He undoubtedly had it coming, for on one occasion at least he went out dancing with another woman during his wife's pregnancy, assuring her that Sally wouldn't mind.

The first outsider admitted as a member of Hugh Lynn's tribe, Charles Thomas's bride, Leslie, found relationships among the Cayces quite different from her experience growing up in a Jewish family in New York, "a family where a lot of things are out in the open, a very emotional family, stable but very interactive, both positive and negative. We give each other criticism and feedback and we argue. In contrast to that, I felt like this was a family that was very touchy on arguing and criticism and interfering, very aware of non-interfering, and I think arguments were minimal. And when any kind of feedback was given, even constructive criticism, it was given a lot of thought before it was let fly. I think that was a Hugh Lynn-and-Sally dynamic, it was not just him. In fact, Hugh Lynn was less like that than any of the other family members. I thought he seemed more open. But as a family, that was sort of their code."

With that trait, Leslie also found a strong sense of family loyalty among the Cayces, a feeling "that they can really trust each other." The code by which they lived was a mixture of Southern gentility and Cayce readings. Leslie noted:

"I think Sally brought a lot of that from her family background, and he brought from the readings the whole philosophy of focusing on the positive. Both Hugh Lynn and Sally were examples of doing that, as much as they could—focusing on the positive. In a family way, focusing on the positive means that you are very wary of all those emotions and negativity. There is the Southern gentility that feeds into that sort of thing, too. I think it was a blending of the two."

Hugh Lynn's attitude toward criticism was also colored by his experience as a child fighting those who made snide critical remarks about his father. Even as president of the A.R.E., he labored to offset criticism from the community. He was not so defensive as to miss the value of criticism, however. "Criticism is something one must learn to live with in this life," he wrote in his diary. "Taken as a basis for reevaluating whatever object is under consideration—even if it is self—can make for real growth. It is not easy, I find, to do this."

Hugh Lynn also introduced a lively sense of humor into his

family time, using it frequently to lighten up the mood during a difficult moment, often by telling a story. "He never told the same story the same way twice," said Greg with a chuckle. "Mother would call him on it, saying 'It was bigger than the last time you told it.' When he told you a story he knew exactly what would make it a better story for you, and he'd stick in a few extras and customize it. That would get him into trouble sometimes when people would get upset because he customized the story. They would say, 'Come on, it wasn't quite that way.' And he'd wink at them and push them off and say, 'Let me tell it the way I want to tell it.'"

While Sally liked her husband's outgoing personality, she sometimes had to bite her tongue when he got carried away during social gatherings. She recalled an evening when their house guests were Raynor C. Johnson, the British author of *The Imprisoned Splendour*, and his wife. Sitting on the porch after dinner, Hugh Lynn dominated the conversation so much that Sally excused herself and went into the house. A few moments later Mrs. Johnson followed her into the kitchen, put her arm around Sally and said, "You know there is a very thin line between the confidence that makes a good speaker and his egotism. And sometimes they stray over the line." Sally never forgot that wise observation. "It made me more tolerant of Hugh Lynn's egotism because no one likes a speaker who doesn't have confidence in what he is saying."

Sally didn't second-guess her husband about his work, however, and so far as her sons could tell, bore up well during his preoccupation with A.R.E. business and his long absences. She was rather like a Chinese dowager, whose home was her unchallenged domain, one friend observed, and Hugh Lynn honored her in this role. "The fact that he was away a lot gave her tremendous influence with us," said Greg. She and Hugh Lynn had worked out their territorial needs, he for doing what he felt right in his work, she for ruling the home. "She saw that he was more effective if she did not edit what he did. She wouldn't add to or subtract from whatever he did. She was just his companion to keep him mentally and physically fit to do that work," Greg concluded.

Their individual territorial rights extended to money as well. Hugh Lynn had frequently remarked on his parents' relationship in terms of money by saying it was his mother who showed common sense in handling the household accounts because Edgar had no instinct for financial management. But how was Edgar's boy with money?

"Just the same way," Sally explained. "His wife handled the

money. He was very unselfish with his money. He usually divided his income with me and he'd say, 'Now I won't ask you what you do with yours and you mustn't ask me what I do with mine.' He helped any number of people [with financial assistance]. I bought groceries and paid the bills with mine, and he helped people with his. He was very generous." If Hugh Lynn related to Sally in some of the same ways that Edgar interacted with Gertrude, Sally modestly diminished the importance of her own role by saying, "I'm not half the woman Mrs. Cayce was. I've never done half as much as she did. She kept house for a houseful of people, and she took the readings twice a day—a remarkable woman."

Sally was nonetheless an influential figure behind the scenes. Hugh Lynn used her as a sounding board. "They would get up early in the morning and I think she would pray and he would meditate, and then they would have breakfast sessions where he would counsel with her and she would counsel with him. He would ask her opinion and say 'This is what's on my plate,' and she would say, 'Have you considered what if . . . ?' Or, 'Maybe this person is trying to do that,' and give him a different point of view or perspective that I felt he couldn't get from other people. And he respected her honesty. She was very candid."

His mother's detachment from day-to-day affairs at A.R.E. allowed her to give objective advice, Greg added. "That objectivity really helped him because everyone else had an iron in the fire." Whether her opinion ever turned him in another direction was hard to know, for Hugh Lynn, a very public person, was too proud to acknowledge his wife's influence—and Sally, basically a shy, private person, was too discreet to claim it.

She would not disclaim the loving, stabilizing influence she had over her sons, however, both of whom did well in school, participating in sports, attending Sunday school, and never particularly rebellious as adolescents. A traveling man could hardly have a more worry-free family life. Hugh Lynn left no doubt of her contribution:

"Without her I could not have done what I have done, there is no question about that. I am very fortunate that I picked her instead of any of the others. She's balanced, stable, and terrific with children."

Also, there was no doubting her priorities. "I think her focus has always been on him," said Leslie. "There were a lot of reasons why she was able to stay home when he did all that traveling and support him the way that she did. I understand to a degree what he meant when he said that he couldn't have done it without her, because he had this base of support there, and she didn't give him a hard time at all about his need to do that." The late Gladys Davis, who knew them both throughout their marriage, said of Sally: "She is a strong, brave person and has made it possible for Hugh Lynn to devote his life to the furtherance of his father's work."

Chapter 16

Public Awakening
to the Sleeping Prophet

Twenty-five years after the Cayce Hospital had been shut down and the building converted to a hotel, it stood on its commanding bluff facing the sea, a bit worse for hard wear, but as sound as ever—and decidedly picturesque. Its most recent occupants, the Virginia Beach Masonic Order, had decorated the interior with symbols peculiar to its mysterious canons. If the manufacturer of Edgar's favorite cigarette had moved in, the decor would have fit. For the Shriners had departed, leaving their camels tethered indelibly in the lobby's colorful murals, palm trees, pyramids and all. The next owner, however, was to be the organization that Edgar and Hugh Lynn had founded.

When he heard that the hospital building was for sale in 1955 for $125,000, Hugh Lynn set out to buy it back and turn it into A.R.E. headquarters. It was a wild dream. The A.R.E. had the equity in the old Cayce home, which had served as headquarters for over twenty years, but the value of that property left Hugh Lynn with a huge sum to raise.

Within A.R.E. circles, Hugh Lynn's judgment came under sharp questioning. The old hospital building, having housed one failure after another, seemed jinxed. Even the realtor admitted that. It had been a resort hotel, a nightclub, a summer theater, a nurses' home during World War II, and a clubhouse for Shriners. It was easy to argue that, all sentimentality aside, this was a white elephant that the A.R.E. could not afford. Would the A.R.E. itself fail, like the Cayce Hospital, if it bought the old building?

"Some people were violently opposed to it. There was no money. I couldn't do anything except get the votes to buy it."

When he put the issue to the board of trustees, he was voted down. But manager Cayce refused to accept that decision.

"We didn't have enough room at Arctic Crescent, no land to expand, no parking space. But they wanted to stay small, add a little bit at a time. I wanted to reach out, all over the world."

The second time he brought up the issue he was voted down again. But Hugh Lynn's determination was greater than the board's resistance. He also went over the board's head and started a prayer vigil. Every day at 11:00 a.m. he led the A.R.E. staff in prayer that God's will might be done. Hugh Lynn had no doubt what God's will was in this case. Before another buyer appeared, he won the board's approval to look for the financial means of acquiring the property. A woman from Florida, Marguerite Briggs, made it possible for Hugh Lynn to sign the sales contract by putting up $5,000. She had made a lot of money as a gladiolus grower, and claimed that once when most growers' blooms were wiped out by a frost, hers were saved after she prayed over them. She later moved to the Beach and lived in rooms on an upper floor of the new headquarters.

In seeking a mortgage, Hugh Lynn traded on his good reputation as a scoutmaster. It served as an entree to the city's most important people, many of whose sons had benefited by his leadership. He had taken his scouts on wonderful tours of the country. Then he went to a bank on whose board Sally's brother, Dr. Taylor served. "There was no favoritism. Waller was a tough businessman," said Sally. "He and his wife would come over for bridge but never talk shop. When Hugh Lynn came home and told me he had borrowed the money to buy back the hospital, I was horrified. Hugh Lynn calmed me down though. It was his confidence that did it. And my brother told me that he made every payment on time—I don't know how."

Hugh Lynn turned over financial management of the A.R.E. that year to Robert A. Adriance, who was vice president of an insurance company before volunteering his services. "The budget of the A.R.E. was about $20,000 then," recalls Adriance, "there were only about five people on the payroll. Hugh Lynn made $300 a month." Five years later in 1961 Adriance was succeeded as treasurer by a certified public accountant, J. Everett Irion, who increased Hugh Lynn's salary to $400 a month. In contrast to the high salaries of many so-called spiritual leaders, Hugh Lynn never drew more than a modest income from the organization he headed. His top salary was $17,000, Irion recalled.

A wealthy real estate man from California and his wife, Joseph and Dorothy Cordak, eventually loaned A.R.E. $80,000 to pay off the

194

mortgage on the old hospital and were repaid without interest. Adriance was another generous contributor. He recalls selling a block of his personal stock for $13,500 and contributing the proceeds to the A.R.E. to make one payment to settle its debt on the headquarters. By renting out rooms on the old building's upper floors, clustering some of them into apartments, some income was generated to help with mortgage payments.

Cordak was a major investor later when Hugh Lynn recommended purchasing the Marshalls Hotel, across the street from the old hospital. Others included William Lord, who later gave his stock to the A.R.E., Rufus Mosely, and Tom Kay, who became manager of the hotel. Hugh Lynn wanted friendly owners who would manage it to the advantage of A.R.E. members.

As for renovating the old hospital, it made a splendid headquarters. Hugh Lynn made his office on the main floor just off the lobby. A small library was established on the opposite side of the lobby. Gladys, business manager Bob Adriance, and a few employees took over the lower levels, where a vault was installed to house the readings safely. "We called it the dungeon," recalled Mary Ellen Carter, who worked part-time as secretary to Hugh Lynn and was later to become editor of *The Searchlight*. The upstairs residential guests included a former concert singer, Lydia J. Schrader Gray, who exchanged her apartment at the old Cayce house for a choice suite on the second floor with a view of the ocean. Lydia moved in her oriental rugs and grandfather's clock and quickly became the *grande dame* of the new headquarters. A striking-looking, chain-smoking widow in her mid-seventies, she collected yellow stamps to be redeemed for lamps and chairs, some of them unfinished, to furnish the place. She took on beautifying the grounds as a personal mission—and gave numerological readings in her apartment, devoting the proceeds to her cause.

"Hugh Lynn couldn't handle her," Mrs. Shelley noted. "He would remark good-naturedly, 'We say we don't endorse psychics, but we have Lydia upstairs.'" Her tobacco habit seemed not to have impaired her longevity. She lived into her nineties and once remarked, "I think I've forgotten how to die."

Ruth Lenoir, another widow, took up residence there also, and for years led the Glad Helpers weekly healing prayer meetings on the top floor. One night an intruder broke into the building looking for a place to sleep. Not knowing anyone lived there, he was awakened by sleep-walking Mrs. Lenoir, a tall, wraith-like figure. Certain that the old place was haunted, he shrieked, waking Ruth, and beat a quick retreat.

A third lady resident was tiny, bird-like Olive Landers, who had previously been involved in Campfire Girls work. As editor of *The Bulletin* in the 1950s and later the A.R.E. *News*, Miss Landers' good-hearted work reflected her adolescent orientation.

A succession of idealistic young people such as Bob Clapp, a schoolteacher, and Henry Bolduc, who was interested in hypnotism, also occupied rooms there in later years. Bolduc recalls that he arrived on the scene one evening and went to Hugh Lynn's house because it was after working hours. "He was all dressed up ready to take his wife out to dinner," recalled Henry, who was then eighteen, "but he was just so nice about it, and took me up to the A.R.E. and fixed me up with a room." Having rented rooms in the old Cayce house to loyal members, the A.R.E. readily filled the upper floors with residents until the organization's growing office staff needed the space. It all helped meet the mortgage payments.

More important than just making its payments, the A.R.E. suddenly took on a new image among its members. Like troops retaking ground lost in an earlier skirmish, its spiritual soldiers enjoyed a sense of triumph. They had regained the heights once held and lost by their illustrious founding father. "Capturing it was a courageous and symbolic step," said Harmon Bro.

If this was a solidifying tactic for the organization internally, it did little to establish the A.R.E. within the local community. Just as Hugh Lynn had once been teased by playmates about his "freak" father, now Hugh Lynn's sons had to endure taunts about the "spook house" on the hill. The A.R.E. would be a long time overcoming that stigma. But Hugh Lynn tried, first by establishing "an image committee," chaired by Mary Ellen Carter. "It was to offset the negative things that were said about us," explained Mrs. Carter. "We were 'the nuts on the hill.'" A former reporter for the local afternoon newspaper, Mrs. Carter tried to become an effective emissary to the community on behalf of the A.R.E. "Hugh Lynn was trying to make us more acceptable in the community and better understood. But we had a hard time convincing the people that we weren't ghost chasers and weren't having seances, which is what people had heard. We felt very uncomfortable with the stigma that we had." As a liaison between the A.R.E. and the local news media, Mrs. Carter inspired a number of interviews with Hugh Lynn that helped to break the ice.

Another of Hugh Lynn's efforts in this direction was the Sunday Forum. Open to the public, the forum offered a speaker on an engaging topic each Sunday afternoon. The lectures were initially given in the spacious entrance lobby, which had been refurbished with funds donated by a Study Group in Dallas, Texas. After the lecture, the guests were invited into the library [now occupied by the Study Group department] for coffee and cookies. When an adjacent building was erected in the 1960s, equipped with a small auditorium, the forum used those facilities. Violet and Jack Shelley, as volunteers, managed the forum for some years. "Jack took up the collection, and we washed the china after everyone left," recalled Mrs. Shelley. "Every Monday Hugh Lynn held a critique, for the idea was to introduce the A.R.E. to the community." He and his brother were among the regular speakers. Edgar Evans gave "one of the best talks I've ever heard him give," Hugh Lynn confided to his diary one stormy winter Sunday in 1964. "The emphasis on philosophy and spiritual concepts was especially good. The rain, a real blowing storm, cut the crowd to about forty-five. Considering the weather this was good." As many as seventy-five sometimes attended.

As interest in the organization grew in later years, a free daily lecture replaced the weekly forum, and continues today.

The same year, 1956, that he bought the hospital, Hugh Lynn received his first telephone call from a New York newspaperman named Jess Stearn. If the 1950s were years of groping, arguing, regrouping, and trying to find a place in the sun for the A.R.E., it was the beginning, too, of a new awakening to the world of the spirit.

The circumstances that led Stearn to call Hugh Lynn can be traced to Harold Reilly's health club in Manhattan. Dr. Reilly one evening introduced two of his regular clients, Stearn and Dave Kahn. Stearn had earlier told Reilly he was working on a Sunday feature story about clairvoyants. When Reilly mentioned that to Kahn, Dave asked, "Are you going to include anything on Cayce?"

"I said, 'Casey who?'

"Kahn said, 'Cayce—C-A-Y-C-E, the greatest mystic who ever lived in America.'

"I told him I'd never heard of him," said Stearn.

Apparently Stearn had not read a popular book by Morey Bernstein, *The Search for Bridey Murphy*, which described Cayce's amazing talents—and his stories of past lives.

A street-wise reporter who had worked on the New York *World-Telegram* before going over to the *Daily News*, Stearn was a feature writer who did human interest stories. Raised by his grandparents in Syracuse, New York—his grandfather was an antique dealer—he grew up in a non-denominational Christian environment, married a Methodist girl, went to Newark for his first newspaper job on the *Star-Ledger*, and then to New York City where the couple and their two children attended a Lutheran church because it was the only

Protestant congregation in their area. Stearn felt no particular allegiance to any denomination or creed. "I came from a very open-minded home. I just believed since I was a teenager in an active Christianity based on the teachings of Christ."

Four years before he heard of Cayce, Stearn had his first encounter with a psychic. At that point, "I didn't believe in any of it. I didn't have anything to do with anyone who went to a fortune teller." In a supper club he was approached by a woman who described herself as a sensitive and asked if he wanted a reading. Stearn brushed her off until she expressed sympathy for his having recently gone through a divorce, with two young children. Jess was amazed that a stranger would know such intimate details of his life, so he got a reading and was told his children would turn out fine—his boy getting involved with law enforcement, his daughter as a healer. She also predicted he would write books, that his third book would become a best-seller and his eighth book would be spread around the world.

While he couldn't know immediately how accurate her predictions would be, the experience aroused Stearn's curiosity about clairvoyance. Later she would be proven right: his son became a policeman, his daughter a doctor, and Jess Stearn became a prolific author.

His early books were devoted more to age-old questions than New Age concepts. First there was *Sisters of the Night*, a variation on the theme of Hugh Lynn's first Broadway show, "Ladies of the Evening." His third book, just like the psychic had predicted, made Jess Stearn a best-selling author. It was *The Sixth Man*, about homosexuality.

That night in Reilly's gym Stearn listened to Kahn talk about Edgar Cayce's ability to diagnose ailments of people at long distance and prescribe remedies. "He didn't say anything about reincarnation at that point, or I probably would have backed off," Stearn recalls. "He told me to call Hugh Lynn for more information."

Stearn got enough information from Hugh Lynn to add a few paragraphs to his article. "I just wrote what they claimed," said Stearn, who didn't get excited about a dead psychic when there were so many live ones around to interview.

Stearn might have forgotten about Cayce meanwhile but for his many conversations with Dr. Reilly. "Harry was like a father to me. I went in three times a week. He had clients like [Edward R.] Stettinius, the secretary of state [under Roosevelt and Truman in 1944-45], Rickenbacker, Boris Karloff, Bing Crosby, Bob Hope—I saw them all. It was probably the classiest gym in America. He told me he was using Cayce's techniques, but he never advertised that because he had many doctors coming to him as clients and he was afraid it might affect his business."

While working on *Door to the Future*, Stearn made his first visit to A.R.E. headquarters. Hugh Lynn had worked hard to persuade Stearn to come see for himself, for by now it was second nature to Hugh Lynn to play the role of super salesman for his father, not just with the people he met on his lecture circuits but those who could make a big difference if they would only look into it.

"I'd do anything that was necessary to get them to do it. It took a good deal where Jess Stearn was concerned—a lot of selling and ego padding and challenging. He was a hard-nosed newspaper reporter, didn't believe in psychics. I'm sure I lied to him to get him to come down here and look, and then I persuaded him to really look at the readings."

After his first visit, Stearn devoted a chapter or two of *The Door to the Future* to Cayce's forecasts of earth changes. That book also introduced Jeanne Dixon to the public, but it was not a big seller. Stearn followed with *Yoga, Youth and Reincarnation*, which took off like a rocket, sold more books than anything he ever wrote, and firmly established him as a New Age author.

Meanwhile in the early 1960s, Hugh Lynn wrote his own book, *Venture Inward*. Tying it to the sudden popularity of psychedelic drugs, he argued that there were better ways of exploring the psyche. Published in hardback by Harper & Row in 1964, it received a glowing review from an unexpected critic, Daniel Poling, editor of the conservative *Christian Herald* magazine, who wrote: "It is a sane and sensible guide to the powers and perils of psychic experience. In my opinion, it is the number one book in its field."

Hugh Lynn undoubtedly earned that accolade by his condemnation of drugs, automatic writing, ouija boards, and Ron Hubbard's Dianetics and Scientology movement. Calling them all "dangerous doorways to the unconscious," Hugh Lynn wrote:

"All the various doorways to the unconscious seem to indicate the existence of areas and powers of the mind we do not yet understand. Fortunately, for the average person, movement through some of the doorways is difficult; thus dangers associated with them are reduced. Ouija boards and moving pencils are tedious and dull. Mescaline is expensive and frequently makes one sick. Mushrooms are hard to secure. There are still too many questions to be answered about LSD for it to be widely used. For the average person perhaps there are better, safer avenues to the inner world."

He recommended meditation and studying one's own dreams

as safe doorways to the inner life. At a time when President Kennedy had launched a program to put men on the moon and explore outer space, Hugh Lynn wrote:

"Venturing into space will surely extend man's knowledge of the universe. Venturing inward to an equally vast unknown area may bring radical, perhaps even greater, changes in his knowledge and understanding of the universe and himself."

The purpose of venturing inward, he said, was not simply greater awareness or self-improvement. The rewards he perceived were:

"Powers of mind and spirit may bring a richer life; control of the negative self, which would destroy man, seems possible; belief in life beyond the period of body confinement can become acceptable; the world of matter can be considered as an extension, a projection, of the world of mind; and, finally, personal experiences of the mind and spirit bring a new kind of relationship with one's fellow men and the Force called God. Indeed, God may be said to take over the life and fulfill His purpose in and through man."

Hugh Lynn was pleased by the generally favorable reaction to his book, especially that of the distinguished Anglican churchman and author, Leslie D. Weatherhead. A member of the Society for Psychical Research in London, Dr. Weatherhead called the book "well written and enlightening." He found it also timely, saying: "I feel certain that soon men will grow tired of the exploration of the physical aspects of the universe and turn to what is vaguely called 'psychic research.' Here a vast continent awaits discovery, with rewards to the honest and sincere investigator, more enriching to the highest welfare of humanity than the exploration of mountain tops or desert wastes, or even the moon and the planets."

Publication of the book attracted national attention to the author when he appeared on NBC's "Today" show in the morning and the "Tonight" show with Jack Paar. It enhanced his reputation locally too. After his book was published, at age fifty-seven, Hugh Lynn was named First Citizen of Virginia Beach for 1964 by the Junior Chamber of Commerce. The Jaycees cited the A.R.E., his book, and "thousands of boy scouts" of Troop 60 as "a few tangible monuments to his contributions." He had been awarded the Silver Beaver Award by the Tidewater Boy Scouts Council in 1959.

Remarkably, his certificate of merit that hangs in city hall pays tribute to his spiritual achievements: "For his unique capacity and selfless effort in developing, after years of study and research, a deep understanding of the mental and spiritual powers of man; for sharing his internationally recognized insights with all manner of men, through individual counseling, participating in church and

200

civic groups and lecturing before university and other audiences; for bringing support, experimentation and study to the psychic science, in the course of which he and all mankind have been elevated to a closer personal identity with the mighty acts of God."

For a man with such an outrageously unconventional occupation to win this award from mainstream businessmen in conservative Virginia was extraordinary. If any doubt remained that he had won the respect of the local dinosaurs, a letter from Sidney S. Kellam, the local chieftain of Harry Byrd's political machine, was among the many congratulatory messages that poured in. "Our city is fortunate to have people like you living here," said Kellam. It was money in the bank of community goodwill for the A.R.E. and its leader.

The success of *Venture Inward* inspired Hugh Lynn to think of writing more books, including one about his father, but it remained for a professional journalist, Jess Stearn, to turn Edgar Cayce into a cult hero. After the success of his yoga book, Stearn began a new book with the working title, *The Psychic Age*, but he couldn't get it to gel. His publisher's sales representative in California suggested that a whole book about Cayce would be more interesting. Stearn agreed, but pointed out that Sugrue had already done such a book. His publisher thought otherwise, because Jess would do it differently, so he abandoned *The Psychic Age* in favor of a Cayce book. That night, after returning to New York from the West Coast, he says he received a telephone call at 1 a.m. from a New York psychic, Madame Bathsheba, whom he had once written about. "She said Edgar Cayce had come to her and told her he was pleased that I was going to write the book, and he said it should be called *The Sleeping Prophet*."

Having discussed his new book idea with no one but his publisher, he was impressed. He went on to Virginia Beach to gather material, this time staying the winter, living in an empty oceanfront hotel, listening to stories told by Hugh Lynn and Gladys, interviewing people who had had readings, and researching the readings. Hugh Lynn tried to steer Jess in the "right" direction:

"I showed him the ones I wanted him to see. I was very careful that he didn't see the ones I didn't want him to see."

Stearn recalls that everyone was helpful. "I was in the old library reading one day when Hugh Lynn showed me a reading that said, 'Be helpful to Stern [sic] when he comes down from New York because he can help the organization financially.' Later he showed me another reading that said, 'Have Kahn tell Stern about the work.' I looked at it and felt water in my stomach because Kahn was the one who first told me about the whole thing. That sort of electrified me."

No one bothered him except the ladies who lived upstairs. They were concerned when they learned that this visiting author didn't believe in reincarnation. "For my own good they set about trying to convince me. This distressed Hugh Lynn because he knew it was annoying me, so he put up a notice that no one was to try to dissuade anyone else of their beliefs. He didn't mention any names."

Completing his research in six months, Jess Stearn knocked out a first draft in three weeks—one chapter a day. When he turned it in, his editor at Doubleday "wasn't crazy about it. I revised and quickened it, which was just normal procedure. I showed it to Hugh Lynn, and he said, 'Well, it's interesting but it's not up to Tom's book.' He didn't object to anything in it though."

The public loved it. The Sleeping Prophet hit the best-seller list and stayed there for months. "My book in three weeks sold more than all the copies of 'There Is a River,'" boasted Jess, still smarting a bit over Hugh Lynn's unfavorable comparison. In twenty-eight weeks it sold 99,000 copies. It was serialized by Ladies Home Journal. The timing of the book during the counter-culture movement of the late 1960s was propitious. To many young people who heard about him, Cayce became a guru. The idea of this straitlaced Presbyterian Sunday school teacher gaining admirers among the hippies delighted Hugh Lynn, who had a special feeling for young people and was willing to spend lots of time counseling those who came to him.

Whether it was just good timing or good journalism, or both, there is no questioning the commanding impact of Stearn's book. At least five books devoted to Cayce had been published between There Is a River in 1942 and Stearn's 1967 hit, but none of them had succeeded sufficiently to make the subject well known. The resounding impact of The Sleeping Prophet could be seen immediately in the increasing number of visitors to A.R.E. headquarters. A.R.E. membership increased so rapidly that Hugh Lynn at last could feel momentum in the upswing. His road trips and lectures and patient counseling had slowly but impressively increased the membership one hundred-fold since his father's death. But overnight, it seemed, fame worked wonders: in the one year following publication of Stearn's book more members joined than in the 20 years previous to that. Membership climbed from 3,000 to 6,600.

It was not Stearn's book alone that did it, of course, but the success of that book had a ripple effect in the publishing trade. Rival publishers rushed into print with Cayce books. Gina Cerminara's Many Mansions, published originally in hardback in 1950, was reprinted in 1967 between paperback covers that emphasized it as "the Edgar Cayce Story." Her book is a lucid account of Cayce's reincarnation theme. Actually, her manuscript was so long that her publisher turned it into two books. *Many Mansions*, followed by *Many Lives, Many Loves*, was destined to inspire many readers, to be published in many languages, and remain in print for decades, a major resource in the building of the Cayce legend. Hugh Lynn's introduction noted that "Dr. Cerminara suggests that 'there is nothing so powerful as an idea whose time has come.' *Many Mansions* certainly has opened the way for what seems to be one such idea."

The plethora of Cayce books in the next few years confirmed his point. But Hugh Lynn didn't just sit back and marvel at this miraculous turn of events. He was instrumental in its happening, for he worked out a deal with a paperback publisher to supply manuscripts. The first book was *Edgar Cayce on Reincarnation* by Noel Langley, a charming, six-foot-five-inch British screenwriter who had moved to Virginia Beach because of his interest in Cayce. A facile writer, Langley had directed the film, *The Search for Bridey Murphy*, from a script he wrote based on Morey Bernstein's 1956 best-seller. The movie flopped after *Life* magazine disparaged its reincarnation theme. Langley was also involved in *The Wizard of Oz*, serving as the last of several directors brought in to produce this classic Judy Garland hit.

Hugh Lynn wisely recognized that Langley was a valuable resource, thus he asked him to write the first of the many Edgar Cayce spin-off books. Langley's approach to reincarnation was less philosophical than dramatic. As Hugh Lynn noted in the introduction, it told stories from readings that dipped into people's past lives and psychological problems. "Such subjects as deep-seated fears, mental blocks, vocational talents, marriage difficulties, child training, etc., are examined in the light of what Edgar Cayce called the 'karmic patterns' arising out of previous lives spent by an individual soul on this earth," said Hugh Lynn.

"I think Hugh Lynn gave him practically all the stories he used, right out of the readings," said Violet Shelley who was then editor of the A.R.E. *Journal* and a friend of Langley's. Included was Hugh Lynn's own story, under the fictitious name, Anthony Hollis, of the girlfriend who ran off with his friend.

Langley's book did extremely well, kicking off the "Edgar Cayce on . . ." series with a bang. It made possible the publication of a number of books by people recruited by Hugh Lynn who had never been authors before, including his brother. Edgar Evans Cayce wrote on the fascinating topic of Atlantis. Again, Hugh Lynn wrote the introduction, explaining that the Atlantis readings on which the book was based were "some of the most controversial readings given during Cayce's remarkable life...describing past lives in Atlantis as if they were experiences in early England or early America....They are the most fantastic, the most bizarre, the most impossible information in the Edgar Cayce files."

Hugh Lynn acknowledged that skepticism might dictate selecting only the readings one could validate to demonstrate that his father was truly psychic rather than simply imagining things. That was out of the question with respect to Atlantis, the so-called lost continent which has never been found. Long before Cayce, the Atlantean legend, dating at least back to Plato in ancient Greece, had intrigued many people. Hugh Lynn tried to establish that his father's information had come from another source: "My brother, the author, and I know that Edgar Cayce did not read Plato's material on Atlantis, or books on Atlantis, and that he, so far as we knew, had absolutely no knowledge of this subject. If his unconscious fabricated this material or wove it together from existing legends and writings, we believe that it is the most amazing example of a telepathic-clairvoyant scanning of existing legends and stories in print or of the minds of persons dealing with the Atlantis theory. As my brother and I have said from time to time, life would be simpler if Edgar Cayce had never mentioned Atlantis."

In a sense, the Cayce brothers had adopted a daring strategy in publishing the incredible Atlantis material on the heels of Stearn's book. Hugh Lynn candidly explained their decision in his introduction: "...before others can point to these readings as unbelievable and impossible, here is the whole story. As the author has pointed out, there is a strange consistency within the hundreds of psychic readings given over a period of twenty years. They will take you back into prerecorded history to lands of myth and legend, and forward into a future of literally earth-shaking changes...[into] a totally new account of man on earth and a new concept of his relationship to God and his fellow men...you may never be able to return to our so-called 'real world of facts' without the nagging suspicion that the fantastic events depicted just might be tainted with truth. Your suspicion may grow into something resembling conviction if Edgar Cayce's predictions for the next few years come to pass."

It was a good gamble. The Atlantis book also did well, selling year in and year out for the next two decades.

A few months later came *Edgar Cayce on Dreams* by Harmon Bro, who had long since received his Ph.D. from the University of Chicago after the acceptance of his dissertation on Cayce entitled:

"The Charisma of the Seer: A study in the phenomonology of religious leadership." A psychologist, Dr. Bro analyzed the many readings in which dreams had been interpreted. "Here is the first popular study of these readings," said Hugh Lynn's introduction. "It is designed not only to present the challenging new concepts on dreams which are contained in this psychic's unusual approach to the subject, but also to enable the reader to apply these ideas in working with his own daily dream material."

About the same time Hugh Lynn had got Bro under contract to do the dream book, he had a call from his traveling companion, Elsie Sechrist, who was then living in Houston. Hugh Lynn valued Elsie for her help in organizing study groups in New York and California, and for her lecturing ability. Now she wanted to be a writer.

As she tells the story, following the success of Stearn's book she began work on a book based on her own acquaintance with Edgar Cayce, whom she had met two years before his death. While writing a chapter about Cayce's ability to interpret dreams, she says that a voice she believes was her guardian angel told her, "Drop this and do a whole book on dreams."

Elsie was intrigued with that idea because all of her life she had been directed or warned by her dreams. As a child in Bristol, Connecticut, she had dreams she knew were important, but she had no one to discuss them with—until she met Edgar, who helped her understand these nocturnal experiences. She had learned to heed her dreams while studying to be a nurse. Engaged at the time, she dreamed one night that her fiance had come to her and confessed that he had been unfaithful. "If you marry me, I'll make your life hell on earth," he said in the dream. She didn't want to believe it but she had to find out—and she discovered that her dream was true. She broke the engagement and soon after met Wilfred (Bill) Sechrist, the man she later married and lived with for fifty-seven years.

Dreams had saved her life and her husband's on several occasions, she felt sure, and so the idea of writing a book on that subject was appealing. When she called Hugh Lynn, he tried to talk her out of it, since he already had Harmon Bro working on a dream book. Also, he had no reason to believe that Elsie could write.

Elsie, who believed that she had been Rembrandt's wife Saskia in a previous life, thought her dream guidance was better than Hugh Lynn's on this subject—and she went ahead with her own dream book.

To his credit, Hugh Lynn didn't stand in her way. Instead, he helped make her book a success by recruiting Noel Langley to turn her material into a smoothly-written manuscript. Hugh Lynn also wrote a foreword in which he paid tribute to the author: "Of the thousands of persons who knew and believed they were helped by Edgar Cayce, Elsie Sechrist . . . has done as much as anyone I know to help bring Edgar Cayce's insights to other thousands who now can test his ideas in their own lives."

Dreams, Your Magic Mirror was published in 1968 as a hardback, the same year that Bro's *Edgar Cayce on Dreams* was published in paperback. A year later, Elsie's book was issued in paperback and sales took off.

"You know it became such a best seller, I made a quarter of a million dollars on that book—and Hugh Lynn never admitted he was wrong," said Elsie.

Dr. Bro and the other authors of the "Edgar Cayce on . . . " series didn't do as well because Hugh Lynn had them locked into book contracts that divided the authors' royalties with the A.R.E.—not a fifty:fifty split, but twenty-five:seventy-five, with his organization getting the lion's share. It was the first major opportunity he had found for fortifying the A.R.E.'s meager finances, and he was determined to make the most of it.

While the book deal showed Hugh Lynn's canny knack for negotiation, he felt sure he was on the right track because some of his father's readings about The Work had said specifically that the organization would benefit by the income from publications. For years he had nursed along the publications branch, getting anyone who could put two sentences together to write booklets which were sold to members for a nominal sum. Mass-market paperback book sales were another league altogether. And the authors in the end did well, too, because their books continued to sell for many years, partially because the A.R.E. developed a book-marketing division that kept the Cayce titles alive and moving.

Dr. Bro followed with a second—and one of the most profound books—in the series, *Edgar Cayce on Religion and Psychic Experience.* As Hugh Lynn described it in the introduction, the book focused on several hundred readings on spiritual laws which were used as the basis of the A.R.E. Study Group program. He recommended it to "ministers of all faiths." Other books that flowed through Hugh Lynn's writing mill included one on prophecy by Mary Ellen Carter,and one on healing by the same author in collaboration with Dr. William A. McGarey, an Arizona physician. "It was Hugh Lynn's idea. I called him one day to see if he had any secretarial work I could do," said Mrs. Carter, a former newspaper feature writer for the Norfolk *Ledger-Dispatch* who had also been a part-time secretary to

Hugh Lynn. "And he said, 'No, but how would you like to write a book?'" Mrs. Carter was thrilled at the prospect. Other books, on health and diet, on the Dead Sea Scrolls, on Jesus, on attitudes and emotions, on ESP, and on prayer followed. Some twenty Cayce books were issued within a few years, most of them inspired by Hugh Lynn.

As editor of this whole series, he had acted swiftly to seize the advantage of popular interest before it waned. It meant working long hours, poring over manuscripts, often in the silence of the night. He was so prone to get up in the wee hours and work that he moved into the guest room. Teenager Charles Thomas, quick to notice that his parents were sleeping apart, questioned his father, who assured him it was not for lack of affection but out of consideration for the boy's mother, whose sleep was disturbed when he restlessly got up and prowled around.

When his publisher, elated over sales, wanted more manuscripts, Hugh Lynn asked the editor of the A.R.E. *Journal,* Violet Shelley, to select some material. A former English teacher who had started out doing volunteer work around headquarters, Violet put together a collection of Edgar's lectures, along with a number of essays she and others had written for the *Journal. The Edgar Cayce Reader* came out in January 1969, followed in six months by *The Edgar Cayce Reader #2,* containing articles chosen—and for the most part written—by Hugh Lynn.

The books overlapped only to a degree, for Cayce had given readings on virtually every topic under the sun. Writing a fresh Cayce book was largely a task of marshalling the information topically from hundreds of separate readings. Unfortunately, some of the books were difficult to read and harder to understand because they were long on quoting passages from readings and short on explanatory narrative.

Nonetheless, the awakening of the book publishing world to the popular appeal of Edgar Cayce had a tremendous impact. It was reflected in subsidiary publications, mostly magazines and the Sunday features sections of daily newspapers. Even the Bible Belt newspapers recognized a good story when it came along, no matter how controversial psychic behavior might be among religious fundamentalists. *The Nashville Tennessean* magazine published a series about the "amazing Kentuckian whose mystical exploits in the realm of healing, clairvoyance, and transience into times past and future still baffle scientists and men of medicine." Up North it was the same. The Detroit *News* magazine said, "the lure of 'the sleeping prophet' is greater in death than life." Even the sophisticated *New*

York Times Book Review couldn't ignore what it dubbed "The Cayce Industry."

Among the literary efforts that benefited by the sudden boom in Cayce books was Hugh Lynn's own, *Venture Inward*, published three years before Stearn's book. Reissued in paperback, it went through seven printings over the next four years and became the springboard for Hugh Lynn's appearance on the "Today" show on NBC television, and other national and local programs.

Not all of his potential authors went gladly to the task. Shirley Winston, a professional singer, said she gave up her musical career to move to Virginia Beach and get into the Cayce readings. "But from the first day I arrived, Hugh Lynn was on my back about doing a book on music. I didn't want to have anything to do with music. He'd say, 'Do some chants.' Well, chanting to an opera singer is like . . ." She shook her head in disgust. "It was very much beneath my dignity. But he kept after me about it and I thought I'd learn one of those darned chants and do the book just to get him off me."

And she did. After writing *Music Is the Bridge*, Shirley said, "Now I'd rather chant than anything. He gave me back music."

In 1971 Hugh Lynn and his brother collaborated on another book, *The Outer Limits of Edgar Cayce's Power*, in which they candidly discussed their father's psychic failures—attempts to find buried treasure and oil, and the kidnapped Lindbergh baby. It was an effort to define the boundaries between the areas in which his psychic gift worked well, such as medical diagnosis, and those in which it misfired. But this book flopped, apparently because people weren't interested in what went wrong so much as they were looking for answers or new insights based on what went right.

On the whole, the quality of the new Cayce literature was mixed, even if the material was promising. Hugh Lynn's own first book, *Venture Inward*, was much better than many of those he nudged into print. If little of the writing would match Sugrue's lyrical prose, it served a different need. It stimulated widespread interest in everything from home remedies and meditation to reincarnation and exploration for the lost continent of Atlantis. It helped birth a renaissance of thought in the United States, a New Age of openness to matters of the spirit.

The success of Stearn's *The Sleeping Prophet* made the author a part of the A.R.E. community. He and Hugh Lynn became quite close—"We were like brothers," says Stearn. The author felt that the book's success had been the fulfillment of another of the long-ago predictions in his first psychic reading—that his eighth book would be read around the world. But there was still another of that

208

psychic's predictions that intrigued Jess. It was that he would become involved in making a movie about Cayce's life. He has been trying to fulfill that forecast ever since.

In 1974 he published his second Cayce book, A *Prophet In His Own Country*, which was a dramatization of the young Edgar Cayce's life. His purpose was to use it as the basis of a film script. The book proved to be a headache to write, however, because he had entered into an agreement in advance with Hugh Lynn: in return for the exclusive cooperation of the A.R.E. hierarchy and family in doing a movie, he would share in the financial returns and consult with them on what he wrote. An informal committee was formed, composed of Gladys Davis and Edgar's two sons, Hugh Lynn and Edgar Evans, to review his manuscript. Stearn said "we had a couple of altercations" over how his father should be portrayed. "Hugh Lynn was trying to protect the aura of his father, but Edgar Evans saw the need to make him look like a human being. He thought I was making his father look too nice."

Although Stearn had moved to Malibu, California, and become acquainted with a number of film celebrities, he found Hollywood much tougher to crack than the book publishing business. He and a young producer, Henry Gellis, who wanted to do the film, couldn't find sufficient investors. They shared that dilemma with many others—writers, directors, and producers—who expressed interest in filming the Cayce story, but couldn't put the project together. It was one of the last great hopes of Hugh Lynn's life—one that he would not live to see fulfilled.

Perhaps as remarkable as the surging interest in Edgar Cayce long after his death is the influence that Hugh Lynn exercised in the shaping of the public image of his father. In all of the scores of books devoted partially or entirely to Cayce, there is almost nothing negative about the man beyond noting a few peculiar failings such as absent-mindedly buying a fishing rod with the rent money. For any public figure in America to become the subject of so much writing without inspiring at least one author's ire or skepticism is a miracle to match some that he himself performed.

This phenomenon can be traced partially to some of the circumstances that inspired the Cayce literature, starting with *There Is a River*. The Cayces loved the author, nursed him, and fed him while he wrote it in their home. And he was grateful to them, especially to Hugh Lynn, who helped him rewrite it to meet his publisher's requirements. This authorized biography then became a prime source for other writers who got interested after Cayce's death made it impossible for them to interview the subject. The best they could do was interview Hugh Lynn and his staff. Thus the second biography, Joseph Millard's *Mystery Man of Miracles* in 1956, is just as adoring as Sugrue's. It was deemed unacceptable around the A.R.E., however, because it claimed too much. Millard wrote that on one occasion Edgar had levitated, which Hugh Lynn and Gladys feared would turn public interest into disbelief, even though Edgar himself had claimed it in an unpublished memoir that he dictated to Gladys. That memoir had been given to Millard by Mae Gimbert after Hugh Lynn, while out of town, instructed her to help him with his research. Mae, whose whole family had had readings from Cayce, talked so freely with the author about their experiences with the psychic that he included much of her personal story in the book. That, too, infuriated Hugh Lynn when he saw the manuscript before it was published. He tried to influence the author and publisher to make changes, without much success. When it was published it was derisively referred to as "Mae's book." Without A.R.E. approval, Millard's book died, with no regrets from Hugh Lynn and Gladys.

Ironically, Hugh Lynn's one setback in dealing with the flood of Cayce books was not a caustic anti-Cayce diatribe, but one he feared was a tad too sensational. It evidently had no ill effect on the public's growing interest in the psychic or his philosophy. Many major publishers released pro-Cayce books; and a film, when it is made, will undoubtedly be based on one of those admiring manuscripts. Not even saints and emperors can expect to fare that well in the modern media.

Chapter 17

Hugh Lynn's Monuments: The Library, the A.R.E. Clinic

The avalanche of Cayce books in the late 1960s and early 1970s inspired a strong show of public interest in the A.R.E., and a need to improve its program and expand its staff. It wasn't enough to welcome visitors and hand them a booklet or two as though the A.R.E. were a museum. But what was it? And what kind of an organization did Hugh Lynn want it to become, now that Edgar Cayce's name was gaining widespread recognition?

Harmon Bro, who had observed the A.R.E.'s maturation for forty years, said Hugh Lynn recognized that he needed to "do much more than proclaim or announce. Evangelism, even for a New Age, would not carry him very far. He needed concrete processes, capable of healing and changing lives."

What kind of processes and what sort of program?

"Here Hugh Lynn came upon a split deep in the American soul, the split between science and religion; the engineer and the saint warring for leadership," said Bro, noting that the readings drew freely on both. "They were painstakingly technical and medical, yet just as earnestly and thoroughly theological." But the A.R.E. would have to tilt in one direction or the other.

"He chose science. He hired psychologists for his top staff, got physicians to do medical research and start an A.R.E. Clinic. He featured the work of an anonymous geologist, and turned to science reporters."

Bro, himself a theologian, may have lamented that choice but he understood Hugh Lynn's preference. Partly it was "because church and synagogue leaders seemed to him amazingly indifferent to the Cayce story. And partly he acted under the pressure of seeing what Americans respected: scientists were the white-coated priests of the present age."

Elsie Sechrist recalled an occasion when Hugh Lynn told her of the advice he received from some consultants. "They told him you can't go on running this organization with just a bunch of housewives. You've got to get some Ph.D.s in here to get credibility." While Elsie says she gave no support to such a change, Hugh Lynn had leaned in this direction from his youth. In the 1930s, when he was accepted at Duke for graduate work in psychology, he said his plan was to get a Ph.D. Tempted away from academia by the lure of national radio's glamour and money, he never enrolled. Returning from the Army, he considered returning to school in order to turn the A.R.E. into a research center.

"I decided not to when I realized I could hire Ph.D.s."

And hire them he did as membership increased and the dues rolled in. Herbert Puryear, a psychology professor from Trinity University in Texas, joined the staff in 1969. An appealing lecturer and able interpreter of the Cayce philosophy, Dr. Puryear soon became a popular speaker at Virginia Beach and on the road. Mark Thurston was another psychologist from Texas, who was to become a prolific writer of A.R.E. books interpreting the readings. Henry Reed, a Princeton psychologist, joined the staff primarily to focus on dream research. And Hugh Lynn's eldest son, Charles Thomas, then a child psychologist teaching at the University of Maryland, joined the staff in 1970, primarily because he was intrigued by this new emphasis on research. The challenge his father offered was to organize youth activities.

Adding four bright Ph.Ds in psychology to his staff might have seemed like overcompensation for his lack of graduate academic work, but Hugh Lynn had taken his training in applied psychology. "He liked reading in psychology and talking with psychologists, though he rarely studied whole systems or pored over journals outside of parapsychology," recalled Dr. Bro, another Ph.D. who was not on the staff but spoke frequently from A.R.E. platforms. Bro wrote several Cayce books, and was part of the long-standing "faculty" that Hugh Lynn built for A.R.E. conferences and field lectures.

Research efforts at headquarters lacked bucks, not brains. Lacking an endowment, the A.R.E. was stretched just meeting current obligations. Nonetheless, some modest psychical research projects were attempted.

Medical research, applying the unconventional Cayce remedies, was an even more troublesome challenge. If he couldn't
212

pique the interest of his own brother-in-law physician, how was he to break through what amounted to a medical boycott? Whenever he did find a receptive doctor, Hugh Lynn went the extra mile to draw him into the work. Such an occasion occurred in 1956 when he went to Phoenix, Arizona to give a talk. Lester Babcoke, his contact in that far outpost, was chauffeuring the honored guest around town the day of his talk, publicizing the event with a hand-lettered sign on the rear of his car. It said: "Ten Million Words From An Unconscious Mind—Hugh Lynn Cayce" and listed Babcoke's phone number. One of the people who spotted Babcoke's sign that day was a doctor's receptionist. The unusual name Cayce rang a bell. It had come up in talk around her office about a book, *Many Mansions*. Slamming on her brakes, she stopped long enough to jot down Lester's phone number—and then went on to work and mentioned it to the young doctors she worked for, William and Gladys McGarey.

The McGareys, intrigued with her news about the Cayce lecture, had been in Phoenix only a year. They had come West with their six children in 1955 from Bill McGarey's native Ohio. During the slow pace of starting a new practice, Bill did a lot of reading, including Gina Cerminara's *Many Mansions*, which explained the philosophy of Edgar Cayce. McGarey had never heard of Cayce, whose ideas sounded pretty revolutionary to a Presbyterian, Republican physician. But he was nonetheless fascinated.

His wife had the same reaction. Accustomed to the mystical side of life from her youth in India, where she had been born and reared, the daughter of Presbyterian medical missionaries, Gladys was attracted by Cayce's philosophy: "I grew up knowing that prayer worked, and that healing was available. And though we didn't work with yogis, there was Sundar Singh, a Christian mystic who visited in our home. He was very much like Paul in the miracles that happened around him, and maybe like St. Francis in that he could communicate with animals. So that part of it was not difficult for me. I knew these things were a reality and I had seen them work."

The concept of reincarnation, however, was hard for her to swallow. But not for her husband, oddly enough, even though he had earlier thought of studying for the ministry: "Until I ran across the concept of reincarnation, nothing in life and its essence made any sense to me. In medical school I had moved away from the church because it seemed to be saying if you don't accept Jesus you are doomed to Hell. But when I heard about reincarnation, everything began to make sense to me. It was a means of explaining how things really worked."

While intrigued with this new way of looking at life, the

213

McGareys were preoccupied with building a family medical practice and raising their family. They weren't searching for a cause or a purpose—they had found it as medical practitioners. But Bill McGarey, who had never heard of Hugh Lynn and thought Edgar was dead, called Babcoke out of curiosity. When Lester offered to bring Hugh Lynn to his office, the doctor agreed to see him.

But Hugh Lynn didn't just drop by and shake hands like a visiting politician. He was more the circuit-riding missionary. "After he arrived we went in the back and sat down on those rickety high stools we had and talked and talked," said Dr. Bill. "A patient would come in and one of us would run out and see the patient in between," said Dr. Gladys. "But I can still see Hugh Lynn perched on one of those stools just giving it to us."

It was an unusual treat for all three of them. Hugh Lynn rarely encountered physicians who asked about his father. The two young doctors liked their forty-eight-year-old visitor instantly. "He was a great salesman for the A.R.E.," recalled Bill.

"Where is tonight's lecture?" he asked.

Hugh Lynn looked at Lester.

"The Oddfellow's Hall," said Lester with a straight face. Bill could hardly suppress a chuckle then and ever after when Lester insisted on booking Hugh Lynn into the Oddfellow's Hall. Obviously, the rent was cheap and the space ample.

After the lecture the McGareys went with the speaker to Brookshires restaurant. By the time they left, the McGareys were thoroughly charmed and inspired. "If there's anything I can do for you, just let me know," said Bill as they bade farewell.

Two weeks later Hugh Lynn took him up on the offer. He asked McGarey to give a talk in Tucson to a group of interested people. The topic was meditation.

"We hadn't done any meditating before that," explained Gladys. "Gladys and I meditated real fast for the next two weeks," laughed Bill, who now meditates each morning and laughs when he recalls his poor performance lecturing on the subject. It had been Hugh Lynn's way of getting the McGareys involved.

The McGareys began attending the annual week-long outdoor A.R.E. conference held at Asilomar in California, taking their children along. One summer Hugh Lynn asked them to teach meditation to a class of children aged five to seven.

"After ten minutes we had said everything we knew to tell them and we had an hour," said Gladys. "One little boy sat there rolling his eyelids inside out and grinning at everyone—with no teeth. Pretty soon all of the kids are turning their eyelids inside out. Afterward we told Hugh Lynn, 'You can ask us to do anything but that.''

What Hugh Lynn had in mind was more to their liking, but nonetheless puzzling.

"Hugh Lynn was really excited about our getting into the physical readings," said Gladys.

Few doctors of any kind showed any interest in those early days. The McGareys recalled an osteopath, Mayo Hotten, and George O'Malley, a Michigan doctor who had tried castor oil packs and later wrote an article for *The Searchlight,* an A.R.E. publication.

"I don't know who was working in the 1950s when we got started, but there was no one deeply involved," said Bill McGarey, "and maybe Hugh Lynn recognized our commitment. I don't know."

Four years after his maiden talk for the organization, Dr. Bill paid his first visit to headquarters in 1960. He learned more about the tiny organization and its growing Study Group program, about dream interpretation and numerology, and he rolled up his sleeves and helped paint the garage behind the old hospital building.

"That's when Hugh Lynn began pushing us to get into the physical readings," said Gladys. "We'd say, 'But Hugh Lynn, your dad was psychic. He could see when to change therapies for different patients. We're not psychic.' And the next year when we saw him he'd start all over again, and we'd say, 'We're not psychic, Hugh Lynn, we can't do that.' This went on for several years."

In 1963 when Hugh Lynn led a group of A.R.E. people on a trip to Egypt, the McGareys went too. They became close friends. "I remember Hugh Lynn [then aged fifty-seven] and Bill and I climbing up the outside of the Great Pyramid to the top—there were just seven of us who did it, and I was the only woman," recalled Dr. Gladys.

"We became so close to him that we felt that we must have certainly known him in a past life," said Dr. Bill.

Hugh Lynn was wearing down the McGareys' resistance and building up their confidence that something could be done. It worked, up to a point. When they returned home, the McGareys opened a small office away from their family practice and called it the A.R.E. Clinic. It was located in one room of a building which housed the Southeast A.R.E. Library, a small reading room where books and lecture tapes were available. Dr. Bill set aside one morning a week from his general practice to see patients there. It never caught on.

"Our purposes were divided," said Gladys, explaining that they were principally conducting a conventional practice. "It just didn't take off."

After a year or so, it "died a natural death."

Several other A.R.E. projects, meanwhile, did materialize in Phoenix. Lester Babcoke began making copies of taped A.R.E. lectures for distribution to members at large, and the McGareys and Babcoke started a printing service for the A.R.E. with a printing press they didn't know what else to do with. Bill had "inherited" the press from a bankrupt printing business in which he had invested. McGarey, who started out as a newspaperman and still had printer's ink in his veins, liked to work around print shops but didn't know how to operate his new press. It was located in a building next to where the Babcokes lived. "Lester looked at it and said, 'Hmm, maybe I can help you.' He got a pressman to come out and get it going the first day, and Lester watched him. The second day Lester took over and operated it himself from then on. So Lester started the Blue River Printers, printing stationery and everything."

Lester sold that venture when Hugh Lynn persuaded him to move to Virginia Beach in 1968 to help organize a printing service for the A.R.E. He also began manufacturing several health appliances—the impedance device and the wet cell—recommended in the Cayce readings. "Lester was what we call a borderline genius," said Gladys.

Hugh Lynn placed a lot of faith in Lester, but one time the new printer set off Cayce's temper. "Lester wasn't too good with the language. He printed a brochure about the A.R.E.," recalled Bill, "and on the front of it he said A.R.E. was located near Norfolk, Virginia, 'the *navel* capital of the world.'" His momentary anger soon turned to laughter.

Hugh Lynn never gave up urging the McGareys to experiment with his father's medical readings. "I told him I couldn't understand the readings," said Dr. Bill. "I couldn't understand why Edgar would say 'Do this' to the patient and the next time he'd say do something else. I couldn't understand why he would change from one therapy to another."

"When the diagnosis was the same," added Dr. Gladys.

"It took quite awhile for us to understand that," said Dr. Bill. "But we started by using castor oil packs on our patients in the late 1950s or early 1960s, and he said why didn't I write something about that."

McGarey liked to write but couldn't afford to take the time to do the research, so Hugh Lynn arranged for a $2,000 grant. The young doctor turned their family practice over to his wife and wrote his first book, *Edgar Cayce and the Palma Christi.* It focused on Cayce's prescription of castor oil for various maladies. McGarey had found
216

from experience that it helped people heal more rapidly, and he was taken by the discovery that the leaf of the castor plant is shaped like a human hand and was called the palm of Christ centuries ago.

By this time the McGareys were making an annual pilgrimage to Virginia Beach. On one visit Bill got acquainted with Jess Stearn, who was in residence working on *The Sleeping Prophet.* On another he met with Hugh Lynn, Bob Adriance, and Everett Irion, and agreed to head the medical research division of the Edgar Cayce Foundation. The group also created an osteopathic research division with Dr. Mayo Hotten in charge.

Hugh Lynn, unfortunately, had no funds to underwrite research. He was barely able to make ends meet for the struggling A.R.E.

"It was very simple," said Dr. Bill. "We didn't ask, 'Is it in the budget to do it?'"

"Hugh Lynn said, 'Do it,' and we'd do it."

In other words, he expected them to perform the research within their own practices, and at their own expense. The McGareys had no hesitancy about it from a financial standpoint, but they were still uncertain how to proceed. Hugh Lynn tried to persuade them to move their practice and their family, six children included, to Virginia Beach, but that held no appeal. The debate as to how and where was not easily resolved. It took a lot of table pounding between Hugh Lynn and Dr. Bill.

In 1968, the McGareys decided to hold a symposium in Arizona and invite other health practitioners to participate for discussions about the unconventional procedures Cayce had recommended. This first meeting drew twenty participants, including Hugh Lynn. When the McGareys repeated it the next year, he returned—and every year afterward until his death sixteen years after the first one. After each symposium, Hugh Lynn and the McGareys took a retreat together to brainstorm how they might do more. The symposium that began so modestly drew over seven hundred participants by the late 1980s.

In 1969, the McGareys took another trip with Hugh Lynn, this time around the world, even visiting Gladys's Aunt Belle in India. Then in her seventies, she had been taking care of the children of lepers for many years.

"She was building a cow shed," said Gladys, "and I asked if she had a cow. She replied, 'No, but if I build the shed, God will provide the cow.' which He later did." It was a lesson in faith that was not lost on the McGareys.

In Israel, they had a turning-point experience. The group was staying overnight in a kibbutz on the shores of the Sea of Galilee.

"Bill and I began talking about the idea of taking our medical group [their family practice] as it was and becoming the A.R.E. Clinic," said Gladys.

It was a risky concept. It might scare away patients who wanted conventional therapies. They talked to Hugh Lynn about it, and to several members of the board of trustees who were also on the trip, among them Robert Jeffries, William Lord, and Robert Adriance, who proved receptive to the idea.

"We figured that numerologically it was a good time because I was forty-nine," recalls Bill, "and I had finished seven seven-year cycles. We thought if we are ever going to do anything about making this real, now is the time to do it."

In 1970, they made the change and notified their patients that their emphasis would be on medical concepts pioneered by Edgar Cayce. They also reorganized in 1973 as a non-profit corporation with three divisions—one treating patients, another for education, and the other conducting basic research.

"Hugh Lynn was involved in all of this. He served on our board. We sometimes had different ideas, and we argued a lot, but we stayed with it until we worked them through and agreed. We came from a pretty conventional medical background, and yet sometimes we had ideas that caused Hugh Lynn to push us back into the conventional mode. There were times when he didn't want us to get too far out, and times when he was concerned that we would," said Gladys.

Things did not run smoothly for another reason: members of the board and Dr. Bill weren't always in agreement about the role of the board. It was undoubtedly difficult for a doctor who was accustomed to being his own boss to contemplate surrendering any authority to outsiders, however well-meaning or persuasive. Hugh Lynn, then sixty-three, had become a father figure and was used to bossing everyone around. So was Dr. Bill. What saved them perhaps was that they could agree on the principal purpose of the clinic.

"What Hugh Lynn wanted more than anything else was to have a place where the concepts, the therapies in the readings could be tested at the clinical level. That was his objective, and that was our objective," said Bill McGarey.

"And he wanted doctors to know about this," said Dr. Gladys. "He wanted the material presented in such a way as to be credible to doctors. Bill started writing the *Medical Research Bulletin* [a quarterly newsletter] in 1970. Hugh Lynn wanted that to be written as a scientific journal, but Bill didn't write scientific journals. So that was

218

an area of a little shove and push. Hugh Lynn wanted it accepted by the medical profession."

"As it seems to have worked out," said Bill, "the only way they are going to accept it is with a baseball bat over their heads."

"And by the opinion of patients," Gladys added.

"They'll be moved by their patients pushing them into doing it," Bill agreed.

As the McGareys ventured into New Age medicine, Hugh Lynn turned to implementing his other big dream. It was no secret that he wanted to build a modern library—one that would become known worldwide as a psychic research center. He had been talking up the idea for years. In 1968 he asked Jim Embleton, a former California real estate broker who had moved to Virginia Beach, to start a fund-raising effort. Embleton sent out a flier to all the members "just as a feeler," and the response was encouraging. Embleton was appointed to the board of trustees, whereupon a committee was named to push the project. Its other members included Edgar Evans Cayce and Bob Adriance. The scale of the project meanwhile grew from a modest library, costing perhaps $75,000, to a combination library and conference center costing around $1 million. After several architects submitted sketches, one was selected who had proposed a building that looked distinctly different from the old hospital and anything else in the area.

"We wanted the feeling of strength and solidarity because it would be housing the readings," recalled Embleton. "Some people said it looked too much like a bank, but we wanted that feeling. You want a bank to look strong because your money is in there. We wanted a solid yet appealing structure that was going to be housing the readings." In 1973 he called the A.R.E. staff together and vowed to raise a million dollars to accomplish it. The board of trustees had given him the green light, with one stipulation: no mortgage. He had to raise the money to pay the construction bills as they came due. If he broke ground before all the money was available, he ran the risk of not being able to finish the job—or as in the case of the Washington Monument, having it stand half-finished for years until enough money materialized. "We signed the contract with the contractor without any money," recalls Embleton. It sounded to the poorly-paid staff like he would need a miracle. Where could he raise that kind of money? Indeed, he would need two miracles. The civic association that represented many residents of the oceanfront neighborhood in which the A.R.E. was located filed suit to block construction, for its members opposed any non-residential construction in that area.

The court ignored the use permit A.R.E. had already obtained and ruled that only the city council could approve the project. Hugh Lynn knew that he had a battle on his hands. He and Embleton organized a petition drive in the area of those who favored the library and inspired four hundred members to deluge City Hall with letters favoring the project. "He worked night and day," recalls Sally, "calling on every member of the city council and all the influential people in town." It came down to a vote of the council. The chamber was packed, not by opponents as is usually the case, but by supporters. And their leader's framed photograph hung on a City Hall corridor wall: Hugh Lynn Cayce, First Citizen for 1965. Every little bit helped. The council voted to build.

Having won the battle on the political front, Hugh Lynn acted like General Patton crossing the Rhine. In the fall of 1973, he called in the bulldozers, put on a hardhat, climbed into the driver's seat, and opened the throttle with glee. For the next two years he bulldozed the skeptics and doubters, just as he had overcome the protesting citizens. He rallied the members nationwide to put it over.

Hugh Lynn's great spirit of enthusiasm inspired the financial miracle he needed. But it was not by corralling a philanthropist or two as much as by inspiring thousands of people of modest means to each "own" a chunk of this new monument. For $42 anyone could purchase one square foot of a library dedicated to mankind. From coast to coast, members and Study Groups held bake sales, garage sales, car washes—anything to keep the builders going. It was an amazing pay-as-you-go feat, watching bricks, mortar, and pledges and cash contributions being trucked in simultaneously. "It was amazing," Embleton remembers, "but each time a payment was due the contractor, the money was there and we paid for it step by step."

What he achieved by Easter Sunday 1975, when the mayor of Virginia Beach gave the dedication address on the front steps of the A.R.E. Library/Conference Center, was something even more important than this beautiful new building. The new library was a visible symbol of the tremendous growth the A.R.E. had enjoyed in the three decades since the death of its founding father, and would continue to enjoy. Membership tripled during the ten years after completion of the library.

It was a symbol also of Hugh Lynn's vision of the A.R.E. as breaking new ground in the field of research and not simply acting as curator of his father's legacy. Librarian Charlotte Schoen explained one dimension of it: "Hugh Lynn's aim was that the library's book collection would contain the outstanding books of all times on every subject covered in the readings."

Again, it was a large order for an organization that had no endowment for this noble purpose, and still doesn't, but many people have contributed individual volumes and the A.R.E. has managed to purchase two valuable collections, those of Egerton Sykes, an English authority on Atlantis who had the world's largest Atlantean collection in private hands; and those of Andrew Jackson Davis, a nineteenth-century American psychic.

Literary research was to be supplemented with research in the readings. Topical abstracts were developed by the staff on many ailments and metaphysical or philosophical questions, using pertinent information found in various readings. These files were circulated free to members. Hugh Lynn urged members to conduct their own research by testing the remedies. He also encouraged the marketing of products manufactured to the specifications of the readings. He and his father had attempted this during the 1930s with two products: Ipsab for the gums; and TIM for hemorrhoids. The effort failed for lack of demand.

A Virginia Beach druggist, Robert Ingram, who knew the Cayce family, filled the gap for many years by formulating remedies, often directly from a copy of the customer's reading, whether it was brought in personally or sent by mail from long distance. Since herbs and other natural ingredients were commonly used then, the prescribed cures weren't considered as unusual as they are today. Ingram said the most popular remedies were inhalants, tonic for hair growth—high-grade crude oil was often recommended—and Ipsab.

When A.R.E. membership started to explode during the 1960s and New Age health concepts began to contend with the conventional drug-based remedies, the commercial potential of the Cayce remedies became apparent—and was tapped eventually by two enterprising A.R.E. members. Tom Johnson, a former computer engineer from New Jersey, founded the Heritage Store in Virginia Beach in 1969 because he thought there ought to be a central source of supply and none was available. Johnson built a successful mail-order business, but not without difficulty from the Food and Drug Administration, which forced him to make no unproved claims for the products—letters to Cayce from cured patients didn't count as proof to the federal government. The A.R.E. sent business his way initially, but disagreements developed over the formulas for some products when Johnson couldn't always find all of the ingredients Cayce had prescribed. A favorite product, Atomidine, was a problem for a time because the firm that manufactured it used three herbs in the same family as Cayce had suggested but not of the same strength. Johnson later traced the right herbs all the way to India.

A competing venture, PMS, was started with A.R.E.'s blessing in 1974 by Adella Scott Wilson with the understanding that all formulas were to be approved by the A.R.E. Undercapitalized, it changed hands and failed to meet the A.R.E.'s expectations for it, to the extent that the A.R.E. considered going into the business itself, at the urging of its executive director. Embleton favored a policy of marketing remedies as it sold books to members. Hugh Lynn took no position openly, letting the board of trustees make the decision against the venture. Embleton said that "Hugh Lynn had the board in his pocket," and it would have done his bidding if he had favored it. The prospect of trouble with the Food and Drug Administration seemed certain, however, for F.D.A. considers the readings to be full of unproven claims for products of questionable value.

Samuel Knoll bought the company in 1982, renamed it Home Health Products, and signed a contract with the A.R.E. promising to uphold the integrity of the ingredients and to pay the A.R.E. a royalty if his venture succeeded. Knoll developed many new products and built a thriving mail-order business with the aid of the A.R.E.'s expanding mailing list. Within a few years the new firm had developed a substantial business that returned royalties to the A.R.E. Hugh Lynn's objective, and more, had been realized.

So one project after another came to fruition, much of it with Hugh Lynn's prodding. He apparently never suffered a major defeat at the hands of his board. Bill Lord thought that was as it should be for efficient management. Involved in managing his own family tanning business in Boston for years before moving to Florida and going into construction, Lord said he and Hugh Lynn shared an interest in how to make things work: "The manager has to get trustees that are compatible. Part of his job is to get trustees he can work with. He did well with that. But you take something as diverse as the A.R.E., it's like the human race. There can't be unanimity of opinion—there shouldn't be. The trustees didn't agree a lot of times. Hugh Lynn wouldn't back down if he thought his way was right. Once in a while there would be a trustee who wouldn't either. They'd sputter once in a while, but we'd laugh it off."

In Phoenix, the A.R.E. Clinic was slow to catch on. But Hugh Lynn had learned long ago that persistence was essential, and the McGareys were learning it, too. Although their training and initial practice had followed conventional standards for the medical profession, they had to learn by trial and error how to work in some of Cayce's methods. It was not enough, however, to introduce castor oil packs, helpful as they proved for a variety of conditions, or suggest dietary changes, the McGareys discovered. They learned to impart a whole new philosophy of healing: It is the patient, not the doctor, who is the healer.

"Healing of the body does not in the final analysis depend upon the therapist," Dr. Bill claimed. "Rather, it is the individual who is ill—the one who brought about the psychological abnormalities in the first place—who must take part in the healing process in order to have the desired result.

"So we understand that every patient who comes to us for aid of one sort or another, and is successful, brings along the key to healing, which is simply the will to get over that problem. If the will is not there, the chances of recovery or true healing are markedly lessened. The mystery of the human body encompasses the power of will or choice which every individual possesses by virtue of his creation as a human being."

Rather than see patients only when they came in with an ailment, the McGareys designed a program intended to inspire healthier habits—exercising, eating nutritious foods, interpreting their dreams to resolve physical and emotional questions, taking massages, colonics, and chiropractic adjustments. It was both preventive and curative.

They called this program the Temple Beautiful, borrowing a term from Cayce's story of prehistoric Egypt. It lasts seventeen days and is conducted in a leased mansion not far from the Clinic. Starting with a conventional physical exam and stress evaluation test, the program includes such unconventional therapies as biofeedback and experimental energy medicine applications. A shorter program lasts nine days.

As the McGareys moved full swing into their holistic approach, they encountered more and more patients who claimed that they had been mistreated by conventional physicians. "We think it's because the emphasis in medicine has moved toward mechanization, specialization, the diagnostics of the disease, rather than caring for the human being in a way that reflects the divine nature of the human being," said William McGarey. "And it has to change."

Hugh Lynn, the McGareys attest, always supported them in this approach, even though the A.R.E. underwrote their program financially for only a few years. They had to prove it then on their own by doing it. In recent years the Clinic obtained strong financial backing from the Fetzer Foundation in order to conduct research on the healing attributes of energy in various forms. Energy medicine, they believe, is the wave of the future. Dramatic success stories have become commonplace.

In 1985, a woman who had been comatose for six weeks as a result of an auto accident was brought to the Clinic strapped into her wheelchair to prevent her falling out. "She couldn't talk, couldn't feed herself, her forehead required a strap just to support it, and we weren't sure she could even see," said Dr. Bill.

They began a variety of therapies: patterning, as developed by the Institute for the Achievement of Human Potential in Philadelphia; acuscope treatments; castor-oil packs; massages; electromagnetic therapy; special diet; and many encouraging words directed at building her confidence. In four weeks she was able to understand directions, had gained weight and strength in her arms and legs. She was sent home with instructions for her husband to work with her.

A year later, returning to Phoenix, she walked into the Clinic and gave everyone a hug. Nearly completely recovered, she gave a talk at the clinic's annual symposium, a living testimonial to the miracles being performed there by the McGareys using Cayce concepts.

Another dramatic case is that of John Freeman, a sixty-two-year-old mechanical engineer from Houston, who refused to accept his doctor's grim sentence of one year to live. Freeman had colon cancer. He had agreed to surgical removal of fifteen inches of his lower bowel but refused chemotherapy as recommended. Instead, he went to the A.R.E. Clinic.

"At first I didn't know that I was being immersed in healing techniques for body, mind, and spirit; it was done so subtly," said Freeman.

John realized he had to change a lot of his ways if he was to save his own life.

"Basically, I had had a bad attitude. I've always fought everything, especially rules that say things must be done in a certain way," he explained.

Before cancer was diagnosed he suffered stomach ailments from the anxiety and turmoil in his life.

"Most of my life I've only been cognizant of my mind, taken my body for granted, and fed my spirit a near-starvation diet. Cancer served as the two-by-four that was laid against my head to get my attention."

He started meditating at the Temple Beautiful, changed his diet, and developed a new attitude toward work. When the old patterns threatened to raise his blood pressure, he stopped and recognized there are better ways. "I stop everything several times a day now and look out the window to watch the birds and squirrels outside. I've slowed my pace."

Six months after leaving the Clinic, he returned to his regular doctor in Texas for a checkup. There was no trace of the cancer. "He was not thrilled that I had taken charge of my own case," said Freeman. "Nonetheless, it feels good to me, handling my own case. I am now doing all the things that I enjoy, just living the way that I want to and feeling good doing so."

Such happy endings serve to validate Cayce's holistic approach, as applied by the McGareys, and promise more breakthroughs to come.

Hugh Lynn's confidence in the McGareys to conduct this pioneering work couldn't have been more fittingly placed. They not only were idealistic young doctors who were open to innovative approaches, but they both had early ambitions to be medical missionaries. They just hadn't thought of finding a mission field in the United States. When asked whether their work at the A.R.E. Clinic, spreading the doctrine of holistic medicine, fulfills their missionary zeal, Dr. Bill replied: "Yes, better than what we would have done otherwise."

"Yes, because we would have been restricted [as clergy]," added Gladys.

Every summer they participate in a conference at A.R.E. headquarters in Virginia Beach on healing. In mid-1987, the McGareys led an A.R.E. conference in Emmitsburg, Maryland attended by over five hundred people. And attendance at the programs held at the Clinic have been higher than ever. People are coming for all sorts of ailments for one main reason: they've lost hope in conventional medicine and have heard of the success stories of the holistic approach.

William and Gladys McGarey are remarkable individuals— competent, caring, compassionate, courageous—and doubly so as a team. Both have become authors and lecturers, working through the A.R.E. and the American Holistic Medical Association, which they helped organize in 1978—Gladys serving as president one term after two terms as vice president. Slowly but surely they began to gain national recognition, at least in New Age circles. But they never forgot who nudged them into it.

"If it hadn't been for Hugh Lynn," notes Dr. Bill, "none of this would have happened—in spite of Edgar Cayce's readings—because Hugh Lynn grabbed the bull by the horns after his father died."

"And he said, 'The world needs to know this,'" Gladys added. "What a dynamo."

"It has given me a lot of insight personally about the

importance of sticking with one's destiny," Bill observed. "While Edgar Cayce was giving these readings, he was being torn apart by the stress of thousands of letters coming in that couldn't be answered, and trying to answer them, and giving as many as twelve readings a day, and trying to do the best that he could. That's why the clarity of his guidance kept coming through in the way that no other psychic has done that I know about—any psychic, no matter who he is. The readings provided the information, but it took someone like Hugh Lynn, who was a salesman..."

"And a charismatic person," injected Gladys.

"He would just take up a free-will offering and sometimes it wasn't even enough to pay his transportation, but it took someone like Hugh Lynn to put it across, someone who was willing to lay down his life to do the things that needed to be done as he saw them."

Chapter 18

The Andrew Dilemma

All of Hugh Lynn's life, Andrew posed a secret dilemma for him—Andrew the disciple, the brother of Peter, the man that Edgar Cayce claimed his son had been in an earlier life. In his youth Hugh Lynn rejected the idea out of hand; but as he came to accept the reincarnation philosophy, he had to come to terms with this formidable identity. It seemed to make him uncomfortable even at age seventy-four, but the name, Andrew, came up repeatedly in our discussions with him, and it became obvious that one could not overlook his Andrew connection if one hoped to understand this complex man.

Hugh Lynn's feeling of intimidation by this identity was understandable. As a boy he was simply overwhelmed by the thought that he had once been one of these legendary figures who marched through the pages of the Bible arm in arm with the Lord Jesus Christ.

"I didn't know what to do with it. It's hard enough being Edgar Cayce's son, but being one of the reincarnated twelve disciples, well I didn't want to try to live up to it at that point in my life or do anything about it. I thought it would be very difficult to live with."

But surely his father, the Bible student, must have been enormously intrigued and proud over the revelation that his son had been one of Jesus' disciples.

"Probably, but you see his very interest in the Bible and belief in it and knowledge confused me, because if he were going to make up something, that's the kind of thing I thought he would make up for me. So I took it with a grain of salt for a long time.

"But also I really didn't want to accept the responsibility. That's a heck of a responsibility, to live up to something like that. I thought it was a little much to lay on me, even if it were true. I wondered whether he was using it to discipline me, to give me a barrier or boundary to being wild. He knew I was going in lots of ways he didn't want me to go. I wondered whether he used it as a checking point—what was I doing acting like this? He was aware of my anger and hate toward him [as an adolescent]."

The Andrew revelation first surfaced only a few months after Edgar's return home from his sojourns in Texas—too soon for Hugh Lynn to have forgiven his father completely.

"I had a violent temper. I enjoyed fighting and he knew that I enjoyed it. I enjoyed firearms and shot and killed things and enjoyed it. I wondered if he was using it as a ploy and he had made it up to hold me in check."

In retrospect, however, Hugh Lynn conceded that his father had never used it in that manner.

"I have no memory of his ever using it in any way connected with morals or discipline or attitudes. The only way in which he ever referred to it was what he knew about Andrew. It was informational only—what he had read, or looked up. Of course, I began to look it up, too."

While Hugh Lynn claimed in later years that he spent his whole life testing the reincarnation theory, it appears that he had accepted it by the time he had finished college. Over that intervening period of five or six years, he had many family dinner-table discussions about life readings, his own included. And he had asked for readings focused on each one of the personalities he was said to have been, Andrew included, for that explosive initial reading had said simply this about his prior "appearances" in the Earth:

"In the appearances we find that in the study of the Courts of the Monks of England, when they were the shut-ins for the study of chemical forces, in the days of Alfred the Great, and this entity's name was Ericson Olaf. This will be found in records as is [were] made by this monk in the study of those elements creating these.

"Before this we find in that of the days of the Crusades in the Holy Land, when there was the quick return of this entity, and as the leader of the invading forces, and carrying then the banner of Him who was the giver of perfect gifts.

"Again in the days when the Prince of Peace walked by the seashore. This entity answered the call, and was one of those followers, as is given in him who brought his brother to the Master, A-N-D-R-E-W [this is how Gladys typed the name].

"In the days before this when the first pharaoh builded in the

228

plains, then we find there this entity is |was| one that will be found in that which represents this entity at present, in the north corner of the second Pyramid, for he was one of these rulers.

"In the days before this we find the entity was among those in the day when the forces of the Universe came together, when there was upon the waters the sound of the coming together of the Sons of God, when the morning stars sang together, and over the face of the waters there was the voice of the glory of the coming of the plane for man's dwelling."

If his reading was to be believed, Hugh Lynn had been not only one of the disciples, but also an Egyptian king, a leader in the Crusades, a monk under Alfred the Great, and among the early settlers when the universe was colonized. What a line-up of heavy hitters.

"In all of these," his reading said, "we find some of this present entity's individuality, and in some, some personalities are brought through."

It doesn't take much imagination to see Hugh Lynn playing each one of these roles. The details about each character were fleshed out a bit in subsequent readings. They revealed that Ericson Olaf had been a Norwegian, a Viking invader probably, who landed in England and there took vows and accepted the Christian faith and adopted the monastic life. Hugh Lynn's personality included certain attributes gained during the monk's reclusive life, this reading said, namely "the ability to concentrate and give the inmost recesses of acquired knowledge in such a manner as |is| understandable to other individuals." The reading added: "Noble calling!"

While this image of him might not have been clear in 1925 just before his eighteenth birthday when he received this reading, it certainly fit him as an adult. For Hugh Lynn was to concentrate much of his adult life on publicizing the "acquired knowledge" of his father through publications that make it "understandable to other individuals." He did it in his own writing and as editor of the "Edgar Cayce On . . ." series of books—a noble calling indeed.

But what about Andrew? This reading said he was "a fisherman on the Sea of Galilee, and became the follower of the Nazarene, the Gift to the World, and the entity sought this out and brought many to the sound of the Living Words as were given to the peoples round about, and the entity was one of those who studied the lessons and had reached that point where the soul knew the awakening and the purpose for which it had set itself in Earth's plane."

As Hugh Lynn, the reading added, he retained Andrew's "desire to ever hold |that which is| acceptable of the Prince of Peace, and the ability of the entity to give much knowledge to others save through such lessons and illustrations as given by the Master."

If this meant nothing to him as a teenager, during his adult years Hugh Lynn loved to lecture on Jesus.

"It's a very personal relationship. I know Him as a human and as a God. Everything I read that is written about Him, I read over and over. I dream about Him. I talk to Him. I think He has talked to me."

Elsie Sechrist, after years of traveling the lecture circuit with him, said her favorite of Hugh Lynn's lectures was, "Jesus Who Became the Christ." She said when he spoke about Jesus, "there was a touch of reverence in his voice which was not apparent in other lectures. There was also an enthusiasm in his voice, as if he were not only convincing you, the listener, but himself as well of the astounding truths and activities of Jesus." She added that he was especially good at answering questions about Jesus and early Christianity. "Hugh Lynn's insight into the nature and life of the Master often awakened within the listener a sudden expansion of the meaning and teachings of Jesus. It was as if his understanding of the Master was transferred to the audience and a sudden greater understanding flooded the consciousness of the listener."

As Hugh Lynn grew older he became freer about discussing his experiences with Jesus, especially with young people because "they understand much more easily than adults. I've often said I'd just like to throw all the adults out of the A.R.E. and just have young people. If they could just support it.

"Souls are souls, but I've found that those that are in young bodies are lighter and freer and more sensitive. Adults have all their prejudices screwed to the floor. They impose their preconceived notions on anything you say. Those now being born are going to be lighter and freer still. They are so honest, so straight."

After the A.R.E. New Year's Conference in 1972, one of the young people in attendance talked to Hugh Lynn privately about the appearance of Jesus in a number of the youth's dreams. His chat with Hugh Lynn was one of the memorable experiences of his life. "For three days afterward," said G. Scott Sparrow, "I felt Jesus' presence so powerfully and tangibly that I regretted having to go to sleep at the end of the days. It was an undeniable presence."

Sparrow, now a professional therapist, said he knows several others who had similar experiences after talking with Hugh Lynn. He is convinced that it was not what Hugh Lynn said but "his radiance and his love for Jesus. Hugh Lynn's mystical relationship with Jesus was his most important teaching tool.

"Hugh Lynn lived as though Jesus might appear any

moment...no matter what Hugh Lynn was doing—whether it was meditating or playing bridge—there was an air of joyful expectation that Jesus might at any moment walk into the room."

Having had several mystical encounters with the Christ at different stages of his life, Hugh Lynn never seemed to lose touch with this reality. "His confidence in Jesus' accessibility seemed directly related to his confidence that he was doing God's work as best he could understand," Sparrow noted. "He accepted that he was only expected to try his best, even if he fell flat on his face from time to time. He was the first to admit that his penchant for anger, for instance, often impeded his ability to serve; and he made a lifelong commitment to harness his fiery temper."

A young woman who worked at A.R.E. one summer recalls her lasting impression of Hugh Lynn: "As a sharing group leader during conferences, I was attending practically all the conferences that summer. He stands out in my mind as the only person I've ever met who really had a relationship with Jesus. I never felt that it was possible to have that kind of thing, alive. It was based on catching him alone in the meditation garden, not just from things he was saying."

On one occasion in 1970 Hugh Lynn's devotion to Jesus triggered an unexpectedly strong reaction to the remarks of a speaker from India with whom he shared the A.R.E. platform. I.C. Sharma speculated that Jesus had learned the yogic technique for not feeling physical pain, perhaps by going out of his body, and thus did not suffer during the crucifixion. Sitting across the platform from Dr. Sharma, Hugh Lynn lost his composure and exclaimed: "You don't know what you are talking about." He would not allow theorizing at the expense of the Christian tradition of Jesus, the suffering servant, and his passion brought tears to the eyes of many in the audience. The moderator quickly concluded the program, and Hugh Lynn, obviously upset, departed straightaway without a word to anyone.

While Hugh Lynn talked freely about his personal relationship with Jesus, he remained silent about Andrew.

"I simply covered it up by keeping those readings out of the public files."

Ken Skidmore, former editor of the A.R.E. *Journal*, recalls that Hugh Lynn, while visiting A.R.E. Camp one summer, was asked by a group of young people why some of his readings were missing.

"I decided it was ridiculous and I put them back in there. I decided that if people discovered my number [341]—and I was sure they would—and they looked it up and asked me about it, I'd say

231

what I always say about it: 'I don't deny it and I don't admit to anything.'"

While Hugh Lynn was wary of admitting to the Andrew identity, some of his associates had no doubt about its authenticity. "Hugh Lynn really had that Andrew consciousness," claimed Meredith Puryear, who knew him the last thirty years of his life. "Andrew's consciousness was, 'Here are five loaves and two fishes, make do.' Hugh Lynn would make do with whatever he had. He did that all his life, and he was marvelous at it." Marilyn Peterson, who worked with him, said one day before he began a lecture she encountered him in his white summer suit and blue shirt, in glowing health, and she said, "Some day someone will write your biography and they will title it, 'Go and Call Your Brother.'" She was alluding to a remark attributed to Jesus in one of the Cayce readings in which Andrew was directed to bring Peter to the Master. "Hugh Lynn narrowed his eyes at me and then beamed," said Marilyn. "But that's what his life was all about—go and call your brother."

Author Mary LaCroix had a mystical experience concerning Hugh Lynn while she was working on her novel, *The Remnant*. A Minnesota farmer's wife, she had never before written a book. But her study of the Bible and the Cayce readings concerning the Essenes' preparation of the Messiah was so moving that she felt called to write a dramatization of those events. Mary had never met Hugh Lynn and knew nothing of his life reading, but when she saw him for the first time along with Ruth Montgomery on a television program, the David Susskind show, she thought he looked like her Uncle Earl. "I just loved him," said Mrs. LaCroix. "I also had an intuitive feeling that he was Andrew. I have no idea how I knew that." When she made her first visit to Virginia Beach and met Hugh Lynn, she discovered he didn't look like Uncle Earl, who was a bigger man. But when someone told her he had been Andrew, she recalled, "I wasn't surprised."

Hugh Lynn was not the only one connected with the A.R.E. who was thought to have been a biblical figure. Meredith recalled a dinner party at her house in San Antonio before she and her husband, Herbert, moved to Virginia in 1968, when, "I had Andrew and John and James and Paul, all at my table. Hugh Lynn made a funny about it because he wouldn't let people take themselves seriously [in those roles]."

He definitely didn't want his biography, which we all assumed would be published during his lifetime, to reveal that he thought he had been Andrew because "a lot of people would consider it ego. But a lot more people would feel it was heresy for me even to talk about it or think about it or let it be written."

So even though he overcame his own initial boyhood antipathy for this idea, Hugh Lynn was sensitive that others might not be so successful.

"My orthodox training in the Disciples of Christ Church and later in the Presbyterian Church simply made it impossible for me to deal with that Palestine incarnation in any factual way, where people could get hold of it. I certainly wasn't ashamed of it, but I didn't want to brag about it either. It was a heavy trip, a heavy load, and required of me a lot of work.

"I can't cover it up from the A.R.E. membership completely and be honest. It's in the readings, and when people say something to me about that I just look at them and never deny it or confirm that. So I leave it like that."

What did he fear?

"There are lots of fundamentalists, and semi-fundamentalists, the whole church area, that I think would be upset, offended by that. I think they would look upon it as an ego trip. Even for me to allow it [to be published], even if it's true, you know, in their minds, it would do us more harm than good and bring criticism of me, and criticism for A.R.E. I've always felt that. And that's why I've never used it. And I think for that reason some people think I'm not really convinced about reincarnation. I am."

When we discussed with Hugh Lynn the biographer's interest in mentioning his fascinating Andrew connection, he tried to talk us out of it because "it just makes it harder for me, more difficult to live up to in that sense. But worse than that, I think people will think you've got an 'ism' going or a cult in which you're attaching yourself to the Master in a very personal way and trying to string onto that. I think any famous names in the reincarnation area do that, and I think we hurt the whole reincarnation concept by that. I know how relatively few famous people there are in the Edgar Cayce readings. Besides, being famous people [in past lives] is most difficult, not easy at all, and some of the most famous are the worst ones, and the greatest failures. But that is not understood by the average person. One of the major criticisms of the reincarnation concept is that everybody thinks they are famous—everybody thinks they were a prince or a king, and there are darn few woodchoppers and scullery maids running around loose. So this [Andrew connection] would be just an additional one, and a bad addition because there are just twelve of them, that's a limited number. It couldn't be more prominent than that, from my point of view. You are picking on twelve, and one of the most active in many respects, one of the most active in the Bible."

Hugh Lynn said he wanted only to be described as one of the multitude of Jesus' followers, in order to place him in that Palestine period so that the influence of his experience with Jesus could be understood as an aspect of his soul's journey. He contended that anyone who had encountered Jesus would have been affected no less than the disciples were. "If you ever ran into Jesus anywhere in Israel in His lifetime, you are as motivated as anyone else by His teachings. If you heard Him talk, by His philosophy, or watched Him heal, and thousands and thousands did, you would have been just as motivated as if you were personally picked by Him by the connection with John. And that's what it was: I was an Essene and I was following John the Baptist. I had been involved in the training."

Hugh Lynn summed up his attitude in this way: "I think it is so much more important to do work that needs to be done *for* the Master than to claim a relationship with Him—so much more important. And my life should reflect that."

Many people thought that it did, he among them:

"I could give you a lot of examples of things out of my life that fit that pattern—personal things that I've done—I've gone back several times to the place where I think Jesus went to study in Persia [Shushtar, Iran], and I've met people there—this Mullah that I think I knew there before. I've had an intimate relationship with the Bible all my life. I responded to my father's doing it, it wasn't that he forced it down me. I loved the Bible, and I memorized long passages. I used to read it more than I do now. I have worked in the church. I believe that worshipping with people helps, particularly at certain times, to be able to sing hymns and pray and listen to inspirational sermons, I think it's a good thing. I've worked in Sunday schools fifteen to twenty years.

"There are a lot of things that indicate my involvement with Christianity and with Jesus, the figure of Jesus, the whole concept of Jesus. The breadth of view of the Christ consciousness, I have said many times, is the most exciting material in the Edgar Cayce readings for me. It is just fascinating. I have instituted archaeological digs on Mount Carmel, raised money and hauled psychics over there and waltzed them around for hours and hours looking for the places where Jesus was trained, where he went to school on Mount Carmel, according to my father. I've done so many things of that sort."

When Hugh Lynn said his Andrew connection imposed a lot of work on him he referred to his life's work, which obviously he thrived on even when it was burdensome. He seems to have coped with it best by keeping in mind an ideal that he expressed in this way: "I work for Jesus, not the A.R.E. The A.R.E. is a vehicle, as is everything else in my life. Once I realized that, either in my imagination or in reality, I've had experiences one after another to push me, drive me, propel me to keep at it. Because it's just that there hasn't been anything that I've tried to do that had any relationship to ideals and purposes that hasn't worked in my life."

Moreover, Hugh Lynn came to believe that it was risky for him not to stay close to Jesus: "When I don't operate on that wavelength in terms of ideals and purposes, I'm dangerous—dangerous to be around and a danger to myself."

What was Andrew, the fisherman, like? He evidently was a zealous, courageous, unconventional believer, and it cost him his life. Originally a follower of that unorthodox desert preacher, John the Baptist, he was also one of the first to become a disciple of Jesus. Then he persuaded his brother, Simon Peter, to join them. It's not hard to visualize Hugh Lynn doing all of these things.

Hugh Lynn saw Andrew as a practical fellow from a middle class family, not wealthy, even though Andrew's and Peter's father was a brother to the wealthy Zebedee. It was Andrew who brought Jesus the boy whose lunch the Master miraculously transformed into the picnic for five thousand. Hugh Lynn said Andrew also found the donkey for Jesus to ride and the children whom Jesus blessed.

"He apparently worked with children a lot. He had children and loved children. Whenever children were involved with Jesus, he was the one who got them or found them."

Hugh Lynn thinks Andrew was younger than Peter and less the leader. "He wasn't a very dynamic or driving kind of person. Peter was that for the family."

Other biblical scenes show him acting as a spokesman with Philip for Greeks who wished to see Jesus, and praying in the upper room after the Crucifixion.

An early historian reported that Andrew later preached in Scythia, an area in Eastern Europe occupied by the nomadic Scythians until they were wiped out by the Goths in the A.D. 100s. Like his two heroes, John the Baptist and Jesus, Andrew was martyred—crucified on an X-shaped cross called the *crux decussata*, or Saint Andrew's cross. He was to become Saint Andrew, the patron saint of Greece and Scotland.

We asked Hugh Lynn if he thought he had met in this life any other disciples or people he had known in Palestine. "A lot of them," he replied, including one woman who had been his daughter in Palestine. "I was very attracted to her. She lived here in Virginia

Beach. She married and moved away." As for others, he said, "Peter didn't show up. I'm still looking for him. He may have decided to sit this one out. Luke, or Lucius, showed up. Not John the Baptist or John, the brother of James. But Zebedee, I think, not the sons. Another one of the disciples turned up—Matthew. He was a Jewish gentleman who was still involved in the marketplace. And Jude showed up. There were a few, not a big list of them." Hugh Lynn declined to identify these persons in this life because that "is a personal matter" and "if they want to talk about it, or don't, that's their prerogative."

He did say that "Matthew," now dead, was a New York businessman who had brought his retarded child to the Cayce Hospital—"a very fine man, very honest, very warm, good man, good with his family, with his child." He was in his thirties, about ten years older than Hugh Lynn. Although he was a Reform Jew, religion was not a major part of his life. Asked if he had experienced any sense of recognition of this man, Hugh Lynn replied, "No, none at all." He said "Matthew" had obtained a life reading out of curiosity and "just shook his head" over the alleged affiliation with Jesus. "His reaction was, 'I don't know what to make of this.' He did not become a Christian."

Whatever his saintly qualities in Palestine 2,000 years ago, "Matthew" apparently was just an ordinary respectable person in this life. But neither was the new "Andrew" a saint, Hugh Lynn was the first to admit. Knowing that he might have worked with Jesus and been one of the founders of the Christian faith—and even believing it, as he did in later years—did not cleanse him of all un-Christian attributes. The violence of Hugh Lynn's temper in middle age was the most visible evidence that he still had inner work to do on his own spiritual quest. He traced his angry side to his Egyptian incarnations, which preceded his appearance as Andrew. His appearance with Jesus had been an effort to calm him down, he once said, but that life hadn't lasted long enough to transform him completely.

He would have to return to the source to be healed.

Chapter 19

The Search for Ra Ta

Within two decades of the death of Edgar Cayce it appeared that Hugh Lynn had achieved his goal of gaining a sense of permanence for the A.R.E. and the reputation of his father. But as the signs of the A.R.E.'s growth became more evident, so did signals of distress within the manager himself. As recognition for The Work edged closer and closer, Hugh Lynn's own sense of well-being deteriorated.

"I had begun to find that I was disliking people, hating people if they did something I didn't like. They were making me angry and I had no control over the hate or the anger. It was making me sick. I was coming apart."

"There were days when I would greet him, 'Hi, Hugh Lynn,' when we passed in the hall and he would look right past me and not say a word," recalled one female employee. "We called him the little king."

Everyone knew that his readings had told of a past life as an Egyptian king who had kicked the high priest out of the country. A.R.E. employees had no trouble visualizing such a scenario. A number of them chose up sides in a sense, identified as either "priest's men or king's men," recalls John Van Auken, who then worked in the press. "I was a king's man."

"When he'd start acting like the old king, I'd react accordingly," said Mae Gimbert, "and he'd say, 'Damn it, Mae, you can make me madder than anyone but Sally.' "

Hugh Lynn recognized that his behavior was out of line but he couldn't seem to correct it. Far from being old enough to become crotchety, he should have been in peak form. He was physically healthy, a robust man in his mid-fifties, and yet he was in trouble emotionally.

"I found myself planning and doing things that were not right, taking advantage of people, hurting people with anger because I didn't like them, because I hated them. I'd get rid of them—people that worked at the A.R.E., people in the membership, people I was dealing with, and I couldn't seem to do anything about it."

By this time the A.R.E. was no longer a one-man and two-secretary operation, of course, but nonetheless Hugh Lynn was still making most of the administrative decisions.

"If I had come apart at that point, the A.R.E. would have come apart."

Fortunately, he had not lost faith in prayer and meditation, nor lost touch with mystical experiences.

"I had this, I don't know what it was, it certainly wasn't a dream or a vision, but it must have been. I didn't remember any of it except what I was told: 'Go to Egypt.'"

Hugh Lynn had done no traveling outside the country since World War II. But his guidance felt right.

"I didn't have any money, so I organized the first A.R.E. tour. I gathered forty-some people together and off we went to Egypt and six other countries around the Mediterranean—Israel, Lebanon, Syria, Jordan, Greece, and Italy. It was nice and cheap traveling in those days [1963]."

And safe. But it wasn't "safe" for an ancient Egyptian soul masquerading as an American spiritual leader.

"In Egypt we went up the Nile to Ramses' great temple at Abu-Simbel, right on the banks of the river, which was rising. We went into a back room where the Gods were supposed to come. There were beautiful carvings on the walls. And we ran the guards out and had a meditation. I led it and said the affirmation, and then I began to smother.

"I decided there were too many people in this little room and imagined all these ladies passing out and our having to drag them out. So I opened my eyes and looked around and they were fine. There was nothing wrong with them. I thought I must be having a heart attack, for I couldn't breathe. I shut my eyes and said the affirmation again. It was like somebody had snatched the thing I was standing on out from under my feet, and I sank—symbolically—and came down into this book-of-life kind of thing. I was in the body of somebody coming from another country with a rope around my neck, and some Egyptians were walking on by me. My feet were tied in dirty, bloody rags. My hands, crossed behind me and tied, were hurting. I was being enslaved by the Egyptians. The Egyptian who was walking by me had a whip, a short-handled whip with leather thongs on it that had rocks and lead in the end of it. I stumbled and he whipped me. The whip came over my shoulder—I'll never forget it—and it took about an inch or so of flesh off my chest. I cursed him.

"It was odd: I knew the language but I didn't know the language I was cursing him in, but he apparently understood it because he hit me with the butt of the whip. It pulled me, and the men just ahead and just behind me, down. I lost consciousness. I hated him, and that hatred was so terrible it was like fire burning inside me.

"Then I was on the scaffold, back in the time of Ramses II in another life. I was on the scaffold chiseling on the walls that our tour group had passed coming in. The artist who had drawn this on the wall was doing some inlay in connection with it, and I would chisel it so it could be filled with gold or something else.

"I could feel the knots of hardened skin on my knees and on my hand where I missed when trying to hit the chisel. I'd hit my hand and it would bleed and become encrusted. It was miserable. I'd stay up there for hours.

"I'll never forget the whip that overseer had. It was on a long staff with a lever thing on the end of it, and he could reach anyone on the scaffold with it. And he hit me on the back—I had chiseled wrong or something. I hated that man with such violence that it raged inside me while I was going through this.

"Then I switched and I was a little boy in a village, and my stomach was swollen. I was dying in my Egyptian mother's arms. The Nile had not flooded that year and the crops had not matured. There was water but nothing to eat. And I died in my mother's arms. I had an Egyptian father and mother but didn't connect them with the present. They must be somewhere.

"This went on and finally I came back [to the meditation] and I knew where my anger and hatred and fear had come from."

Hugh Lynn, interestingly enough, having initially rejected the idea that he had been an ancient Egyptian ruler, now had no trouble believing that he had had more than one demeaning life as a slave.

Having come to a new understanding of the cause of his anger, how was he to be rid of it?

"I prayed about this very hard. I couldn't stand myself. In Israel, we went then to Galilee and to Capernaum, a village on the north coast of the Sea of Galilee, the most beautiful spot in the world. The guide was telling us about Capernaum, what they think was Peter's house all the way back in the time of Jesus.

"I turned around and walked down to the water. There is a wall there on the seacoast. Beyond it is grassy and there are trees. And as I stood there, a light formed, taller than I and oval shaped. It moved over until it began to encompass me. It was the greatest peace I've ever felt. I was so joyous that in my mind I wanted to know if I could go and get Sally. I knew—I don't know how I knew, there were no words spoken—that I could do it. And I ran and got her, pulled her away from the group and walked down there by the Sea of Galilee and stood in the same place. And it enveloped us both. And I was healed."

Was it a modern miracle? Hugh Lynn didn't attempt to classify the experience, only to describe its results for him.

"I have had far, far better control over my fears and my angers and my hates since then. I can still get irritated, but it's not the deep-seated fears and angers of the past when I could get so angry that I could destroy a person without batting an eye. I mean just get rid of them, or turn away from them, not deal with them. No scruples whatsoever. It was very dangerous, and successful. You play people against people. A lot of businesses are run this way—competition, playing people against each other."

But if he, his soul, had manifested as Andrew in Jesus' time, why had that hatred not been healed then?

"There was too much violence. It was so short, and the Essenes of whom I [as Andrew] was a part were so warlike. Do you realize what they were doing? They were playing footsie with the Zealots in attempting to overthrow the Jewish church. And if they overthrew Rome in the process, that was fine. They were vitriolic and determined to destroy the Jewish church. That's why Caiaphas was so harsh with Jesus.

"There was violence all around. The Essene group was fomenting a revolution, financing it, and taking part and attacking. Zealots, Essenes and all kinds of people—tax collectors, fishermen—followed him. It was a conglomerate mixture for a very good purpose, I'm sure. But the Egyptian hatreds are still coming out. The early church was not a happy one. It was exciting, challenging, but also in a state of upheaval—arguments and attacks.

"John, the first Essene leader, was violent—shouting, ranting and raving—a fire-and-brimstone man. And he reached out to so many different kinds of people it was a job adjusting to the people you ran around with.

"Then after the death of Jesus, the divisions within the church were drastic—the fight between Peter and Paul, arguments within the early church. The disciples scattered. Some went to India, I think, looking for where He was. Some went to Persia. That's where I was. Some went to Egypt. I've been back to the place I went, I think,

Shushtar, Iran. We've [the United States] since been thrown out of there completely."

Hugh Lynn said he had no sense of *deja vu* while visiting the Holy Land, but that this experience with the Light had a profound effect on him. He not only mellowed in later years but gained a more realistic picture of himself. "After the trip I think he tried to work with himself," said Mae Gimbert.

"I hadn't known for years that people were afraid of me, that some people hated me automatically without knowing why—people I'd meet all over the country. And when I 'act like Egypt,' people climb trees and rebel and fight and oppose anything, it doesn't matter what it is. I could be so obviously right about something and yet have it opposed if I try to do it, if it comes across in that [Egyptian] image."

Hugh Lynn said in this life, trying to build the A.R.E., he had to learn not to give orders but to seek help from people. Given his nature, it was hard.

"It was a fascinating kind of karma, a karma of having to ask and plead, beg people to do something rather than telling them to do it and expecting it to be done instantaneously.

"It's never occurred to me in my life—and this is a horrible thing to say—that people won't do what I ask of them. It never occurs to me that there is any *reason* to say 'No,' and [I tend to think] they say, 'No,' just for aggravation's sake.

"But when I switch to that other personality, it works like a charm."

Didn't Hugh Lynn realize that he also inspired a lot of love in people?

"Yes, when I'm in that other personality. But I have to dress up in another costume, get into that other category, which is caring and loving and believing in and wanting to help people."

He frequently explained these contrasting aspects of himself in astrological terms: "Again, that fish (Pisces)." It tends to swim one direction and suddenly flip over and go the opposite way, he would say, as though seeing himself acting like that.

"It's funny how it works, but an interesting life, though— exciting, fascinating. Living it has been a joy."

Returning from the Middle East in April 1963, Hugh Lynn headed out across the United States on his annual speaking tour, this time for ten weeks. His itinerary took him into the South, the Midwest, and the Far West, and not just the major cities. As *The Bulletin* reported, he went first to California for "one- and two-day stands in Palo Alto, San Jose, Santa Cruz, and Sacramento, followed by a five-day conference in Los Angeles." From there he went to San

Diego and swung through the Southwest—Tucson, Albuquerque, Phoenix—and on into Texas—El Paso, San Antonio, Dallas, Fort Worth, Corpus Christi, and Houston. With no rest stops in between, Hugh Lynn headed for the Deep South:

"...there will be one-day stands in New Orleans, Birmingham, Nashville, Hopkinsville, Indianapolis, Chicago, Sioux City, two days in Kansas City, one each in Denver and Spokane, three days in Portland, Oregon, one day in Coos Bay, three in Seattle, two in San Francisco, possibly another stop or two not yet fixed, bringing him on June 16 to Asilomar on the Monterey Peninsula in California, where a week's workshop will be held."

Only a man of remarkable dedication and purpose voluntarily submits to such a strenuous road test—thirty cities and two week-long conferences in seventy-one days. And any man who includes Coos Bay, Oregon, on a national tour isn't saying "No" to any requests.

Of his far-flung journeys that year, his "return" to Egypt and to Israel was without a doubt the most meaningful to him personally. It marked, also, the beginning of a great new adventure for him and the A.R.E.—a search for roots in antiquity.

Three years later, in 1966, he organized a return to Israel for the purpose of looking for evidence of the Essene community that the Cayce readings had described on Mt. Carmel. He was accompanied by Dr. William McGarey of Phoenix, Shane Miller of New York, Rudolph Johnson of Dallas, Ruben Miller of Norfolk, and Bob Adriance of Virginia Beach, who later wrote of the trip:

"The Cayce readings report that 'the school of prophets was established in Carmel during Elijah's time; these were called, then, Essenes, and those that were students of what ye would call astrology, numerology, phrenology and those phases of that study of the return of individuals, or [re]incarnation.'...Thus there is much of a very intriguing nature about the whole story of Elijah, and John, the Essenes, Mt. Carmel, the Mother Mary and the Christ, particularly when, two years after Edgar Cayce's death, a Bedouin shepherd boy unearthed scrolls telling a great deal concerning the hitherto obscure sect, the Essenes....With the growth of the state of Israel and of Haifa on Mt. Carmel, in particular, it might soon become impossible to find any evidence that a community following the description of the Essenes ever existed. Hugh Lynn and the author [Adriance] laid plans accordingly for a three-week stay in Israel to learn all possible about the Essene Mt. Carmel story from the locale itself and from historians."

Armed with cameras and shovels, the group uncovered mounds

of old pottery. "Hugh Lynn was the prime archaeologist with his digging," McGarey noted in his diary, "which produced the top of a jug and the two handles, intact, and all the portions of the body of the same pottery jar or jug." He added that Hugh Lynn found an old coin but sprained his right foot prowling around one ruin. Dr. McGarey wrapped Hugh Lynn's ankle with a castor oil pack, which remained on for the night. Next morning, he noted, "It seemed considerably improved after the use of prayer, healing hands, and castor oil, so we headed out...."

The expedition was fascinating but proved inconclusive. To verify the Cayce readings' story of the Essene community would require a complete archaeological excavation, and that would be expensive, assuming permission were granted. Adriance reported confidence that someday "mankind will learn of a group who for centuries prepared for the birth of a child with the perfection of God, the Messiah, the Christ. There is almost certainly more to be told of the story of the nativity."

The quest for evidence to support Cayce's stories of ancient events had just begun. Actually, it had been initiated a few years earlier by a graduate student, Marjorie Hansen, who had gone to Egypt with a woman friend to look for the Hall of Records described in the Cayce readings. The records were said to have been buried in a hidden underground chamber near the left paw of the Sphinx. Edgar Evans Cayce recalls that the twenty-seven-year-old Miss Hansen and friend "stayed at the Y and bored eight holes in front of the Sphinx—I don't know how they got permission, maybe their good looks—and that was the first exploration in Egypt." The authorities charged her $300 (Hansen paid in travelers checks) and assigned workmen to punch holes through the floor of the Sphinx Temple about ten feet deep and one meter apart.

Instead of a chamber or tunnels beneath the Sphinx, she hit water about four feet down. But Hansen observed in a report to the Edgar Cayce Foundation that "the inner contours of the two forepaws have been filled in with large limestone blocks which are visible where the outer double casing of brickwork is incomplete." She argued that this alone justified "a thorough examination," because none of these blocks had been moved in search of hidden chambers. Indeed, she pointed out that little is really known about this mysterious desert monument, and that "who built it or why is mainly conjecture. Foundation deposits containing such information were usually placed under most temples; so possibly some such might be found under one of the large limestone blocks composing the paws." These blocks had been covered with brickwork many years ago when drifting sand had been cleared from the base of the Sphinx. She advocated "a thorough examination."

The implication was clear: if further excavation turned up records left by the builders of the Sphinx, the legendary Hall of Records might also be found.

Logic was on her side, and Hugh Lynn wanted to believe it; but circumstances were not. The A.R.E and the Edgar Cayce Foundation had no resources to launch an archaeological dig in Egypt and no connections or experience in the field. Hugh Lynn, however, had an inner feeling of rightness on his side and would spend the rest of his life in hot pursuit of the evidence of Ra Ta. But he needed help. He found it in the unlikely person of a college dropout named Mark Lehner.

"Mark was a college student during the 1960s in California and was involved in a lot of student protest activity at Berkeley and around there. He was pursuing a girl and caught her at our Asilomar conference. She dragged him into a meditation class I was giving. It enabled me to look at him, and I saw somebody that I thought I recognized.

"So I asked him to come to Virginia Beach. He came right at the time in 1972 that Charles Thomas [Cayce, who had joined the staff as director of youth activities] was taking a youth group to Egypt and Europe. Mark wanted very much to go, so I gave him the trip."

Lehner recalls experiencing an extraordinary attraction when the group reached the Great Pyramid: "I went out to the Giza Plateau with the group and then went out to the pyramids again by myself and sat for a while in the King's Chamber in the Great Pyramid. I wandered around the cemeteries that are outside the pyramid, and something plugged into me about that place. I vowed that I would be back in a year."

Hugh Lynn knew what Lehner's experience meant as soon as the group returned home.

"He was really turned on. He said he wanted to go back, and I knew he was going to have to go back when I saw him. I thought, 'This is the man who can find what we are looking for.'"

Hugh Lynn was no less excited than Lehner. He wanted to find the trail of an ancient pharaoh not mentioned in academic circles. What he hoped Lehner might discover would be a whole prehistoric civilization. Such a discovery, he had no doubt, would dazzle the modern world no less than the discovery of the Dead Sea Scrolls. It would be proof positive that Edgar Cayce had been more than a good storyteller and medical diagnostician. He would be recognized at last as the greatest mystic of modern times.

244

Lehner, an unlettered youngster from rural America, hardly looked the part of a modern Schliemann, the discoverer of ancient Troy. He needed an education, credentials, travel expenses, experience. Like Shaw's Professor Higgins, Hugh Lynn set out to transform his young protege and make it all come true. Lehner had what he most needed: imagination and motivation. Hugh Lynn would wave his wand to produce the rest.

"He asked if I thought they'd take him at the university in Cairo. He told me he had some good grades and some very bad grades, and he asked if I'd write him a letter of recommendation. I wrote to the dean of admissions who turned out to be somebody who had read all the A.R.E books. He said he'd love to have Mark."

In preparation, Lehner recalled. "I enthusiastically researched the Cayce readings on Egypt." He pieced together fragments from many readings given for people who were said to have been in Egypt. His narrative, *The Egyptian Heritage*, was published in booklet form by the A.R.E. Press. "The readings describe not only a civilization in Egypt in 10,500 B.C. but also, preceding that, the lost civilization of Atlantis, which was in its final days, according to the Cayce information, when the Sphinx and the pyramids were being built. And as I researched, I found it to be a coherent scheme, internally consistent, developed over twenty years of psychic readings."

If Edgar Cayce had merely been spinning a fanciful yarn over that long a period, it was astonishing that he had not contradicted himself occasionally. His consistency as much as anything convinced this young explorer that Ra Ta, the high priest of that ancient Egyptian kingdom, was not a mythical product of Edgar Cayce's imagination.

Archaeologists had concluded years before that the Great Pyramid had been built around 2500 B.C. during the reign of a pharaoh named Kufu. The Cayce readings disagreed: "Edgar Cayce said that Hermes built or designed the Great Pyramid," Lehner found, "but he didn't say who Hermes was. He said Hermes helped the high priest, Ra Ta, build the pyramid in 10,500 B.C."

The readings also identified Edgar as having been Ra Ta, the high priest, and Hugh Lynn as a king named Araaraart. But where was the evidence? Lehner picked up a trail in the oral tradition of the region: "Arab legends from hundreds of years ago say that Hermes was the architect who built the Great Pyramid, and that it was built as a repository of knowledge in its dimensions before the Great Flood. That's one legend that parallels the Cayce readings."

As Lehner searched the Cayce archives, Hugh Lynn looked for the means of underwriting his young explorer. Mark had an artistic bent and tried to earn as much as he could.

"He painted Egyptian scenes on big conch shells and sold them and made some money, but not enough. An A.R.E. couple came to our house one day and I was showing them his shells, some of his sculpting, and they said, 'This is the kind of boy we'd like to help.' I said, 'That's interesting because he does need help.'"

Lehner's benefactors were Arch and Ann Ogden, who lived in Florida. "It's very important, in my opinion right now," Hugh Lynn told the Ogdens, "for the A.R.E. to have a man in Cairo."

A long-time A.R.E. member who served as president of the Edgar Cayce Foundation, Arch Ogden was a modest man and a generous philanthropist by virtue of having the income from a successful family business. He agreed with Hugh Lynn's grand strategy and didn't blanch at the estimated college expenses: $3500 a year.

"So they put Mark through two years at the American University in Cairo."

For young Lehner it was an adventure that exceeded the American collegiate protest marches of the 1960s. When he returned to Cairo in the fall of 1973, the United States and Egypt had broken off diplomatic relations. Egypt was on the brink of revolution or disintegration. Student riots had closed Cairo's universities twice that year already. Mass trials of subversives were starting when Lehner arrived in September. Egypt's President Anwar Sadat, under pressure from Libya's President Kaddafi to unite with his country, kept Kaddafi at bay, but in October attacked Israel. Israeli air raids that struck the outskirts of Cairo sent American tourists fleeing and caused suspension of classes at the university once again, but Lehner wrote Hugh Lynn that he was staying on and using his time to study Arabic and Arabian history. He also worked as an aide to an NBC correspondent in the Egyptian capital. His chief regret was that the Egyptian Museum closed during the fighting.

By year's end, Egypt and the United States resumed diplomatic relations. Hugh Lynn was relieved that the Yom Kippur war lasted less than three weeks. Even war in the Middle East could not be allowed to torpedo the search for Ra Ta. As Lehner was getting acclimated to Cairo, Hugh Lynn was traveling on the other side of the border, in Israel and Iran. When he returned home, Hugh Lynn began writing Mark long, encouraging letters. They had the flavor of a doting father:

"Now that the cease-fire has been put into effect, perhaps it won't be necessary for you to move out at all and you can carry on with your activities there. It will take time for you to get adjusted and begin to get ahold of the language and until you do get the language under some kind of control, communication will be only sketchy. Once you begin to think and dream in Arabic everything will be easier and it shouldn't be too hard for you....

"You have everything it takes to make this venture a rewarding one: Brains, determination and internal drive which I think may very well come from the so-called past and certainly good goals based on sound ideals."

As for his own exploratory trip to ancient Persia, with Arch Ogden and Rufus Mosely, an airline pilot who often flew the route from New York to Cairo, he wrote Lehner: "In Iran we were able to see in some detail the area around Shushtar [about seventy-five miles east of the Iraq border]. My thinking on this matter isn't so much tied up with the City in the Hills and Plains, though of course that is the archaeological focus, a spot 7½ miles southwest of Shushtar.... What is exciting for me, Mark, is that I think the Shushtar area may well have been the scene of Jesus' incarnation as Zend. Later I think, as Jesus, he may have returned as a student before he went on to India and then back to Egypt. Later because of what he told the disciples, I think several of them went to the Shushtar area and later still, Shushtar became one of the early Christian missionary centers."

Hugh Lynn believed that as Andrew, he had been there before. He thought it all tied in with some statements in the readings but admitted "they are vague and tenuous." He nonetheless found it very exciting. "It is putting all of the little pieces of the immense puzzle together that becomes so fascinating," he told Mark.

Lehner justified Cayce's confidence. He made straight A's his first semester, and he fell in love with Egypt and its ancient culture. He also fell in love with a pretty Egyptian dancer, a Coptic Christian who had already graduated in psychology from the American University. Her name was Suzanne.

Even before Lehner was graduated, he became involved in archaeological activities and acquainted with American scholars at various digs. But since any group or organization that wishes to conduct archaeological exploration in Egypt must obtain permission from the government's Ministry of Culture, he made the acquaintance of key officials, too, including Zahi Hawass, chief inspector of the Giza pyramids. After obtaining his degree in anthropology, Mark got a job as secretary to Hassan Ragab, head of the Papyrus Institute. Ragab, a former diplomat, had spent years in research in order to reintroduce papyrus to Egypt. Mark was hired to help him write a book on the subject of papyrus and to handle his foreign correspondence. He also helped paint reproductions of ancient Egyptian paintings on papyrus. One can visualize the number of portraits of the gorgeous Nefertiti hanging in American living rooms, souvenirs of a grand trip to the Valley of the Nile, painted by a talented lad from Minot, North Dakota.

In 1976, the Edgar Cayce Foundation broadened its archaeological program by contributing $2500 to the Nag Hammadi dig, a project undertaken by the Claremont Graduate School's Institute for Antiquity and Christianity in cooperation with Brigham Young University. Nag Hammadi had already yielded a valuable collection of fourth-century manuscripts. Hugh Lynn recalled:

"The Nag Hammadi Scrolls were found about the same time as the Dead Sea Scrolls [1947]. They contained the earliest writings of the earliest monks—the book of Melchizedek, the book of Enoch. The writings have been translated, a big project, in one book. I wrote a review of the book and told everybody that it mentioned several incarnations of Jesus, referring to Melchizedek and Hermes. But I said it's going to be very difficult for you to read—they ate it like hotcakes. It was a good gimmick and sold a lot of books.

"We gave a little money to the Hammadi dig and got Mark on that dig for a summer. He made sketches and he made a name for himself."

Claremont in return offered the A.R.E. the use of instruments lent by the University of California. But the A.R.E. was in no position to use such equipment on its own. It had to operate through other agencies already conducting operations in Egypt, such as the American Research Center in Egypt, which operates under the auspices of Columbia University to conduct archaeological exploratory work in the country.

"We gave them a little money and Mark got attached [to the ARCE] and set up with the Sphinx project."

The project was to document the Sphinx, describing architecturally the shape and size of every aspect of this mysterious stone monument. It would make Mark Lehner the world's leading expert on the Sphinx. More important to Hugh Lynn, it gave his man in Cairo the leverage to search for the evidence of Ra Ta and the legendary Hall of Records.

The Egypt project, as it was called around the A.R.E., appealed to Edgar Evans Cayce, an engineer, no less than to his brother. As young fellows both had participated in several explorations for treasure which the readings said had been buried in Virginia—never with any success. But the prospect of turning up an ancient Egyptian treasure trove brought Edgar Evans into the adventure. When he

248

read that the Stanford Research Institute was conducting exploratory work around the pyramids, using instruments that could detect underground cavities, he sensed a great opportunity. "I suggested to Hugh Lynn, since these people were over there, we ought to get in touch with them. If they have all this equipment over there, here was a chance to prove, once and for all, whether there is anything there or not. They can check by the Sphinx's paw to see whether there is a cavity there. Hugh Lynn agreed with me."

SRI had already spent two years at Giza in search of passages in and under the pyramids. An SRI official, Lambert Dolphin, whom Lehner had met in Egypt, came to Virginia Beach and worked out an agreement for the Edgar Cayce Foundation to finance a remote sensing survey of the Sphinx. Edgar Evans said Hugh Lynn raised $70,000 to $100,000 for the Egypt project. The work was approved by the Egyptian authorities and went forward in 1977-78, with Lehner participating as the Edgar Cayce Foundation's "man in Cairo." It is amazing how swiftly these elements had fallen together.

Using devices that measure electrical resistance and acoustical effects, SRI identified five major anomalies—deviations from the norm in the rock structure—which indicated the possibility of underground cavities.

"And they found them in the places Dad said they would be. I used SRI's report to raise money. It cost us a lot to get into Egypt—it was like knocking down the door to get in the gate. If you've got scientific backing from SRI, you've got scientists over there whom you pay a lot of money. But we got Mark Lehner into that project, and into the Sphinx."

Using precision drills to explore these five areas found in the floor of the Sphinx and the Sphinx temple, the scientists dropped a boroscope camera and tiny light down the shaft but found "only natural fissures and small Swiss cheese-like cavities," Lehner reported.

When the funding ran out, SRI packed up and returned to the United States. Like the Cayce Petroleum Co., SRI and the Foundation had nothing but dry wells when they ran out of money. Discouraging as these inconclusive results were, Hugh Lynn had no sense of defeat. He would stay with the search as long as it took, building alliances with other groups and individuals. One of the latter was the Egyptian chief inspector at Giza, Hawass, whom he had met through Lehner in 1975.

In 1980, Hawass accommodated the A.R.E by conducting an excavation in front of the Sphinx temple. A core drilling through fifty feet of debris struck red granite instead of the natural limestone bedrock from which the Sphinx had been carved. Since the granite had to have been imported, this discovery raised questions about why it was placed there and what more might be found if a dig were permitted. Such an operation would require approval at a higher government level. If Zahi Hawass was to advance within the government, to further his own career and open doors for Hugh Lynn's project, he could best do it on the wings of higher education at an American Ivy League college. His patron cleared the way:

"I got him a scholarship at the University of Pennsylvania in Egyptology, to get his Ph.D. I got the scholarship through an A.R.E. person who happens to be on the Fulbright scholarship board. He has aided Mark to work on the Sphinx, and I'm very appreciative."

More than returning a favor or expecting one in this life, Hugh Lynn sensed some past-life connections.

"I believe in following through on things, not just in this life but when they relate to other lives, because I think of it as all of a piece. I want to get all the eggs together rather than separated. If I'm going to have an omelette I need some eggs. That's the way I've lived this life. The reincarnation concepts have brought that about and extended my view, stretched my view of everything."

There was another Egyptian, a teenager named Nufa, who brought memories of another lifetime to him.

"He showed up every day at the Sphinx. He wanted more than anything else to learn English so he could become a tourist guide for Americans and other English-speaking visitors."

As Nufa remembers it, he saw Hugh Lynn sitting near the Sphinx, watching a drilling operation. "I had seen him there other days, just sitting. He had on a large wide-brimmed hat and was just sitting in the hot sun. His hair was so white, and I thought he would get a sunstroke."

Nufa tried to sell him a tour of the pyramids. Hugh Lynn just laughed but struck up a conversation with the lad, who told him he was studying English and wanted to practice. They talked and played chess.

"That first day I knew that I knew him," said Hugh Lynn, "but I didn't know from where. In my hotel room as I went to bed I asked how I knew him. And I had a dream about him. In the dream he actually prevented somebody from killing me in Egypt, probably in the period of Ra Ta [when Hugh Lynn was said to have been the king]. He was just an ordinary soldier. The dream was a fight scene. My men had lost track of me. And some other men were trying to kill me and were getting close with their spears. And this boy and a few others were shouting after our men who were supposed to come but hadn't
250

arrived. One man with a spear got to me, and this young soldier got between me and the spear and they drove it through him.

"My men came up, drove them off, but this boy died in my arms as I said, 'Live, I can give you anything in the world that you want. Live.' That was my dream.

"The next morning down at the Sphinx he showed up and I said, 'What would you like more than anything else in the world?' He said, 'I want to go to America.' I didn't say anything more to him—so many Egyptians want to go to America—and he didn't know it but I started working then to get him to America. It took quite a few years, but I got him over here and got him in a community college and got him a job."

Nufa later married an American girl, Elaine Guidry, an A.R.E. member who had an amazing experience not long after the wedding. She began to experience a strange fear whenever Nufa was late getting home, or wasn't home when she arrived thinking he would be there.

Oddly enough, neither Nufa nor Elaine knew about Hugh Lynn's past-life dream until after they married. He told them about it during a visit to their home not long thereafter. Elaine said hearing about the death scene in the dream had a powerful emotional effect on her: "I could hardly breathe. My entire body was tingling and I knew that I had heard truth. I could only stare into his eyes because the emotion came only partly from his words. The room and Nufa seemed not to exist. I saw in Hugh Lynn's eyes that king who long ago knelt in the street with blood covering him and made a promise to a dying friend."

In the weeks that followed Elaine was no longer gripped with fear in Nufa's absence. "To this very day it has not recurred." Elaine became convinced that her fear had been triggered by a karmic memory of the loss of Nufa in ancient Egypt. "I often wonder about the feelings of loss that I experienced that fateful day when the house remained empty because Nufa had died saving the life of our king."

Elaine also made a connection in her own mind about strange markings on her husband's body: "I noticed two rather round but jagged discolorations on Nufa's skin, one on his chest and the other on his back. I asked if he remembered anything in connection with these scars, but he insisted that he had them since birth and laughed when I suggested that they were caused by a spear in ancient Egypt."

Nufa and Elaine's marriage lasted only three years, but they remained friends, convinced that they had played out a role in which they had been cast centuries before. Hugh Lynn, having made his defender a promise in ancient times, had paid his karmic debt.

If he could find Nufa in that sea of humanity called Cairo, after all these years, he thought surely he could find Ra Ta. He said, "I'm never giving up there. It is very important. If we get back to the old kingdom there, it is going to make history look like...." Hugh Lynn shook his head and smiled as though anticipating the tremendous impact such a discovery would have. What did he hope to find?

"We are looking for records—this is what the readings say—of the pyramids themselves and the Sphinx. We are looking for the Atlantean records which are buried there. We are looking for Hermes' records and his prophecy of his next incarnation as Jesus. I think they are there, in front of the Sphinx. The Sphinx is guarding them. We are playing for all the marbles."

Chapter 20

A New Edgar Cayce?

The longer his quest to verify the Ra Ta myth with a stunning archaeological discovery continued without success, the worse Hugh Lynn's dilemma became about calling on other psychics for help. Why not use a living psychic to supplement the information the dead Edgar Cayce had given? Hugh Lynn was not closed to the idea, but whom could he trust?

Besides, for years following his father's death there had been discussion among A.R.E. members about the advisability of finding a "new Edgar Cayce." People with some unusual sensitivity showed up frequently. One woman, Betty McCain, even gave readings at A.R.E. for quite a while and gained considerable respect. Hugh Lynn thought she was pretty good. All of her readings are still preserved in the archives of the Edgar Cayce Foundation, but no attempt to index or evaluate them—a tedious and expensive task—was ever made.

Another promising psychic, Ray Stanford, was accorded the A.R.E. forum. The McGareys, who experimented with psychic readings for their patients and for members of their family from time to time, were impressed with his talent and invited him to Phoenix. "He came for Thanksgiving weekend," recalls Dr. Gladys with a smile, "and stayed [in the McGareys' house] for four years." Hugh Lynn became disenchanted with him, but Stanford gained a following when he formed his own organization.

When it came to the quest for Ra Ta, there seemed no end to the parade of psychics who came forth with information, much of it not unlike Cayce's Ra Ta legend. Most of it was unsolicited but nonetheless intriguing. "I have reams of psychic information," said Lehner in 1985, "triangulations on maps, projections of passages done by dowsers, big fat files full of it." Hugh Lynn was ambivalent about how to deal with such supplementary information. On one occasion, however, he got excited about the prospect of hitting archaeological pay dirt.

In 1974, a year after his trip to Iran, while lecturing in Toronto, he met J. Norman Emerson, an anthropologist who worked with a Canadian psychic, George McMullen. Dr. Emerson had published several articles on intuitive archaeology. Hugh Lynn was so intrigued that he and Sally and the Ogdens went to Vancouver to visit the psychic. They took along pottery shards they had picked up in Iran, and on Mount Carmel, where he and his associates had searched for possible ruins of an Essene temple described in the readings. He wanted to see if McMullen could get any images from them. As Hugh Lynn told the A.R.E. board of trustees later, "these were shards which relate to meaningful projects for future explorations."

Hugh Lynn placed the shards before McMullen without explanation. The psychic held each one and reported his impressions. Hugh Lynn thought his statements were so "very accurate and convincing" that he made plans to include McMullen and Emerson in a return visit to the Middle East. Near Shushtar were several noteworthy ruins, including Daniel's tomb, and, "the possibility of taking a capable sensitive with us was intriguing."

In the fall of 1975, he returned to Iran and Egypt with McMullen, Dr. Emerson, the Ogdens, and Sally—an expedition that cost the Edgar Cayce Foundation about $17,000, all of it covered by contributions earmarked for this venture by such donors as Rufus Mosely and his wife.

It was very appealing to Hugh Lynn to work with a man of Dr. Emerson's credentials, which might serve to validate his unorthodox quest as well as to provide a test of psychic archaeology. Emerson reciprocated the feeling: "I was happy to be given the opportunity to work with the A.R.E., whose motivation and integrity I considered to be outstanding," he wrote later. "My own research had convinced me that in intuitive studies the problem of motivation was one of extreme importance—that it must be 'of the highest' and directed toward the good of humanity." He said he rejects any proposal motivated by "greed or personal gain." On that, too, Hugh Lynn and he saw eye-to-eye.

The party went first to Giza, which Hugh Lynn regarded as a "warm-up" for more important research in Iran. After a period of immersion in Egyptian archaeology and prehistory at the Cairo Museum, McMullen spent a day around the Sphinx and another around the pyramids of Giza. Afterward he described the location of ancient water systems, pools, baths, and luxurious vegetation adjacent to the Sphinx. Hugh Lynn said a number of McMullen's ideas coincided with the Cayce readings.

Most intriguing, McMullen saw an underground chamber containing records in the direction of the Nile. The exact spot, he said, was where two shadows overlap at sunset in late October—the shadows of the head of Sphinx and the top of the Great Pyramid. The problem with locating that spot was complicated by having to calculate the original height of both structures. "George was able to provide helpful information about the height of the pyramid capstone and on the dimensions of the Sphinx's original crown, now completely missing," said Dr. Emerson. "The proof will be in the digging."

In Iran, after a hot, dusty, bone-shaking jeep ride to remote Shushtar in search of a cave mentioned in the readings, McMullen pinpointed several locations that were blocked by landslides. One of them, he said, had been a healing and instructional center. The healing teacher who had lived there had been an early incarnation of Jesus. A dig there would recover important ancient tablets, he added.

While McMullen's psychic tips were fascinating, there was no opportunity for excavation to verify them. Both Egypt and Iran exercise tight control over digs, and the A.R.E. lacked funding to pursue either one even if permission were granted. Frustrating as were the results, McMullen's intuitive work left Hugh Lynn more convinced that he was on the right track, especially since other clairvoyants tended to confirm that the shifting desert sands obscure an unknown ancient culture.

In 1978 he sent a map of the Mount Carmel area in Israel to a number of psychics, inviting their participation in researching the origins of the Essenes. But Egypt remained the primary target area. One woman psychic went there on an A.R.E. tour and told Lehner that the Ra Ta culture, as well as Atlantis, had been thought-form civilizations: "They were very real, she said, but they existed at a higher frequency, on another dimensional level than we are on here in our physical bodies." That might explain why archaeologists had never found a trace of either civilization. But her theory did not discourage the Ra Ta investigators because she agreed with Cayce that an actual Hall of Records existed and had been buried at the time of the construction of the Great Pyramid. She thought the records of Atlantis had been produced by the seers of the Middle Kingdom around 2500 B.C.

A well-known psychic, Ingo Swann, whose participation was

solicited by Ogden, seemed interested in another possible expedition to Persia (Iran). Instead, Ogden took a new psychic, Al Miner, to Egypt at his own expense. Having underwritten Lehner's education in Cairo, Ogden had no hesitancy in investing further in the Egypt project. He commissioned Miner, who lived near him in Florida, to give about twenty readings on Egypt. Others who shared his enthusiasm for Miner were a Virginia Beach couple, Ursula and Joseph Jahoda, who were close to Hugh Lynn and backed the Egypt project financially. The Jahodas had so much confidence in Miner's clairvoyant gift that they used him repeatedly for readings for their family and their business as well as recommending him to others, Hugh Lynn included.

The closest Hugh Lynn came to involvement was when Arch Ogden persuaded him to observe a reading from Al Miner. It was given in the privacy of the Ogdens' motor home in the parking lot of the Marshalls Hotel across the street from A.R.E. headquarters. Arch had brought Al and his wife, Lucy, to the A.R.E. in an effort to break down Hugh Lynn's resistance. Accompanied by Herbert Puryear, one of his top A.R.E. lieutenants, Hugh Lynn watched as Al lay down on the Ogdens' travel bed, put himself under hypnosis just like Edgar Cayce had done, and began to communicate from another realm or another level of consciousness. The entity that comes through Miner, Lama Sing, greeted the president of the A.R.E. and his associate and the president of the Edgar Cayce Foundation, who conducted the reading, and answered their questions. Hugh Lynn posed only one: How does one know whether a psychic's information is valid?

Lama Sing said one can only judge by the fruits, the results. As he left, Hugh Lynn is said to have mumbled, "The same thing my father said forty years ago." He later had dinner with the Ogdens and the Miners and split a huge ice cream sundae with the Miners' six-year-old daughter, Angel. But close as he was to the Ogdens and the Jahodas, all of whom who helped Miner organize his own foundation and become established as a professional psychic, he avoided official contact and denied him any recognition. Puryear, on the other hand, was so impressed with Miner's gift that he obtained a number of readings for himself and his family, some of them given on the Puryears' living room couch, usually with the stipulation that they not be recorded. Others on the A.R.E. staff quietly obtained Lama Sing readings during the 1970s and 1980s.

Hugh Lynn remained wary. Over the years he had encountered countless so-called psychics, some outright frauds among them, but many who were sincere if not as clairvoyant as they believed they were. He had traveled the world interviewing noted psychics, and one more unknown psychic was no cause for excitement on his part. During our dialogues, in fact, he made unflattering references to most psychics other than his father, pointing out what he considered to be their fatal flaws. Arthur Ford, for example, he faulted as an alcoholic. One of the wisecracks of the period was that the A.R.E.'s eleventh commandment was, "Thou shalt have no other psychics before me."

When Hugh Lynn was interviewed by *Metro* magazine editor Robert S. Friedman in 1974 and asked why the A.R.E. had a reputation for discouraging other psychics, he replied: "Well, that's the rumor, not the fact. The A.R.E. is greatly interested in and greatly concerned with the development that is taking place in the whole psychic field and very interested. And I am certainly personally sympathetic with the problems and the opportunities of people who are psychically gifted. But we are not in a position at the present time to investigate thoroughly and carry through the kind of experimentation and training that we feel would be necessary and important in the development of psychic gifts. Consequently, as an official policy, we presently do not recommend or promote any psychic or any kind of occult or metaphysical practices. We try to maintain an attitude of research and of careful evaluation in checking experimentally in the whole field. We use Edgar Cayce's material as a platform, as a springboard for research in many directions."

He added that anyone who is gifted with clairvoyance needs to consider their diet, and how to meditate, and to work with meditation groups in order to become better psychics. "We are moving toward a research program that would include investigation of psychic sensitivity and the development of psychic sensitives in a frame of reference that we feel would be very helpful."

One area of research in which A.R.E. participates, he noted, is to "work with our own dreams." A.R.E. conducts seminars to help people learn how to work with their dreams. Indeed, dream research became a major emphasis at A.R.E. under a young Ph.D. from Princeton, Henry Reed. But money for research was always short, so psychic investigation of any kind was minimal.

Hugh Lynn wasn't the only one who was wary of employing other psychics. So was his board of trustees, said William Lord: "It was a perplexing question [for the board]. Edgar Cayce insisted on going to headquarters, which was a symbol of the Christ Consciousness. He said, 'Why go to anybody else?' A lot of psychics have a channel or a guide. Maybe it's Aunt Mary, but Aunt Mary doesn't know any more dead than she did when she was alive. So why go to anybody but headquarters? We had a feeling that a lot of it was channeled. And to test all these people takes a great deal of time. We felt that it was unsafe because we weren't sure about the source of the information. Some would be good sometimes, some would be lousy."

As for Hugh Lynn's attitude, Bill Lord said that he "was single-minded about pushing what he had, Cayce's readings. Why should he divert himself? Yes, he brought in other psychics and was quite open-minded about it, but he realized that they didn't have the depth that Edgar Cayce had. The psychic stuff was only giving him problems."

If Hugh Lynn's attitude was not always consistent, there may have been a hidden factor. Perhaps he didn't want another psychic sharing the glory if the legendary Atlantean records were uncovered in Egypt with the aid of a living clairvoyant who could be interviewed, written up, even lionized. A dead psychic's zealous son might find it hard to compete.

Finally, there was the question of timing. The Cayce readings and Miner's Lama Sing readings on Egypt not only agreed about the buried records, but predicted that they would be found only when the human race was ready for the information. The implication seemed to be that as of today, the warlike tendency of people and nations precludes discovering the secrets of Atlantis, some of which evidently had led to the destruction of that civilization. Hugh Lynn was gambling that it would happen on his watch, and that sole credit would go to Edgar Cayce.

After his death in 1982, the Ra Ta mystery deepened when Mark Lehner made the first attempt ever to carbon-date the Great Pyramid. The trick was to find tiny bits of carbon from wood fragments in the mortar between the blocks. Gathering fifteen samples from top to bottom of the huge structure, he sent them to two laboratories for analysis, one in Zurich, the other at Southern Methodist University in Dallas. The results were baffling because they confirmed neither the conventional theory that the Great Pyramid was built around 2500 B.C nor the Cayce date, 10,500 B.C. The radiocarbon dates on the average, Lehner reported, indicated that it was nearly four hundred years older than Egyptologists believe.

The range of dates and the location of the mortar for specific samples only compounded the puzzlement. "We have a spread of nine hundred years from the earliest to the latest date on the Great Pyramid," Lehner told A.R.E. officials. No one had ever thought it took that long to build it. More mystifying was the discovery that "the oldest ones are at the top and the youngest ones are at the bottom," which led to the joking conclusion among the radiocarbon experts that the Great Pyramid had been built from the top down.

What would Edgar Cayce—or a successor psychic at A.R.E.— have to say about this? One is left to speculate. Hugh Lynn's answer was always a determined push for tangible evidence—a tunnel, an underground chamber, a cache of artifacts that would dazzle and inform the skeptics.

While his Egypt project gave The Work a tremendously satisfying international dimension for him, its frustrations and the requisite globetrotting also added great stress to his already heavy workload as president of the A.R.E. Sooner or later something had to give.

Chapter 21

Passing the Torch

Shortly before his seventieth birthday, Hugh Lynn suffered the first major physical setback of his adult life. For most of his life he had enjoyed robust health, even overcoming a youthful dependency on eyeglasses. But now his body rebelled against the overload it had been carrying for years. While taking a massage in the physical therapy rooms at A.R.E. headquarters, he felt an ache in his left arm. The nurse took his blood pressure, 190/98, but he attributed the curious reading to the effect of the massage. He dressed and walked down the hill to the Library/Conference Center to attend the noontime meditation. Whatever his discomfort, he wasn't going to let it interfere with meditation. "He meditated pretty much every day for fifty years," said Charles Thomas. As he sat down in the auditorium behind his son, Hugh Lynn's pain grew ominously worse.

"It filled my chest. I realized I was having a heart attack. I touched Charles Thomas on the shoulder. He followed me out of the auditorium and took me to the hospital."

For the next three days, he lay immobilized in the intensive care unit at Virginia Beach General, his chest pains deadened by drugs under the care of a heart specialist recommended by his brother-in-law.

"I asked myself, 'Are you afraid of dying?'"

More than thirty years before he had faced down death during the Battle of the Bulge. But he couldn't say he hadn't been afraid. And when he learned of his father's death, he had suffered anxiety, fear, and even loss of faith in God. On another occasion years later, he had received numerous dream warnings of imminent death in an auto accident and feared only that he would leave his work

261

unfinished. Even now, lying in the hospital wondering how much longer he had, listening to the night sounds of death around him, Hugh Lynn re-experienced those wartime doubts about the nature of reality: Is there a God out there? Has He gone away and left us in this crazy world? And his focus suddenly shifted to the physical. Moved to a semi-private room, he began making brief entries in a diary:

March 6: "Heart seems to have stabilized, my doctor R. Gormly, recommended by W. Taylor and R. Brewer, assures me. Two weeks here, then a period of quiet at home."

March 7: Hospital service excellent. A.R.E. members on staff drop in—cards pour in—just a very few visitors."

March 8: "Jim D., a real estate agent, showed up. He had a bad one. As a roommate he is fun."

March 9: "Talked to Ecken [then fifty-nine]. He is considering by-pass surgery for his clogged arteries—they may try medication."

Some days he made no entry other than the word "hospital."

March 12: "Jim D. left. He has lots of medication. So far I have none."

March 13: "Ecken will try medication for a couple of weeks."

March 16: "My birthday was celebrated in the hospital. My mild heart attack came as a warning, I think, to slow down. Tomorrow I've been here two weeks and I go home for a rest, all schedules involving me have been cancelled."

March 17: "Came home before noon from hospital."

March 18: "This is the 100th anniversary of Edgar Cayce's birthday. Charles Thomas, Gladys and Sarah Hesson, Dad's sister, are in Hopkinsville for three days of celebration. Charles Thomas spoke to groups—library, high school, clubs and Liberty Church. The contract for the [motion] picture came. Henry Gellis paid $50,000 plus for [film] rights to A Prophet in His Own Country by Jess Stearn."

The payment was for an exclusive consulting agreement. The money was divided five ways among Hugh Lynn, Edgar Evans, Gladys, Stearn, and the Edgar Cayce Foundation. Stearn says he declined to collect his share.

Hugh Lynn was not bed-ridden. His doctor advised exercise and fresh air. Anticipating the arrival of spring, he had his garden plowed and limed. And he began thinking about what it would mean to slow down.

March 23: "A day with slides—talk with Charles Thomas—a longer walk—exercise—work on design book—prayer—I'll start meditation tomorrow—for two, yes almost three [weeks] it has been only prayer."

262

March 24: "Today I start reworking and finishing my book on fear. Leslie and Charles Thomas will be here tonight to view slides of early trips, wedding reception, etc."

The wedding of Charles Thomas and Leslie Goodman in January had given Hugh Lynn great satisfaction.

March 25: "The slides were good—wedding reception at the farm, old pictures by Charlie Dillman, including Mother, Dad, Judy [Chandler], Edgar Evans's family. Saw Dr. today—going OK."

March 26: "Busy day in yard. Frank plowed garden twice—lime and fertilizer. Dan worked with me on wood pile—good shape. Bridge Ecken & Kat.

March 27: Busy time with maps, books, magazines. Finished clean up on wood pile. Ordered cinder blocks & manure for garden."

March 30: "Today I go for stress checkup in hospital with Dr. present. Plan to get seeds for garden on way home."

March 31: "The stress test seemed to go very well. There were no indications of irregularities."

April 1: "The A.R.E. Board of Trustees meets tonight. It's the first one I've missed. Charles Thomas will attend. He brought the movie check. 3 rows of garden have been planted."

April 2: "Both Board meetings A.R.E. & E.C.F. seemed to have gone smoothly."

April 4: "Back to writing today—detail of prayer and mediation & some further work on Fear of Death [chapter in Faces of Fear]. Going smoothly, I feel. Walked for 30 minutes."

April 6: "Start therapy today at hospital. Go with Ecken."

April 7: "Charles Thomas leaves for West Coast, will see Jess and Henry [Gellis, the film producer]."

April 8: "Appointment with Dr. Gormly. Report on stress test was excellent. Can drive now short distances and go out to dinner."

April 9: "Second exercise trip to hospital yesterday. Ecken picks me up. Bridge with Gail tonight."

April 10 (Easter): "A quiet time today for meditation and prayer. A beautiful day. Study for chapter on Med. for book. Work in garden—lunch—walked a mile or more. Saw last of 'Jesus of Nazareth.'"

April 11: "Lots of exercise today—hospital, walk with dog [Sunshine], ping-pong and horseshoes with Frank. Slept for 9 hours."

April 12: "A little writing, a trip to grocery, library, bank, appliance after lunch with Kim, walk, and a lot of garden—planted lima beans, squash, greens and flowers."

For much of that spring, Hugh Lynn divided his time between working on his book, writing in longhand for his secretary Norrene to pick up and return, typed; and working in his garden. He and Sally played a lot of bridge, went out to dinner occasionally, and attended a concert by the Virginia Symphony Pops Orchestra—"The symphony was good music—and Benny Goodman, a short swing session at end, good and fun." And he thought a lot about the future, especially after the following unusual experience:

"After my heart attack I woke up one morning remembering a dream. It wasn't a dream, it was a vision or an actual out-of-body experience. But I was remembering as if it had been a dream. I'd been at a meeting, an enormous meeting. The people at the meeting were the people who put together the A.R.E.—my father was there, Mother was there, Charles Thomas, my wife, everybody. Key people in the A.R.E. from all over the country, everywhere. Some I haven't seen yet, that are coming. Some that I've seen since having the dream that I had not seen before. What was going on was that my father and Morton Blumenthal were trying to tell me that after all of the conflict that had taken place [between them] over the first association [the National Association of Investigators], they had gotten together again. Morton said, 'You know, Hugh Lynn, this whole thing was planned before we all came this time. We all had our jobs to do. Some of us didn't do as well as others. But we all had a job to do. I was supposed to put up some money and start a hospital and get you to Virginia Beach and all that. But we've made peace. We're all right. It's like having money in the bank. So you can write a check on it now. Anything you want to do, there will be enough energy to get it through because of what's going on over here. It'll happen. It was planned before we all came.'

"What Morton was saying to me, and what I believe really, is that it was planned beforehand, and people come in at different wavelengths and on different levels. All have an opportunity and a job. There are certain things they can do and can't do, some just a little bit, some a whole lot.

"Then after Morton talked, Dad said, 'Hugh Lynn, we're at peace. Anything you can dream of can happen.' And they all smiled. I came out of this meeting remembering it and going over in my head what they had said to me. I knew I had to come back to my body, but I had been to this place before—I go to school there—I've been going to school there for a long time."

During his three months' convalescence at home—Hugh Lynn returned to the office for a half-day's work in early June—he and his family and friends discussed his future. Some thought he should retire. He deserved it. At the very least he should reduce his workload and change his lifestyle if he cared to live much longer. But after that dream experience, he thought maybe the best was yet to come. How could he retire now? It was a time to change his approach perhaps, but not to give it all up.

"I made up my mind when I had that heart attack that I was going to get myself in shape and stay here awhile. I couldn't see quitting right in the middle of all this fascinating stuff that was happening."

But any change affected his top subordinates and possibly the future of The Work. Herbert Puryear, the A.R.E. director of education, who had come to lunch with him on April 28, thought he was entitled to succeed Hugh Lynn, if and when the president vacated his office. Hugh Lynn told him that he and Charles Thomas should share in directing the organization in his absence, after which some decisions would have to be made.

"I guess you and Tommy will have to fight it out," Puryear is said to have been told by Hugh Lynn.

It was no contest. "Herb and Hugh Lynn never saw eye to eye on anything," said Meredith Puryear, "and yet I don't think there was any man living that Herb respected more or wanted more to be accepted by than Hugh Lynn."

Hugh Lynn plainly favored a family succession. He had already designated Charles Thomas as his stand-in during the board of trustees' meeting that month. But for now Hugh Lynn had no intention of bowing out, just because he was seventy and had a heart condition.

"I plan to be around as long as I can function normally," he was still saying four years later.

He confided few of his private thoughts to his diary, but occasionally dropped hints:

May 20: "Charles Thomas for dinner—first discussion."

May 27: "First time A.R.E.—1 hour with Norrene & Charles Thomas. Played golf 9 holes—Jim, Jerry & Bob A."

May 29 (Sunday): "Lunch Charles Thomas—talk."

May 30 (Memorial Day): "Talked with Ecken—A.R.E.—Gail, etc."

The line of succession from father to son, a third generation Cayce to head The Work, was nearing confirmation. Those most immediately involved, family and colleagues, were being advised. Only Puryear was not told.

May 31: "Lunch with Everett [Irion, business manager and treasurer of the A.R.E.]."

June 6 (Monday): "Back to office—may try just half a day until weekend—Board meetings."

June 9: "Sphinx committee meeting—to consider SRI proposal."

June 10 (Friday): "Trustees first meeting tonite—I'll resign as

President of A.R.E. and become ch. of Board."

June 11 (Saturday): "All day trustees, A.R.E. Foundation trustees at nite."

June 12 (Sunday): "Board's at Charles Thomas and Leslie's |farm| for barbecue lunch."

Five days later, June 18, 1976, the board ratified Hugh Lynn's plan of succession. William Lord, a long-time board member, said there was no disagreement, "None whatsoever." Charles Thomas Cayce, at age 34, was elevated to president of the A.R.E. While it is hard to imagine the board rejecting Hugh Lynn's choice, Puryear was not considered a suitable replacement. "Herb was a good idea man, he was a good draw, a charismatic figure for A.R.E.," said one board member of that period, Jim Embleton, "but he was not a good administrator. He just didn't have the practicality that you need to get things done in a job like that." Bill Lord said, "Herb did a lot for the A.R.E. But it would have been the worst thing for Herb to put him in as a manager |president|. Everybody recognized that except Herb." The decision hit Puryear hard. "I don't think Herb ever got over that," Meredith Puryear said, but he nonetheless worked well with Charles Thomas for five more years before "the lid blew off" and he suddenly resigned.

The decision favoring Charles Thomas answered the big question that had hovered over the organization for years: after Hugh Lynn, who will lead? It was a plan that also gave every appearance of sparing the A.R.E.'s aging leader much of the stressful detail of day-to-day management.

Just as Hugh Lynn was quite different from his father, Charles Thomas was quite different from his. And not all the board members were convinced he could handle the job. Hugh Lynn would be a hard act to follow. Charles Thomas was more reserved and less naturally outgoing than Hugh Lynn, but he had grown up with a deep love for his father and apparently none of the anger or resentment that Hugh Lynn had to overcome with Edgar. But what of his own reservations as a young man toward the A.R.E.?

"My earliest memories of the A.R.E. are of visiting the house on Arctic Crescent. I remember Tom Sugrue in a wheelchair on the front lawn by the lake and a dozen or so people sitting around. And Eula Allen's son and several other kids and I playing around, trying to catch turtles. I remember cutting the grass down there when the lawn mower was bigger than I was.

"There was nothing strange about the A.R.E. then. It was where Dad worked and the people were very friendly, didn't seem strange. They always made a lot of me, hugging me, friendly to me. There were

266

people in our home, and I remember being fascinated with people like Tom Sugrue and Harold Reilly being at the same dinner table and they would hold forth. I didn't know what they were talking about but I knew they were powerful characters and I enjoyed it without really understanding it. And Hugh Lynn, I could tell, was one of them. There was no sense of awe on his part. He was a peer with them and I remember feeling proud of that, and that these people were a part of our family and were famous somehow."

As Charles Thomas grew older, his perception changed, especially after the A.R.E. took over the old Cayce hospital building for its headquarters when he was fourteen.

"After the A.R.E. moved, it was a different proposition. Then it was my friends in school talking about 'the spook house on the hill.' The place even felt spooky to me. It was bigger and we weren't using the whole building. That plus the peer pressure made me aware that there was something different about our family and my father's work. I would ask Hugh Lynn about it, and he was terrific. He would listen and tell me stories about his difficulties and his embarrassments, about his father reading his mind and other stories. Somehow that was reassuring to me.

"But there were other people around A.R.E. who were psychic, like the ladies in that first Search for God group—Esther Wynne, Florence Edmonds, Eula Allen, Hannah Miller, Ruth Lenoir—eight or ten of these ladies who were just as psychic as they could be. I remember Hannah Miller, a big friendly lady, hugging me one day after I had caught a fish and had come up to tell Dad about it—and I hadn't told a soul. She hugged me and whispered something about this fish, and I pushed away from her big bosom and thought, What is going on here? I remember feeling real uneasiness, although she was very friendly.

"That kind of thing happened a number of times. I would ask Hugh Lynn about it and he was very gentle and understanding, I think mainly because he had been through it worse than I was going through it. It wasn't that people teased me much openly [about the A.R.E.], but I was always afraid they were going to. Dad was very sensitive to that because he had been through it. I think he made an extra effort with Greg and me to plug into our activities."

About the same time Tommy was given a copy of his life reading for the first time. "I remember being very frustrated and upset that this reading was given when I was a few hours old and that someone could know me that well. Also that there could be a plan or pattern. Then almost immediately I felt a sense of relief and encouragement and optimism that my reading was a confirmationof the accuracy of the readings Edgar Cayce gave."

That meant a lot to him simply because "up until I was a teenager, my personal beliefs and my family life was very much tied up with the A.R.E. I went to A.R.E. lectures regularly. We had regular meditation times and discussions about dreams at the breakfast table. The diet my mother worked with was very much along the lines of the readings."

About that age he also realized that such things were not a part of the lives of his school mates. "I became very embarrassed about. my association with my strange grandfather and the A.R.E., and I disassociated myself from all of this for a number of years through high school, college and the first part of graduate school."

One thing sure, he was not going to follow in his father's footsteps. Tommy announced that he was going to be a doctor, an ambition that he felt from the age of six. When he entered Hampden-Sydney, a small Presbyterian men's school in Virginia, he was intent on preparing for medical school. During his senior year at Hampden-Sydney, however, he wavered, thinking he might prefer the ministry. He thought also he might combine the two and become a medical missionary. His younger brother Greg recalls when Charles Thomas, home for the weekend from college, would sit up late in front of the fireplace talking with Hugh Lynn about his career. "Dad would talk to him about a career in A.R.E. He didn't do that with me." Charles Thomas says he felt no pressure from his father to work at the A.R.E., but Hugh Lynn evidently had that in mind for a long time. But he knew that Charles Thomas must be free to make his own vocational choices.

Instead of medicine or the ministry, Tommy chose psychology—much to Hugh Lynn's delight. He earned his Ph.D. in 1968 after doing graduate work at the University of California at Berkeley and at the University of Mississippi, then took a teaching position at the University of Maryland. That was followed by an overseas job for the State Department as an educational consultant looking over American schools in Germany, Italy, Pakistan, and Turkey.

When Charles Thomas returned to the United States, Hugh Lynn enticed him with talk of the rush of hippies that had adopted Edgar Cayce as a cult hero and moved to Virginia Beach to hang out. More than an interesting challenge, many of them needed help. Clearly, the time had come to launch a youth activities program. "We talked about a camp. My training had been in child psychology, and I think he carved out a thing he thought I would be interested in."

Charles Thomas no longer felt the urge to keep a safe distance from the A.R.E. One thing that helped to turn him around was that a distinguished psychology professor at Hampden-Sydney, an honors graduate of Harvard, had occasionally inquired about The Work in such a way as to convey his respect for Hugh Lynn and his field. "He said in so many words, 'There is something to this. There are more states of consciousness than when we are wide awake, and we haven't gotten around to figuring them out yet.' I didn't take the bait at that point, but that clearly made an impression on me."

Another influential faculty member was "Holy Joe" Clower, as the boys called him. He had been a classmate of Hugh Lynn's at Washington & Lee, had married Hugh Lynn and Sally, and become their minister at the Presbyterian Church before leaving the pulpit for teaching. "He told me he disagreed with Hugh Lynn's theology [of reincarnation] but said he had never seen more Christian human beings than Hugh Lynn and his father. He'd give examples of Hugh Lynn giving money to alcoholics when Joe was his minister. He said whenever he needed ten dollars to provide people with a hot meal, Hugh Lynn didn't have it but he could always get it."

On one occasion, Clower invited Hugh Lynn to speak at the college. Although an accomplished speaker by then, he admitted to some anxiety. "Even though he has only a half-year left there, what Tommy thinks, and how he feels, is important to me," he wrote in his diary before driving to the college. "It is so easy for me to remember the many times I felt defensive, apologetic for my father, even ashamed. It is not easy to keep from being on the defensive, overly careful so that I lose the naturalness and enthusiasm about the work I am doing. I may never know how well I succeed or fail. How strange to be talking to a whole auditorium full of boys and not caring what a one of them thinks—except *one*. Maybe that even is wrong. If I care about all, the one may be O.K."

The talk went smoothly, he felt, and later he had lunch with a group of students—"rather formal, Tommy was only one without coat and tie. Not much conversation." But an evening bull session with thirty-five or forty students lasted two hours. What was Tommy's reaction? "He was carefully reserved but seemed pleased."

What came across to Charles Thomas was that his professors respected the nature of The Work "and didn't think it was a scam." So when it became obvious that a job was there to be done that appealed to him, this time he took the bait. He volunteered his services—"Hugh Lynn never asked me"—but with a clear understanding that it would be for only a year. He made no commitment concerning a career of the A.R.E. but for some years he had been meditating daily and working with his dreams. "I had become a convert."

Once he was on board, Hugh Lynn played his hand carefully, indulging his son's impatience with such administrative chores as preparing budgets in order to free him to do what he enjoyed most, working with young people. During the summer he left headquarters to manage the camp on a mountain farm on the edge of Jefferson National Forest in southwestern Virginia. And during the rest of the year he lived on a ten-acre farm which he populated with chickens, lambs and geese. He clearly seemed more at home in his jeans, working outdoors, than in coat and tie.

The youth activities program was fun but a heavy responsibility. The camp had been initiated in 1958 at Virginia Beach by Bob Clapp, a former teacher. It consisted of creative activities for youngsters while their parents attended lectures during week-long conferences. One of the youngsters who attended the first camp program, John LaPrell, was so helped by it, his mother thought, that she offered Hugh Lynn the chance to build a summer camp on her farm near Rural Retreat, Virginia.

Although the A.R.E. had no money to build facilities, the old scoutmaster jumped at Mary LaPrell's offer. Again, it was a loaves-and-fishes situation requiring a miracle or two. Starting with tents and pit toilets, Hugh Lynn inspired a year-by-year construction program with volunteer carpenters until the camp evolved into a collection of rustic cabins, mess hall, square-dance pavilion, and meditation grove that each summer drew hundreds of young people together—and bonded many of them into a unique spiritual fraternity.

Perhaps it was the mystique of A.R.E. Camp, but Charles Thomas was soon hooked. At camp he also was attracted to Leslie, a vivacious camp counselor whom he married five years later. Leslie recalls meeting Hugh Lynn there: "He came up to camp several times during the summer. He was very relaxed. He just sat at the picnic table next to the dining hall and hung out with the kids, and talked to anybody who happened to sit down next to him. Very low key. The kids just gravitated to him, he always had kids around him. And he square-danced, and he told stories, mostly about his dad and what it was like to be with a father who had all this psychic ability that he couldn't get away with a thing—and the kids loved that."

Hugh Lynn said he preferred working with young people. Mark Lehner was just one of many that he spotted and worked with over the years. "I saw him just sort of tag or pick out people at the beach who were in their late teens or early twenties who needed help, and he responded on that level; or needed inspiration and he would respond on that level," said Leslie. "There were a lot like that. It was

270

as though he had antennae that were always up."

To have enlisted Charles Thomas into developing a Youth Activities department, then, was much more than finding a niche in which his son might learn the ropes. It was to manage and build a cherished outreach.

If Charles Thomas harbored thoughts of moving on to other career opportunities, Hugh Lynn's heart attack, catapulting him into the leadership role, virtually closed out his options.

Though pleased over his son's willingness to move into the presidency, Hugh Lynn had not thought in terms of relinquishing power. He would follow his doctor's orders and walk two miles a day. And he would turn over his *title to* Charles Thomas, but not his office on the first floor at A.R.E. headquarters. The new president would have to do the best he could in the small upstairs office from which he had guided Youth Activities. Old monarchs seldom surrender their thrones.

When Charles Thomas's secretary tried to fend off distracting visitors for the new president, she was helpless before Hugh Lynn. "He'd walk in unannounced and say, 'I'd like to see my son.' I'd say, 'He's tied up but I guess he'll see you,'" Lindy Meunier recalls.

"I'll tell you there was friction," recalls Charles Thomas. "Hugh Lynn saying that I could be president, and then his feeling comfortable with that, were two different operations. He tried his darnedest, but he would get frustrated at not having all the reins in his office. He was used to just making things happen. He would come up to my office, and I would disagree with him on something or there was some bureaucratic red tape, and he had no qualms about losing his temper with me or whoever was around, beat the desk, fly off the handle. He wouldn't stay mad, which was great, but it was sort of awkward because people still respected him. For them it was like having two bosses and trying to do the best they could by both of us. It was screwy. There were people here who said they were working for Hugh Lynn; they'd listen to what I had to say, but they'd do what Hugh Lynn told them to do."

The little king still had clout. His impulse to command, to "get things done," he traced to his Egyptian heritage. Indeed, he saw the entire organization in an Egyptian perspective: "The structure of A.R.E. is bedded in Egypt. And all the counselors and all of the people on the board, and my ability, so far as it exists, of leadership, the ability to manage comes out of that Egyptian period. My personality comes out of Palestine, when I'm in good spirits—that's the strong part of me; this other one [in Egypt] is the negative, painful one. But it's the management aspect—it knows how to get things

271

done, anything, and I think that is one of the best angles on my whole character—the range of things I have attempted to do, because there isn't anything I wouldn't try if I thought it would be helpful to The Work."

One of Hugh Lynn's key loyalists was the treasurer, Everett Irion, who thought part of his job was to facilitate Hugh Lynn's objectives. Often no one but Everett knew how much was being spent for what. As long as Hugh Lynn had Everett's cooperation, he could still find ways to get things done.

"There was no subterfuge, with Hugh Lynn doing things behind my back," said Charles Thomas. "He was just out and out frustrated, and said so to me over and over. He had a hard time letting go. But it was natural. He was just an old horse in harness.

"It was hard for everybody, for me, for him, for Sally, hard for the people working at the A.R.E. That went on for five years, and I don't think it ever got any better for him or for me. It got a little better in the sense that some of the people who were working for him or were psychologically connected to him left. Everett changed [gave up the treasurer's post, which was assumed by Fred Davidson, a contemporary of Charles Thomas's, and later by Verna Brainard, a tough-minded former corporate comptroller. And that was the key—when Hugh Lynn no longer had the purse strings, no longer had access to the money to do what he wanted to do, that burned him up and added to his frustration."

As Hugh Lynn returned to work full-time, he became too busy to keep up his diary. One of his last entries said:

July 1: Good checkup with Gormly—Sunshine died today. He was a member of our family—we will miss him.

By Independence Day 1977, he was lecturing morning and afternoon some days, evenings others, conducting meetings on the Egyptian project, and trying to finish his book, *Faces of Fear*. He finally sent it to his publisher, but it came back unaccepted. When his youngest son stopped by to see him one day, Sally told Greg that his father was in his study and that he was "very worried." When Greg asked him what was troubling him, Hugh Lynn told him that his book had been rejected because they didn't understand one chapter in particular. Stumped over how to fix it, he asked Greg to read it. Sally recalls hearing their conversation: "Greg said, 'No wonder they didn't accept it. You've written a whole chapter here and you haven't said a word.' I was horrified when Greg said that, but Hugh Lynn said to him, 'Well, what are we going to do about it?' Greg said, 'I'm going to re-write it for you.' Hugh Lynn took it beautifully, and I thought that was such a compliment to a father who would take criticism from his

272

son. Greg took it and re-wrote it, and they accepted it and the book was published."

By year's end he was on the road again, lecturing, raising money, inspiring the flock, and seeing more of the world. One place he wanted most to visit again was China. For the past decade during the Cultural Revolution, entry into China had been impossible. He had been there once, during a memorable round-the-world tour in 1969. Now China was opening up to Westerners and Hugh Lynn wanted to go back. And there was also the Middle East.

If he needed any justification for globetrotting, he managed it by turning a tidy profit for the A.R.E. from his travels.

"I developed, with Norrene Leary's help, a whole tour business. We earn $15,000 to $20,000 a year from A.R.E. tours. And it does our members a lot of good."

For a time he led at least one adventure abroad each year. It seemed almost as regular an occurrence as his annual lecture tour around the States had been. His travels also served to minimize his personal frustration over losing absolute power, at least for a few weeks at a stretch.

Chapter 22
'It's Been A Good Life'

Hugh Lynn's zeal for the Ra Ta mission was so strong and persistent that he scheduled another Egyptian safari on the heels of a strenuous journey to China in the fall of 1980. Returning from the Orient, he had scarcely time to pack clean laundry before catching a jet for Cairo. It was to be his briefest and final trip to the Valley of the Nile. His seventy-three-year-old body simply rebelled. Suffering from a stabbing pain, he began passing blood. An American doctor who was traveling with him advised returning home immediately. Reluctantly, Hugh Lynn cancelled his itinerary and flew back to Virginia.

The diagnosis was serious: a large kidney stone.

The surgery was swift: the left kidney removed.

The lab report the worst: malignant.

The prognosis: Cautiously favorable, for there was no sign of cancer elsewhere. The doctors told him they thought they had got it all.

Hugh Lynn acted on that hopeful assumption. He would tell few people outside his immediate family. No need to worry anyone needlessly. "I think he thought he could lick it," says son Greg. Moreover, having to admit that he had cancer was more embarrassing to Hugh Lynn than the prospect of death was frightening. But he slowed down for awhile. And he discussed his condition with Drs. William and Gladys McGarey from the A.R.E. Clinic in Phoenix. They urged him to come to Arizona and take their full therapeutic program, based on Cayce principles of healing, which already had helped many people. "He told us that he had to decide whether he was going to make the transition and come back, or stick around," said Gladys.

During the months following his surgery he went to the hospital periodically for a CAT scan and came to our house frequently on Sunday afternoons to talk out his life for this biography, giving his listeners no clue that his time might be suddenly foreshortened. Evidently he believed that he still had control over the length of his own lifespan. But he was secretly fearful because of a dream that had waked him in the middle of the night about a month before. This is how he described the dream to us:

"I was with Sally in a very small place. There was a knock on the door. I opened the door. There was a man wearing a business suit standing there. I'd read my father's dream of this symbol [Edgar Cayce had said the dream symbol for death was not an old man carrying a scythe but a younger man in a business suit.] and I knew it was death. I backed up and sat down. He didn't look at me, he looked at Sally on my left. He walked into the room and I got up and got between him and Sally and said, 'I'm ready any time.' He smiled faintly and kept looking right on through me over my shoulder at Sally, and I kept telling him, 'I understand. If this is the time, I will begin to get ready.' But he never looked at me, never looked me in the eye. He just looked at her. So I gently pushed him out the door—he never let me touch him, he just backed up—and I closed the door."

Hugh Lynn was so troubled by this dream that he swore us to secrecy "until something goes one way or the other." He was afraid not for himself—"I have no fear of death"—but for his devoted wife.

"I haven't told Sally about the dream, of course."

He made a point of scheduling more time to talk with his sons, not just his successor at the A.R.E., but also Greg, who had moved from California, where he had been teaching school, to Virginia Beach during his father's illness. Greg had majored in philosophy at Randolph Macon College and planned a career in college administration, with the intent of applying the Cayce philosophy in his personal life, but without joining his father and brother in working at the A.R.E. Having enticed one son into the organization, Hugh Lynn had never offered Greg a permanent position there. "Dad regularly scheduled lunch with me, and we would just listen to one another. I felt like he was trying to make up ground for time he had missed or skipped, and I really appreciated that. I think he thought the clock was ticking. I didn't feel any sense of urgency, but I think he did."

While Hugh Lynn seemed to have no fear of death during his last years, he acknowledged concern that he might end up physically incapacitated.

"I plan to be around as long as I can function normally. When I begin to crack up, if necessary, I would kill myself in a moment. I don't plan on staying. I wouldn't want to bother somebody else with it, so I'd just do it. I have no intention of suffering through cranky old age and doddering around. I know I'll have enough brains to figure out how to do it, but I don't think I'll do it that way. I think God is going to let me go quickly, either with a heart attack or in my sleep."

He said he liked Elsie Sechrist's remark about death.

"She says, 'What I want to do is become a piece of really ripe fruit and drop on the ground and squash all at once.' That's a beautiful description of death, to be very, very ripe and squash."

That summer, 1981, he resumed traveling and lecturing, this time to Germany, ignoring the tearful pleading of his wife and his secretary, Norrene, that the exertion would be harmful. But Hugh Lynn had been restless during his convalescence. He wanted to return to action. The thought of being confined by illness was worse to him than risking death. "One was a restriction and the other was just a change, and the restriction was hard because he went full speed all the time," said Greg. "He only knew one gear."

He returned from his German lecture tour sporting a beautiful Mercedes Benz automobile, a used model that he had bought for a song to replace the battered little VW Beetle he had been driving. It was one of the few times in his life that he had indulged his elegant taste.

That summer he and Sally took a cruise ship through the scenic Inland Passage along the Pacific Northwest coast of Canada to Alaska, a gift of the board of trustees designed to force him to slow down and get some rest. It lasted only as long as the ship was at sea. In August, he headed out again, this time to China, the land for which he and Sally felt strong romantic connections. Leading twenty-six A.R.E. members for three weeks in the stifling summer heat and dust of inland China was not exactly a second honeymoon, and probably not what Hugh Lynn's doctors would have recommended, but there was something about this mysterious and long-forbidden land that tugged at him and wouldn't let him go. Besides, Hugh Lynn loved traveling and felt eager to remain active as long as he was able.

The following March, however, during a routine check-up at the hospital, the technicians detected what everyone hoped they would never find. Hugh Lynn called me and said he had something to tell us. Over Sunday brunch at our house, he and Sally revealed the family secret.

"Several weeks ago they discovered a spot on my liver, and then they discovered a spot on my head."

Hugh Lynn talked optimistically, even cheerfully, as though this were merely another nuisance he had to put up with. But his use of the expression "a spot on my head" had a ring of unreality to it. He couldn't, it appears, bring himself to say, or perhaps to believe, that the cancer had reached his brain.

In a letter to Jess Stearn he used the same expression: "They found spots in the liver and eventually spots in the head. They punctured the liver to get the tissue to check exactly what kind of sarcoma it might be. The spots are very tiny. In fact, in taking the biopsies on the liver, they had great difficulty, having to make five punctures before they could even get a hold of one or two cells. I have undergone ten radiation treatments for the spots in the head. As you know, it is much safer to radiate the head than anywhere else in the body."

The most noticeable change in his appearance was that he lost some of his hair in the process. But he expressed optimism to everyone:

"We have caught this whole thing very, very early. While the chances generally go up and down depending on the individual, I see no problem in handling this. I am sure so much is tied up in attitudes about all of this. Isabelle Adriance did a wonderful job of recovering from cancer [of the colon] and is just as healthy as she can be. I will, of course, be following everything from the Edgar Cayce readings that seems to fit whatever type of cancer they come up with."

He had talked again with the McGareys by phone in Phoenix. They urged him to come immediately. He considered doing it, but decided to stay in Virginia Beach and follow his local physician's directions.

"I didn't see much point in isolating myself [in Phoenix]. I can get everything he has here, and I can be near the children and my grandchildren and see them, and I look forward to that with great anticipation."

"I think he decided it was his time to go," said Gladys McGarey, "and if he had come out to the Clinic and died it would have been considered a failure [for the A.R.E facility and the Cayce approach]. He'd made his decision, and it was okay, and this was the way he was going to do it. I think it was according to plan."

Hugh Lynn also took the rare step of asking the Glad Helpers Prayer Group to intercede for him. Meredith Puryear, nominal leader of that group, recalled his attending one of their meetings that spring and saying, " 'I don't usually ask groups to pray for me, but for the first time maybe in my life I am going to ask this group to pray for me.' He came two or three times and sat in my chair [for laying on of

278

hands]. Honestly I did not feel that it was that serious. I'm very sensitive when I do a laying on of hands with people, and I really felt that it was relatively minor."

Before beginning the radiation treatments, Charles Thomas and Leslie took him and Sally to their beach cottage on the North Carolina coast for a weekend. Hugh Lynn rode with his daughter-in-law, who has a vivid memory of their conversation:

"On that trip down to Whalehead, we took the long route, and Hugh Lynn talked a lot about his future plans. This was in April, right before he was going to start the radiation therapy. He had plans to do both the A.M.A. version and the readings' version. I feel sure he thought he was going to make it. Mostly what he talked about was the Health Center. He wanted to see it happen during his lifetime."

The Health Center, planned as a combination spa and research facility, was the next building project he wanted to undertake on the A.R.E. campus.

On this last family outing for Hugh Lynn, he took a stroll down the beach with his first grandchild, two-year-old Corinne. As Leslie recalled with delight: "They were gone a long time, maybe two hours, and when they came back she was perfectly happy, talking about their adventures of finding this and that, and how they got tired and went off into the dunes and fell asleep. She had never done anything like that with anyone. That was just a few months before he died."

By early May, when he talked freely with us about his cancer, he was mentally prepared for the most difficult phase of his therapy.

"Next Thursday [May 6] I go in for chemotherapy."

Many of his admirers wondered aloud why Hugh Lynn chose the path of conventional treatment rather than the alternatives the McGareys were applying, based on his father's readings. In Hugh Lynn's own mind he was doing that, too.

"I'm stepping up my regular therapy to three massages a week, a colonic every week, two osteopathic adjustments, and attending the Glad Helpers healing prayer group. I've given up Scotch—all alcoholic beverages, even wine—and I'm following the Cayce diet."

His own philosophy of healing was another factor in his decision:

"My attitude toward healing comes from the readings that say all energy is from one source. All healing is simply the awakening, the quickening of the divine energies within the person. Now that can be done with a knife or massage or prayer or anything else, and that four million volts or whatever I got through my head was just as much God's energy as my prayer. It's just a matter of adapting or adjusting. My business is to try to use that which will quicken or awaken the

279

Divine within me and thus bring about the healing."

More than that, Hugh Lynn took a fatalistic attitude toward his condition. He said his attitude toward his illness had been helped by his experience in a Search for God study group that met at his house for many years.

"I've been working for forty years on that first affirmation, 'Not my will but Thine be done, oh Lord.' If Jesus wants me to stay here and work a while longer, I'll stay. If not, I'll be going somewhere else. Death and dying don't bother me."

Following brunch Sally went home, admonishing us not to keep Hugh Lynn too long. He stayed much of the afternoon.

"I don't plan on getting morbid about this or backing up. I'm breezing right along."

When I asked if he had a philosophy of illness, he replied:

"Yes, and it's a very complicated subject. It's not a matter of just illness. I would spell it down into the direct meaning of suffering. I have tried to think about that, talk about it, and tried to figure it out. I don't know that anyone has really settled it. There are people who believe that God is punishing them, and that He has destined that they suffer and die. All these things happen to them, but I don't believe God operates like that.

"But how does He operate? What are His laws?

"We are faced with three sets of laws—spiritual, mental, and physical. If we break any of these, we pay. We have to meet what we break. That's what I think Dad meant when he said we face only ourselves. This means that if I eat the wrong things, it is going to hurt me. If I drink the wrong things, smoke the wrong things, it is going to hurt me and I'm going to suffer at that point.

"It also means, if I understand it, that if I break a mental law that is critical—and Dad moves from that directly over into the psychosomatic approach—not only does it hurt the mental and incapacitate you to deal with things at a mental balance, but it makes you physically sick. It affects, it destroys tissue—anger, hate, fear.

"So these mental laws have to be obeyed-laws of commitment to integrity and balance and positiveness, just as in the terms of the physical laws. We have to keep a clean healthy mind. If we don't, we're going to suffer at that level. And it's going to be even more painful frequently because it brings emotional as well as mental chaos, and it eats us up.

"But spiritual laws are worse still if we break them, if we are egotistical, or if we are impatient, unkind, unthoughtful. The simple fruits of the spirit. These are the spiritual laws. If we break them we are going to suffer.

"Now suffering is something we build, with the mind as the builder, in the earth plane. I don't fully understand what this means. I think the earth plane is much broader than we know. In other words, when we die we are not free of the earth plane. It's at a different vibration, a different level, but it is still the earth.

"This needs a lot of thinking and work, but every life reading contains the statement about the planes of consciousness between lives in the earth. Those are physical—not the flesh, but this finer pattern that gets out of body. This finer body is moving faster, but it's still in the realm of vibration in matter. It's much broader than people know. That's not heaven. This is not the spiritual life. Many people get hung up on this. They think that when they die they are in heaven. They may be in hell, but they are not in heaven. Hell's a lot easier to get into than heaven, apparently.

"I need to know a lot more about this, but I've been working with it, thinking about it. Of course what it does is set up the whole karmic pattern. Karma is the cause and effect coming from one life to another. I think we all misjudge the fact that karma is some action, that you have to have action to get karma.

"But if you think some thought, you get karma. You get karma of your mind. Jesus was very specific about this about adultery. If you even think about it, He said, you've already committed it. You don't have to do it, perform. And you don't pay for the act, you pay for the thought. That makes it kind of sticky.

"Suffering begins to show up in several guises. I think God has thoughtfully arranged it so that we grow through suffering, if we will. We can learn through suffering. The earth becomes a school in which we begin to grow physically, mentally, and spiritually as a whole. We are total beings, not separate pieces. Suffering is fascinating."

Earlier, Hugh Lynn had talked about suffering in terms of how we relate to others.

"You can't do anything to a person without getting involved in it and spending a lot of time meeting it all and working it all out. It is absolutely as Jesus said, whatever you sow you reap. You build situations that work it out. It's the basis of suffering, I'm sure. It's not punishment, it's cause and effect. It's the fairness of the law. That has grown on me through the years in looking at the readings, watching case after case, and looking at my own life. So I have set about this time to handle as many of these negative forces as I can handle."

What about grace?

"Grace for me is acceptance of God's love. It's always there. It's flowing. He doesn't dish it out by the spoonful. It's always coming. But you and I get some things in the way. We are either too egotistical or greedy or too full of anger that we block off what is flowing to us. It never reaches us. We can't accept it. And for me, grace is God's love. This, by the way, is how the Catholics define it—the acceptance of God's love. As you do this, you come under the law of grace.

"I think this is what Jesus demonstrated when people accepted His love and were instantaneously freed of petty conceptions and were healed. They accepted God's love and it healed them. So Grace is coming to that point where you need to be freed of the self, and can be.

"Most suffering is not in the body, but in the emotions and in the mind."

The Cayce readings are full of references to past lives in explaining present ailments—the karmic connection—so we asked Hugh Lynn: is it conceivable or could you conceivably trace your condition or the condition of that cancerous kidney to anger in some previous life?

"I haven't gone that far with it. I've laughed about it, that I got all my Egyptian karma wrapped up in my kidney and brought it back and got rid of it. But that's not quite true, I don't think. I've been very much involved in Egypt."

It did seem an amazing circumstance that Hugh Lynn would become aware of his condition while in Egypt.

"Well, the symptoms were pathological—pain and suffering. I had created a lot of suffering in Egypt, all with good intentions of course [he laughed]."

While Hugh Lynn sounded optimistic about being healed, his mind was very much on trying to heal relationships lest they haunt him in yet another life. He credited the concept of reincarnation with having stretched his whole philosophy and given him a new perspective on human relations.

"It ceases to be a case of who were you, but what did you do? And what did you not do that you should have done, which you can now straighten out? Lives becomes like days of the week or minutes of the day—they make up a total life, the life of the soul. Life is not just this one experience but the total experience of many, many, many lives, all feeding in together. Any little point of consciousness is an illusion of reality. Reality is much broader and with many more dimensions."

When Hugh Lynn lapsed into philosophizing, he seldom talked about the abstract. Often he returned to relationships, for he saw them as a vehicle for soul growth.

"If you believe in this and think it works, you solve things as you go. I'm working with the laws as I understand them. I'm trying to work with karmic problems, to straighten out, to heal the things I left undone and the things I did. And I left many things undone in various places.

"I think it's ridiculous to sit around and think about it unless you are going to do something about it. You can conjecture about these things but unless they work out. . . . I'm not sure you can make it all up. . . but I'm trying to work, not only understand, but work with whatever understanding I have, and as I work with it I think I get more.

"Most people in any given life—and I'm sure I must have had lots of mediocre lives like everybody else—don't know enough or don't have the energy to be very bad or to be very good. They just sort of react and move along fairly level. They have a build-up in the mind of good things and bad things, but they never act them out or put them into action. I think that saves most of us or we'd go down the drink very quickly. That's just a theory I'm playing with, from what I know about karma and reincarnation and the laws, because for me it is not a theory any longer. You say, 'Well, it may be true and it's intellectually very stimulating and raises a lot of questions about survival and philosophy and the will and grace,' but it's something that you work with, that you use. You put it into operation in your life. You never miss anything you build. You always deal with it. It goes with you.

"I'm getting ready to work on one right now. Besides Tom Sugrue, there has been no man in America that I have had more difficulty with than Harmon Bro. Except for my father, but that doesn't count. But I'm going to work that out. I'm going to heal that."

Hugh Lynn said he and Dr. Bro had quarreled over a manuscript Harmon had written about his youthful experiences with Edgar Cayce, which included an argument in which Edgar and young Bro had come to blows. Harmon said he had knocked Edgar down once, although others doubt that it ever happened, explained Hugh Lynn. What angered Hugh Lynn, he went on, was that Harmon had hurt his father by being angry and obnoxious.

"I had a hard time forgiving him and trying to work with that."

Their differences were not suppressed.

"When we discussed it, we discussed it at the top of our voices. We closed all the doors and screamed at each other. And I can scream just as loud as he can."

Hugh Lynn had high praise for Bro as a teacher, lecturer, and writer, but he thought it important not to hide his own struggle with Harmon, like that with Sugrue, another brilliant man.

"Harmon and I've talked about it and we decided we are going to straighten it out. It has to be a mutual thing, you can't do it one-sidedly. If the other person refuses, you can do your part and then turn it loose. But they will stay in the condition they are in.

"Tom and I worked at it. The readings said we had settled it. That was a glorious day, to know it was finished."

Although he was not aways agreeable and seldom conventional, Hugh Lynn seems to have come through his controversial life without making any sworn enemies. Bill Lord said the only people who might be considered in the enemy camp were religious fundamentalists who considered the doctrine of reincarnation anti-Christian. "He had trouble with fundamentalists who called up and said, 'You're doing the work of the devil,'" said Lord. "Nobody likes that, but he'd just brush that aside."

Henry Vaughan recalled a stir of fundamentalist resentment in Selma, Alabama, in 1979 when the town fathers considered a proposal for erecting a historical marker in front of the downtown store in which Edgar Cayce once had his studio. "The word 'psychic' in most quarters in Selma is thought to be roughly synonymous with 'of the devil.' But when I proposed that Hugh Lynn Cayce be the main speaker, there was not a ripple of dissent. Then came the inevitable reaction," said Henry. "When word got around that the legend on the marker would include the word 'God' along with 'gifted psychic,' some people objected strenuously, and took their righteous indignation to the city council, insisting that the project be scrapped. A preacher and several of his flock had prayer in the store that used to be the Cayce Art Co., and a group from a Sunday school class visited my home. It was quite a stir."

Vaughan loaned copies of a book, Unto the Churches, by the Rev. Richard Drummond, a Presbyterian clergyman, which integrates the Cayce philosophy with Christian teachings, and "after much discussion the furor subsided." And when Hugh Lynn arrived with Gladys for the event, he received no cat-calls but a homecoming welcome. "He even spent some time with an old college classmate and worked out a karmic relationship that had worried him," added Henry.

At the close of his speech to the Selma Chamber of Commerce, Hugh Lynn was approached by an elderly woman who recalled that her husband had received a reading and followed its advice after his doctor had given him a year to live. He lived another forty-three years, she said. "I'll never forget your father, and I bless him every day." Hugh Lynn was deeply touched. His life experience was discovering new friends rather than engaging old enemies.

Such fierce emotions as he experienced with both Sugrue and Bro he traced to earlier troubles in other lives, but also to the close connection between love and hate.

"You love and hate at the same time. Everybody does. You can't just love a person—you've got to hate them a little bit, too. You kid yourself if you think you just love. You can't love unless you hate so that you have something to contrast it with."

The day after he told us the bad news about his health, he asked Everett Irion to lunch. More than the treasurer of the A.R.E., Irion had been one of Hugh Lynn's confidants. Hugh Lynn had induced Irion to give up his work in Dallas as a CPA and join the staff of the A.R.E. in the early 1960s. They were the same age, seventy-five, and had weathered the same A.R.E. financial crises together—Irion keeping the A.R.E.'s books and accounts for twenty years, Hugh Lynn raising the money from affluent friends to cover the annual deficits, sometimes spending for purposes no one but Everett knew anything about.

"Everett," Hugh Lynn said over lunch that day, "how would you pray for me?"

Irion, a quiet-spoken man from Arkansas, fondled his bolo tie and thought for a moment, took a long drag on his cigarette, and replied: "I wouldn't pray for you, Hugh Lynn, I would pray for The Work. You and I will be gone someday, but The Work will go on. I would pray for The Work."

Hugh Lynn nodded approvingly. Everett was right. The Work would go on without him.

The next day Hugh Lynn entered the hospital for chemotherapy. He never came out. The disease was spreading rapidly. Dr. Bill McGarey, who saw him a month later, recalls: "He was sitting in a chair and had lost a lot of weight and was hardly able to talk.

"I said, 'Hugh Lynn, are you going to stick around?' He didn't really say anything but he nodded his head. I suppose I really felt that he was going to get over the problem."

Hugh Lynn received lots of prayers once word of his condition spread. Meredith Puryear visited him regularly, announcing herself as his sister in order to gain admittance, and knelt by his bedside. Even Rolling Thunder, a Cherokee medicine man from Nevada, went to the hospital to perform a shamanic ritual on his behalf—causing quite a stir among the hospital's nurses and orderlies.

I telephoned him at the hospital early one evening just to say hello. It was evident that his condition had worsened but he had not given up.

"I'm going to get right," he said. "I'll see you."

In June when the board of trustees convened, Herbert Puryear made another unexpected bid for the presidency. He urged the board to move Charles Thomas into the chairmanship of the board and name Puryear the new president. With Hugh Lynn near death, his timing couldn't have been worse. This time, however, he had apparently acted on the advice of an Arizona psychic he had met six months before. Unknown to the board, Puryear had received a reading from this woman and been encouraged to seek the presidency. "I think she thought she would become the resident psychic," said Meredith. The board once again turned him down.

When Meredith visited Hugh Lynn that month she realized how grave his condition had become. "During those last two weeks he was very much out of his body. He had lost so much weight." She developed a theory to account for the change: "What I think happened was that Hugh Lynn decided he was ready to go. I think he did not want to deal with all the stuff that came up at that time and his choice was simply to leave."

On Independence Day 1982, he made one more out-of-body trip and never returned.

There was no funeral or burial for Hugh Lynn. He had wanted to be cremated, but acceded to the wishes of Sally, who opposed cremation, and committed his remains to medical research. Memorial services at the First Presbyterian Church and at the A.R.E. drew large crowds. Virginia's largest daily newspaper, the Norfolk *Virginian-Pilot*, paid tribute to Hugh Lynn for building the A.R.E. into "an international organization that will survive his own death" and for his major contribution to the human-potential movement. The newspaper's editorial noted that his achievements in dream analysis and metaphysics "necessitated his sailing against winds of public doubt most of his life. In braving skepticism, he was never an exhibitionist and claimed no special psychic gifts. If he was something of a zealot of a New Age, he was also an inspiring, captivating human being of this age.

"Like his father, he lived unpretentiously, was deeply devoted to his family and to helping young people even while globetrotting as an untiring investigator of psychic phenomena. For a man with such an unconventional legacy, Hugh Lynn's formula for life was most conventional—love for one's fellow man. His father's clairvoyance, offering no higher vision, had confirmed that this was how life is to be lived."

Seven months after his death, Leslie Cayce had a vivid dream about Hugh Lynn. It was not her first since his passing but it was so striking that she woke her husband at 5:00 a.m. to tell him about it. "I dreamt that I was by his bedside and he reached over and took my hand and was fumbling with a special kind of handshake, and it was specifically my left hand and he was reaching over my right to get my left. And either nonverbally or verbally the message was, 'This is for Charles Thomas.' Then he told me something about myself and I woke up."

Charles Thomas asked her to tell him the dream twice. Ten days later, when the Study Group that meets at the Cayces' house came together, he revealed that before Hugh Lynn died they had agreed in secret on three signals by which he would attempt to communicate from the other side. Even his wife had not known this, he explained, and then told the group about her dream. One of the agreed signals was the Boy Scout two-finger handshake, which Eagle scout Cayce recognized from Leslie's description of her dream. The old scoutmaster had delivered the message.

Scott Sparrow, unaware of Leslie's dream, also had a handshake dream about Hugh Lynn that seemed to convey a message.

That should surprise no one, for Hugh Lynn in his last days saw himself as a messenger, and The Work basically as delivering a message that would lead people into a state of higher consciousness.

"What's happening really is a revolution in thought about the mental and spiritual potential of the human race. It's probably the only thing that is going to save us, as people are awakened to their own potential. If we depend on the government, we are in trouble. If we depend on our fellow man, we're in trouble. And if we're going to depend on hoping that things are going to turn out all right, we're in trouble. It's a pretty tense, pressuring time. So many things are on a collision course. We are reaching points of no return with the pollution of water and air, not to mention the danger of atomic war. It's beyond us to know what to do about that—what are we going to do with all the atomic waste? Do you realize how many of these reactors are located on earthquake faults all over the world? We could suddenly have a decent earthquake and everything would be polluted. And people say the oceans are dying, the plankton is at a point of no renewal. And the economic confusion is terrific. We are on a collision course in so many ways."

In addition, there were his father's forecasts of drastic earthquakes before the end of the century, which Hugh Lynn had published in a book called *Earth Changes*. But Hugh Lynn did not think chaos was unavoidable.

"I think what we are here for is to quicken and awaken man to his predicament and to his real potential and to alert him. I think that is where God said He would meet every man and deal with him on an individual basis, and we've got to rely on that. The time is rapidly approaching. We are no longer walking, we are galloping toward all

287

this business."

The purpose of his father's prophecies, he thought, was to help the world forestall catastrophe. His message was clear and simple like the Boy Scout motto, "Be prepared." It was:

"When people begin to pray, to live by spiritual law instead of the law of the jungle, things can be changed, things can be turned around. But it takes a lot of people to do that. It takes evolved people to do that, to stop our ego trips and live more spiritually."

The proof, of course, is in the living. Hugh Lynn's work with young people seemed designed to help them fulfill the potential of their better natures. Sometimes it worked, and sometimes not. Charles Thomas said he occasionally sees a man around the Beach who fits the description of the town drunk. "Hugh Lynn used to work with him in the Boy Scouts. He and I would go get this boy special when we were going on an overnight hike. The boy would have nothing, but Hugh Lynn would have packed a pack for him because they didn't have things together enough at home for him. Over and over we would get that boy, and there were others, any number of them that he was working with in the process of scouting."

One time on an airplane Charles Thomas encountered a man his age he hadn't seen since high school who told him what his father had done for him. He was an ex-scout who had joined a tough gang in later adolescence and began drinking while still in high school. One day Hugh Lynn took off work to go to the school to watch a wrestling match in which Charles Thomas was participating. During a break in the contest, Hugh Lynn went to the rest room and was followed in by this former scout, who was tipsy from drinking beer. The boy staggered up to the urinal next to Hugh Lynn and began to bump his head on the tile wall and then glanced over and recognized his old scoutmaster.

"Hugh Lynn," he said, "turned to me, grabbed me by the shoulders, and just looked me in the eye for a long moment or two. He didn't say a word, just left. He didn't need to. I didn't take another drink."

Charles Thomas said his father had never told him that story, which had a happy ending. The man, now a dentist in Florida, said, "Hugh Lynn literally turned my life around."

Chapter 23
'I'll Be Back'

A year before his death Hugh Lynn talked about his intentions in the event of his passing. Not content to attune one life for maximum productivity, he was already planning the next one. On one occasion, he even entered into a solemn agreement with a young couple in hopes of expediting his own reincarnation. He couldn't recall precisely when this happened except that it was "during the time Miss Wynne was alive." Esther Wynne died in 1959 when Hugh Lynn was fifty-two.

"She and I were beginning to take auto trips to help organize Search for God groups. Someone volunteered some information about me—people were always volunteering information, the most outlandish stuff you ever heard of, over the telephone, in the mail, from people who just wanted to tell me things about myself and everything else under the sun. This person warned me, I think on the basis of astrology, of an impending auto accident. And following this, two or three people dreamed that I was in an auto accident. You never know how these things start, whether somebody thinks of it and others pick it up from some pattern that is supposed to exist in your numerology or your astrology, or whatnot. Then other people pick that up. It's very difficult to sort these things out.

"I became concerned over this incident because it sounded as if I were really going to have a problem. I began to pray about it as we got closer and closer to the trip Miss Wynne and I were scheduled to take to upper New York state. All the psychic information I got was that this was a dangerous time. This was an important trip we had planned for a long time. But I finally wondered whether this was something I should not do—you know, Dad was dead, and things were not going very well. We were working on the Search for God material, but it wasn't going very well.

"I wondered whether I ought to go [die] and come back quickly and get going again, because this whole thing was a pattern. I wondered what I ought to do about it. I didn't get any answers in my prayers about whether I should go on this trip and be very, very careful, or whether I shouldn't go at all. I finally decided, just to be on the safe side, I would see if I could set up a pattern.

"I went to a young couple that I admired who were having children. They were certainly good people. As it turned out they were pretty weak people [they later divorced], and I would have had a rough time had I been born to them if I had died and come right back.

"I set up some symbols for myself that are in my life seal and in my readings. There is a particular cross that I used to carry in my pocket. And there is a place—I don't know where it is, or even if it is on the earth, or what it is—but I visualize it. I've been going there in my dreams for years and years. I use that cross and that place, and I described them to this young couple as we talked. I asked them if they would agree to meditate and concentrate on these symbols and pray, and would they be willing to have me as a child if I came back, if I could arrange it, because I wanted to come back quickly and I wanted to be involved in The Work. I wanted to be able to carry on. I had lots to do."

Hugh Lynn said he didn't mention this astounding reincarnation scenario to anyone else, least of all to his wife. As for the young couple, he said:

"They were surprised and sort of upset."

What upset them was the prospect of his death in a car wreck.

"After I had talked to them, Miss Wynne came to me and said she had had a worry dream, as she called it. She had become uncomfortable about the trip. She didn't know why, but she didn't think we should go on that trip. So we cancelled."

Did Miss Wynne know anything of the accident predictions? "Nothing."

How did he feel about this decision?

"Relieved. I didn't want to...you know, it's funny when people have premonitions like that. I think they are warnings in order to balance things like that. But if it's likely to happen, it will happen anyway. And maybe I should go and come back, I don't know."

Had Hugh Lynn ever heard of anyone doing this before?

"No, but I didn't see why it couldn't be done. I still don't. I think some people have some choice. I think the choice is based on your performance, what you do and where you go, what the opportunities are, and whether you can set up a pattern and then pray about being able, if this be God's will, to be incarnated as their child."

Wouldn't such a quick return be unusual?

"No, there are examples of that in the readings, especially when people are killed in accidents or war. I think there are a great many kids from Vietnam who are coming back rapidly. Ian Stevenson [author of many books based on his reincarnation research] has a lot of cases of fast returns from strong emotion. So I don't know that this is so unusual or difficult. The Tibetan Buddhist concept is that you return very quickly. So it's not all that unusual, but I didn't know all that then."

Why was Hugh Lynn so anxious to come right back?

"To work. I could see there was a lot that needed doing. I didn't want to go away, but if I was going, I wanted to make arrangements to get back. It's that simple. I didn't want to leave it up to the old pattern because it could be a long time."

When Hugh Lynn had his heart attack and later contracted cancer, he still had the feeling that in the event of his death he would want to return quickly. But he made no comparable arrangements.

"Things may be in a shape where I don't have to rush back. Maybe I can rest for a little while, or do other things."

Events at the A.R.E. immediately following his death were not likely to have been reassuring to him. They certainly tested his successor severely. Some members of the board of trustees who were older than Charles Thomas had seen him grow up and were not at all sure he had yet gained the managerial skill or maturity to run the organization. The five years that Hugh Lynn had served as chairman of the board had given him time to get adjusted to the duties and operations, but always with the knowledge that his father had the board under control. Hugh Lynn had prepared his son to carry on in every way, except by stepping aside entirely and allowing Charles Thomas to cope for himself. Now the young president suddenly had to do just that.

For a time it was a period of retrenchment. An experimental elementary school using Cayce methods, subsidized by the A.R.E. and launched with Hugh Lynn's blessing and Charles Thomas's approval by his successor as youth activities director, Robert Witt, was shut down by orders of the board, lest it become a financial burden. A plan for building a community of A.R.E. members south of the city near Charles Thomas's farm, which he favored, was dropped. Dr. Puryear, passed over in the succession, abruptly resigned two months after Hugh Lynn's death.

Charles Thomas showed perseverance through it all, attending to managerial details, adopting administrative reforms and trying direct-mail promotional practices to build membership. He told one visitor that he felt strongly that he needed to take hold and lead the A.R.E. because he thought he had failed in a similar task in ancient Egypt. He was determined that it wouldn't happen again.

But within a few years his uncertain launching period seemed long gone. By the time he turned forty, Edgar Cayce's grandson had hit his stride as the spokesman for another generation in the spiritual renaissance his father had helped inspire. New people by the thousands flocked to Virginia Beach to attend lectures and conferences based on Cayce concepts. Membership in the A.R.E., which had jumped from several hundred to 20,000 or so during Hugh Lynn's lifetime, now headed toward 100,000.

As with Hugh Lynn, who was such an effective activist in the New Age expansionist movement, Charles Thomas chose a "make-it-happen" role for himself. He seemed to be following in his father's footsteps when he persuaded actress Shirley MacLaine to launch a national tour of seminars at Virginia Beach, giving credit to Edgar Cayce for starting her on her spiritual quest; contracted with a prestigious publisher, Harper & Row, to bring out a new series of quality New Age books based on Cayce concepts on dreams, reincarnation, healing, expanding one's psychic powers, and others designed to reach a whole new generation; reactivated Atlantic University with a graduate degree program in transpersonal psychology; traveled the Hollywood circuit trying to put together a Cayce film; and became a popular speaker at New Age conferences from coast to coast.

Although seemingly ill-suited to the demands of the executive life, and admittedly more comfortable feeding his lambs or hoeing his garden, he raised salaries, improved working conditions for employees, expanded the size of the staff, computerized the Cayce readings and other operations for efficiency, and launched a membership magazine, *Venture Inward*, that turned out to be extremely popular.

Just as Hugh Lynn worked in the shadow of his father's fame, Charles Thomas may never equal the charisma of Hugh Lynn, nor match the gifts of his grandfather. But like each of them, he has done what he felt it was his to do, grasping the mystical baton from his fallen predecessor, running his lap with a sense of cosmic purpose. Hugh Lynn would be pleased, even persuaded perhaps that he needn't rush back to salvage The Work. In his later days, indeed, he thought of his soul's journey beyond the endeavors of this lifetime.

"I think there is so much in the universe. And, too, I think I have more and more quit trying to make my own life pattern and tried to turn it over to Him. What does He want me to do? What am I supposed to do? I think more and more I've tried to put that first in my life, rather than just trying to make up my own mind, because I figure that I don't know much and I need guidance and help, and I pray for it all the time. I may be just imagining, I don't know, but I feel like I'm working for Him, I'm not working for myself. I don't try to do what I would want done but what I think He would want done if He were in the same kind of position, because I think there is a lot going on—and I'm doing the best I can. And I'm trying to do it on all kinds of levels."

What did Hugh Lynn think happened ordinarily between incarnations?

"I think the first thing we have to deal with, and it's extremely difficult, is that it is not a time dimension. So what goes on there is a kind of experience without time and without space. Now there are dimensions of consciousness, and I think the dimensions we have set up—the patterns, the ideals, purposes, goals—and how well we have worked at them, move us to a certain level of consciousness. I think we continue then to experience the level of consciousness and communicate at the level of consciousness that we have set for ourselves in the unconscious levels of our mind.

"I think at a certain point we are drawn, or have some choice after we reach certain levels—and these are not up and down levels, but they are out and all over the place—from certain levels you can choose schools, so to speak, places you go to strengthen a weakness, or for cleansing, or for understanding a particular direction. These are mental levels of activity.

"One of them, for example, would have to do with how you mobilize, how you work with energy in the earth. It has to do with vigor. If it's negative it has to do with violence. It has to do with action and movement and force and energy of various kinds.

"Another one would have to do with love, with the dimensions of love, with all the ways that love can be expressed in the earth. Remember, these are mental planes, they are intellectual, of the mind.

"Another one might well have to do with vision, the breadth of vision, the universality of points of view, the oneness of all force, the oneness of all people, all races and religions.

"Another would be a place of purification where you could go to free yourself of thought patterns that are cluttering your life—a cleansing, a purification.

"I think you have choices, and then you come back into the earth plane when you are ready. You pick or are drawn to those who will help you in your next program, so to speak. You go to school, then you come out and try to put it to work. That's what I think."

Did Hugh Lynn have any sense of what he might have done between incarnations?

"Yes, at a negative level I had experiences that related to energy and drive that gave me an involvement with violence. That led me into a whole series of wars, and I enjoyed fighting. I got caught on that and didn't get it very well worked out between times. I enjoyed it so, that I kept coming back to enjoy more wars. I wrestled with it in life after life. I started fighting in Egypt, went on into the Crusade period, became a Viking raiding England. In each one of those I tried to get out, to stop, but I got involved. I enjoyed it. There was a pattern there.

"Now what that pattern gives me this time is a lot of energy, a lot of drive, a lot of persistence. I'm very persistent about anything I do. I've had to get over, in a simpler fashion this time, fighting. It brought anger and hate and fear and impatience—that's the fault I have this time that gets me into more trouble, I'm impatient. I have to do something about it. I have to relax and be quiet about it. If I don't, I blast things and it makes people unhappy, makes me unhappy. It hurts, and I hurt myself.

"There is another aspect I have been through, an experience that deals with a great concern of universal points of view. I don't have any religious prejudice left. I'm very interested in people everywhere. I've developed this, spent time and energy at it. I've tried to interest other people in it and tried to broaden this pattern, even though I was enmeshed in a Christian pattern. I have read about modern religions. I'm familiar with Mohammedanism and Hinduism and Taoism, not in depth, but I've read a lot about them. And about Joseph Smith and the Mormons, and Christian Science. It's fascinating. So I've explored through reading and talking to people who are in those religions and enjoyed it and had a rapport with them."

Hugh Lynn considered these to be two counter-balancing patterns, one negative, one positive.

"I've been to the plane where the mind is trained and involved but I haven't done very well with it. So I've kept plodding at that, it's something I have to keep working on. Mine is not a great, penetrating mind, not very subtle, just the average."

In some respects, his life seemed single-minded, devoted to one objective to the exclusion of other interests—to advance the name of Edgar Cayce. However, he achieved much more. As Robert J. Jeffries, a member of the A.R.E. board of trustees during Hugh Lynn's last years, put it: "He left us a heritage every bit as important as the readings themselves. His visible monument will be the enduring structure and programs which make The Work available and meaningful to future generations. The awakening of public awareness to human spirituality will ultimately be recognized as his greatest contribution."

Bill Lord agreed: "The work that has been created here was his greatest achievement. He was responsible for it. He could have ruined it, but it grew and developed. He had to do it his own way. What he lacked in organization, he made up for in determination. He got the job done, but it wasn't the way they do it at the Harvard Business School. He got it done with determination, persistence, and enthusiasm. He kept hammering until he got it, and he had enough enthusiasm to attract people to help him."

Jess Stearn summed it up this way:

"I think the Hugh Lynn story is one of a man with single-minded determination, with one idea in mind, that he was the apostle for his father and his father's work. He was close to his father, and his father told him that Hugh Lynn was going to carry on his work, and he believed this. And he was going to bring this before the world. And Hugh Lynn completely effaced himself. He took on the thankless job of making the rounds of the publishers and the TV stations and the radio stations. And he wasn't an accomplished speaker at that time—he became an accomplished speaker by practice and determination—but back then he would stammer and draw on his notes.

"He did everything that was humanly possible to advance his father's name and his father's work. As I told him once after the success of my book [The Sleeping Prophet], when everyone was attributing the renaissance of Edgar Cayce to me, I told him that without him there would have been no me because he held up the torch all those bleak years."

He was, indeed, a torch carrier extraordinaire. And not just a success in the world's terms and within his own organization. As Manly P. Hall, president of the Philosophical Research Society, put it, "He was very sensitive about maintaining a high ethical standard; there was no compromising and no willingness to deviate for advantage, fame, or distinction. I thought he was one of the most sincere men in the field that I've ever known."

If there is any question about who won the inner battle for his soul, the little king or the devoted disciple, it seems apparent. As he went about his father's business, Hugh Lynn was an apostle first and last—for his father, and for their Father and ours.

"I'll be back," he said.

Anyone who knew Hugh Lynn can hardly wait to see what adventures his soul will chart the next time around.

Appendix

Life Readings: 'The Karma of Each Must Be Met'

Hugh Lynn Cayce received over 50 readings from Edgar Cayce during the thirty-eight years that they lived and worked together, the first one when he was a child and the last not long before his father's death. Only a few people received more readings than Hugh Lynn. The purposes of so many readings were as varied as Hugh Lynn's life was rich, from exploring his stormy days as a beleaguered Egyptian potentate twelve thousand years ago to seeking advice for a happy marriage to a Southern belle, from suggestions for taking a group of scouts on a transcontinental adventure to advice when he faced the military draft.

Of all these psychic discourses, the one that undoubtedly had the strongest impact on Edgar's eldest son was his first life reading. An adolescent at the time, he had received several physical readings prior to that, but he knew nothing of life readings and their underlying reincarnation scenario. His father had given only ten of these horoscope or life readings before doing this one for his son. It was given soon after the Cayces moved from Alabama to Ohio. The conductor, a Dayton man, Linden Shroyer, worked with the Cayces by asking the questions while Cayce was in a trance. Later, Mrs. Cayce assumed the conductor's role.

The text of that discourse, exactly as recorded by Cayce's secretary, Gladys Davis, follows, complete with a code number designating its otherwise unidentified recipient to protect his privacy:

This Psychic Reading given by Edgar Cayce at Phillips Hotel, Room 115, Dayton, Ohio, this 10th day of December 1923, in accordance with request made by parents.

PRESENT

Edgar Cayce; Linden Shroyer, Conductor; Gladys Davis, Steno. Mrs. Edgar Cayce & Edgar Evans Cayce [age five].

READING
[341]
Born March 16, 1907
[3:15 P.M., CST] at
Bowling Green, Ky.

Time of Reading ....Street
3:30 P.M .....Alabama.
[Horoscope suggestion]

EC: We see the soul and spirit completed this present entity at 3:23 in the afternoon. We find as this:

Without the will of the entity taken into consideration, under those forces of Jupiter, Mercury, Mars, Neptune, Venus, with afflictions of Saturn with the assistance or ascendency of Uranus in the latter days more than in the earlier sojourn here.

We find under this influence one strong of body, well balanced in body and mind.

One given to study of the many phases of development, both in the mental and physical plane.

One with the affliction of Saturn, under conjunction of Mercury and Mars, has the affliction in fire and firearms to the detriment of the body. One that must use the will force in the use of firearms in the coming year, when Mars is nearest, and with the latter days of that year will be under the afflictions of Saturn, and this body may be wary of the use of those in his own hands.

One that the injunctions [conjunctions] from Venus, Mars, and Jupiter will bring many petty warrior troubles in affairs of the heart.

One whose life-love will enter after years of maturity.

One whose greater forte will lie in that of literature; writer, composer, historian, or compiler of data for such works.

One who should, with the mind and will, develop the mind or

mental forces toward such development of self for this present plane.

One that may choose through will force, and the assistance of the natural elements, in its (this entity's) development through other planes, or by natural forces reach the higher developments through mental and spiritual forces.

One that will do well to keep ever present in its inner soul that the law of Him who giveth life everlasting is the greatest force in the physical plane, and to rely upon that force and not upon self, else this entity would become as the drifting clouds, blown about as the sifting waves, and the desert sands, for with the loss of self's support, through faith in Him, would be the declining forces in this entity's development, which has gone exceedingly far.

Many and varied forces, we see, enter into this development, being upon the cusps, and under many constellations, in the new of the Moon, and with the Sun's ray bright in the Heavens, and one whose coming and going will ever bring joy to those who contact this entity, when will force guides it in the natural elements.

In the appearances, we find that in the study of the courts of the Monks of England, when they were the shut-ins for the study of chemical forces, in the days of Alfred the Great [848?-900 A.D.], and this entity's name was Ericson Olif [?] [Ericson, Olaf?]. This will be found in records as is [were] made by this monk in the study of those elements creating these.

Before this we find in that of the days of the Crusade [Crusades 1096-1291] in the Holy Land, when there was the quick return of this entity, and as the leader of the invading forces, and carrying then the banner of Him who was the giver of perfect gifts.

Again in the days when the Prince of Peace walked by the seashore. This entity answered the call, and was one of those followers, as is given in him who brought his brother to the Master, A-N-D-R-E-W.

In the days before this when the first pharaoh builded in the plains, then we find there this entity is [was] one that will be found in that which represents this entity at present, in the North Corner of the second Pyramid, for he was one of these rulers [Ra Ta period].

In the days before this we find the entity was among those in the day when the forces of the Universe came together, when there was upon the waters the sound of the coming together of the Sons of God, when the morning stars sang together, and over the face of the waters there was the voice of the glory of the coming of the plane for man's dwelling.

In all of these we find some of this present entity's individuality, and in some, some personalities are brought through.

First: That of the love of outdoor. All nature.

Second: The geometrical inclinations of mind to weight and measure happenings, space and time by geometrical conclusions.

Next, the love of the Master, with the love of others to gain that knowledge.

In the next, the defending of personal principles at any cost.

The next, the closeness of individual study.

Edgar Cayce gave initial life readings for each of the other members of his household about the same time, first for Edgar Evans, then Gladys and his wife, Gertrude, followed by Hugh Lynn. While these earliest life readings revealed prior lives in some of the same countries, it was not until later readings that the first connections were established among all of them in ancient Egypt. Gladys, for example, was initially told only that she had had a brief incarnation "in the rule of the second ruler of that land, when the glory of the country was near its height." Gertrude learned only that she had lived "in the land of the Nomads in the hill country of the first pharaohs." Hugh Lynn's reading was slightly more informative, claiming that he had been "one of these (Egyptian) rulers," but there was no basis for believing that he and his parents and Gladys had been closely associated. Edgar's reading and subsequent readings for all of them and others filled in details of their prior associations. Sometimes this information emerged spontaneously, at other times through lists of questions as in the following reading excerpt, 341-9, given on June 2, 1925:

Mrs. Cayce: You will have before you the life reading given on [341] on February 28, 1925 [341-8], on the earthly existence in Egypt as Raaaart, and the associations with same. You will tell us at what period, as counted by man, in the world's history this was, and what the entity accomplished at this time.

Mr. C: Yes, we have this sojourn in the earth's plane. This is rather A-r-a-a-r-a-a-r-t [GD's note: In the suggestion Mrs. Cayce pronounced it R, then spelled the rest and in the first paragraph Mr. Cayce spelled the same again, as he did in 341-8], and the time as we find is, as counted by man, eleven thousand and sixteen (11,016) years before the Prince of Peace came into this land.

As to that accomplished, we find this in one of the highest civilizations of this country in its present position, for we find this same country had been submerged for nearly a quarter of a million years since the civilization had been in this portion of country, and the peoples as had overrun the country in the various changes by invasions from the east and north, and this ruler, Araaraart, being then the second of the northern kings, and followed in the rule of the father, Arart, and began the rule, or took the position as the leader in his sixteenth year and ruled over these peoples for ninety-eight years. The country, as we find, was brought to a higher state of understanding with the surrounding nations, and there was much of the religious ceremonies practiced in this time, much of this being brought in from the northern country and of the religions as existed in this same country through the religion of that of the one taken as the companion, for there were many taken, and with the unearthing of the tribal rites and ceremonies, the coalition of these truths we find were correlated with these peoples as were gathered about this ruler, and much of the architectural forces were set in motion. As we see, the first foundations of the emblematical condition as is set in the Sphinx was begun in this rule, for this, as we see, has remained the mystery of the ages.

In the accomplishments then, we have as these in Araaraart. This: Much of the sealing of the peoples' abilities in being drawn together for benefits of the masses rather than classes, for we find, though this ruler worshiped by many, yet remaining much in that same spirit as is found in the better classes of the ones serving Higher Forces than self, which is service to fellow man. The monuments as were unearthed and added to from time to time, we find are some still existent, though many buried beneath shifting sands. Others underneath sands that became the bed of the seas that overflowed this country.

Q. Did this ruler have any other names or titles?

A. There were many titles given in the various dialects of the peoples. This is one as will be found recorded with that of the other rulers. Araaraart, known as one of the household of rulers in the Egyptian forces. One of good stature. One of goodly countenance, for we find this entity of the larger peoples as came in from the north during the reign of one preceding this entity.

The accomplishment is in the sealing of the religious rites and of giving of the laws to be used by these peoples in this great land.

Q. Was this entity, as history gives it, one of the Pharaohs, or Rameses?

A. As one of Pharaohs of which there were more than three thousand. This coming, as given, in the eleven thousand and thirteen to sixteen years before the Prince of Peace came into this country— coming in during the second year, see?

Q. You will now have before you the individuals, as I name them, and you will tell us whether or not these individuals lived in Egypt at this time, and if they were associated with this entity, and in what capacity.

Author's note: Mrs. Cayce proceeded to name friends and associates. Edgar thus identified Fred Batterson, Hugh Lynn's friend from Selma, as Ralij, a younger brother of Araaraart and the Prince of Ibex; Morton Blumenthal as Aarat, father of Araaraart; Edgar as the High Priest, Ra Ta, who was banished by Araaraart; Gertrude as Isis, daughter of a priest and a temple dancer "in high favor" with Araaraart until banished with the High Priest after having a sexual relationship with him.

When Mrs. Cayce asked why Ra Ta fell into disfavor, the reply was: "It being permissable for the Priest to have only one wife, and this High Priest taking of the daughters of the second sacrificial priest and a favorite to the King, as the concubine to the Priest, this brought in the forces of rebellion, and the banishment when the offspring was presented in the temple." Gladys was that offspring, Iso, the love child of the dancer and Ra Ta who was taken from her parents when they were banished. This situation, the reading said, "brought constant consternation to the king," as to whether he was justified in exiling them. He had followed the advice of his councilor.

Gladys later added an ironic footnote. The councilor in this life was a man who "left his own wife and took a common-law wife, since his wife would not give him a divorce, and had two sons by her. No doubt he suffered greatly, because he really loved the common-law wife and wanted very much to marry her." Gladys considered this "a good example of those 'jots and tittles' of which the Bible speaks," for the councilor had recommended exiling Ra Ta "because of a sin for which he became guilty himself later."

Gladys applied the same karmic principle to herself from a past life in France. Edgar gave two readings one day, one for her and one for himself, and sketched out a melancholy romance in which a French girl [Gladys] took the exiled English Duke of York as her lover and gave birth to a child (Edgar) out of wedlock. This was a brief incarnation for Edgar, who died at age five after his mother left the baby in the care of others and entered a convent. Years after receiving this reading, Gladys said she spent much of her present life taking care of Mr. Cayce's needs to redeem her neglect during their French connection.

The karmic links within the Cayce household became clearer in Gertrude's second life reading. The text follows:

This Psychic Reading given by Edgar Cayce at his office, 322 Grafton Avenue, Dayton, Ohio, this 7th day of March 1925, in accordance with request made by self—Mrs. |538|.

PRESENT

Edgar Cayce; Mrs. Edgar Cayce, Conductor; Gladys Davis, Steno.

READING
|538|
Born February 22, 1880
at Hopkinsville, Ky.

Time of Reading   . . . .
12:40 P.M.—Dayton Time   . . . . Ohio

Mrs. C: You will give the relation of this entity and the Universe, and the Universal Forces, giving the conditions that are as personalities latent and exhibiting in the present life. Also the former appearances in the earth's plane, giving time, place, and the name, and that in that life which built or retarded the development for the entity, giving the abilities of the present entity and to that |that to| which it may attain, and how.

Mr. C: Yes, we have the entity here, and those relations with the Universe, and those conditions as relate to appearances in the present earth plane and those in the earth plane in other appearances, with the urges and conditions as created and merited in those relations, with abilities and the how.

Many of these conditions we have had before. These, as we have at present, show the relation as approached from a different viewpoint, or angle.

In this then, we find the relations in the present sphere taken from those of Mercury, Jupiter, Venus and of Uranus, and the entity then has those urges as are made with the relations of these conditions in earth's plane, and in the urges as received by accentuation of conditions received from other sphere than earth's sphere or plane.

Then, we have one given to the conditions that are exceptional in many ways. One not understood by many. One that brings much joy to many through the influence of the forces in Venus and in

303

Jupiter. One who has mental forces far beyond that as has been developed in the present plane.

One that brings much of the forces of antagonism to many through some conditions as received through urges, as will be found, from appearances in earth's plane.

One who is decided in likes and dislikes, whether of individuals or of places, things or conditions. One that under such conditions often brings more worry to self than to others. One tending to be in a manner recluse in self, often keeping many things that would prove beneficial in manner, were they expressed to others. This pertains to mental abilities, the urges, the worries, the many conditions. One capable in many lines, either in that of artistic forces as applied to inanimate conditions, or of those pertaining to the improvement in other forces as applied from others' work. [She spent years doing retouching in her husband's photo studio.] One, then, a good critic in many ways. One that is very bombastic, however, in dislike in criticism. One that finds in the joy of the elemental forces of earth's plane the greatest enjoyment in the earth's plane. One showing much patience under conditions where the relation is to self and to others.

As to the appearances, these we have much to deal with in the present plane, and these conditions under which the development was made in other planes has its effect in the present. Hence we find there are many conditions relating to those through which the entity passes in this present time.

Then, in the one before this, we find in the land now France, and during the period when the English ruler [Charles II] was in exile in that land on account of conditions that existed in that field. The entity then in that of Lurline [Maezie? in 538-5] Annose [?] in the courtesan to the exiled ruler, and assisted in his return to the land, and in this found favor in the eyes of many. In the present sphere we find this is shown in the ability of the entity to appear and to gain in that being in a manner extra in attention to strangers, and that such brings much to the entity. As to the personality gained and exhibited in the entity, the love of the finer things in earth's plane of the beautiful, and of playing the courtesan to many.

[Author's note: Gladys added a footnote in which she quoted Mrs. Cayce as having thought that "the French incarnation in which I 'played the courtesan'" might have been responsible for her physical ailments in this life. "Perhaps even the early tuberculosis, of which I was cured by the readings, was a karmic condition from the past, since the readings say that all illness stems from sin," Gertrude said. "You remember in Edgar's life reading (294-8) it was explained that he and I had much to work out in this life."]

In the one before this we find in the period of the rule as was shown in Greece, when the law or understanding was given by the Socrates, and the entity then in that household and of that family, and suffered much by the persecution as was brought on by the position that the entity occupied in that household, yet the greater urge for knowledge and understanding comes in the present plane from that incarnation in earth's sphere. The name then was Normaline, and the entity was the second daughter to that philosopher of the day. In the urge and the personality, the seeking today of those philosophic questions as propounded, and such easily understood, for each must be passed on that same principle as was then set—right for all and no exception in the rule.

In the one before this, we find in the land of the Normads [nomads], or in the outer edge of now Arabian deserts [Persia-Arabia: Uhjltd period], and the entity then the follower in that of the Bedouins, and given as the most beautiful of that group to which the entity then belonged. The name then in that of Inxa, and the entity then ruled many through the power of the eye over the condition created in the minds of those whom this would subjugate to her way of reason.

[Author's note: Years later Gertrude went blind in her right eye, and Gladys noted that Mrs. Cayce thought it was "no doubt a direct result of my misusing my eyes in my Persian-Arabian incarnation, to subjugate others to my way of reasoning."]

In the personality as exhibited today, we find in the patience and persistence in the condition, thought or felt to be aright, still able to control many through the eye and expression of same.

In the one before this we find in the Egyptian forces [Ra Ta period], and the entity sought, after the Egyptian entrance a sudden return again, or sought quick entrance again into earth's plane. In the Egyptian forces the entity was of the household of the assistance to the one becoming the leader in the religious cult [294], and being of beautiful figure and form, and giving the condition to him who was the leader brought through her seductive forces much troubles to self and that entity. This bringing banishment to the group brought distress and physical suffering to each, in that the entity set about to bring the enmity of many, and in the present we find grudges easily held and that the entity must overcome to reach the development that will bring the best, whether of mental, physical or spiritual forces. As to the name at that period, we find in Isris [later known as Isis—see 294-147 though 294-153.] and there are found even to this day many of the plastic forces in that country of the entity, though we find this was 10,996 earth years before the Prince of Peace came.

The abilities of the entity lie in those spheres of each to acquire the musical ability, the ability to symmetrize body and music in dance, to give much to peoples through that manner, yet in that as has been set in the present plane these yet may be acquired in no small degree. Time will soon approach when this may be effected, and the entity will through the will of self have the building of will's forces in self to acquire development in this earth's plane.

Then, to use all these, let the entity gain that understanding that self must be made as naught, would we manifest the spiritual elements in the physical plane, and that it is hard to kick against the pricks that would bring only the condemnation of self, that each thought, action, deed, must be met, and that paid for. With the mind, soul and body must earth's inhabitant magnify Him, the giver of all good and perfect Gifts, and in making the will one with His, even as Him who became the Light, the Truth, the Way, may we approach the Heavenly throne.

We are through for the present.

If Edgar Cayce in trance was painfully candid with others, he did not spare himself either. This honest impartiality is one aspect of his psychic readings that argues for believability. Here is his own first comprehensive life reading:

294-8
M. 46 yrs.
Clairvoyant
(formerly a Photographer)
Protestant

This Psychic Reading given by Edgar Cayce at Phillips Hotel, Room 115, Dayton, Ohio, in a series of five readings beginning February 9th, 1924, 1 on 2/12/24, 2 on 2/13/24, and 1 on 2/16/24.
Request made by Edgar Cayce himself.

PRESENT
Edgar Cayce; Linden Shroyer, Conductor; Gladys Davis, Steno.

READING
Edgar Cayce
[Born 3/18/77, in Christian Co., Ky., near Hopkinsville]
[2:30 P.M., CST.]

Time of Reading   2411½ E. Fifth Street,
11:40 A.M.   Dayton, Ohio
(Horoscope suggestion, with request for past lives, etc.)

EC: There is much we have given relative to this before. We have the conditions as have been, as are, and will be. In this, without reference to that as has been given, for in giving the conditions in the various phases of the past experience there will be much that will show the various phases of the past experience there will be much that will show the various phases of the developing in the different stages, the conditions as given then will be those as with reference to the effect that the planets and their satellites and spheres have upon the present life and plane, without reference to the will.

Then, with the will, and also the developing with will and the planetary or astrological effect in the various planes as have gone before; in the present, as in this plane, we find the condition as brought to the earth plane was from that of the attitudes as held by those to and through whom the present entity was and is made manifest upon the earth plane by the relativity of force and the attraction of likes; the attitude of those earthly parents towards conditions that brought the relations to the stage of the developing of the entity that came, and through that stage the entity chose the mode of manifesting in the earth plane. Hence the condition of the parents upon the earth plane, or duty that is due each of its earthly offsprings, for all are under that bond of duty to be made the channel of the manifesting of this force through the entity's actions towards his offspring.

As to the condition from the astrological standpoint, we find this entity almost entirely influenced by, and came from that in the last plane of Uranus, with Neptune, Venus and Jupiter. Afflictions in Mars and of the Sagittarius, Capricornus, Gemini Sun and Moon in the various stages, for with the ultra forces, as of Uranus and Neptune, come much of the influence of the various planes, given in strength with Jupiter and Mercury.

As to the influences this gives then without reference to the will:

One that will always be either very good or very bad, very wicked or very much given to good works. Ultra in all forces. Very poor, very rich. One scaling to the heights in intellectual ability and capacity, or groveling in the dregs of self-condemnation, influenced at such times by those forces either coming as afflictions from the various phases of developing, from which the entity has received its experience, or controlled by will as exercised in the present sphere.

307

One ever within the scope or sphere of firearms, yet just without.

One saved spiritually, mentally and financially often through a great amount of waters, for it was from the beginning, and will be so unto the end of time, as time is reckoned from the earthy plane, for this entity we find was first manifest in the earth plane through the waters as was on the earth, and above the earth. Hence through these elements and forces is the spiritual, mental and financial, these three phases of spiritual life, mental life and financial life manifest in the earth plane.

One who finds much in the scope of sphere of intrigue in secret love affairs. One given often to the conditions that have to do with the affairs of the heart, and of those relations that have to do with sex.

One that finds the greater strength in spiritual forces and developing.

One given to make manifest in the present plane much of the forces of psychic and occult forces, reaching the greater height of developing in such plane in those forces when that of Jupiter, with Uranus and Neptune, come within the scope of the Sun's influence upon the earth plane and forces.

One that will bring, through such manifestations, joy, peace and quiet to the masses and multitudes through individual efforts.

One who, after the present year passes the place of that of Pisces and Sun's rays on the twentieth of present month, will go forward to developing much of the psychic and occult forces to the great numbers that have become interested in developing of such phenomena.

One who will on the nineteenth of March, this year, reach the place or plane where the present years and the present developing reaches the turn for the developing, or the wield of those influences in Sagittarius, Capricornus and Gemini that may bring destructive forces without will's manifestation upon that day.

In the developing as regards will force in the present plane, with conditions, there have been many conditions that have been hindered by the effect of the will, and others that have been assisted. Keep the will in that of the spiritual development, if the physical would manifest to the better advantage in the present plane, keeping this ever before, that all work in present plane will be judged to the individual and the classes, masses, as to the individual's manifestation of spiritual forces in and through the individual action in and before men. Ever keeping the mind clear to the developing of the Uranian forces that often manifest in the present plane, which will in the present plane reach in the present and coming two years the

308

influence of the Neptune and Mercury forces, carry the body, unless will is exercised against such conditions, to many places beyond this present bounds, or across many waters. Keep the developing then to that force as is given in that of Uranus, Neptune and Jupiter, whose greater influence as is upon the earth plane, and beware of the influences in Venus forces, for with Mars' affliction would bring sudden destruction to the physical in the early fall of present year.

As to the vocation, this in the present plane may be directed in any channel through will. The better condition, as given, in that of astrological forces, would be toward those of psychic and occult, or teaching or developing along the lines of such plane to give the manifestation of such forces to the populace.

In the plane as of others:

In the one [incarnation (author's insert)] before this, we find in the present place of the physical plane sojourn, but in that of the soldier in the British forces as were in the force that developed the surrounding plains. The name, John Bainbridge, and in that life we find the birth in Cornwall, England, and the training in the Canadian forces as taken by that country, and the drifting into the present plain as known as American, or United America, and the life was lost then in the waters as in the crossing of the river at the time the battle was fought near the present sojourn [Dayton, Ohio]. In this, as that given just previous to the present appearance upon this plane, in which the body's sojourn was near unto that at present, we find the body's or the entity's and body's condition is then entered upon that of the Saturn forces [see 5755-1 or 6/27/38], and the life as was manifested then in the plane was as that of the adventurer, when the forces of the king [James I?], under whose rule this entity was a subject, entered in the force, or in the colonization of the country, was the first appearance upon this present sphere's plane or scope [the United States?], and was connected with that in the group that were landing in the East coast of the new country, now known as Virginia, and near where is now the resort known as Virginia Beach. When this raid was made, this John Bainbridge was carried in this raid to the Southern coasts of the country; escaped, and with the forces then going in the inland way, and making the surrounding of the places in which the present sphere's plane has seen much of the same country, and developing [Ky., Ohio?], and finally making the way to the fort then on the Great Lakes [near what later was known as Ft. Dearborn], now in place known as Chicago, and from that fort entered the fray [with the Indians?] in which the crossing was later attempted in the Ohio River [see 1/10/33 ltr. under 299-1 in re memory of boy in barber shop], and there met death, as known in the earth plane. The body was known as under two names [John Bainbridge and ?], and was never wed during that sojourn upon the plane, though was in many escapades that have to do with those of the nature of the relations with the opposite sex. In the developing upon the present plane, we have much of the personality as shown in present spheres, as from that of the ability to take cognizance of detail, especially in following instructions as given from other minds or source of information.

[GD's note: "In later years EC said he felt that his poverty in this lifetime, his trouble in obtaining and holding onto money, resulted from his improper use of money in his early American life as John Bainbridge."]

In that previous to this, we find in the Courts of the French, when Louis the 15th was King, and in the [care of the] Royal Guard was this entity's sphere, which was of short duration, so far as years go upon the earth plane. This entity, then, was [under the care of] the attendant upon the Royal Court [4121], and who was the Guard of the household of that Ruler, and [who] lost the elements of life, as known, in the defense of those [who had been placed under his care] under whose care they were placed, as both lost the elements of physical life, in the defense. In the forces or personal conditions as seen in present sphere from this sojourn, we find that of the intense defense of those principles that to the entity's inmost soul or force is the right. In the name, we find that of Ralph Dahl [Dale?] (See 1001-7 on 9/7/30 indicating that Louis 15th & 294 had same grandfather?)] . . . . Or was Louis 15th grandfather of John Bainbridge?]

In the condition that was previous to this, we find in the force as was manifest when the Trojan rule was in that fair country, to whom the nations of the world have looked for the beauty in culture, art and refinement of the physical, mental and material force, and in that we find again the soldier and the defender of the gate, as was the place where the physical or material destruction came to the body. In the experience of that plane, we find these cover many and various stages. Those of the student, chemist, the sculptor and the artisan, as well as of the soldier and defender in the last days. In that we find the name Xenon, and there is, and has been, and will be many more in the present sphere that were in contact with that plane's forces, that the contact will be, has been brought in the present sphere. In this, we find those present forces exhibited through that of the art, and the love of the beautiful in any and every form, especially those that partake of human form Divine.

In that before this we have that plane in which is now known as the Arabian plane. In this we find this entity's developing under that of Uhjltd, and there are many of the conditions, personality,

310

knowledge, understanding, thought, referenced as is and will be in the passing of the plane of today. For we find there are many upon this earth's plane, and in different locations, who were associated with this entity at that time.

In the entity's force of that day, we find this entity one of power, prestige, royalty, and the leader in many raids or wars as made upon the surrounding peoples, tribes or nations. This we find the most outstanding of that period, in the connection as was shown in the war as made on the Persian ruler, Croesus.

|GD's note: *Subsequent readings indicated a line of rulers called Croesus. 538-9 indicated a "quick return" into the Uhjltd period from the Egypt Ra Ta period. This suggests that the Uhjltd period, or the Croesus II period, was somewhere between seven and nine thousand B.C.*|

Uhjltd led the expedition into that country. The force under this leadership was successful in the bringing of submission to the rule of the nation which Uhjltd led. And the developing in that plane was with the suffering of bodily ills from injuries received in the escape from the force as connived from the weaknesses of the physical to make this Uhjltd a slave in bondage. His escape and sojourn upon the plains, with those surrounding him, was the developing stage, and the first of that developing known in present earth plane as psychic force. For, with the developing as received in the plane just before this |in prehistory Egypt as the priest Ra-Ta|, as we shall see, this Uhjltd sojourn was the continuation of the one found at that time.

The passing of the portion of the entity again into nazova |nirvana?| was through the wounds and infections as received upon the plain, in the vicinity of the well about which the three palm trees stood, which has remained in the inner being of the soul's developing force. And not until that entity is again united with this entity will the developing upon this or other planes be as efficient, or as good, as it should be . . . .

|GD's note: *Wife's readings 538-9, 538-31, and 538-32 explain the close relationship of 294, 538 and 288 in that Uhjltd sojourn.*| |5717-5 *says: Present remains of what was once this body |294| may still be seen—a thing of fact—in the cave still existing seven and one quarter miles southwest of Shushtar, Arabia.* |Author's note: *Hugh Lynn's attempt to locate this cave with the help of a Canadian psychic is told in Chapter 20.*|

In the plane before this, we find that as known in the dynasty of the Rameses or Pharaohs in Egypt, and in the Court and rule of the Second Pharaoh or Rameses, and was at that time the High Priest of the cult as gave the religious element and force in the age, and reached the heights in that dynasty; yet was cut short in the allowing of physical forces and desires to enter in, and the taking of the

311

daughter |538| of the order of the one who offered the sacrifices for the priest's force, and going or leaving the shores of this country brought the destructive elements to the body. That same entity that was taken is at present in this earth's plane, the companion and mate as should be in the present sphere |538|, and in this Court we find there was the study of the religious cults, the isms, schisms as would be termed in this day and plane. The High Priest |294| who gave the elements of the religious force, and in this dynasty or reign of this Pharaoh |341| did the religious cult reach its height, as given through this priest, though he became the outcast, but for the good as had been accomplished by this individual was in the resting place of the King, and the force as manifest in the present is the delving into the whys and wherefores of all who express a different mode of manifesting the hope that lies within the human breast of the life after the passing from the earth's plane. This, we see, manifests in the present. As to those forces that have brought this condition that the entity is in, the elements as brought the destructive force to self in the two, again we find that the karma of each must be met, |294 and 538| and in this plane overcome if each would enter in.

In that before this, we find in the beginning, when the first of the elements were given, and the forces set in motion that brought about the sphere as we find called earth plane, and when the morning stars sang together, and the whispering winds brought the news of the coming of man's indwelling, |the coming| of the spirit of the Creator, and he, man, became the living soul. The entity came into being with this multitude. As to the experiences as have been given in this plane, the earth, and the often sojourn upon this plane, we find all summed in this:

Take this thou hast in hand and make and mould it into the present plane's development, that thyself and others may know that God is God, and demands of His creatures that of the knowledge of self, that they may better serve their fellows, and in so doing present themselves as the ever giving force, bringing others to the knowledge of Him.

There are many other influences as have been shed abroad in the earth's plane from the entity's sojourn there. These are given that all may know and understand that the record of each soul is kept in and unto that Great Day.

Be not deceived. Be not overcome, but overcome evil with good.

INDEX

A

A Search for God, 116-17

A.M.A. *Journal*, 137

A.R.E., 8, 105, 157-178; Camp, 231; Congress, 109, 164; destiny, 159, 264; founded, 105; Egyptian connection, 271; growth of, 119, 158, 202, 292; headquarters, 193-94; Library/ Conference Center, 219-20; Press, 245; printing services, 216

A.R.E. Clinic, 211, 215; med. symposium, 217-18, 222, 275

Adriance, Robert, 168, 194-5, 217-19, 242-43

Allen, Eula, 267

American Holistic Medical Association, 225

American magazine, 136

American University, Cairo, 246

Andrew, the apostle, 227-236, 240, 247

Association for Research and Enlightenment. See A.R.E.

Atlantic University, 98-99, 101, 163

Atlantis, 203-204, 221, 255

Atomidine, 137, 221

Automatic writing, 171

automatism, 37

B

Babcoke, Lester, 213-14, 216

Baraff, Jim, 173

Bathsheba, Madame, 201

Batterson, Fred, 68

Battle of the Bulge, 151

Benesch, Samuel, 150

Bernstein, Morey, 197

Black Book, The, 168

Blumenthal, Adeline, 93

Blumenthal, Edwin, 63, 93

Blumenthal, Morton, 62-6, 92-107, 111, 264

Bolduc, Henry, 196

Bonney, Marjorie J., 175-76

Boston Clinical Research Society, 31

Bowling Green Medical Society, 34

Bowling Green studio fire, 29

Boy Scouts: Troop 60, 200; Tidewater Council, 200, 288

Bradley, Franklin F., 94

Brainard, Verna, 272

Brennan, Father, 138

Brewer, Robert, M.D., 262

Briggs, Marguerite, 194

Brigham Young University, 248

Bro, Harmon H., 147, 158-59, 166, 169, 196, 204-206, 211, 283

Bro, June, 158

Bro, Marguerite, 147

Brown, Tim, 93

Brown, William Mosely, 99

Bulletin, 109, 196, 241

Burroughs, Woodland, 133

Byrd, Harry F., 99, 201

C

Carter, Mary Ellen, 195, 206-207

Cayce Art Co., 33, 284

Cayce ancestors, 13-14

Cayce film, 208

Cayce Historical Memorial, 157

Cayce Hospital, 91, 94, 96, 99; collapse, 100-101, 103, 107; reacquired, 193-94

Cayce mystique, 13

Cayce Petroleum Co., est., 46; founders, 49

Cayce remedies, 221

Cayce, Annie (aunt), 45

Cayce, Carrie Major (grandmother), 29

Cayce, Charles Thomas (son), 18-19; born, 146, 181-190; joins A.R.E. staff, 244, 263; A.R.E. president, 265-272, 279; dream message from father, 287-88

Cayce, Clint (great uncle), 46

Cayce, Corinne (granddaughter), 184, 279

Cayce, Edgar: arrests, 110, 113; biography of, 77, 138, 141-43; Blumenthal break, 100-107; born, 15; Cayce Art Co., 32-33, 49, 53; Cayce Petroleum, 45-49, 54; children, 28-29, 38; church life, 35-36; death forecast, 146; death, 152; disciplines son, 38; dream of future, 114-15; Egyptian love triangle, 59; father's ghost, 134-35; fearful of gift, 28; hires Gladys, 53; incarnations, 245, 302, 309-312; last days, 151; letters to Hugh Lynn, 80-88; life readings begin, 55; marries, 18; Medical Society meeting, 34-35; messages from, 170; moves to Dayton, 54; moves to Virginia Beach, 65; National Assn. of Investigators, 63, 74, 103; partners with Ketchum, 29-31; prophecies, 288; psychic childhood experiences, 15-18; saves son's sight, 33-34; saves wife's life, 32; studio burns, 29; study group work, 106, 109, 115-117; uniqueness of gift, 161-63

Cayce, Edgar Evans (brother): born, 38; burned, 74; college grad, 141; inheritance, 181-82; author, 203; film script, 209, 219, 243; Egypt project, 248-9; 262

Cayce, Gertrude Evans (mother): marriage, 18; TB, 32; The Hill, 41-44; love for Edgar, 51-52, 80, 104; arrested, 109-10, 113, 135-36; death, 152-54; 190; incarnations, 297-306

Cayce, Gregory J. (son), 181-90, 272, 276-77

Cayce, Hugh Lynn: adolescent hijinks, 42-43; ambitions, 95; Andrew incarnation, 227-36; anger, 50-51, 236-41; Army service, 147-54; arrests, 110, 113-14; astrological chart, 27; attraction for mother, 50, 57, 59, 127-29; author, 199, 208; automatic writing, 37; blinded, 33-34; book editor, 203-10; born, 27; business school, 66; cancer, 275-286; college life, 71-88; death of brother, 28; death, not fearing, 276-77; death, of parents, 152-53; death, of, 286; delinquency, 43-44; drafted, 146;

—dreams about: message for son, 287-88; scouting, 120; death, 276, 289; Earth changes, 287; eulogies, 286, 295; family's togetherness, 33, 35; fighting spirit, 294; First Citizen Award, 200; first romance, 67-69; heart attack, 261; hunting, marksmanship, 42; husband role, 185-90; idealism, 95; incarnations, 57-59, 93, 96, 139, 149, 227-40, 245, 250-52, 299-302; inheritance, 181-82; Jesus experiences, 23-25, 230-31; karmic

relationships, 59, 88, 94, 179, 241; kidney stone, 21; Light, use of, 172; experience at Capernum, 239-40; loaves and fishes miracle, 23; married, 139; mother's qualities, 52; New York life, 126-29; Norfolk Business College, 66; Ouija board experiences, 36; out-of-body experiences, 22, 171, 179, 264; parental role, 181-89; parents' relationship, 51; parents, relations with, 52, 82; Persian flashback, 149-50, 172;
—philosophy of: abundance, 23; A.R.E.'s destiny, 264; between incarnations, 145, 293; suffering, 281; telepathy, 172; grace, 281; healing relationships, 282; illness, 280; love, hate, 285; overcoming faults, 152-53; parenthood, 145; venturing inward, purpose of, 200; prep school, 59-62; psychics, other, 253-59; Ra Ta, search for, 252; radio program, 119-25;
—readings, on: past lives, 56-59; marriage, 139-141; parenting, 145; reincarnate, plan to, 290-91; reincarnation, 92; religious views, 294; salary, 194; courtship, 131-39; Scouts, 108, 120, 200; Search for God, 116-17; self-hypnosis, 177; study group cooperation, 115-16; study groups started, 106; succession, 264-66, 271-73;
—Sugrue, Thomas, relationship: antagonism, 71-74; friendship, 77; nursing, 136-38; love for, 179; working together, 92-93; taunted about father, 35; telepathy, 172; Texas trip, 47-49; The Work, 287; There Is a River, rewriting, 141-43;
Cayce, Leslie B. "Squire" (grandfather), 14, 44-45, 134-35
Cayce, Leslie Goodman (daughter-in-law), 8, 181-90, 263, 270, 279, 286
Cayce, Milton Porter (brother), 28
Cayce, Sally Taylor (wife), courtship of, 131-47; 153-57; building family, 181-90; 240, 254, 264, 272, 276-80
Cayce, Sarah (aunt), 45
Cayce, Thomas Jefferson (great-grandfather), 14-15, 19; reincarnated as, 146
Caycey, Shadrach, 13
Cerminara, Gina, 141
Chandler, Judy, 127
Channon, Patricia, 178
Christian Century, 147
Christian Endeavor, 36
Christian Herald, 199
Church, Disciples of Christ, 233
Church, First Christian (Selma), 35
Church, First Presbyterian (Virginia Beach), 66, 286
Church, Star of the Sea Catholic, 138
Church, Virginia Beach Baptist, 65
Clapp, Bob, 196, 270
Clower, Rev. Joseph B., 139, 152, 269
Cochran, Lin, 172
Cochran, Tony, 172
Condon, Eddie, 178
Cordak, Joseph and Dorothy, 194-95
Crosby, Bing, 148, 198
Crump phenomenon, 133-34

D
Davidson, Fred, 272
Davis, Andrew Jackson, 161, 221
Davis, Gladys, 10; hired by Cayce, 53; life readings, 65, 67, 93; ideals for The Work, 104, 107; arrested, 109-110, 113; holds A.R.E. together,

157-58; indexes readings, 165; marriages, 182, 190, 195; Cayce film, 209, 262; incarnations, 297-311
Davis, Mildred, 107, 109-110
Detroit News, 207
Devlin, Patricia, 100
Dianetics, 199
Dietrich case, 30
Dixon, Jeanne, 199
Dobbins, Dr., 111
Dolphin, Lambert, 249
Door to the Future, 199
Dreams, Your Magic Mirror (Sechrist), 206
Drummond, Richard, 284
Duke University, 124

E
Earth Changes, 287
Eddy, Mary Baker, 161
Edgar Cayce and the Palma Christi (McGarey), 216
Edgar Cayce Foundation, 9, 158, 217, 243, 244, 248-49, 253, 262
Edgar Cayce on Dreams (Bro), 204
Edgar Cayce on Reincarnation (Langley), 203
Edgar Cayce on Religion and Psychic Experience (Bro), 206
Edgar Cayce Publishing Co., 158
Edgar Cayce Reader, 1 and 2, 207
Edmonds, Florence, 171, 267
Egypt project, 242-259
Egyptian Heritage, The (Lehner), 245
Ellington, Helen, 104
Embleton, James, 219-220, 222, 266
Emerson, J. Norman, 254
Epstein, Bill, 150
Essenes, 232, 240, 242
Evans, Elizabeth "Lizzie" (grandmother), 42
Evans, Hugh (uncle), 44
Evans, Lynn (uncle), 41

F
Faces of Fear, 263, 272
Fetzer Foundation, 223
Fletcher, 134
Food and Drug Administration, 221-22
Ford, Arthur, 134, 257
Freeman, John, 224
Friedman, Robert S., 10, 257

G
Garrett, Eileen, 161
Gay, Dr. S., 33
Gellis, Henry, 209
Ghosts, 31-32, 134-35
Gimbert, Mae. *See* St. Clair
Glad Helpers, 109, 195, 278-79
Gormly, J. R., M.D., 262
Gray, Lydia, J. Schrader, 195
Gray, Mamie, 127
Great Pyramid, carbon-dating, 258
Guidry, Elaine, 251-2

H
Hall of Records, Egypt, 243-44, 248, 252, 255
Hall, Manly P., 174, 295
Hampden-Sydney College, 268
Hansen, Marjorie, 243-44

Hardwicke, Henry, M.D., 111, 119, 122
Harper & Row, 199, 292
Harper's magazine, 169
Harvard University, 159
Hawass, Zahi, 247, 249-250
Heritage Store, 221
Hesson, Sarah (aunt), 262
Holmes, D.B., 161
Holt, Henry, Publishing Co., 141
Home Health Products, 222
Hope, Bob, 198
Hotten, Mayo, 215
House, Carrie, 42
House, Doris, 131
House, Thomas B., M.D., 91
House, Tommy, 42, 87
Hubbard, L. Ron, 199
Hurkos, Peter, 16
Hypnosis, 150

I

Impedance device, 216
Imprisoned Splendour, The (Johnson), 189
Ingram, Robert, 221
Institute for Antiquity and Christianity, 248
Institute for the Achievement of Human Potential, 224
Ipsab, 221
Irion, J. Everett, 194, 217, 272, 285

J

Jahoda, Ursula and Joseph, 256
James, William, 161
Jeffries, Robert J., 218, 294
Jesus experience, 23-24,
Johnson, Raynor C., 189
Johnson, Rudolph, 24, 242
Johnson, Tom, 221
Jones, H.H., 104
Junior Chamber of Commerce, Virginia Beach, 200

K

Kahn, David, 46-9, 71, 93, 100-101, 148
Kahn, Lucille, 93, 109, 125, 148
Karloff, Boris, 198
Kay, Tom, 195
Kellam, Sidney S., 201
Ketchum, Wesley H., 29-31
Kettering, Charles F., 60
Kettering, Gene, 60
Knoll, Samuel, 222
Kunz, Dora, 161

L

LaCroix, Mary, 127, 232
Lama Sing, 256, 258
Lammers, Arthur, 54-57
Landers, Olive, 196
Langley, Noel, 203
LaPrell, John, 270
LaPrell, Mary, 270
Layne Al, 53
Leary, Norrene, 263, 265
Lehner, Mark, 244-258
Lehner, Suzanne, 247
Lenoir, Ruth, 171, 195, 267
Life readings, first ones, 57

Lord, William, 195, 218, 257-58, 266, 284, 295
Lydic, Lyman A., 94

M

MacLaine, Shirley, 292
Madigan, Jessica, 174-77
Many Lives, Many Loves (Cerminara), 203
Many Mansions (Cerminara), 141, 202
Marshalls Hotel, 195, 256
Martin, W.H., 46
Masonic Order, Virginia Beach, 193
McCain, Betty, 253
McChesney, Wallace H., 103-104
McGarey, Gladys, M.D., 213, 222-26, 253, 275, 278
McGarey, William A., M.D., 174, 213, 222-26, 242-3, 275, 278, 285
McMullen, George, 254
Meade, Fort George, 146
Medical Research Bulletin, 218
Metro magazine, 257
Meunier, Lindy, 271
Millard, Joseph, 210
Miller, Hannah, 267
Miller, Ruben, 242
Miller, Shane, 242
Mind Science Foundation, 16
Miner, Allen J., 256, 258
Miner, Angel, 256
Miner, Lucy, 256
Miracle Man of Virginia Beach, 147
Montgomery, Ruth, 232
Moraine Park School, 59, 62, 64
Mosely, Rufus, 195, 247, 254
Muddie. *See* Gertrude Cayce
Music Is the Bridge (Winston), 208
Mysteries of the Mind, 119
Mystery Man of Miracles (Millard), 210

N

Nag Hammadi, 248
Nashville Tennessean, 207
National Association of Investigators, 63, 74, 103
Mutual Network, 119
New Tomorrow, 92
New York Herald-Tribune, 110
New York Times Book Review, 208
Noe, Mr., 29
Norfolk Business College, 66
Norfolk *Virginian-Pilot*, 286
Nufa, 250-2

O

O'Malley, George, 215
Ogden, Arch and Ann, 246-47, 254, 256
Oil drilling, 45-47
Other Side, The 171
Ouija board, 37, 171
Out-of-body experiences, 22, 171, 179, 264
Outer Limits of Edgar Cayce's Power, The (with E. E. Cayce), 208

P

Paar, Jack, 200
Papyrus Institute, 247
Patton, Gen. George, 48
Peterson, Marilyn, 232
Philosophical Research Society, 174, 295

Pierson, David, 54
Pike, Bishop James, 170
PMS, 222
Poling, Daniel, 199
Pratt, Laurie, 27
Price, Wym, 173
Prophet in His Own Country, A (Stearn), 209, 262
Psychic ability, causes of, 16
Pungo store, 134
Puryear, Herbert, 212, 232, 256, 265-66, 285-86, 291
Puryear, Meredith, 232, 265-66, 278, 285-86

Q
Queen Mary, 149

R
Ragab, Hassan, 247
Randolph-Macon College, 276
Readings, preserved, 159-160; indexed, 165
Reed, Henry, 212, 257
Reilly, Harold J., 111, 137, 197, 267
Reincarnation, theory of, 58
Remnant, The (LaCroix), 127
Rhine, J.B., 124, 159
Rickenbacker, Eddie, 198
Ringle, Cecil, 48
Ringle, Leonora, 48
Rolling Thunder, 285
Rooney, Mickey, 148

S
Salter, Gray, 42
Sanders, M. C., 46
Saturday Review of Literature, 148
Scattergood, Rev. Frank H., 104
Schoen, Charlotte, 220
Schwab, Charles, 126
Scientology, 199
Search for Bridey Murphy, The, (Bernstein), 141
Search for God Study Group, 106, 289
Searchlight, 164, 195
Sechrist, Elsie, 169, 175-76, 205-206, 212, 230, 277
Secret Teachings of All Ages, The (Hall), 174
Self-hypnosis, 177
Selma Chamber of Commerce, 284
Sharma, I.C., 231
Shelley, Jack, 197
Shelley, Violet M., 163, 195, 207
Shelton, Vaughan, 168
Sherman, Harold, 121
Shroyer, Linden, 297, 306
Sisters of the Night (Stearn), 198
Sixth Man, The (Stearn), 198
Skidmore, Ken, 231
Sleeping Prophet, The, (Stearn) 168, 295
Sloane, William, 141
Slutz, Fred, 62
Slutz, Leland, 61
Smith, Kate, 42
Society for Psychical Research, 161, 200
Socrates, daughter of, 305
Southern Methodist University, 258
Sparrow, G. Scott, 230, 287
Spiritual renaissance, 163, 166
St. Clair, Mae Gimbert, 178, 210, 237, 241

Stanford Research Institute, 249
Stanford, Ray, 253
Starling of the White House (Sugrue), 148
Starling, William, 148
Stearn, Jess, 168, 197-201, 208-209, 217, 262, 278, 295
Stettinius, Edward. R., 198
Stevenson, Ian, M.D., 291
Stier, Jery V., 174, 177
Stone, Henry, 133
Stranger in the Earth (Sugrue), 168
Study Group movement, 115-7
Such Is the Kingdom (Sugrue), 138
Sugrue, Thomas, college, 71-88; 110; illness, 136-9; Cayce biography, 141-3; magazine work, 148, 151; A.R.E. work, 160, 162-4; death, 178-79; 266-7
Sunday Forum, 196
Susskind, David, 232
Swann, Ingo, 255
Sykes, Egerton, 221

T
Taylor, Waller, M.D., 131, 194, 262
Telepathy, 172
The Work, called to, 19, 25,
Theosophical Society, 161
There Is a River (Sugrue), 77
Thurston, Mark, 212
TIM, 221
Tresslar, Mr., 31
Turner, Albert E., 182
Twigg, Ena, 170

U
University of California, 248
University of Chicago, 204
University of Pennsylvania, 250
Unto the Churches (Drummond), 284
Uvani, 162

V
Van Auken, John, 237
Vaughan, Henry, 284
Venture Inward magazine, 292
Venture Inward, 199, 208

W
Warner, Lucien, 119
Washington & Lee University, 71
Watch for the Morning (Sugrue), 169
Weatherhead, Leslie D., 200
Western State Hospital, 91
Wet-cell appliance, 137
Williamson, Malcolm, 36
Willis, Berry D., Jr., 108
Wilmore, Les, 182
Wilson, Adella Scott, 222
Winston, Shirley, 208
Witt, Robert, 291
Wood, C.V., Jr. 16
WOR, radio station, 119
Wright, Orville and Wilbur, 61
Wynne, Esther, 104, 267, 289-290

Y
Yoga, Youth and Reincarnation (Stearn), 199